Bring it on!

vol.1

Baek HyeKyung

ice
Kunion

WORDS FROM THE CREATOR

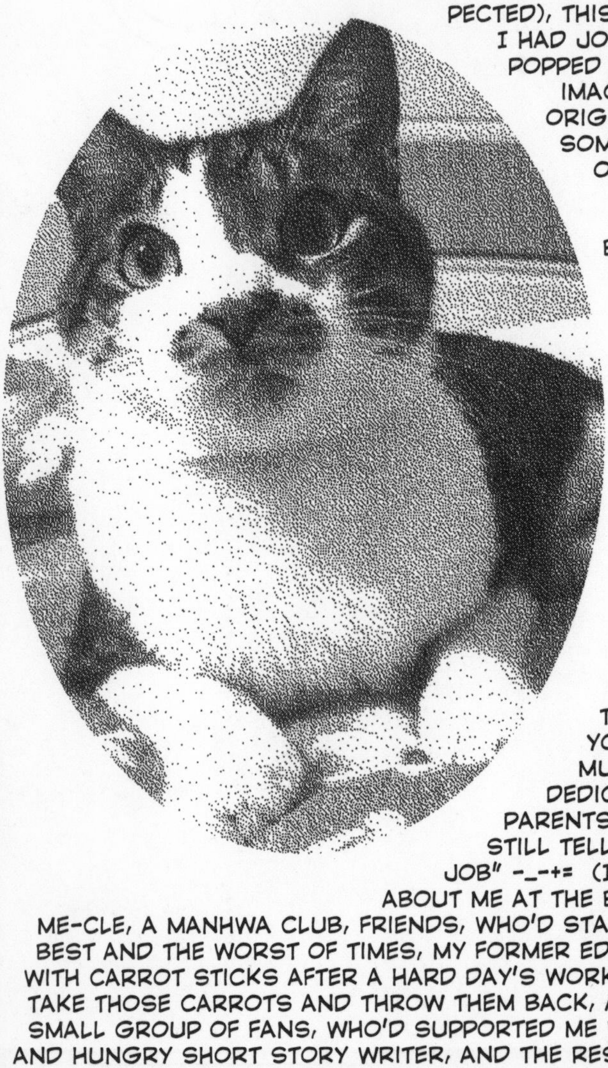

WHILE I WAS AGONIZING OVER HOW TO BEST UTILIZE MY LIMITED ABILITIES TO WRITE AN AWESOME STORY ('CUZ THE PUBLISHER'S GO AHEAD WAS A BIT UNEXPECTED), THIS ONE PARTICULAR STORY I HAD JOTTED DOWN YEARS AGO POPPED INTO MY HEAD. HARD TO IMAGINE NOW, BUT IT WAS ORIGINALLY A VERY DARK AND SOMBER TALE, WHERE EVERYONE ENDS UP MEETING A TRAGIC DEATH. ^^; FORTUNATELY, LIFE'S BEEN BETTER TO ME SINCE THE TIME OF THE FIRST DRAFT, AND THE STORY STARTED TO TAKE ON A MORE CHEERFUL AND OPTIMISTIC TURN. AFTER SEVERAL REWRITES, ALL THAT REMAINED FROM THE FIRST DRAFT WAS THAT THE PROTAGONISTS WERE HIGH SCHOOL STUDENTS. (INCIDENTALLY, SEUNG-SUH CHARACTER WAS ORIGINALLY ALSO A GIRL ;;) I HAD A GREAT TIME DRAWING AND WRITING THIS STORY, AND I HOPE YOU GUYS HAVE JUST AS MUCH FUN READING IT. I DEDICATE THIS SERIES TO MY PARENTS WHO FROM TIME TO TIME STILL TELL ME TO "FIND A NORMAL JOB" -_-+= (I KNOW YOU GUYS BRAG ABOUT ME AT THE BAKERY, TEE HEE), TO MY ME-CLE, A MANHWA CLUB, FRIENDS, WHO'D STAND BY ME THROUGH THE BEST AND THE WORST OF TIMES, MY FORMER EDITOR WHO'D REWARD ME WITH CARROT STICKS AFTER A HARD DAY'S WORK, MY NEW EDITOR, WHO'D TAKE THOSE CARROTS AND THROW THEM BACK, AND MOST OF ALL, TO MY SMALL GROUP OF FANS, WHO'D SUPPORTED ME WHEN I WAS BUT A COLD AND HUNGRY SHORT STORY WRITER, AND THE REST OF YOU ALL OUT THERE, WATCHING OUT FOR ME, THANK YOU. I WON'T LET YOU DOWN.

HYE-KYUNG BAEK

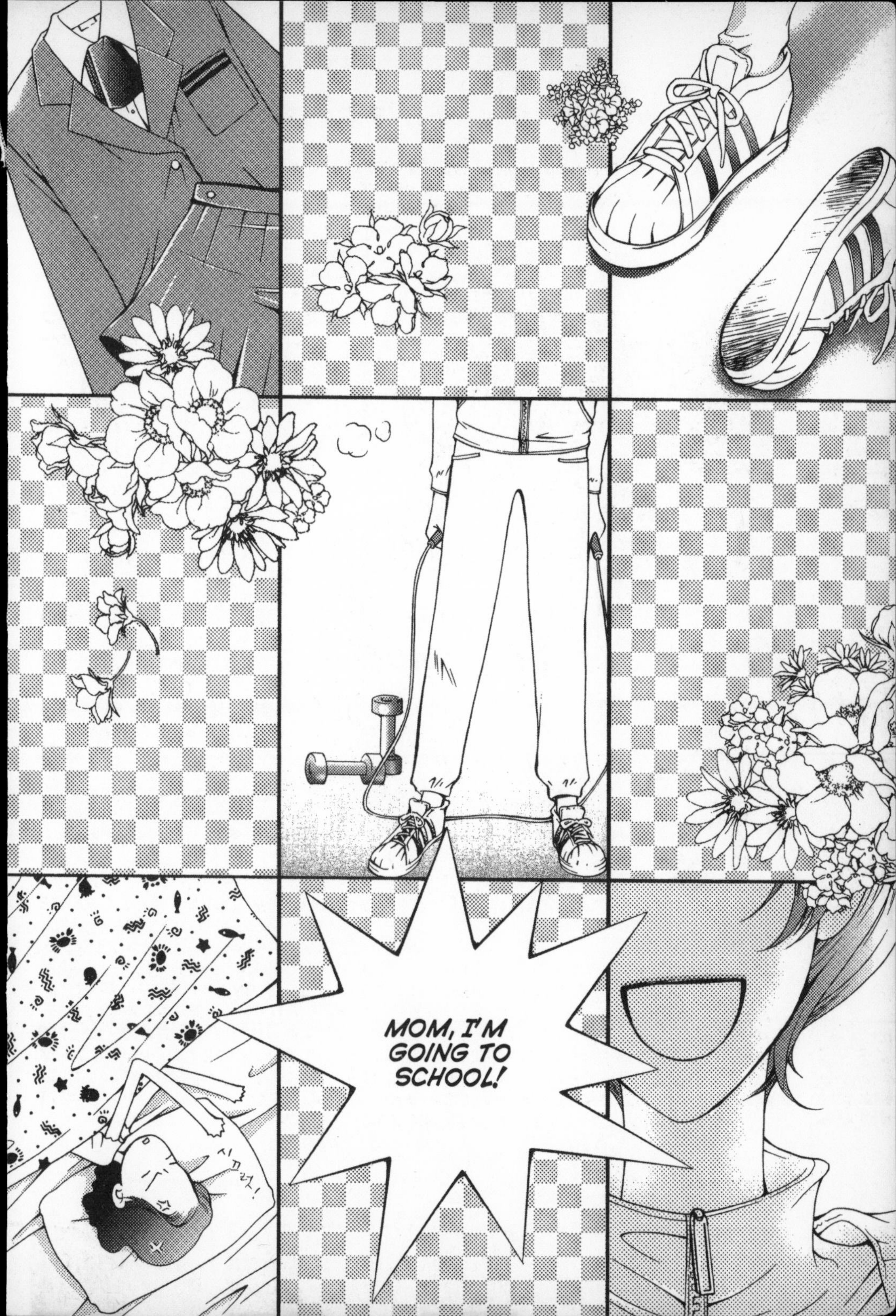
시끄러!
MOM, I'M GOING TO SCHOOL!

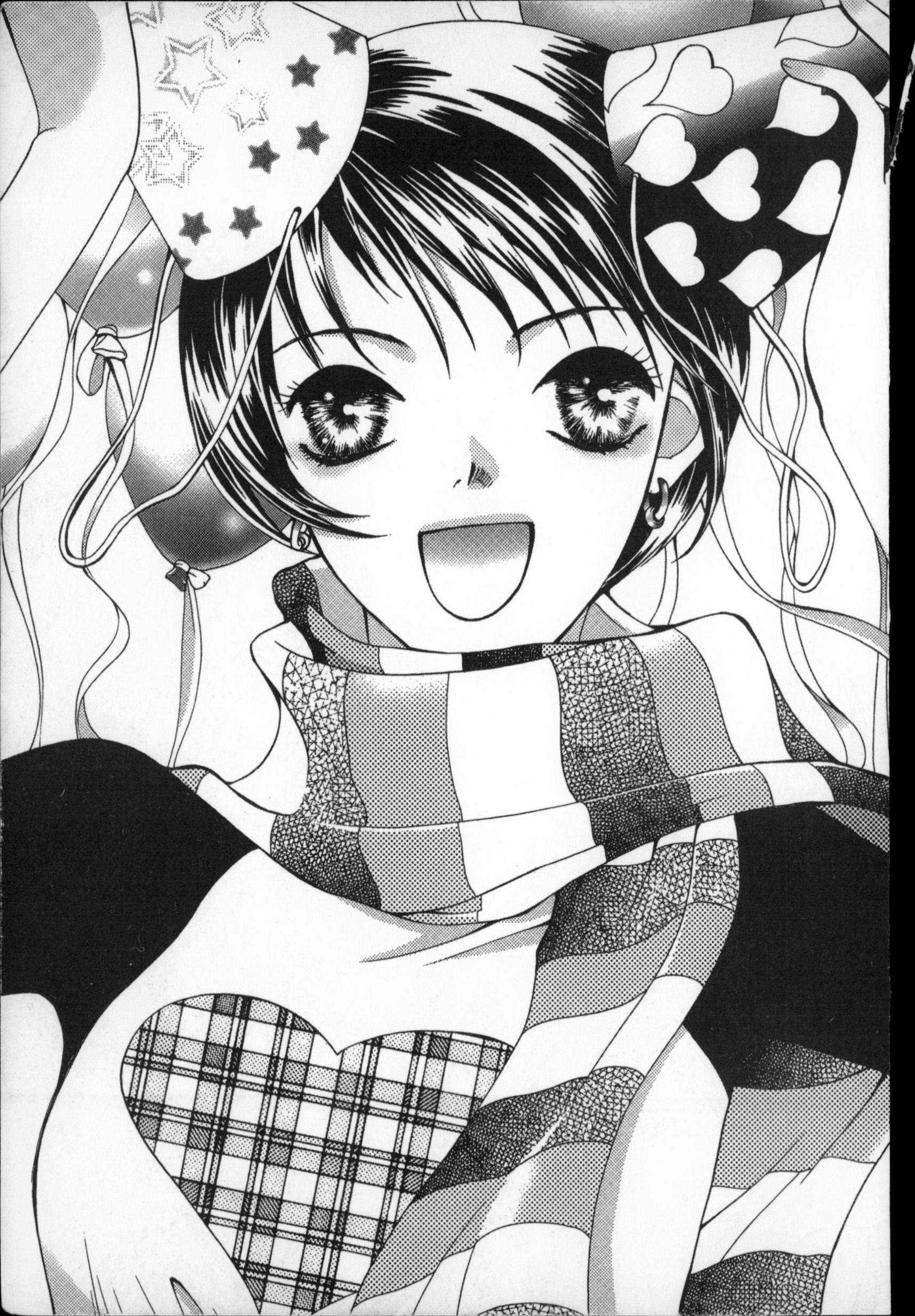

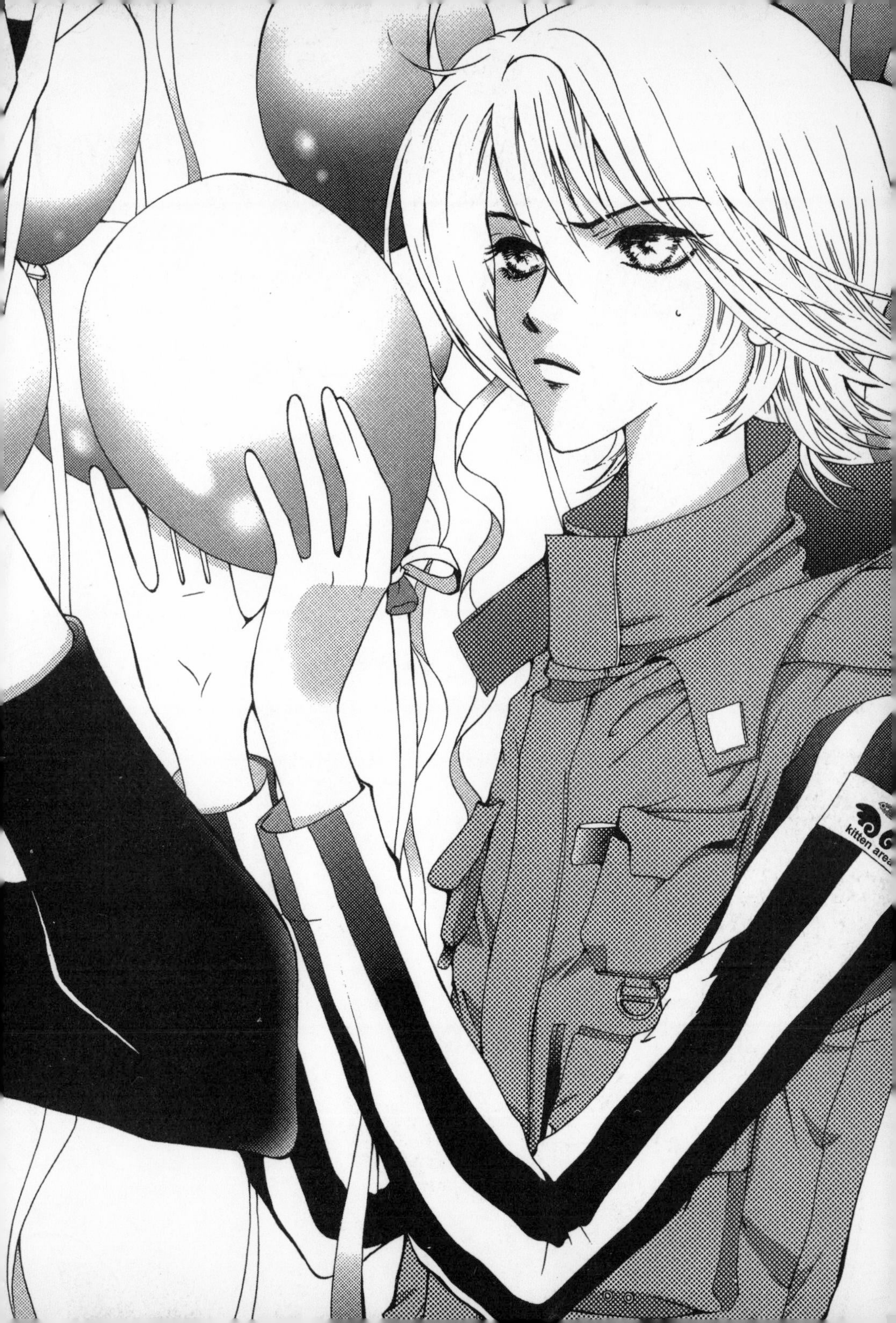
kitten area

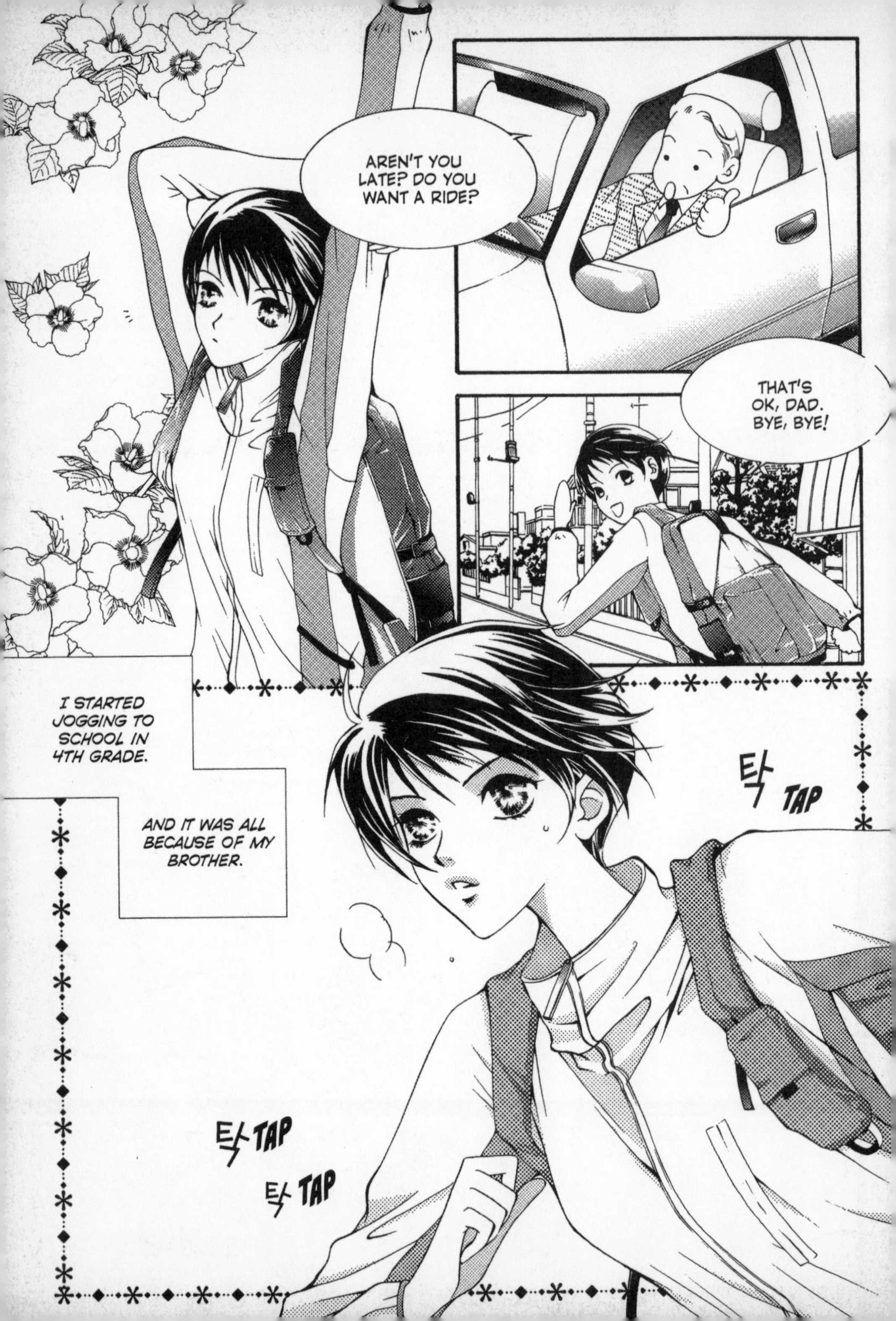
ARE'NT YOU LATE? DO YOU WANT A RIDE?
THAT'S OK, DAD. BYE, BYE!
I STARTED JOGGING TO SCHOOL IN 4TH GRADE.
탁 TAP
AND IT WAS ALL BECAUSE OF MY BROTHER.
탁 TAP
탁 TAP

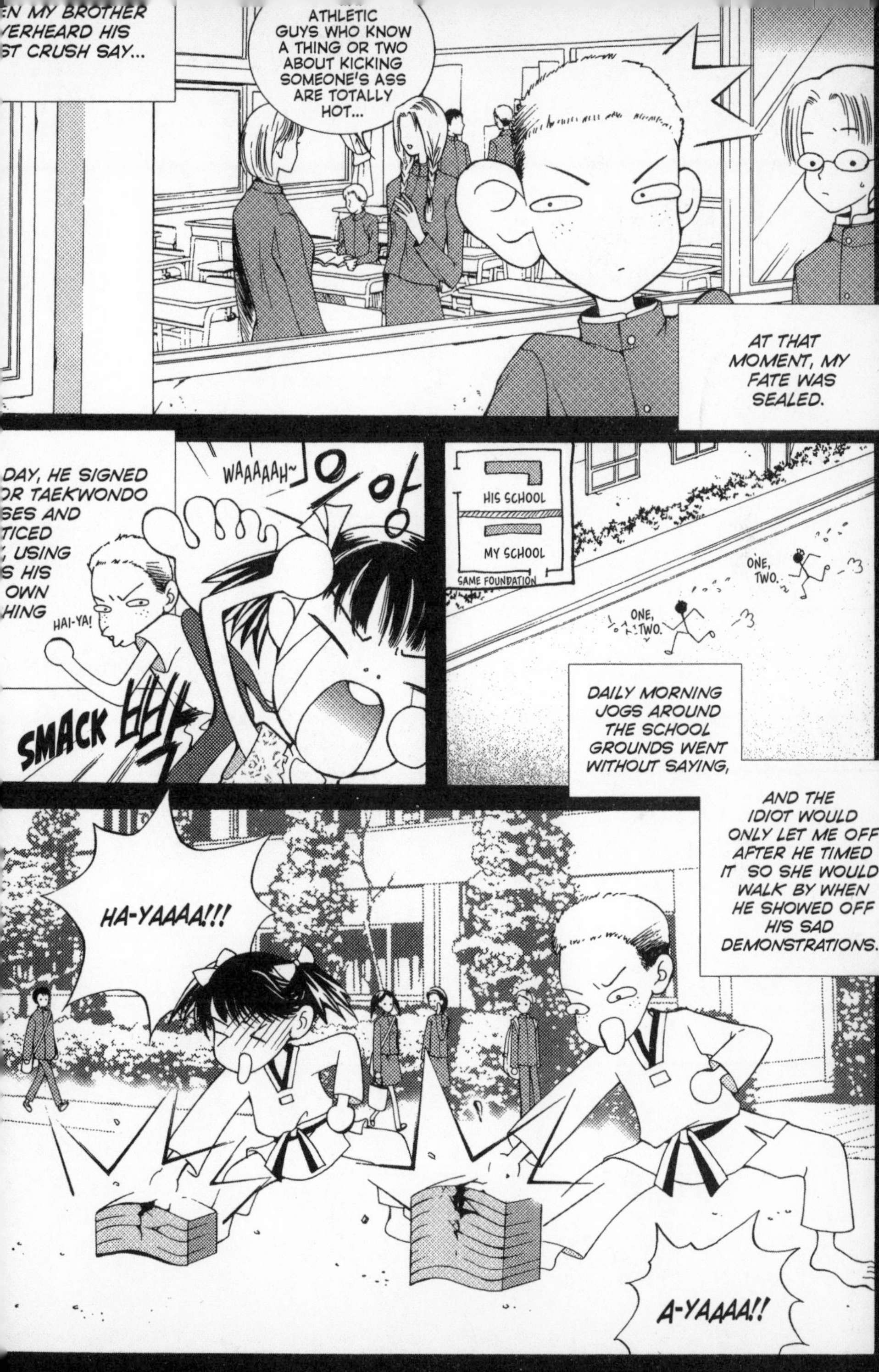

EN MY BROTHER VERHEARD HIS ST CRUSH SAY...
ATHLETIC GUYS WHO KNOW A THING OR TWO ABOUT KICKING SOMEONE'S ASS ARE TOTALLY HOT...
AT THAT MOMENT, MY FATE WAS SEALED.
DAY, HE SIGNED OR TAEKWONDO SES AND TICED , USING S HIS OWN HING
HAI-YA!
WAAAAAH~
으앙
SMACK
HIS SCHOOL
MY SCHOOL
SAME FOUNDATION
ONE, TWO.
ONE, TWO.
DAILY MORNING JOGS AROUND THE SCHOOL GROUNDS WENT WITHOUT SAYING,
AND THE IDIOT WOULD ONLY LET ME OFF AFTER HE TIMED IT SO SHE WOULD WALK BY WHEN HE SHOWED OFF HIS SAD DEMONSTRATIONS.
HA-YAAAA!!!
A-YAAAA!!

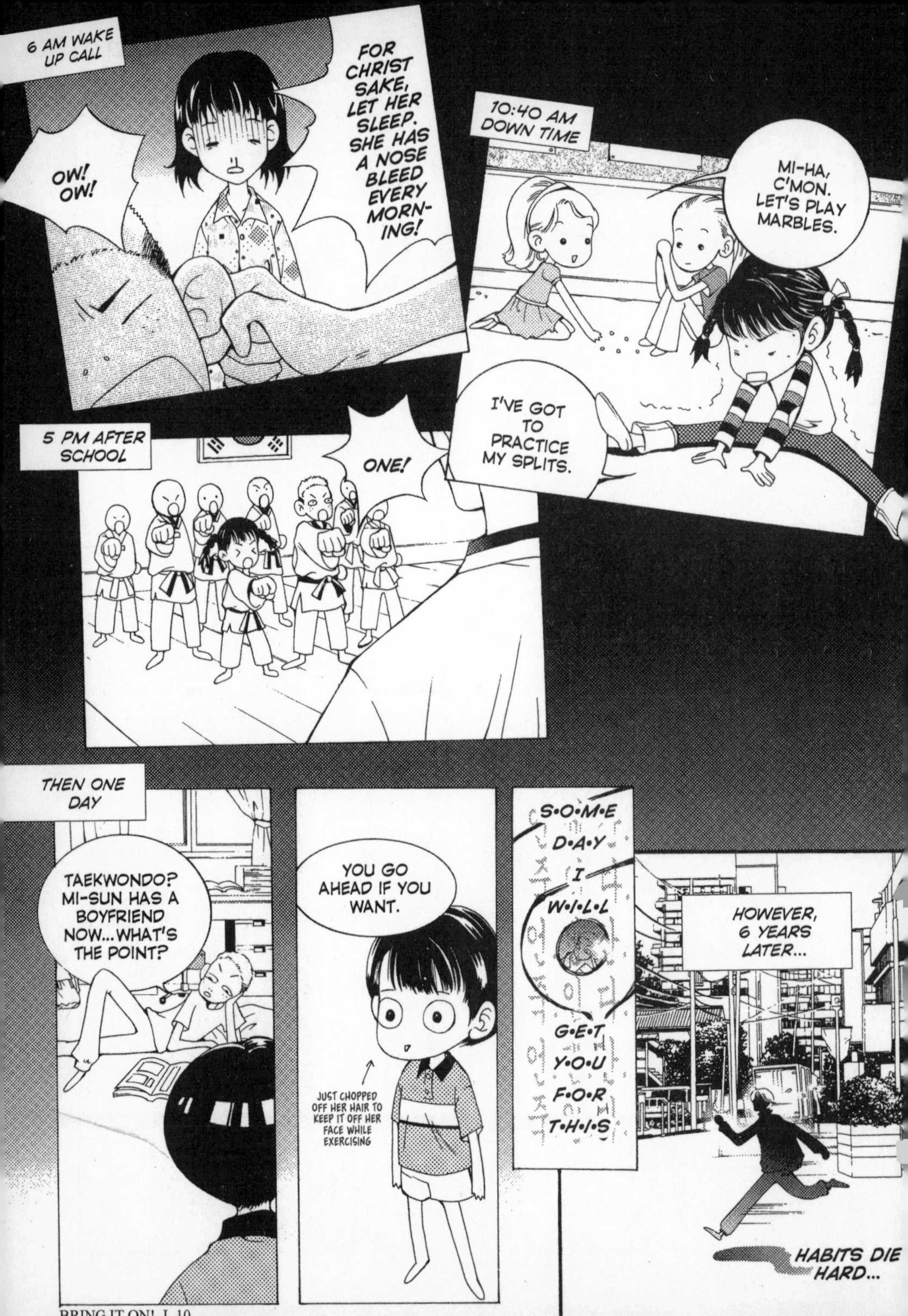
6 AM WAKE UP CALL
OW! OW!
FOR CHRIST SAKE, LET HER SLEEP. SHE HAS A NOSE BLEED EVERY MORN-ING!
10:40 AM DOWN TIME
MI-HA, C'MON. LET'S PLAY MARBLES.
I'VE GOT TO PRACTICE MY SPLITS.
5 PM AFTER SCHOOL
ONE!
THEN ONE DAY
TAEKWONDO? MI-SUN HAS A BOYFRIEND NOW...WHAT'S THE POINT?
YOU GO AHEAD IF YOU WANT.
JUST CHOPPED OFF HER HAIR TO KEEP IT OFF HER FACE WHILE EXERCISING
S•O•M•E D•A•Y I W•I•L•L G•E•T Y•O•U F•O•R T•H•I•S
HOWEVER, 6 YEARS LATER...
HABITS DIE HARD...

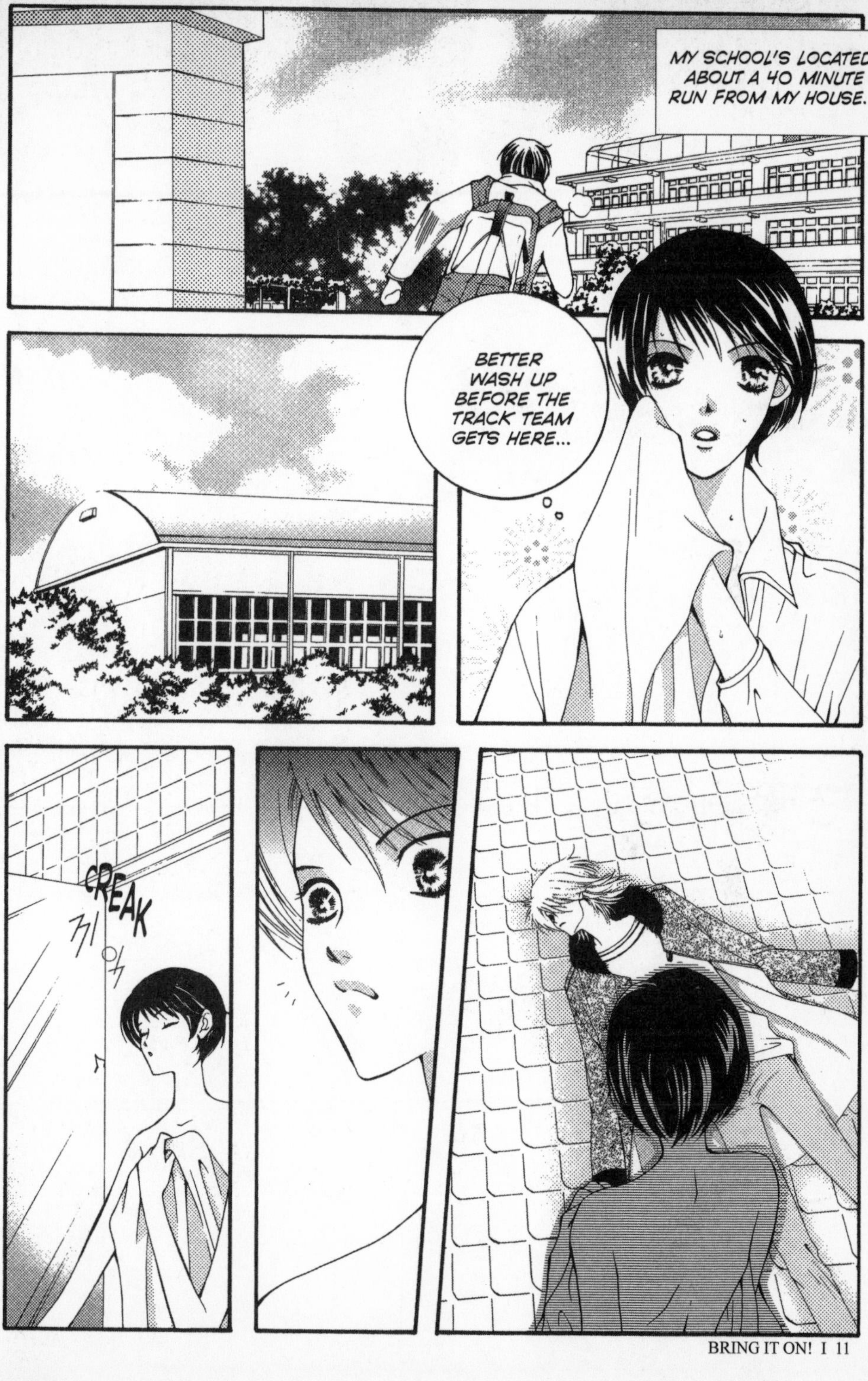
MY SCHOOL'S LOCATED ABOUT A 40 MINUTE RUN FROM MY HOUSE.
BETTER WASH UP BEFORE THE TRACK TEAM GETS HERE...
CREAK

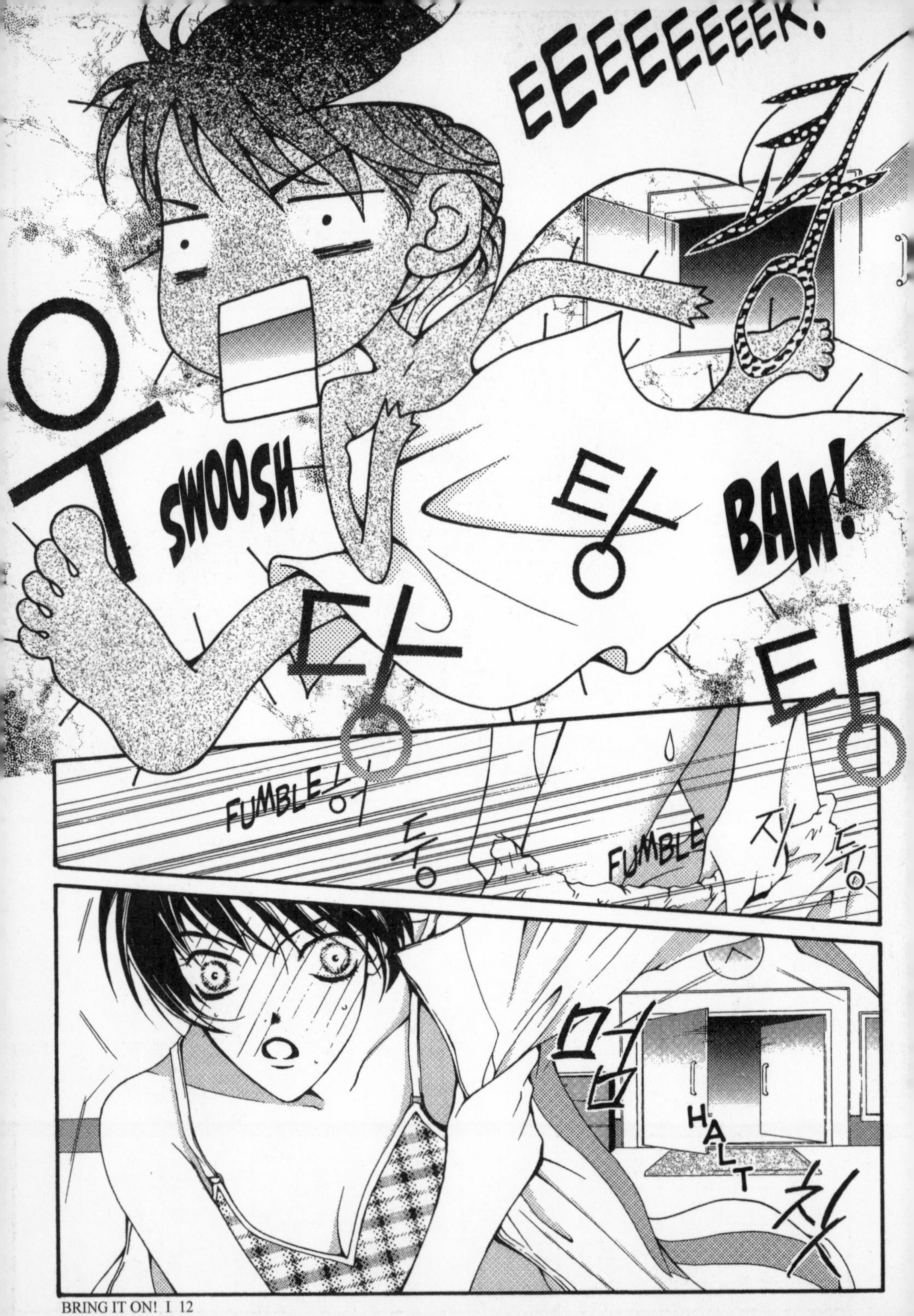
EEEEEEEEEK!
SWOOSH
BAM!
FUMBLE
FUMBLE
HALT

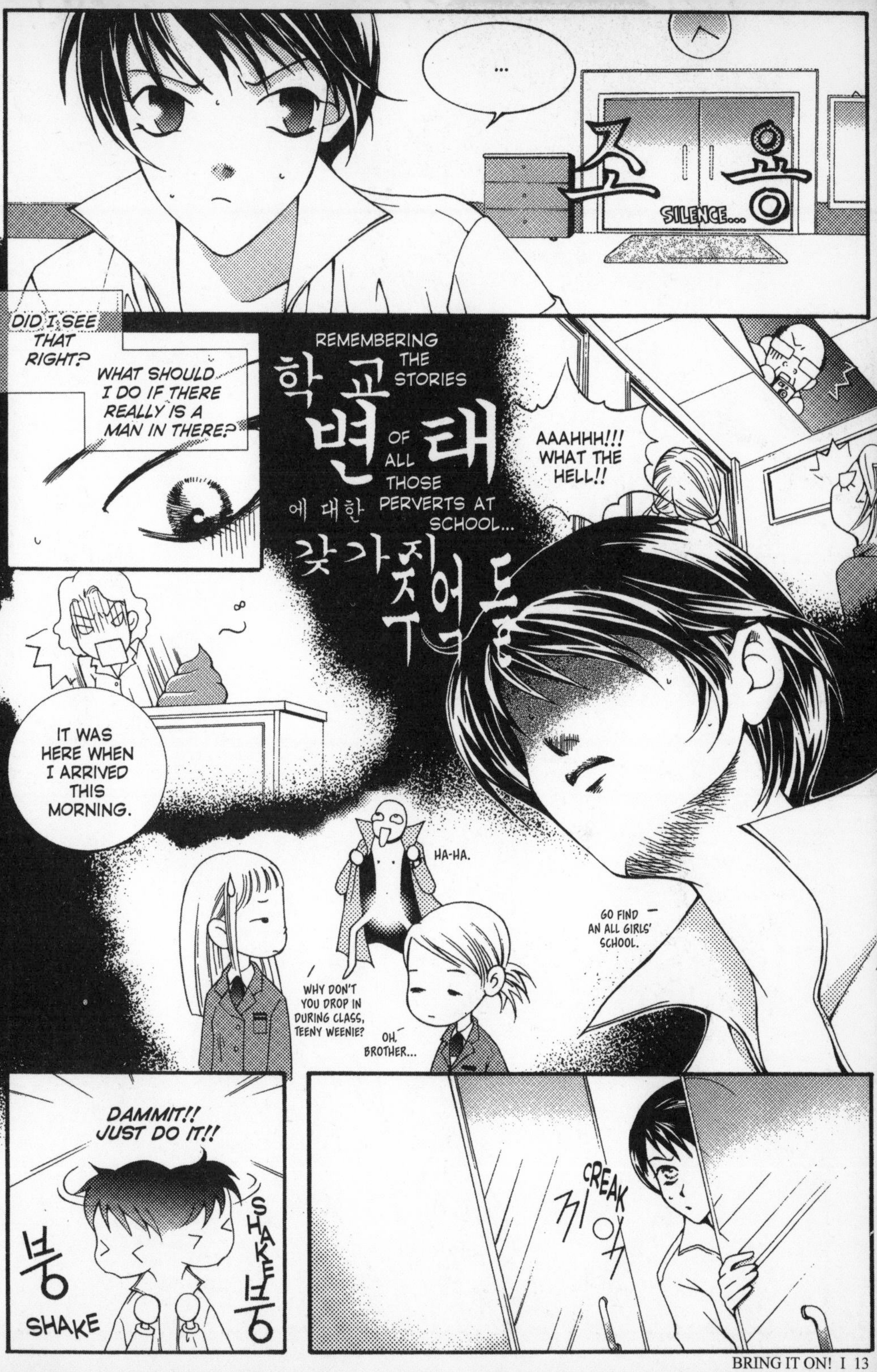
...
조용
SILENCE...
DID I SEE THAT RIGHT?
WHAT SHOULD I DO IF THERE REALLY IS A MAN IN THERE?
학교 변태에 대한 갖가지 추억들
REMEMBERING THE STORIES OF ALL THOSE PERVERTS AT SCHOOL...
AAAHHH!!! WHAT THE HELL!!
IT WAS HERE WHEN I ARRIVED THIS MORNING.
HA-HA.
WHY DON'T YOU DROP IN DURING CLASS, TEENY WEENIE?
OH, BROTHER...
GO FIND AN ALL GIRLS' SCHOOL.
DAMMIT!! JUST DO IT!!
붕
SHAKE
SHAKE
붕
CREAK

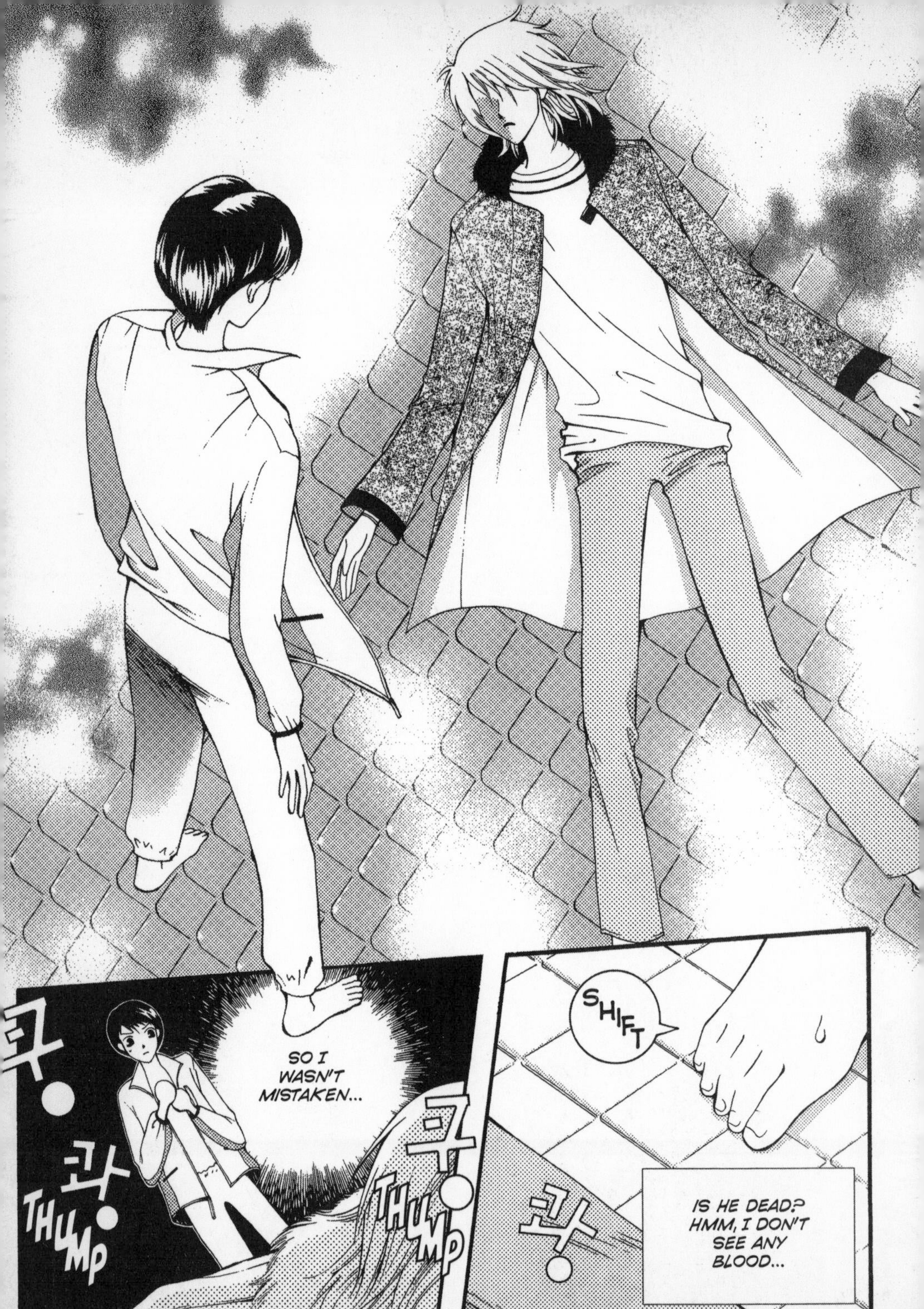
쿠•콰•
THUMP
SO I WASN'T MISTAKEN...
쿠•
THUMP
SHIFT
콰•
IS HE DEAD? HMM, I DON'T SEE ANY BLOOD...

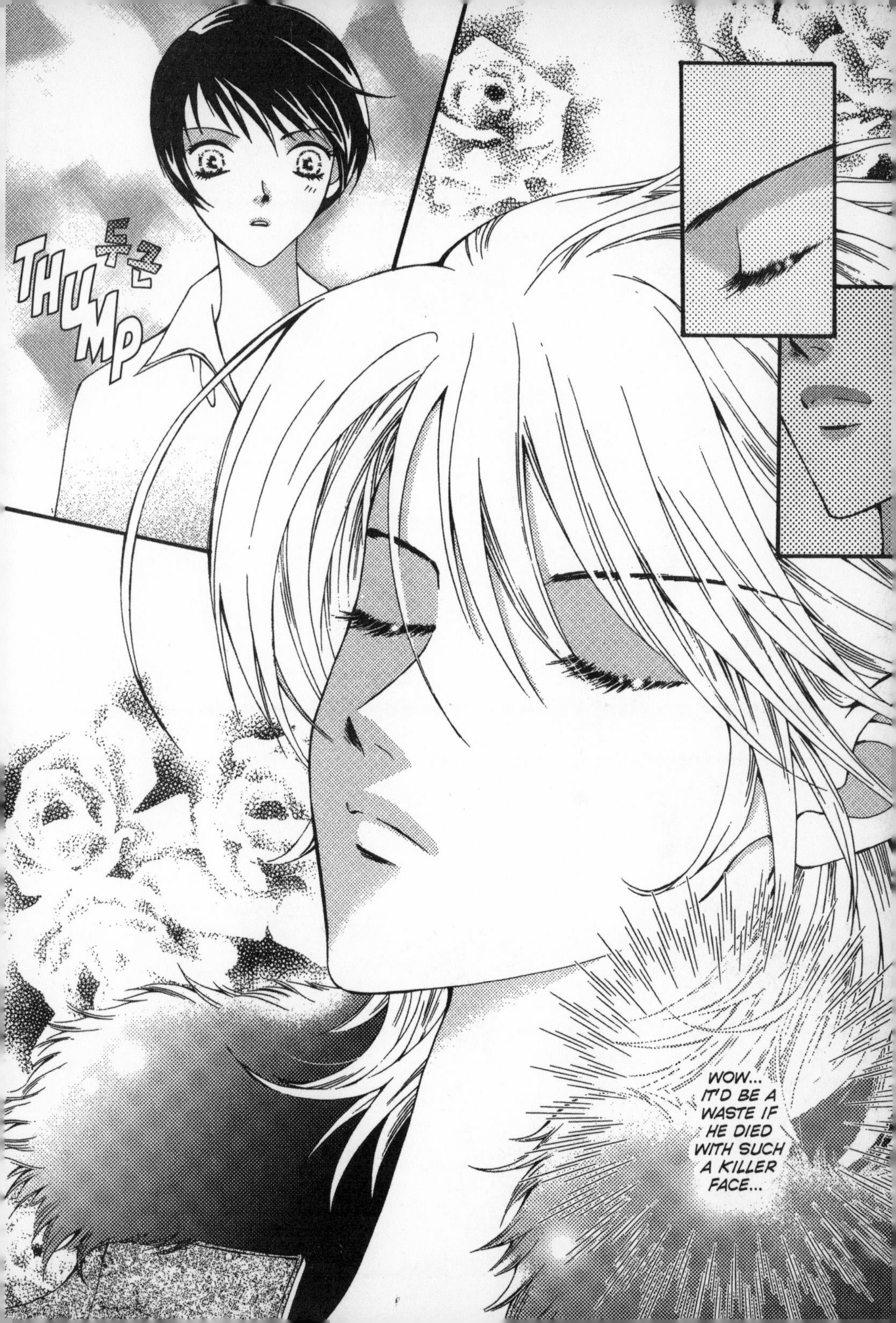
THUMP
두근
WOW... IT'D BE A WASTE IF HE DIED WITH SUCH A KILLER FACE...

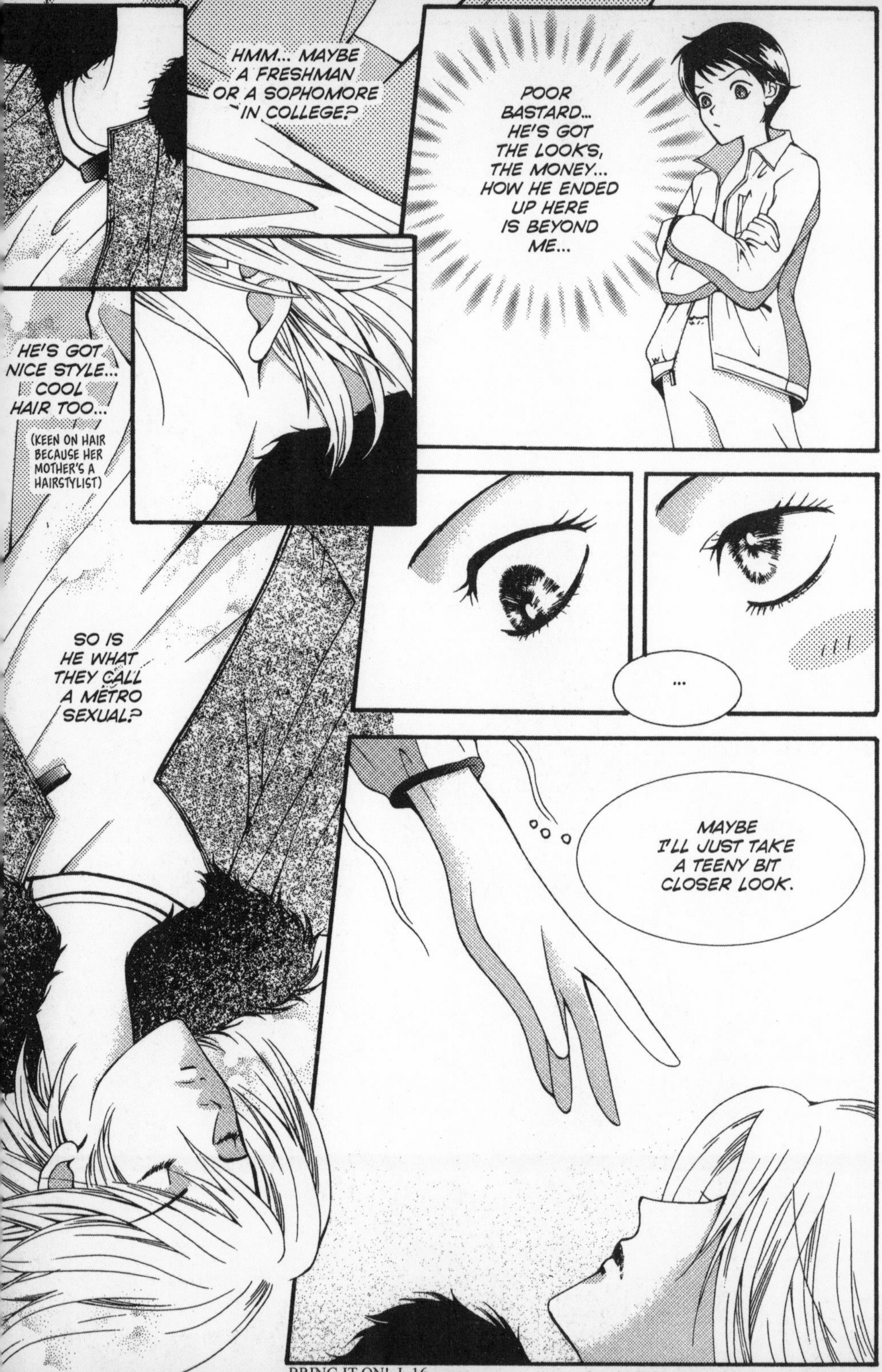
HMM... MAYBE A FRESHMAN OR A SOPHOMORE IN COLLEGE?
POOR BASTARD... HE'S GOT THE LOOKS, THE MONEY... HOW HE ENDED UP HERE IS BEYOND ME...
HE'S GOT NICE STYLE... COOL HAIR TOO...
(KEEN ON HAIR BECAUSE HER MOTHER'S A HAIRSTYLIST)
...
SO IS HE WHAT THEY CALL A METRO SEXUAL?
MAYBE I'LL JUST TAKE A TEENY BIT CLOSER LOOK.

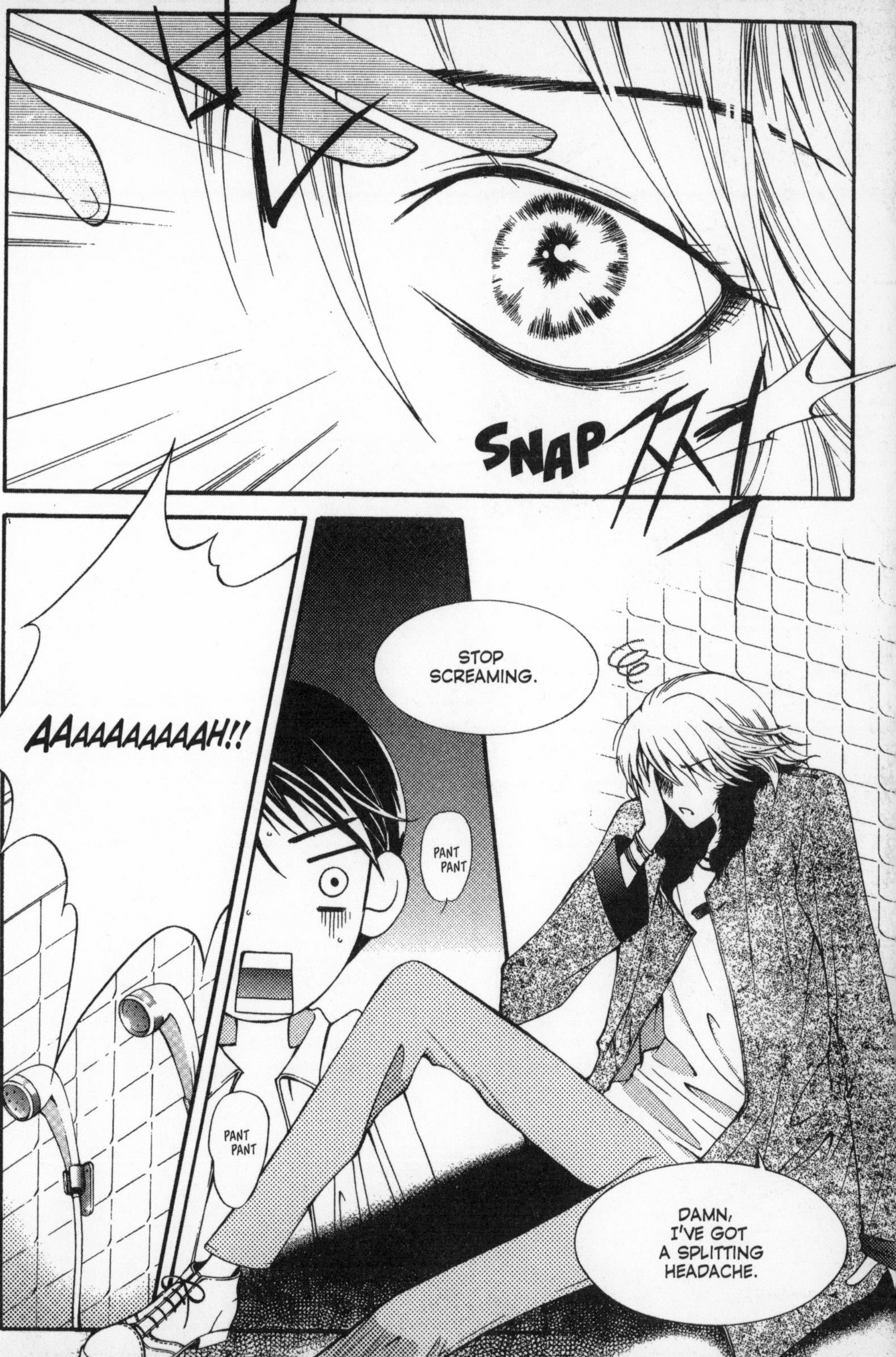
SNAP
AAAAAAAAAAH!!
STOP SCREAMING.
PANT PANT
PANT PANT
DAMN, I'VE GOT A SPLITTING HEADACHE.

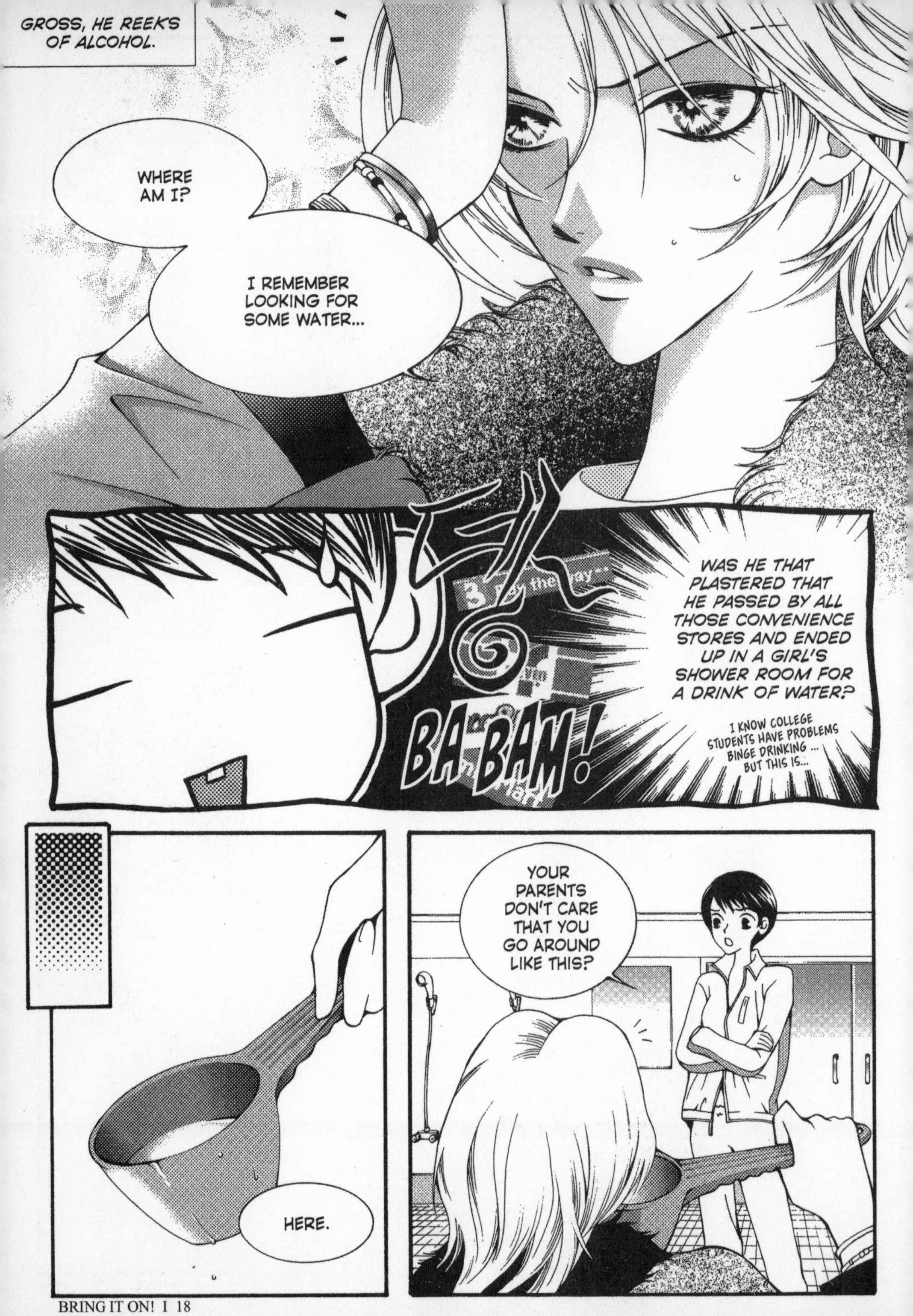
GROSS, HE REEKS OF ALCOHOL.
WHERE AM I?
I REMEMBER LOOKING FOR SOME WATER...
BA-BAM!
WAS HE THAT PLASTERED THAT HE PASSED BY ALL THOSE CONVENIENCE STORES AND ENDED UP IN A GIRL'S SHOWER ROOM FOR A DRINK OF WATER?
I KNOW COLLEGE STUDENTS HAVE PROBLEMS BINGE DRINKING ... BUT THIS IS...
HERE.
YOUR PARENTS DON'T CARE THAT YOU GO AROUND LIKE THIS?

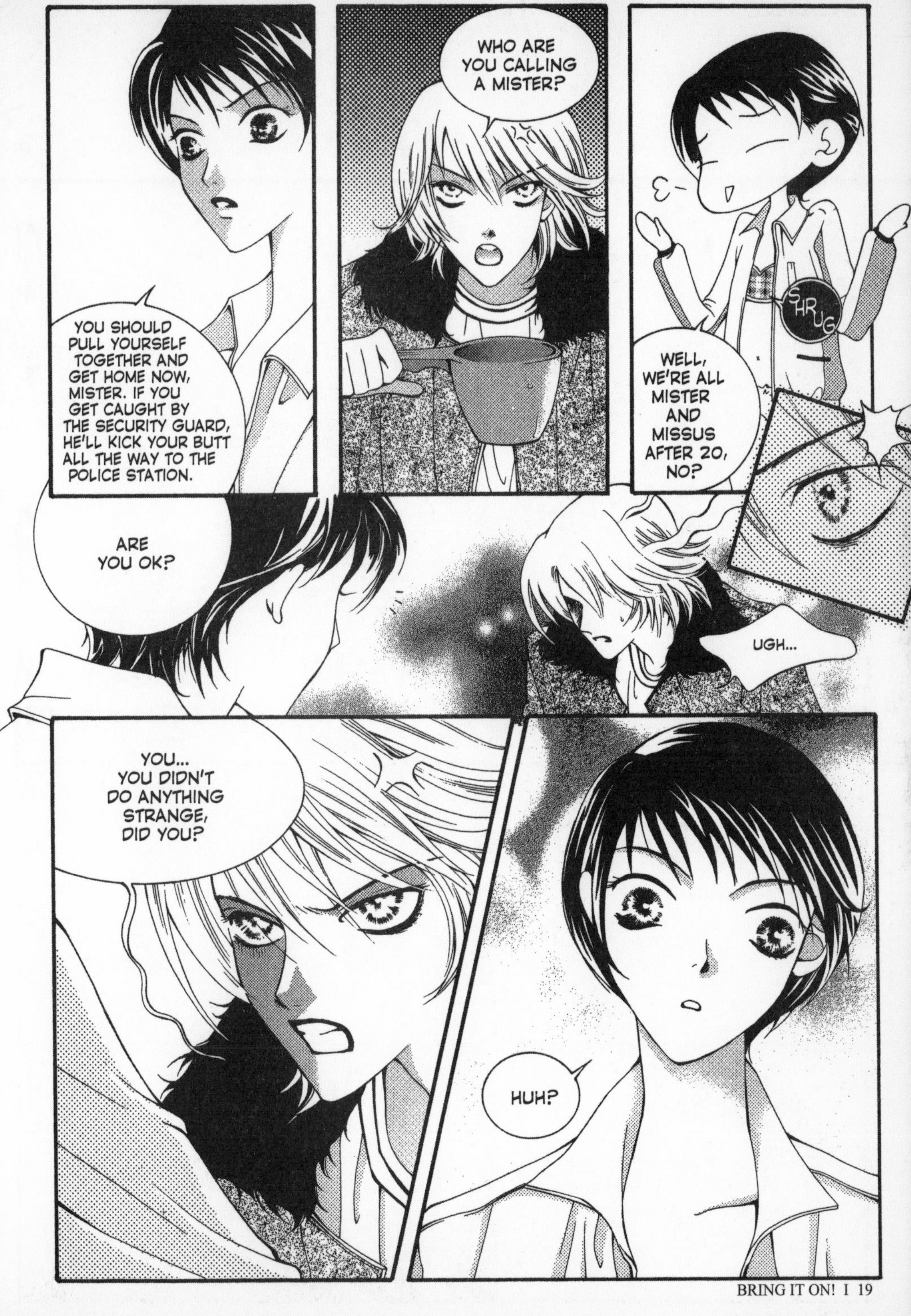
YOU SHOULD PULL YOURSELF TOGETHER AND GET HOME NOW, MISTER. IF YOU GET CAUGHT BY THE SECURITY GUARD, HE'LL KICK YOUR BUTT ALL THE WAY TO THE POLICE STATION.
WHO ARE YOU CALLING A MISTER?
SHRUG
WELL, WE'RE ALL MISTER AND MISSUS AFTER 20, NO?
ARE YOU OK?
UGH...
YOU... YOU DIDN'T DO ANYTHING STRANGE, DID YOU?
HUH?

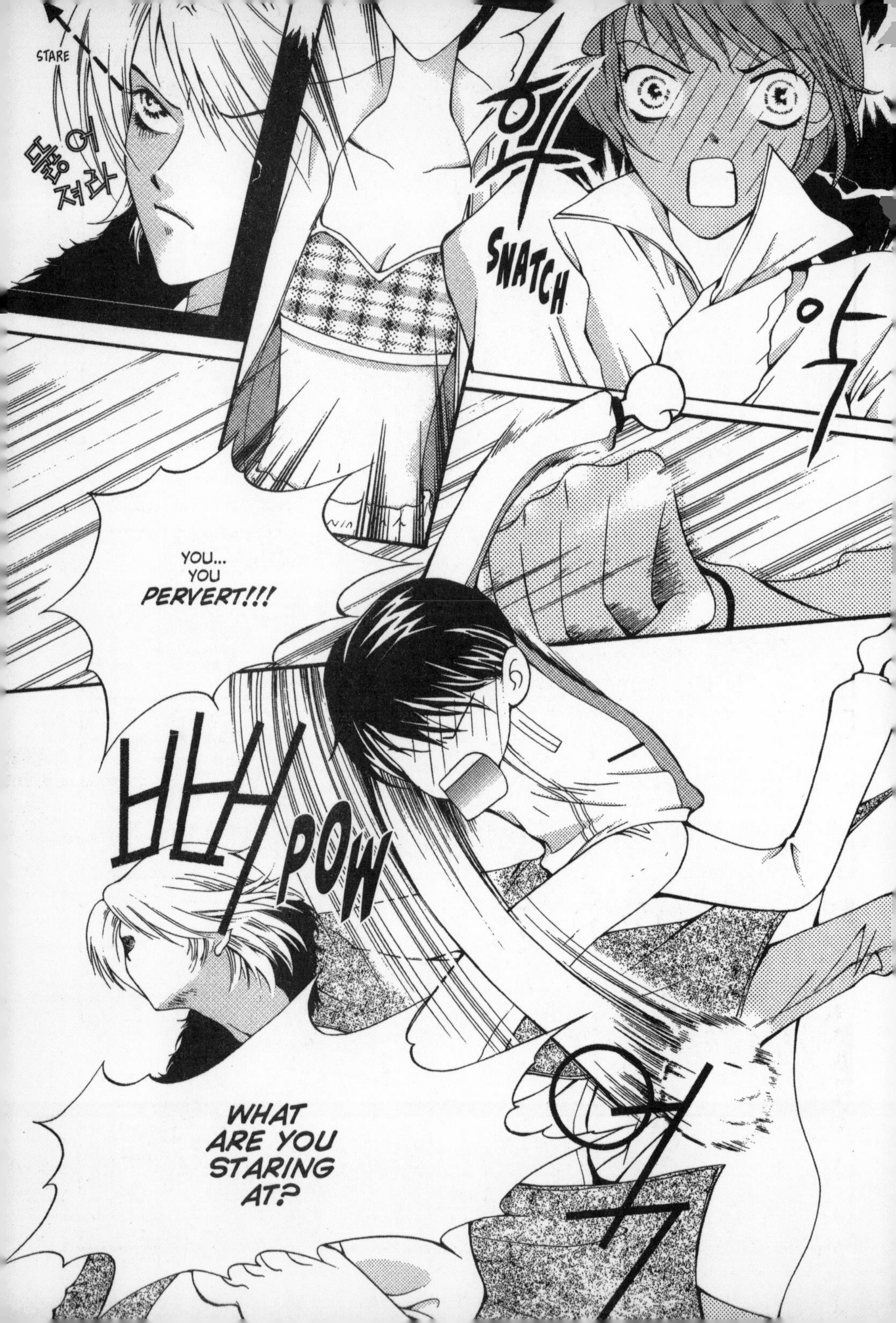
STARE
뚫어져라
확
SNATCH
악
YOU... YOU PERVERT!!!
빠
POW
WHAT ARE YOU STARING AT?
억

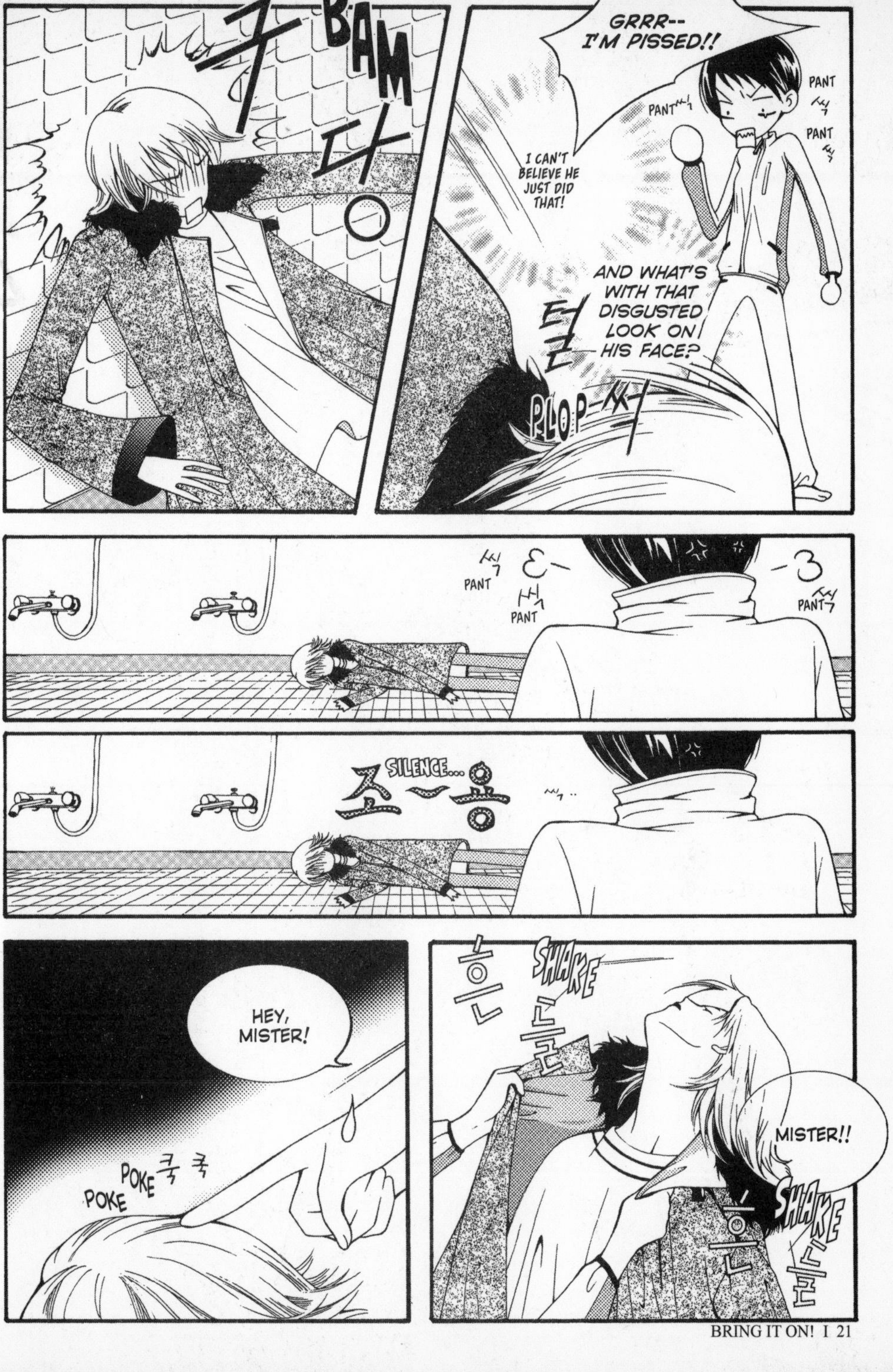
BAM
GRRR-- I'M PISSED!!
I CAN'T BELIEVE HE JUST DID THAT!
PANT
PANT
PANT
AND WHAT'S WITH THAT DISGUSTED LOOK ON HIS FACE?
PLOP
PANT
PANT
PANT
SILENCE...
HEY, MISTER!
POKE
POKE
SHAKE
MISTER!!
SHAKE

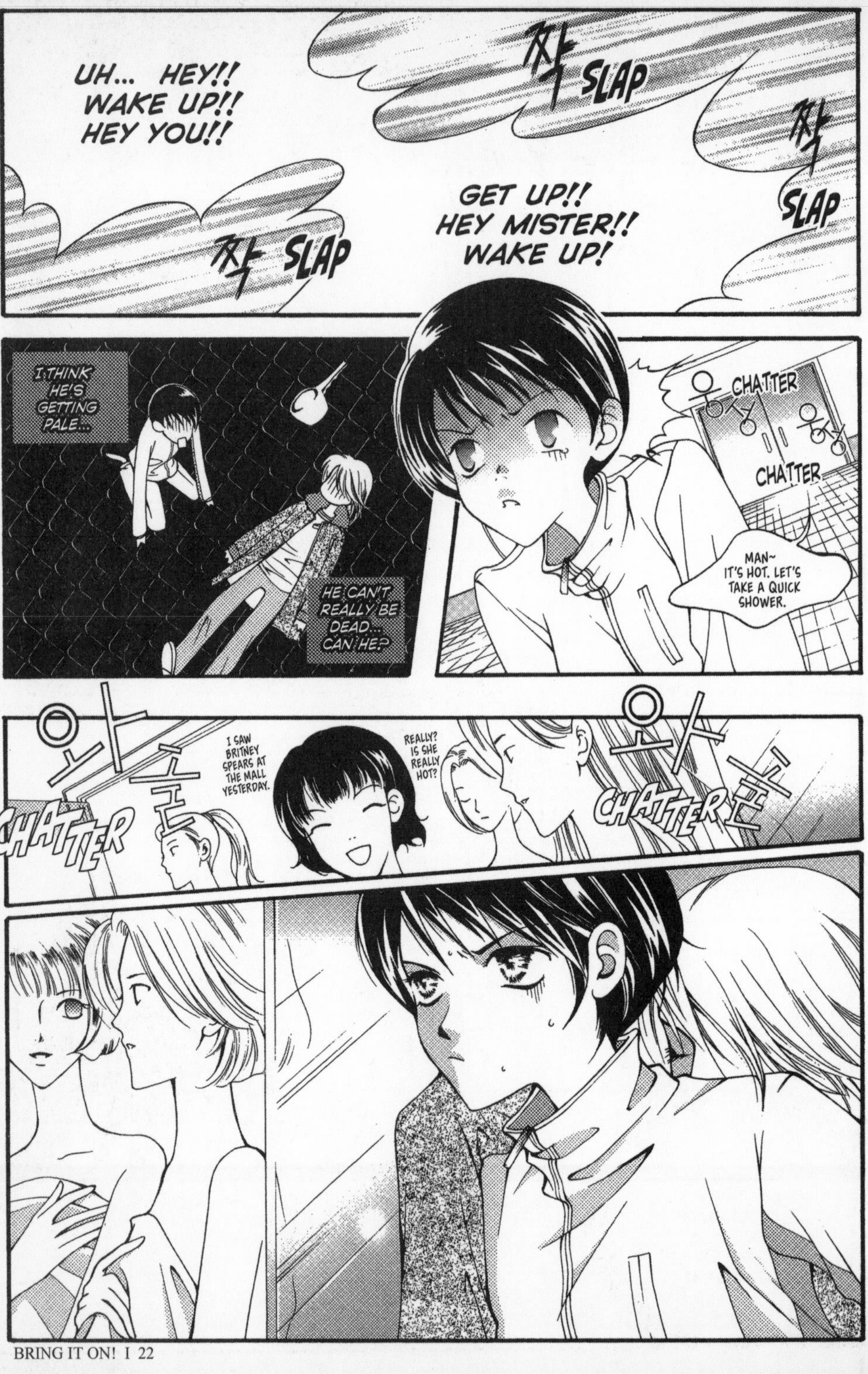
UH... HEY!!
WAKE UP!!
HEY YOU!!
짝 SLAP
짝 SLAP
GET UP!!
HEY MISTER!!
WAKE UP!
짝 SLAP
I THINK HE'S GETTING PALE...
HE CAN'T REALLY BE DEAD... CAN HE?
웅성 CHATTER
웅성 CHATTER
MAN~ IT'S HOT. LET'S TAKE A QUICK SHOWER.
와글 CHATTER
I SAW BRITNEY SPEARS AT THE MALL YESTERDAY.
REALLY? IS SHE REALLY HOT?
와글 CHATTER

SHOOT

TAP TAP TAP TAP

SHIT. I'M RUNNING WITH A GROWN MAN ON MY BACK.

I MEAN REALLY, IS THIS WHAT A NORMAL 17-YEAR-OLD GIRL SHOULD DO ON A REGULAR BASIS?!

THIS IS ALL MY BROTHER'S FAULT!!

MIHA~ I'M TOO PLASTERED TO WALK. COME FETCH ME, WOULD YA?

COLLEGE FRESHMAN YEAR

HEEY THERE PERRITTY LADY~ WANNA BAAR HOP WITH ME? MY TREAT... HIC.

SHUT UP!!

THANKS TO MY INSANE STRENGTH, I'VE NOW KILLED SOMEONE!

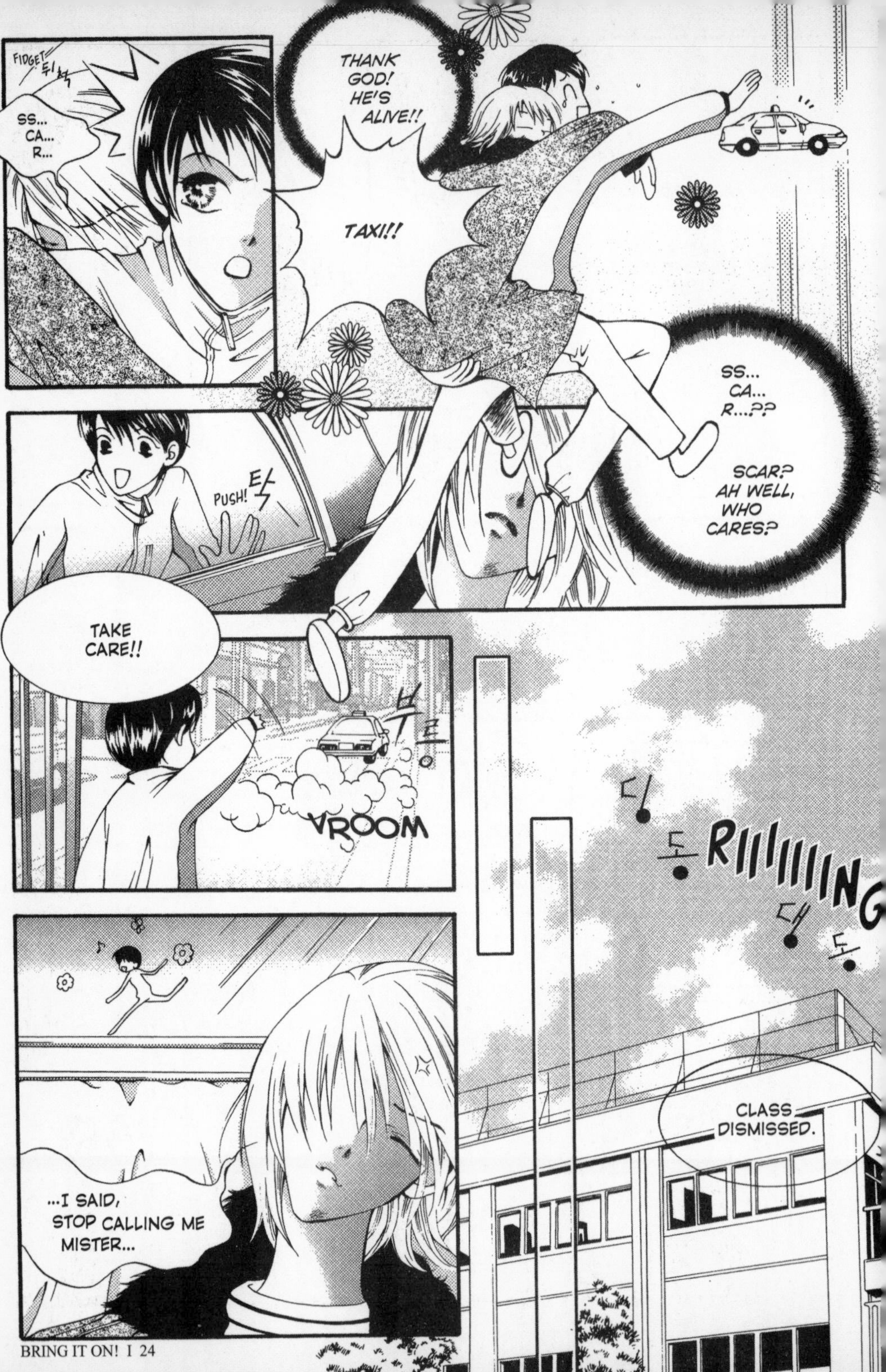
FIDGET
SS... CA... R...
THANK GOD! HE'S ALIVE!!
TAXI!!
SS... CA... R...??
SCAR? AH WELL, WHO CARES?
PUSH!
TAKE CARE!!
VROOM
...I SAID, STOP CALLING ME MISTER...
RIIIIIING
CLASS DISMISSED.

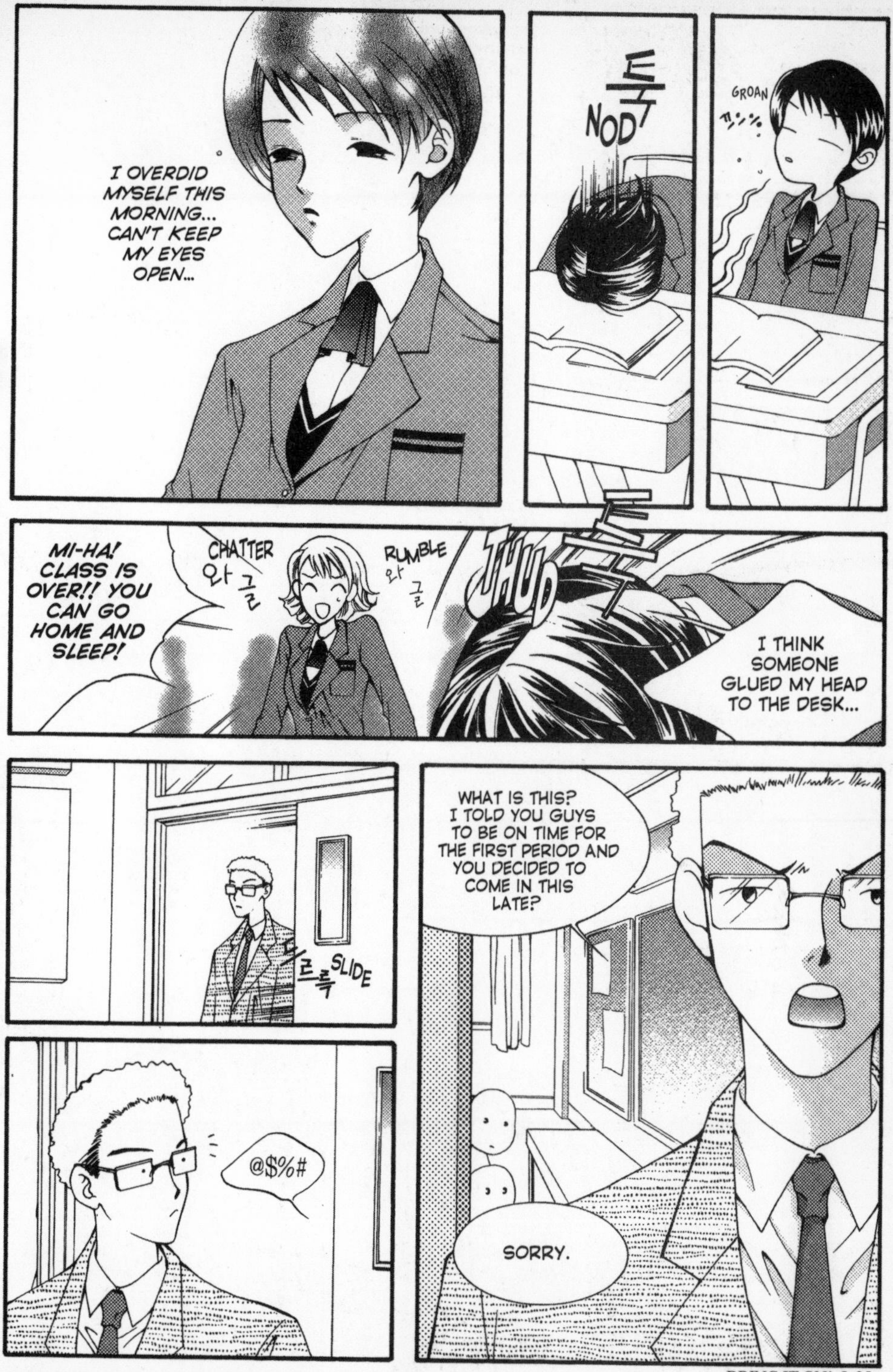

I OVERDID MYSELF THIS MORNING... CAN'T KEEP MY EYES OPEN...
NOD
GROAN
MI-HA! CLASS IS OVER!! YOU CAN GO HOME AND SLEEP!
CHATTER 와글
RUMBLE 와글
THUD
I THINK SOMEONE GLUED MY HEAD TO THE DESK...
SLIDE
@$%#
WHAT IS THIS? I TOLD YOU GUYS TO BE ON TIME FOR THE FIRST PERIOD AND YOU DECIDED TO COME IN THIS LATE?
SORRY.

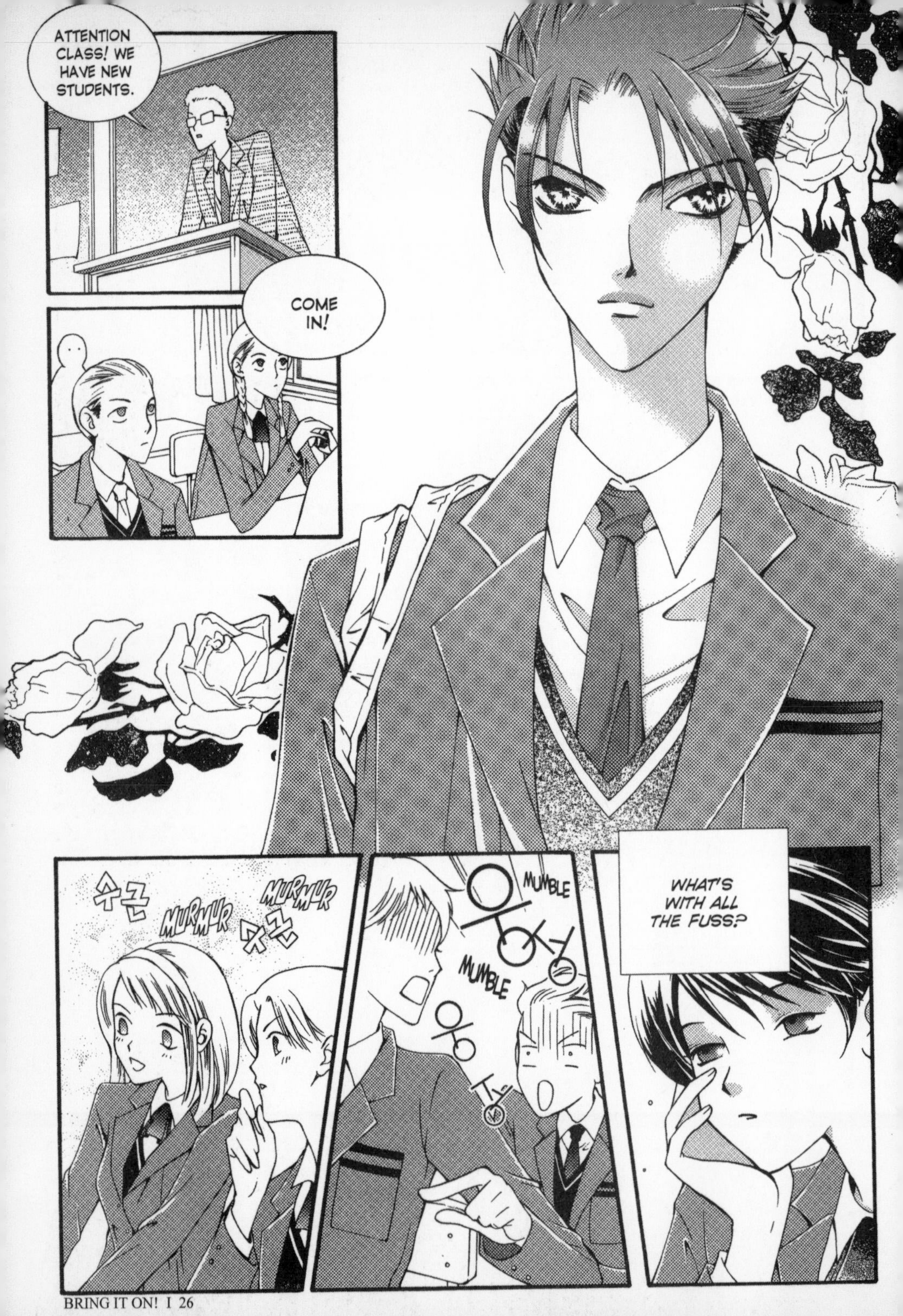
ATTENTION CLASS! WE HAVE NEW STUDENTS.
COME IN!
MURMUR
MURMUR
MUMBLE
MUMBLE
WHAT'S WITH ALL THE FUSS?

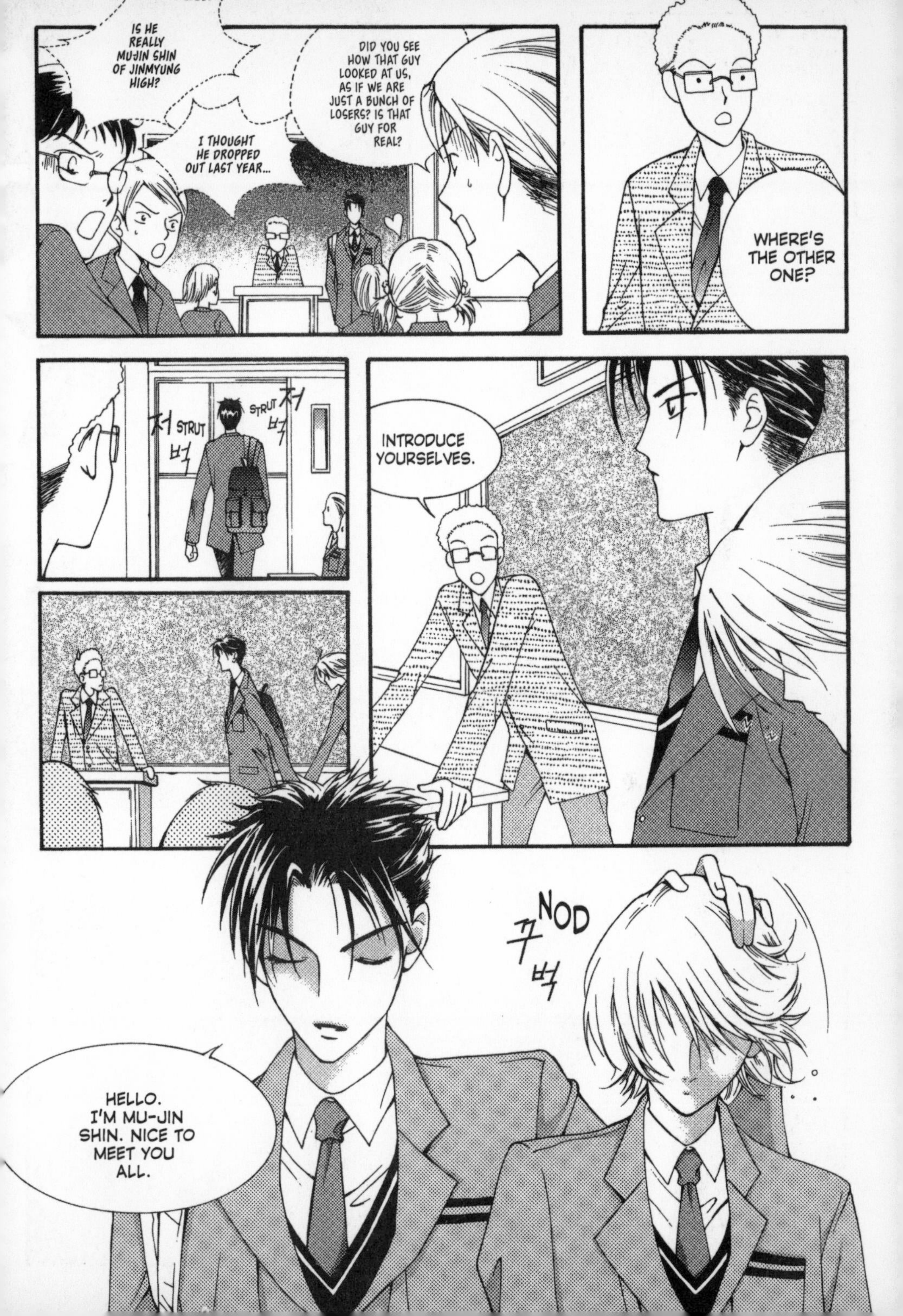
IS HE REALLY MUJIN SHIN OF JINMYUNG HIGH?
I THOUGHT HE DROPPED OUT LAST YEAR...
DID YOU SEE HOW THAT GUY LOOKED AT US, AS IF WE ARE JUST A BUNCH OF LOSERS? IS THAT GUY FOR REAL?
WHERE'S THE OTHER ONE?
저벅 STRUT
STRUT 저벅
INTRODUCE YOURSELVES.
꾸벅 NOD
HELLO. I'M MU-JIN SHIN. NICE TO MEET YOU ALL.

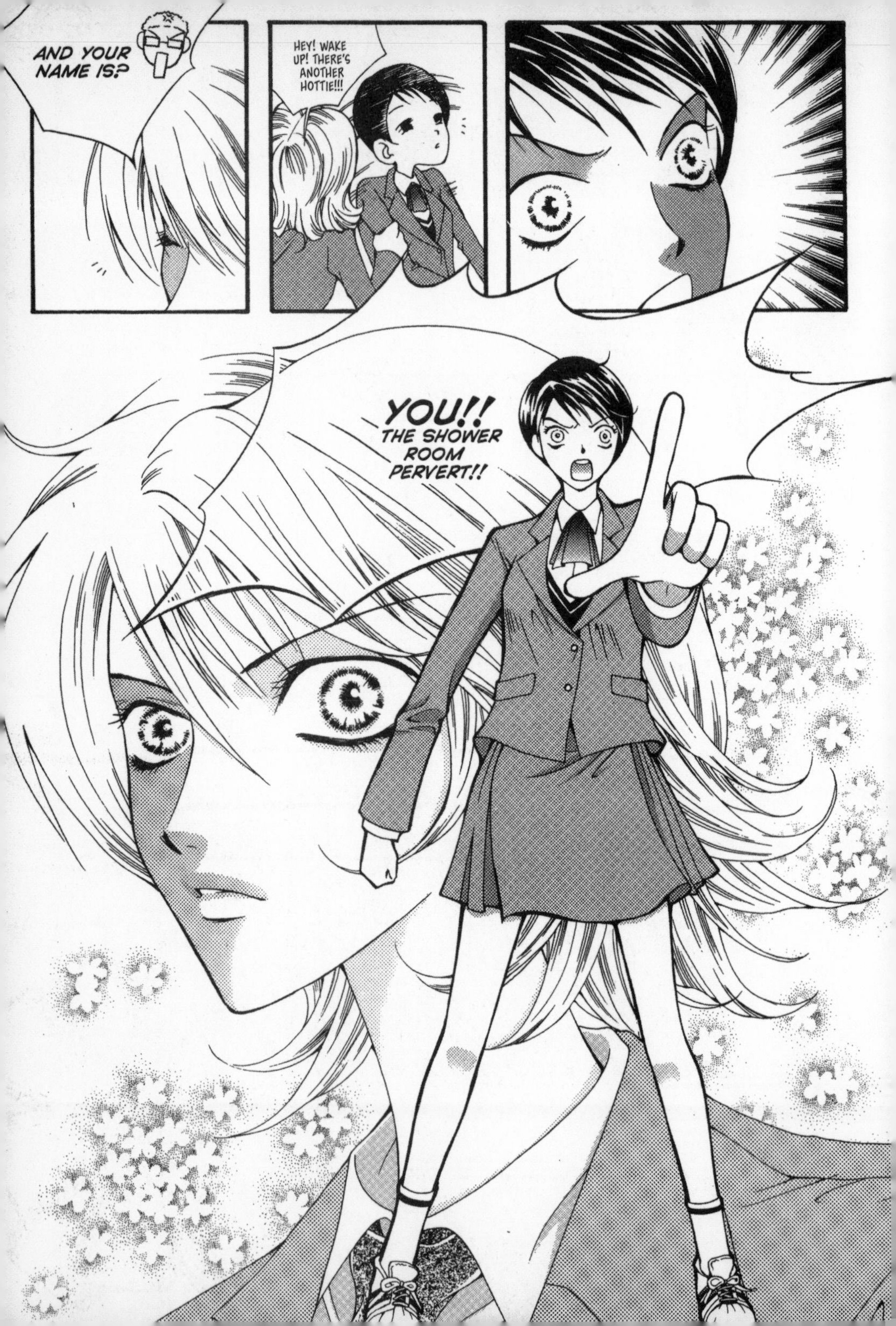
AND YOUR NAME IS?
HEY! WAKE UP! THERE'S ANOTHER HOTTIE!!!
YOU!! THE SHOWER ROOM PERVERT!!

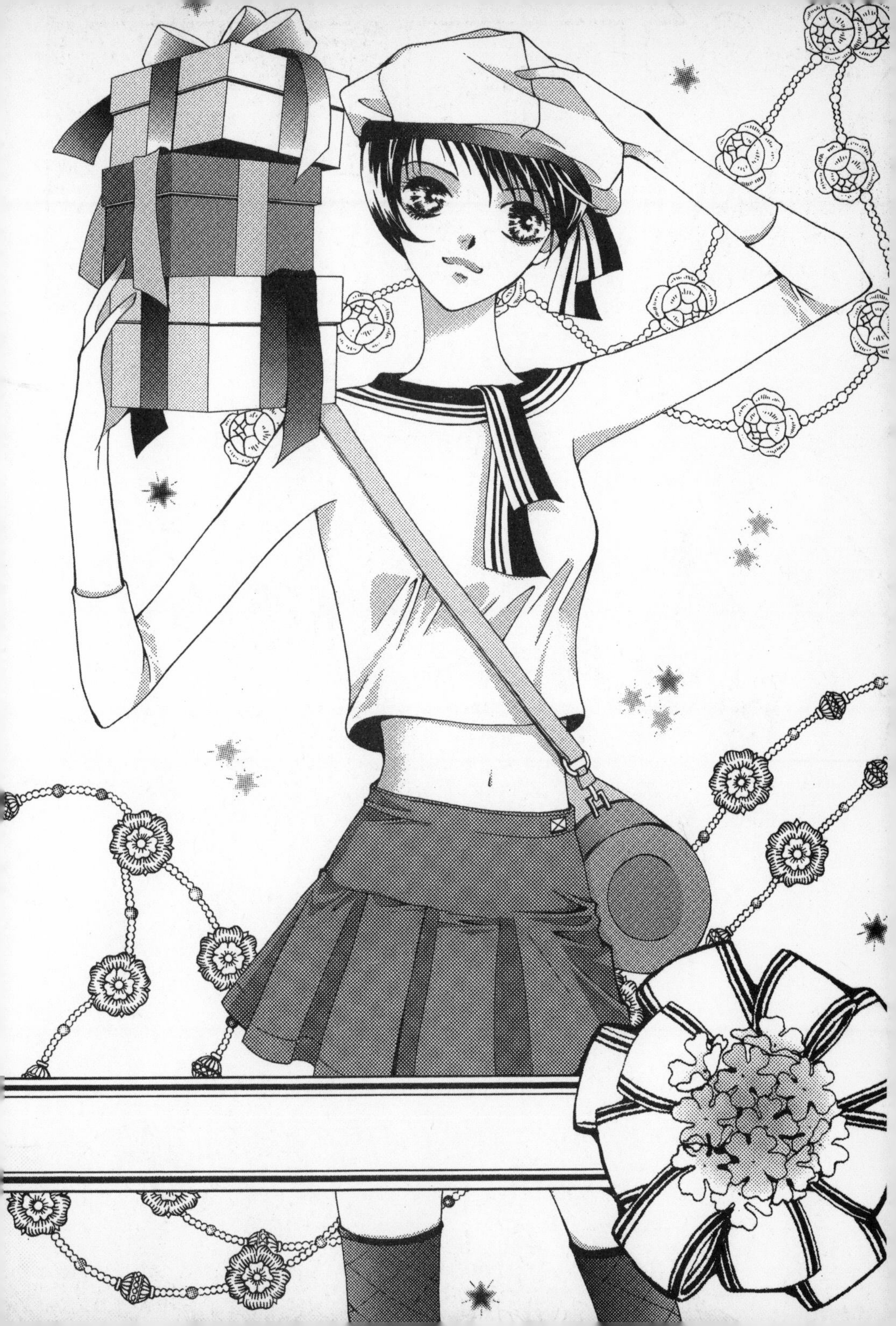

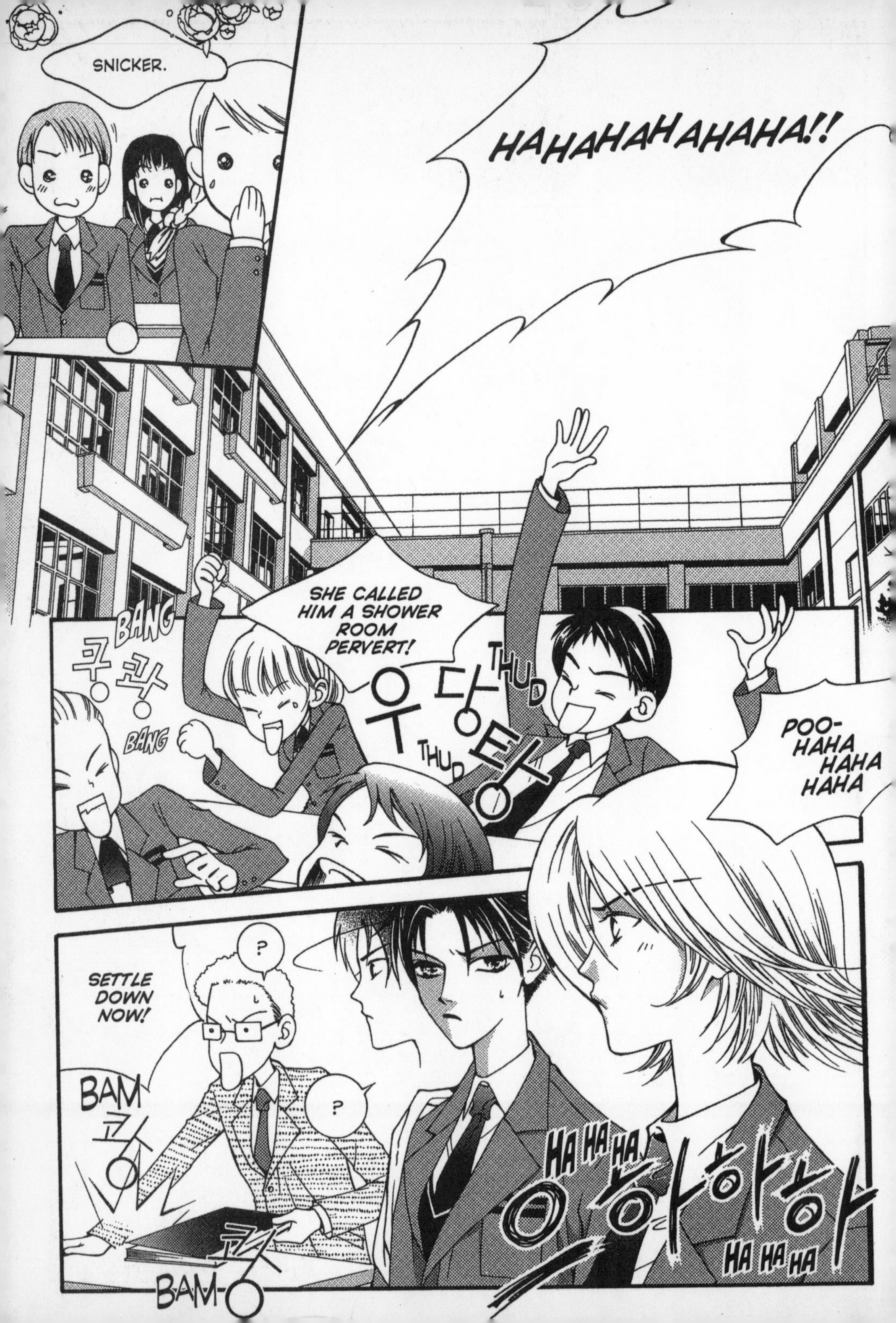
SNICKER.
HAHAHAHAHAHA!!
BANG
쿵쾅
BANG
SHE CALLED HIM A SHOWER ROOM PERVERT!
우당탕
THUD
THUD
POO-HAHA HAHA HAHA
SETTLE DOWN NOW!
?
?
BAM
쾅
쾅
BAM
HA HA HA
으하하하
HA HA HA

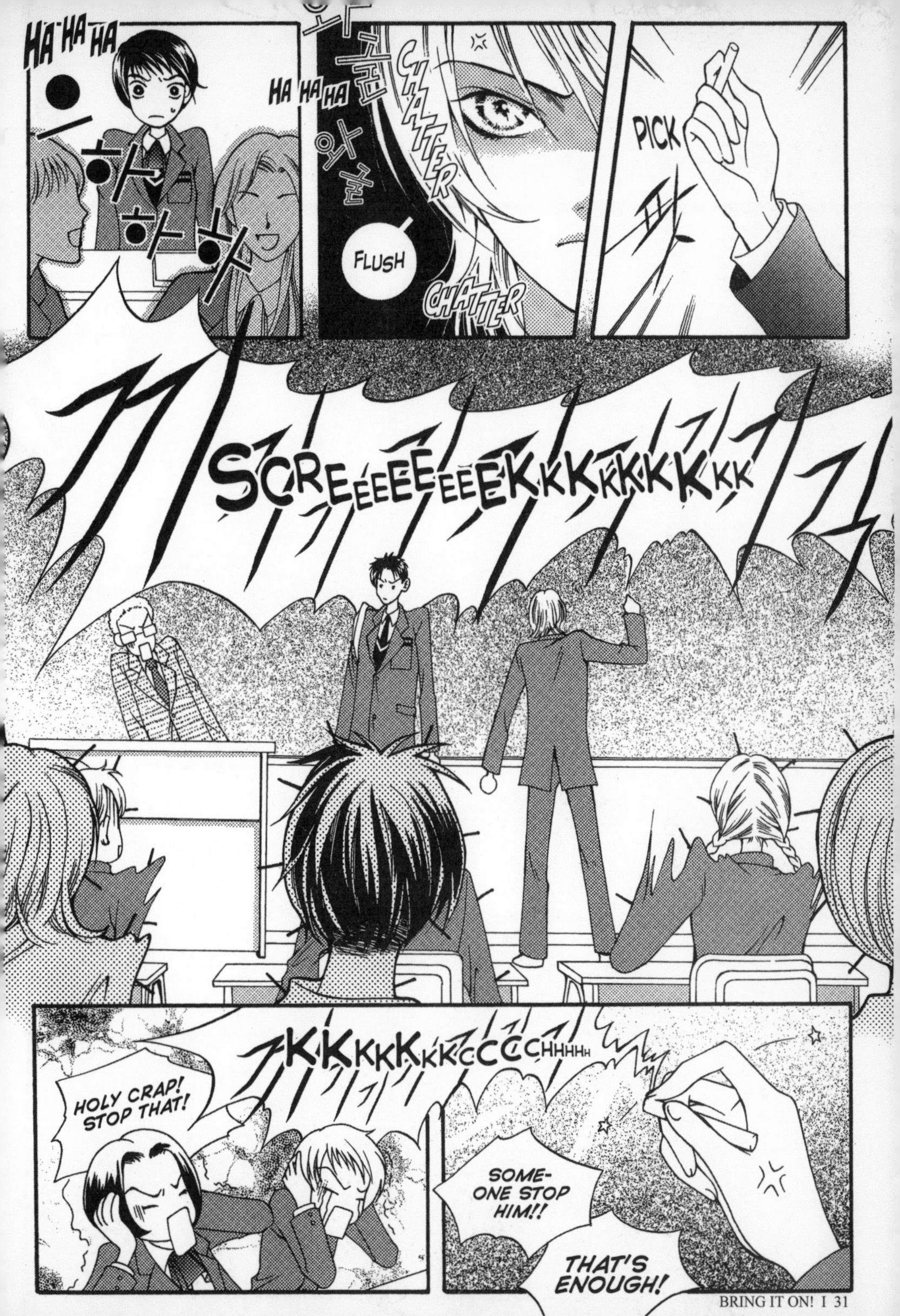
HA-HA-HA
HA HA HA
CHATTER
FLUSH
CHATTER
PICK
SCREEEEEEEEEEKKKKKKKKK
KKKKKKKCCCCHHHHH
HOLY CRAP! STOP THAT!
SOME-ONE STOP HIM!!
THAT'S ENOUGH!

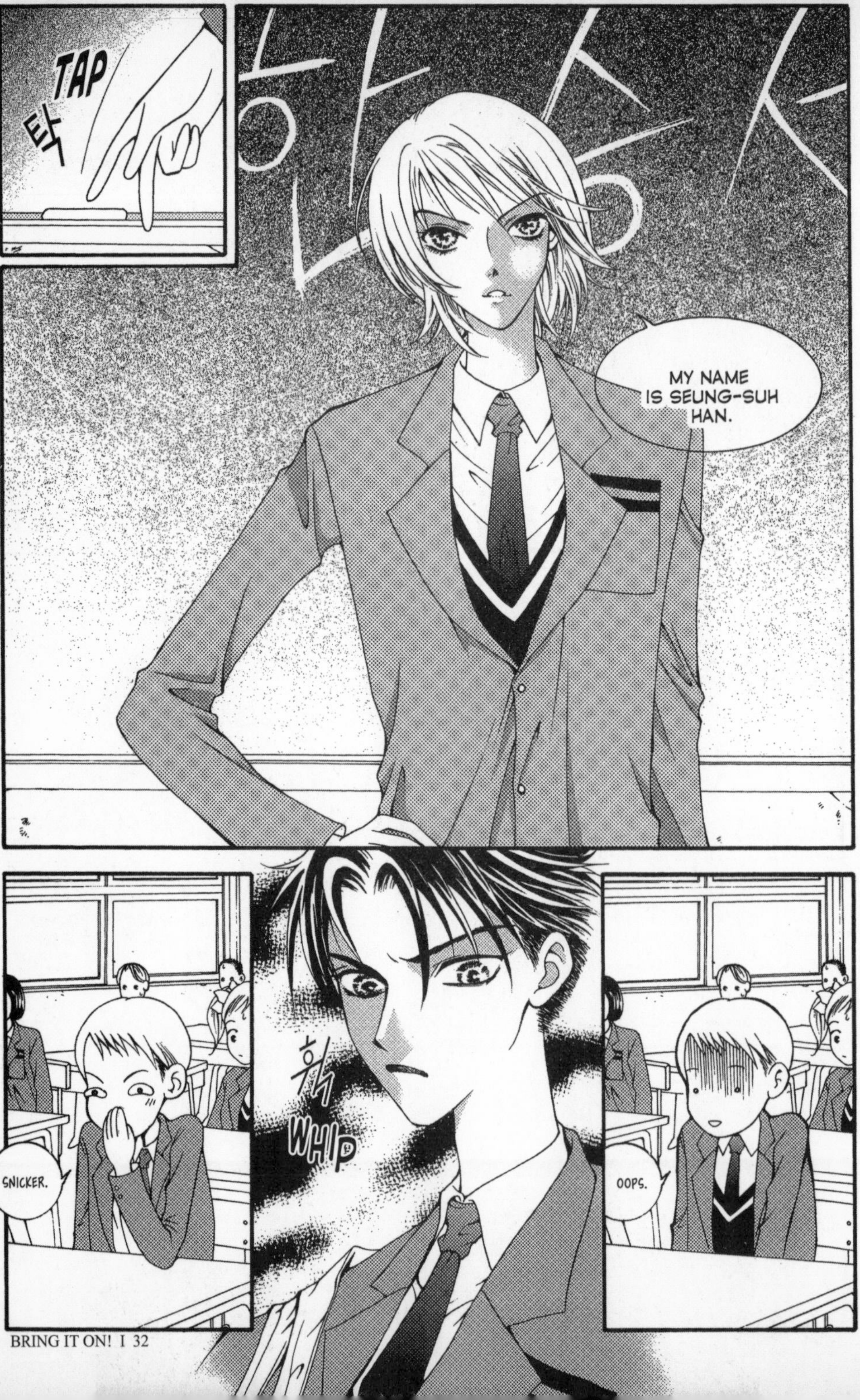
TAP
탁
MY NAME IS SEUNG-SUH HAN.
SNICKER.
휙
WHIP
OOPS.

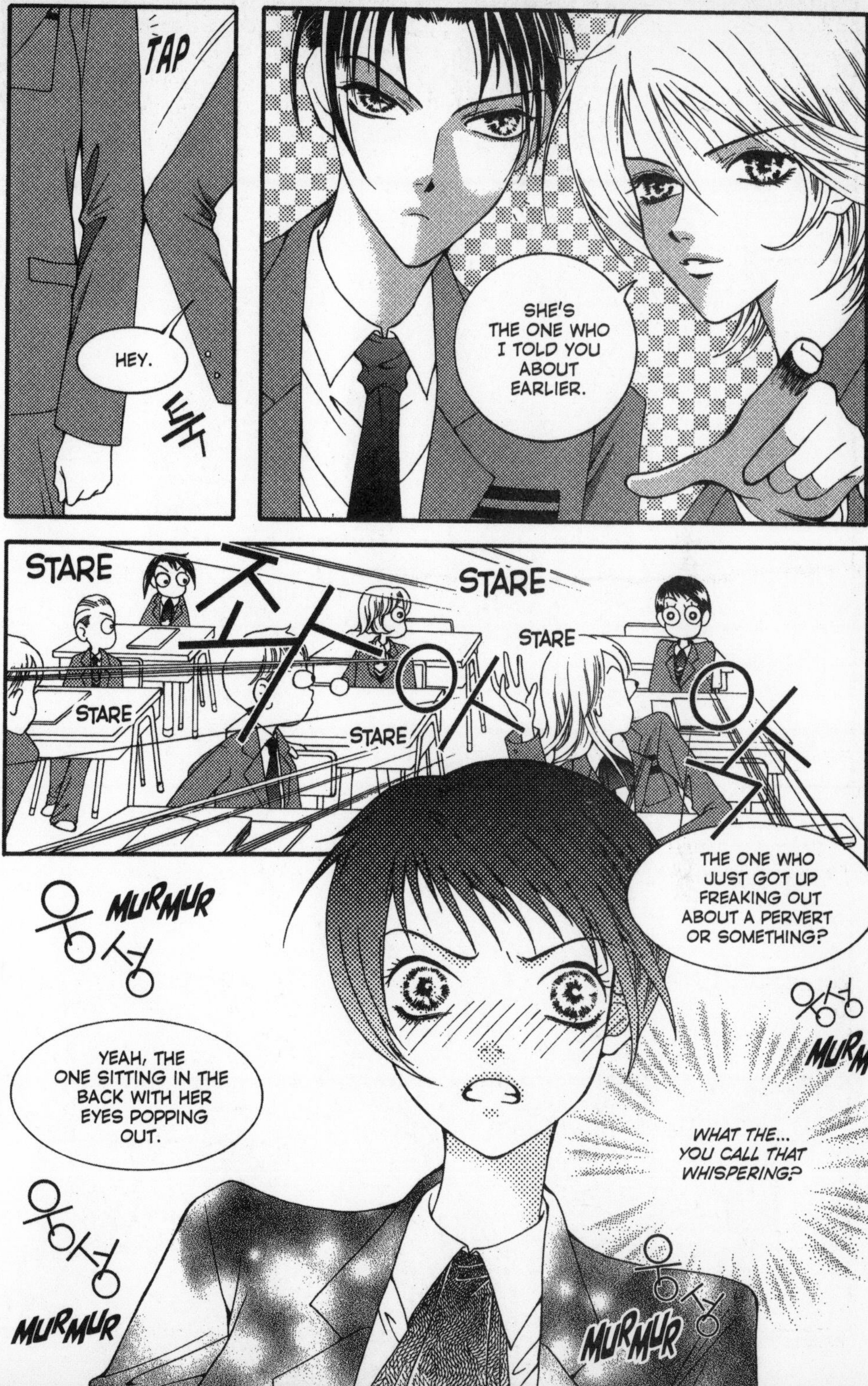
TAP
HEY.
SHE'S THE ONE WHO I TOLD YOU ABOUT EARLIER.
STARE
STARE
STARE
STARE
STARE
MURMUR
THE ONE WHO JUST GOT UP FREAKING OUT ABOUT A PERVERT OR SOMETHING?
MURMUR
YEAH, THE ONE SITTING IN THE BACK WITH HER EYES POPPING OUT.
WHAT THE... YOU CALL THAT WHISPERING?
MURMUR
MURMUR

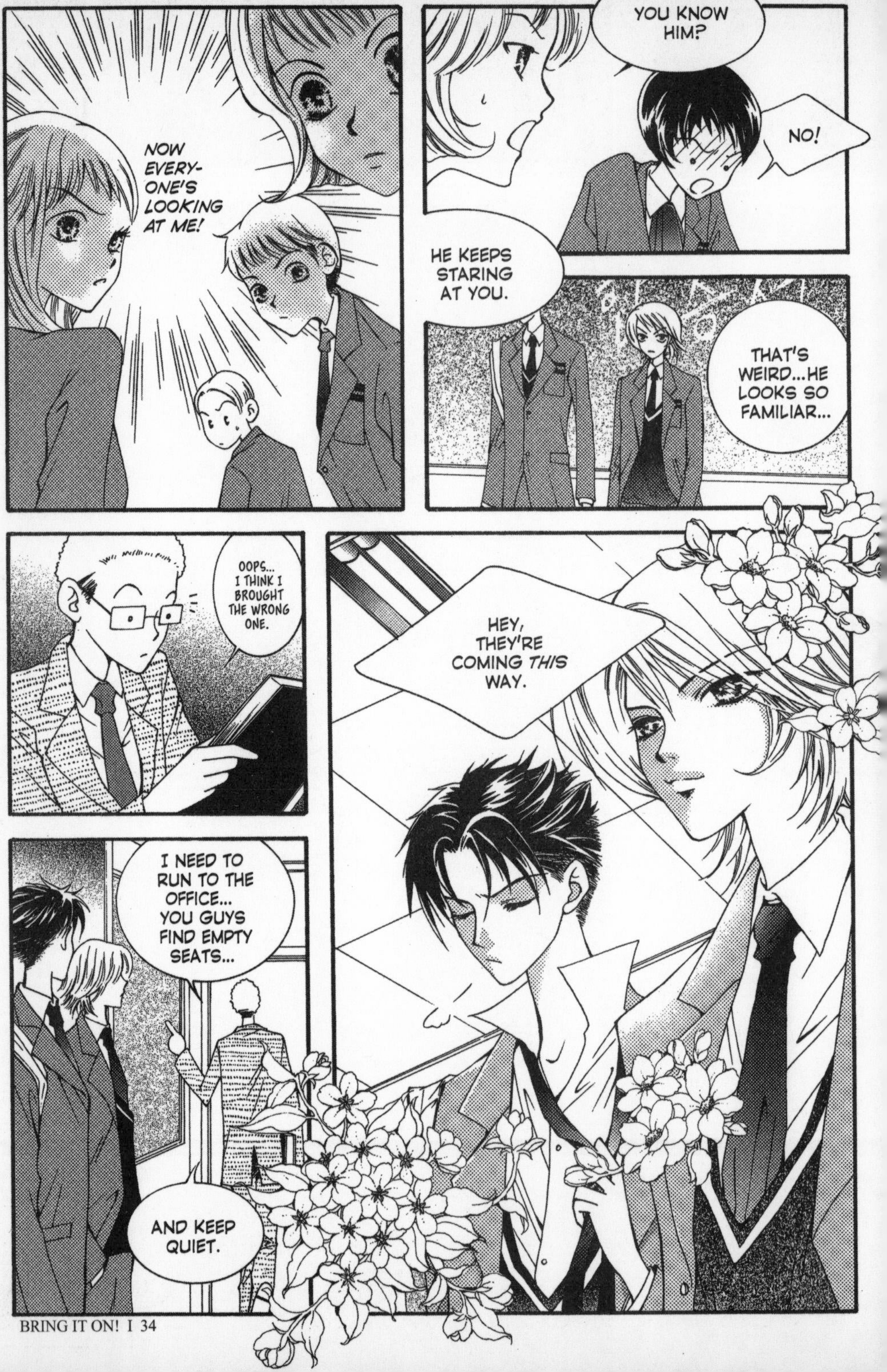
NOW EVERY-ONE'S LOOKING AT ME!
YOU KNOW HIM?
NO!
HE KEEPS STARING AT YOU.
THAT'S WEIRD...HE LOOKS SO FAMILIAR...
OOPS... I THINK I BROUGHT THE WRONG ONE.
I NEED TO RUN TO THE OFFICE... YOU GUYS FIND EMPTY SEATS...
AND KEEP QUIET.
HEY, THEY'RE COMING *THIS* WAY.

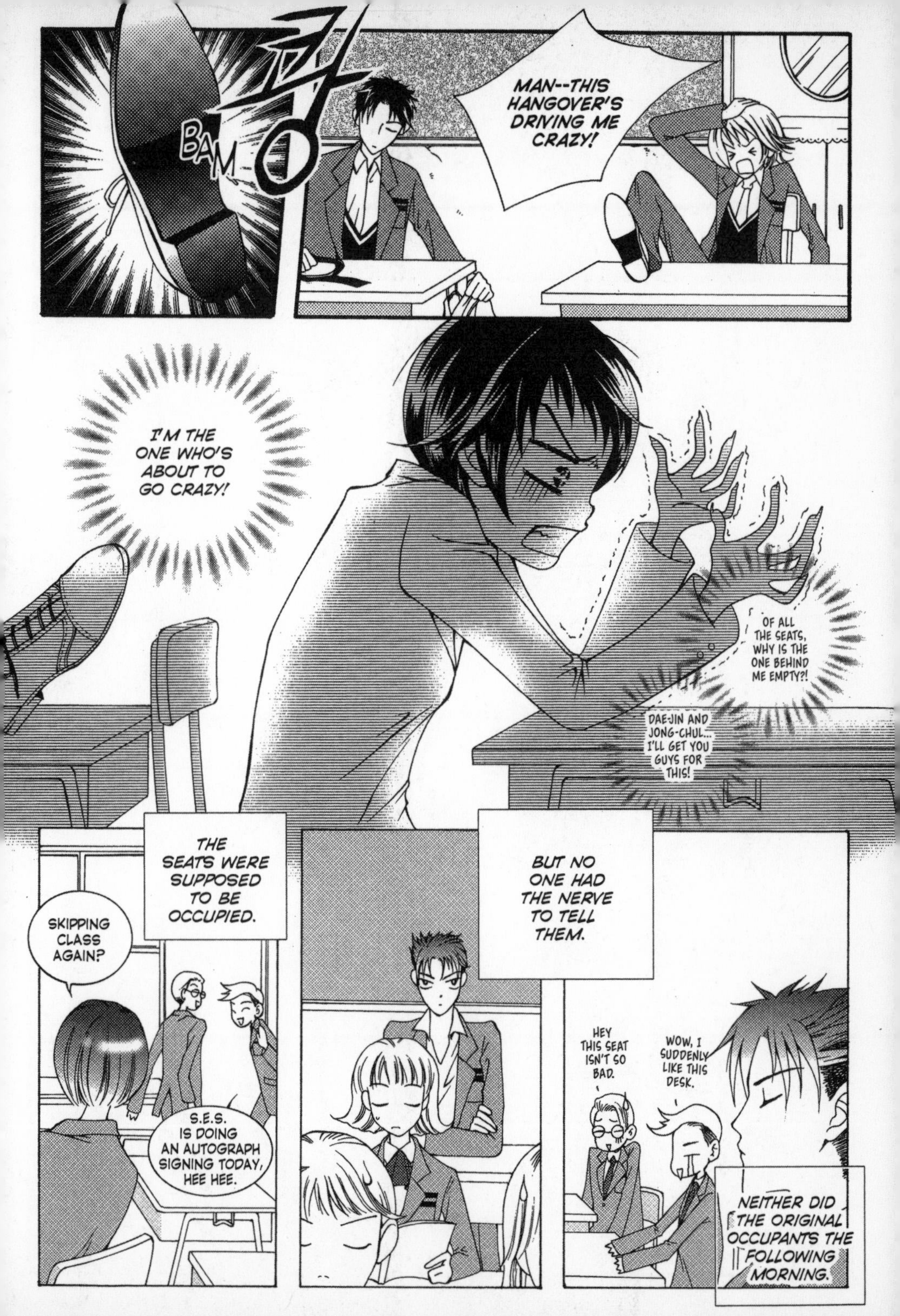
BAM
MAN--THIS HANGOVER'S DRIVING ME CRAZY!
I'M THE ONE WHO'S ABOUT TO GO CRAZY!
OF ALL THE SEATS, WHY IS THE ONE BEHIND ME EMPTY?!
DAE-JIN AND JONG-CHUL... I'LL GET YOU GUYS FOR THIS!
THE SEATS WERE SUPPOSED TO BE OCCUPIED.
SKIPPING CLASS AGAIN?
S.E.S. IS DOING AN AUTOGRAPH SIGNING TODAY, HEE HEE.
BUT NO ONE HAD THE NERVE TO TELL THEM.
HEY THIS SEAT ISN'T SO BAD.
WOW, I SUDDENLY LIKE THIS DESK.
NEITHER DID THE ORIGINAL OCCUPANTS THE FOLLOWING MORNING.

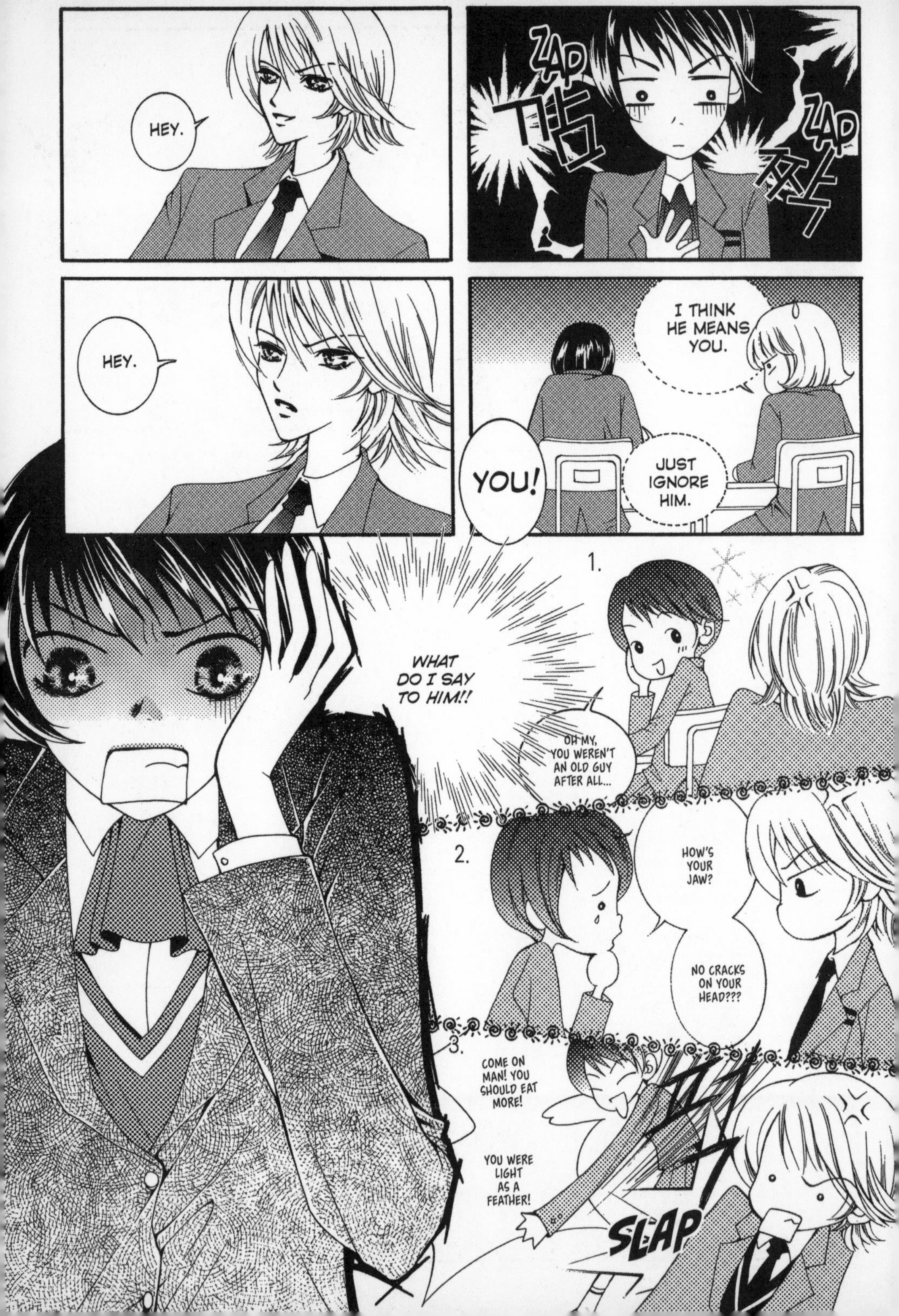
HEY.
ZAP
ZAP
HEY.
I THINK HE MEANS YOU.
YOU!
JUST IGNORE HIM.
WHAT DO I SAY TO HIM!!
1.
OH MY, YOU WEREN'T AN OLD GUY AFTER ALL...
2.
HOW'S YOUR JAW?
NO CRACKS ON YOUR HEAD???
3.
COME ON MAN! YOU SHOULD EAT MORE!
YOU WERE LIGHT AS A FEATHER!
SLAP

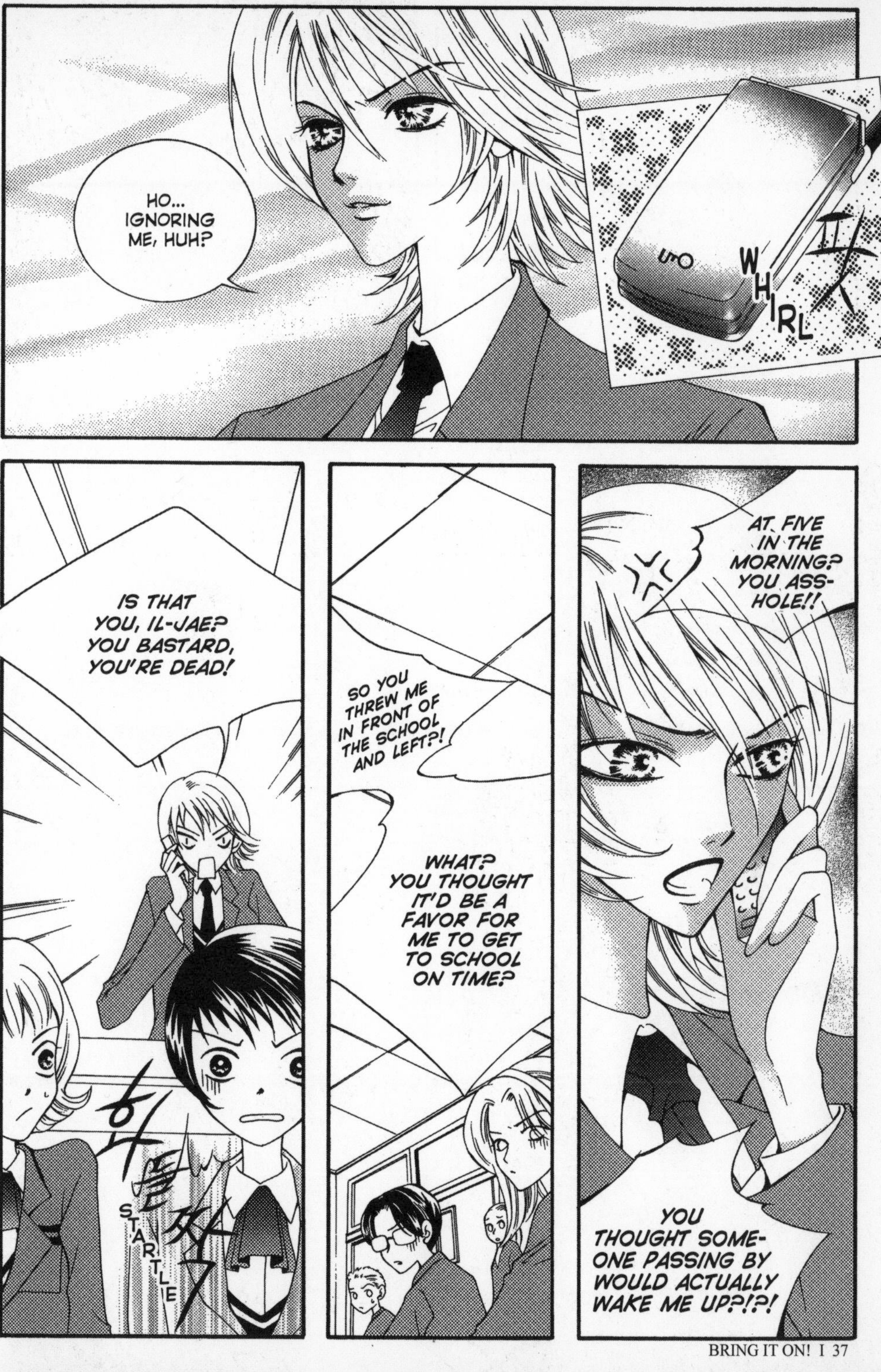
HO... IGNORING ME, HUH?
WHIRL
IS THAT YOU, IL-JAE? YOU BASTARD, YOU'RE DEAD!
STARTLE
SO YOU THREW ME IN FRONT OF THE SCHOOL AND LEFT?!
WHAT? YOU THOUGHT IT'D BE A FAVOR FOR ME TO GET TO SCHOOL ON TIME?
AT FIVE IN THE MORNING? YOU ASS-HOLE!!
YOU THOUGHT SOME-ONE PASSING BY WOULD ACTUALLY WAKE ME UP?!?!

YEAH, YOU'RE RIGHT, IT'S NOT REALLY *ALL* YOUR FAULT.

SOMEONE THREW ME IN A CAB AND I RODE AROUND THE ENTIRE CITY UNCONSCIOUS AND FINALLY CAME TO SCHOOL.

STARE STARE

STARE

STARE

WHEN I CAME TO, THE DRIVER WAS CRYING WITH THE CAB PULLED OVER 'CUZ THE METER HAD MAXED OUT AT $999.99.

WHY DON'T YOU JUST GO ANNOUNCE IT OVER THE INTERCOM?

I DON'T THINK ENOUGH PEOPLE HEARD YOU.

MU-JIN? YEAH, HE'S HERE.

YEAH, FINE. SEE YOU LATER.

HE WENT AROUND LOOKING FOR ME, AND WHEN I CALLED HIM, HE BROUGHT ME MY UNIFORM.

CLICK

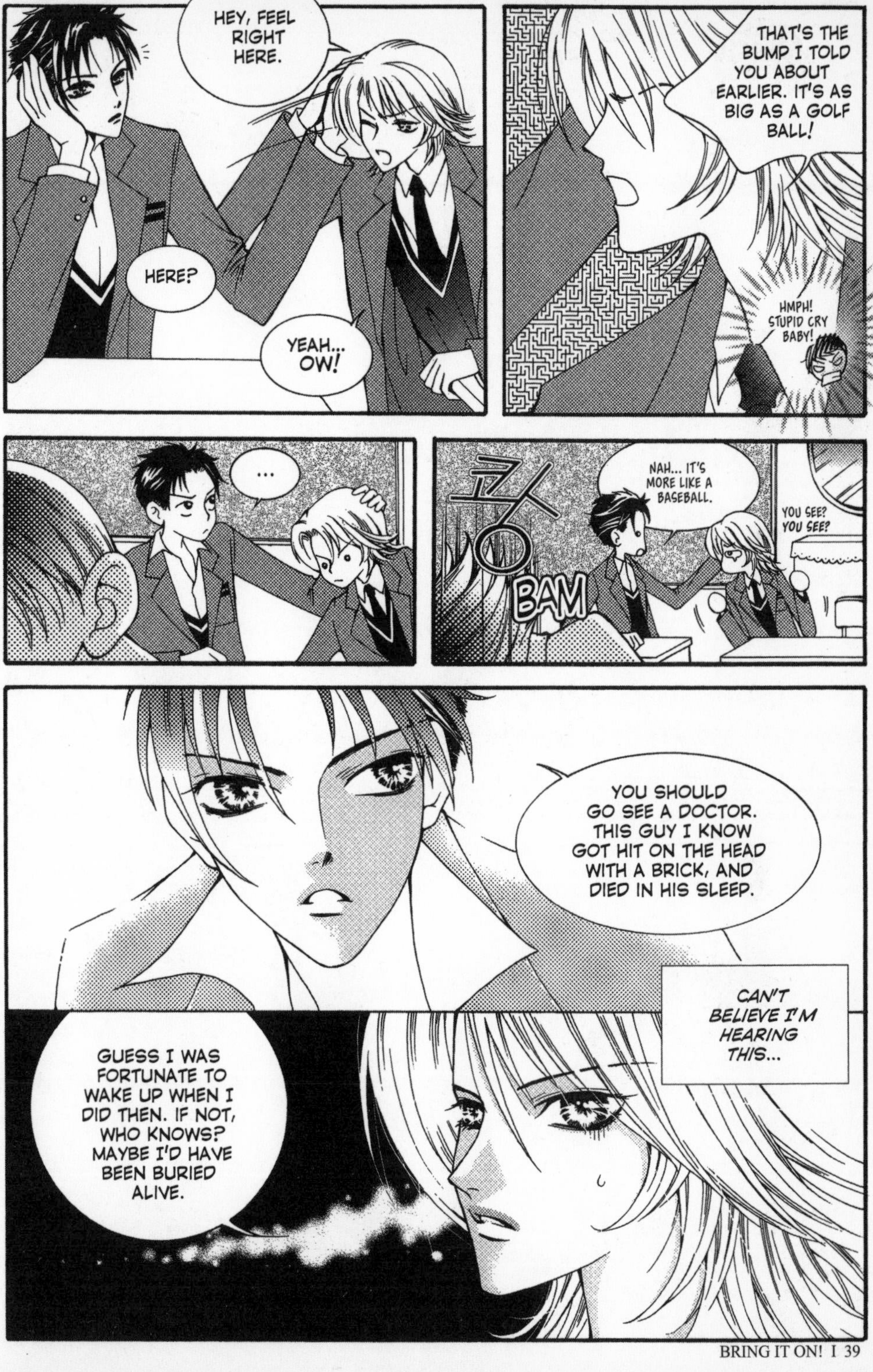
HEY, FEEL RIGHT HERE.
HERE?
YEAH... OW!
THAT'S THE BUMP I TOLD YOU ABOUT EARLIER. IT'S AS BIG AS A GOLF BALL!
HMPH! STUPID CRY BABY!
...
BAM
NAH... IT'S MORE LIKE A BASEBALL.
YOU SEE? YOU SEE?
YOU SHOULD GO SEE A DOCTOR. THIS GUY I KNOW GOT HIT ON THE HEAD WITH A BRICK, AND DIED IN HIS SLEEP.
CAN'T BELIEVE I'M HEARING THIS...
GUESS I WAS FORTUNATE TO WAKE UP WHEN I DID THEN. IF NOT, WHO KNOWS? MAYBE I'D HAVE BEEN BURIED ALIVE.

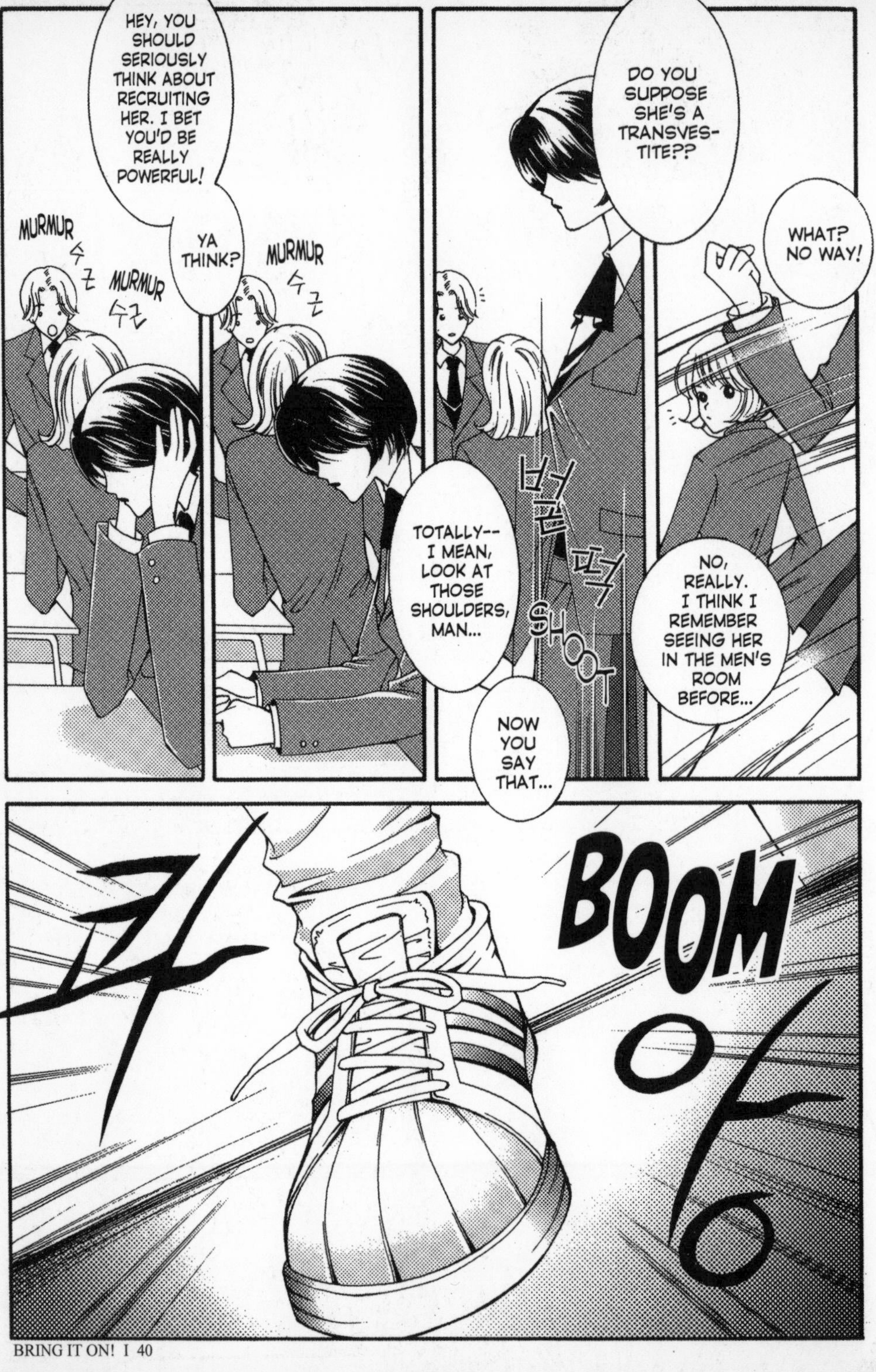
MURMUR
수군
MURMUR
수군
HEY, YOU SHOULD SERIOUSLY THINK ABOUT RECRUITING HER. I BET YOU'D BE REALLY POWERFUL!
YA THINK?
MURMUR
수군
TOTALLY-- I MEAN, LOOK AT THOSE SHOULDERS, MAN...
DO YOU SUPPOSE SHE'S A TRANSVES-TITE??
SHOOT
NOW YOU SAY THAT...
WHAT? NO WAY!
NO, REALLY. I THINK I REMEMBER SEEING HER IN THE MEN'S ROOM BEFORE...
BOOM

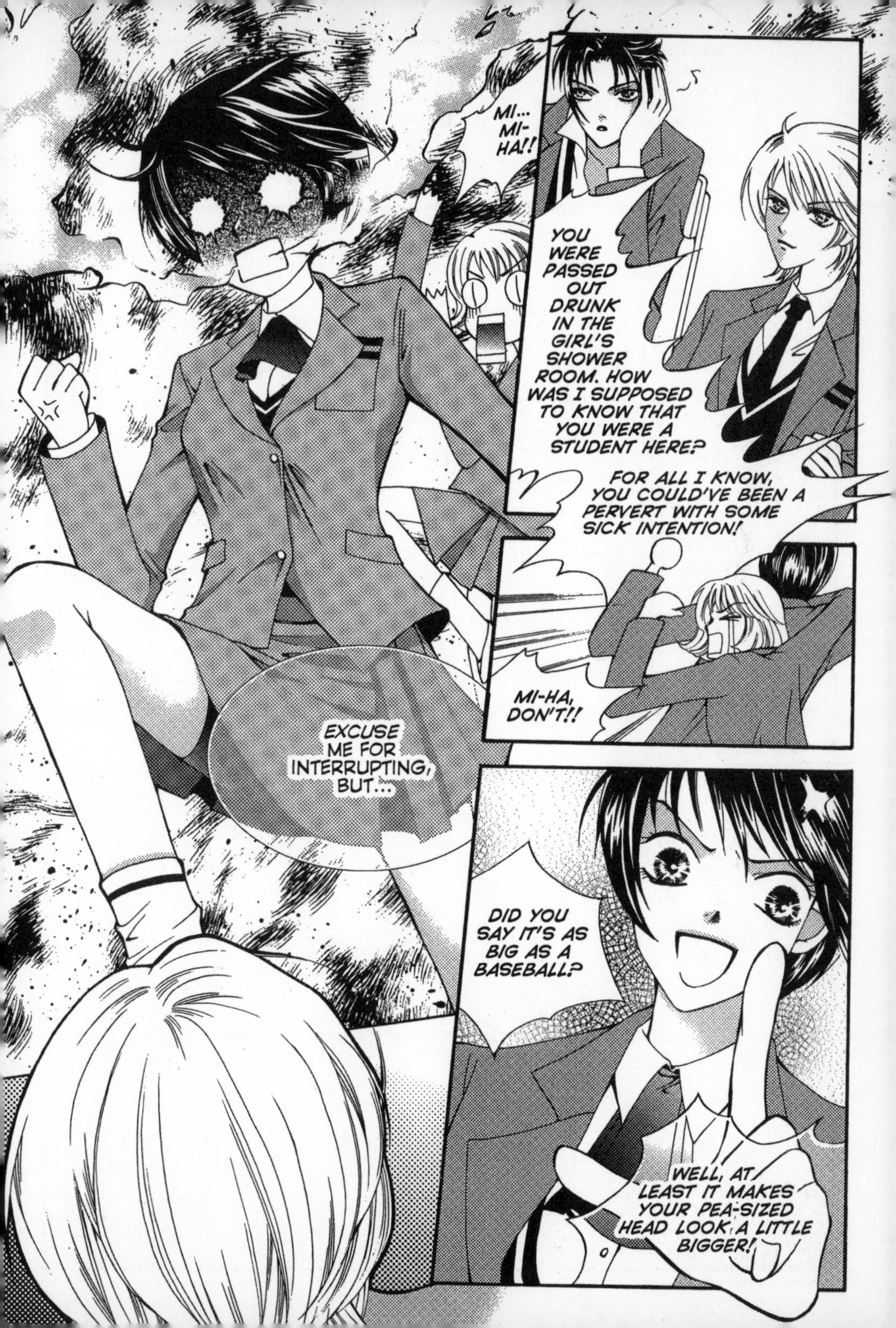
MI... MI-HA!!
EXCUSE ME FOR INTERRUPTING, BUT...
YOU WERE PASSED OUT DRUNK IN THE GIRL'S SHOWER ROOM. HOW WAS I SUPPOSED TO KNOW THAT YOU WERE A STUDENT HERE?
FOR ALL I KNOW, YOU COULD'VE BEEN A PERVERT WITH SOME SICK INTENTION!
MI-HA, DON'T!!
DID YOU SAY IT'S AS BIG AS A BASEBALL?
WELL, AT LEAST IT MAKES YOUR PEA-SIZED HEAD LOOK A LITTLE BIGGER!

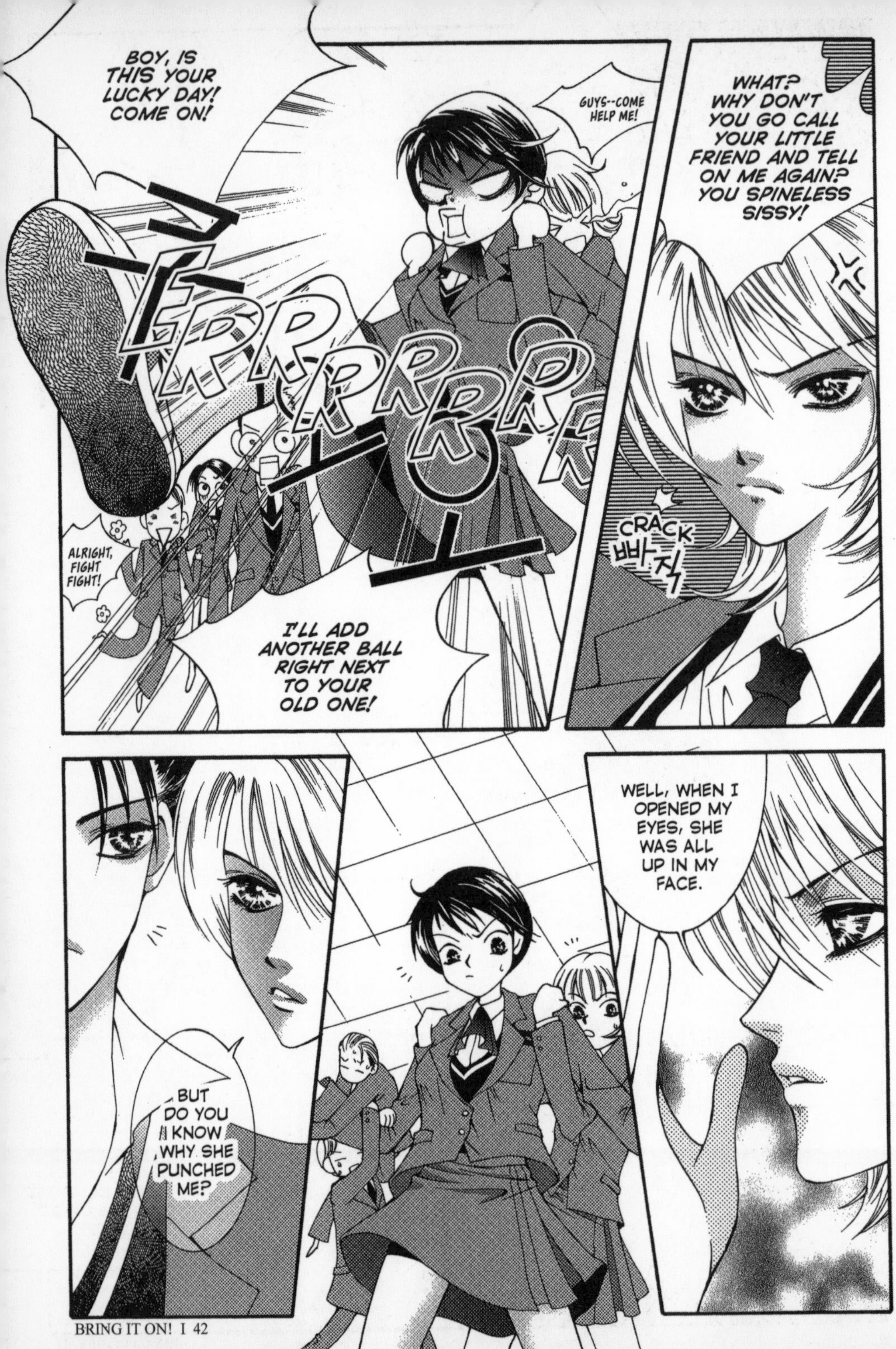
BOY, IS THIS YOUR LUCKY DAY! COME ON!
GUYS--COME HELP ME!
ALRIGHT, FIGHT FIGHT!
I'LL ADD ANOTHER BALL RIGHT NEXT TO YOUR OLD ONE!
WHAT? WHY DON'T YOU GO CALL YOUR LITTLE FRIEND AND TELL ON ME AGAIN? YOU SPINELESS SISSY!
CRACK
빠직
...BUT DO YOU KNOW WHY SHE PUNCHED ME?
WELL, WHEN I OPENED MY EYES, SHE WAS ALL UP IN MY FACE.

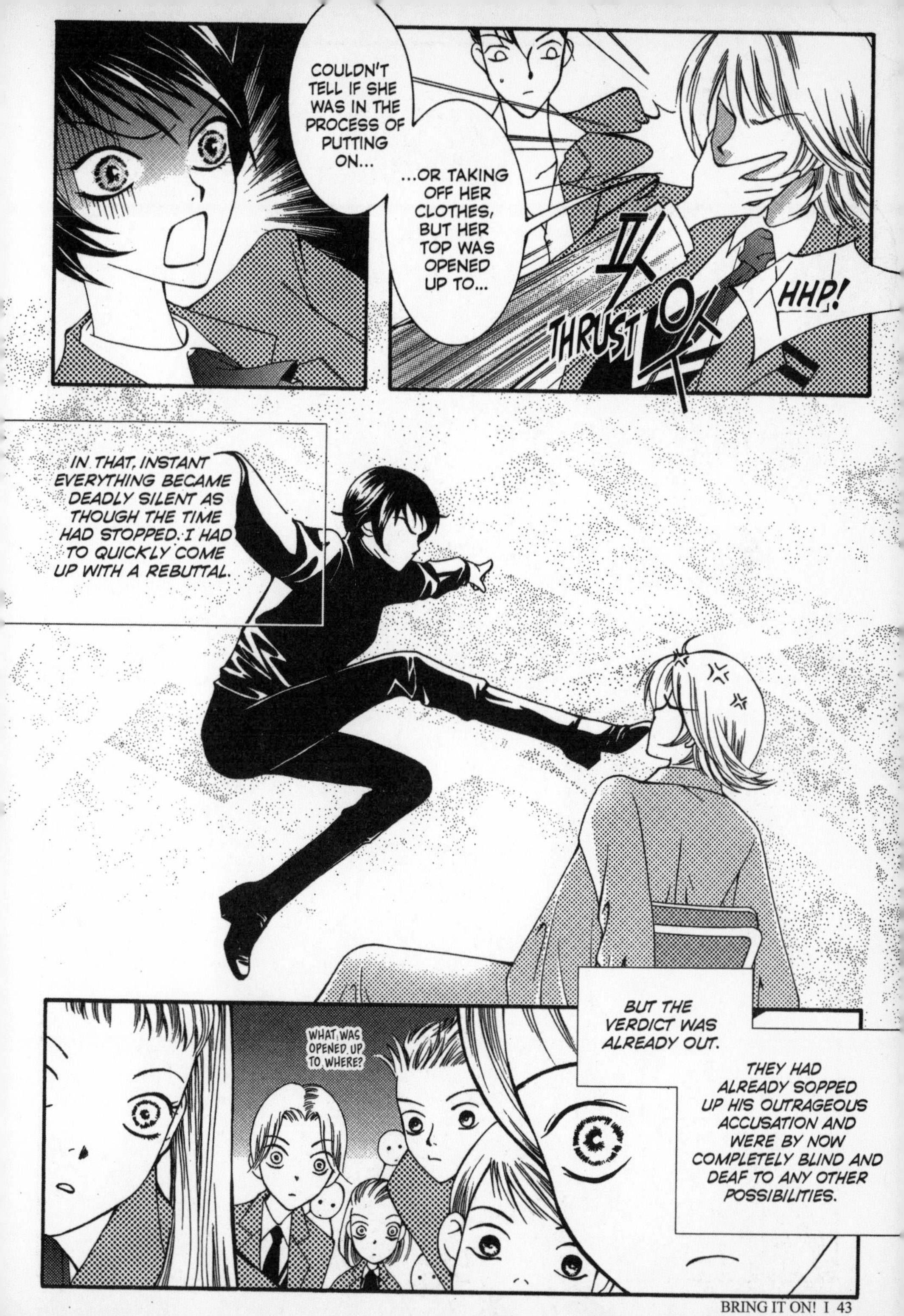

COULDN'T TELL IF SHE WAS IN THE PROCESS OF PUTTING ON...
...OR TAKING OFF HER CLOTHES, BUT HER TOP WAS OPENED UP TO...
THRUST
HHP!
IN THAT, INSTANT EVERYTHING BECAME DEADLY SILENT AS THOUGH THE TIME HAD STOPPED. I HAD TO QUICKLY COME UP WITH A REBUTTAL.
WHAT WAS OPENED UP TO WHERE?
BUT THE VERDICT WAS ALREADY OUT.
THEY HAD ALREADY SOPPED UP HIS OUTRAGEOUS ACCUSATION AND WERE BY NOW COMPLETELY BLIND AND DEAF TO ANY OTHER POSSIBILITIES.

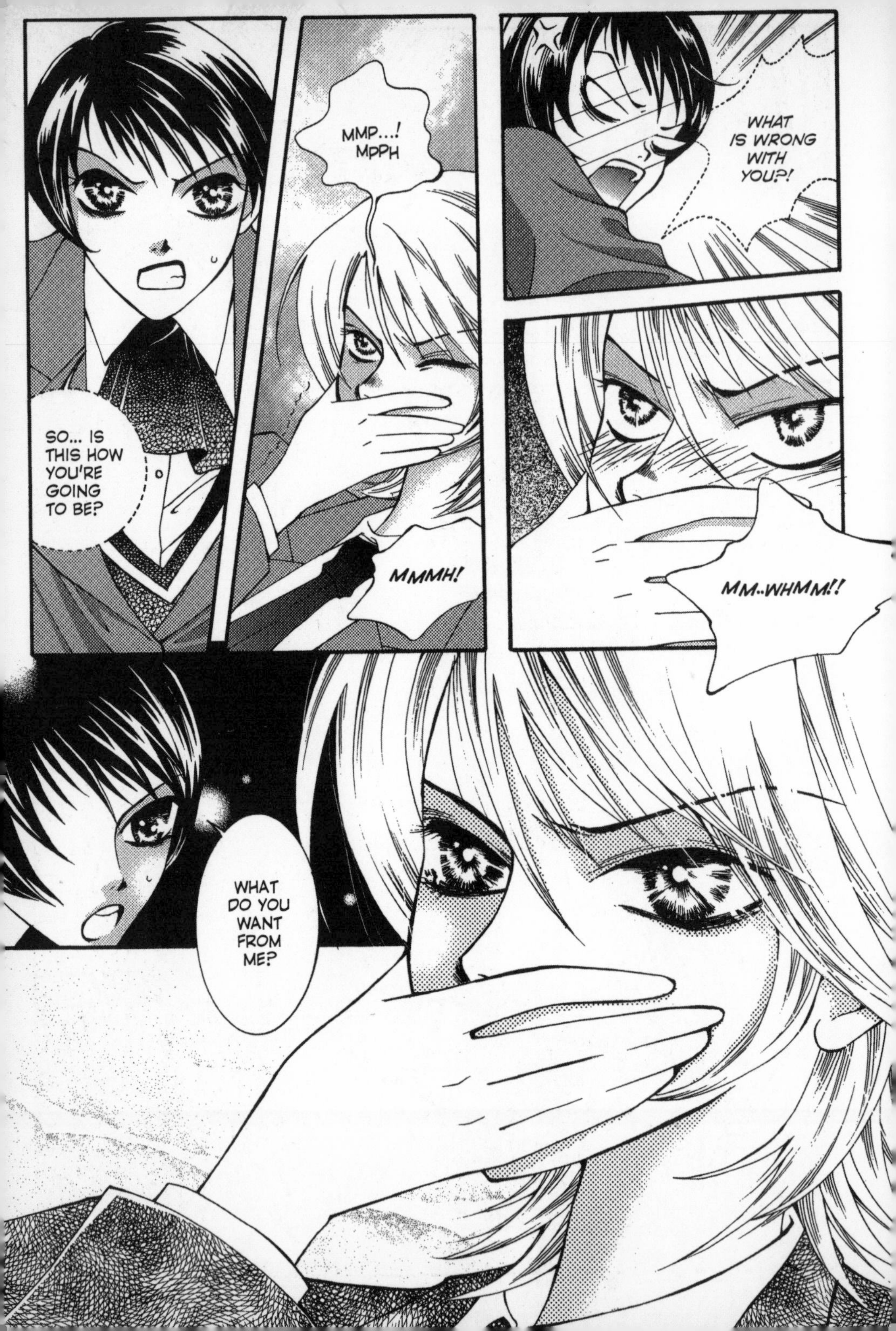
SO... IS THIS HOW YOU'RE GOING TO BE?
MMP...! MPPH
MMMH!
WHAT IS WRONG WITH YOU?!
MM..WHMM!!
WHAT DO YOU WANT FROM ME?

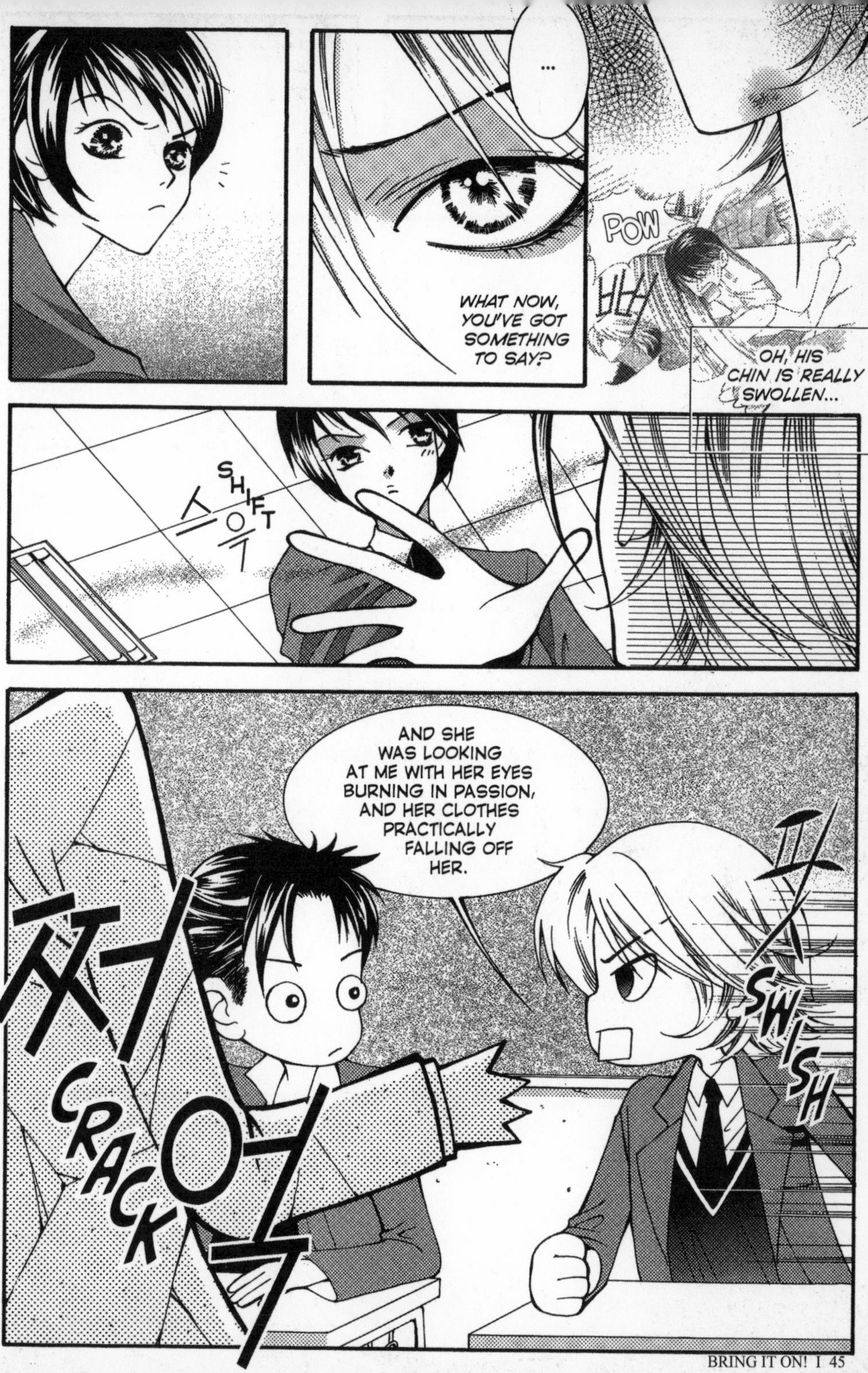
...
WHAT NOW, YOU'VE GOT SOMETHING TO SAY?
POW
OH, HIS CHIN IS REALLY SWOLLEN...
SHIFT
AND SHE WAS LOOKING AT ME WITH HER EYES BURNING IN PASSION, AND HER CLOTHES PRACTICALLY FALLING OFF HER.
SWISH
CRACK

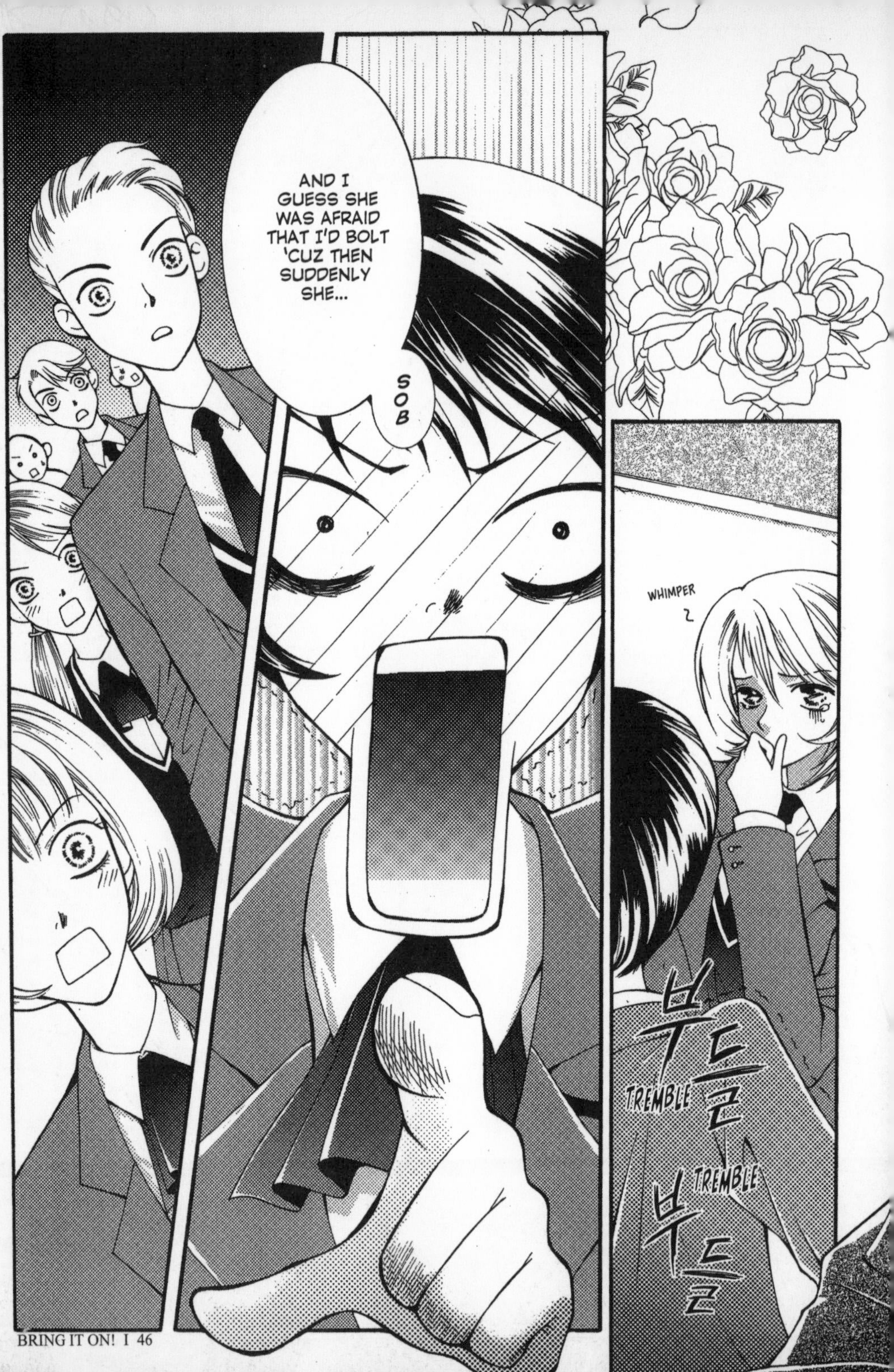
AND I GUESS SHE WAS AFRAID THAT I'D BOLT 'CUZ THEN SUDDENLY SHE...
SOB
WHIMPER
부들
TREMBLE
부들
TREMBLE

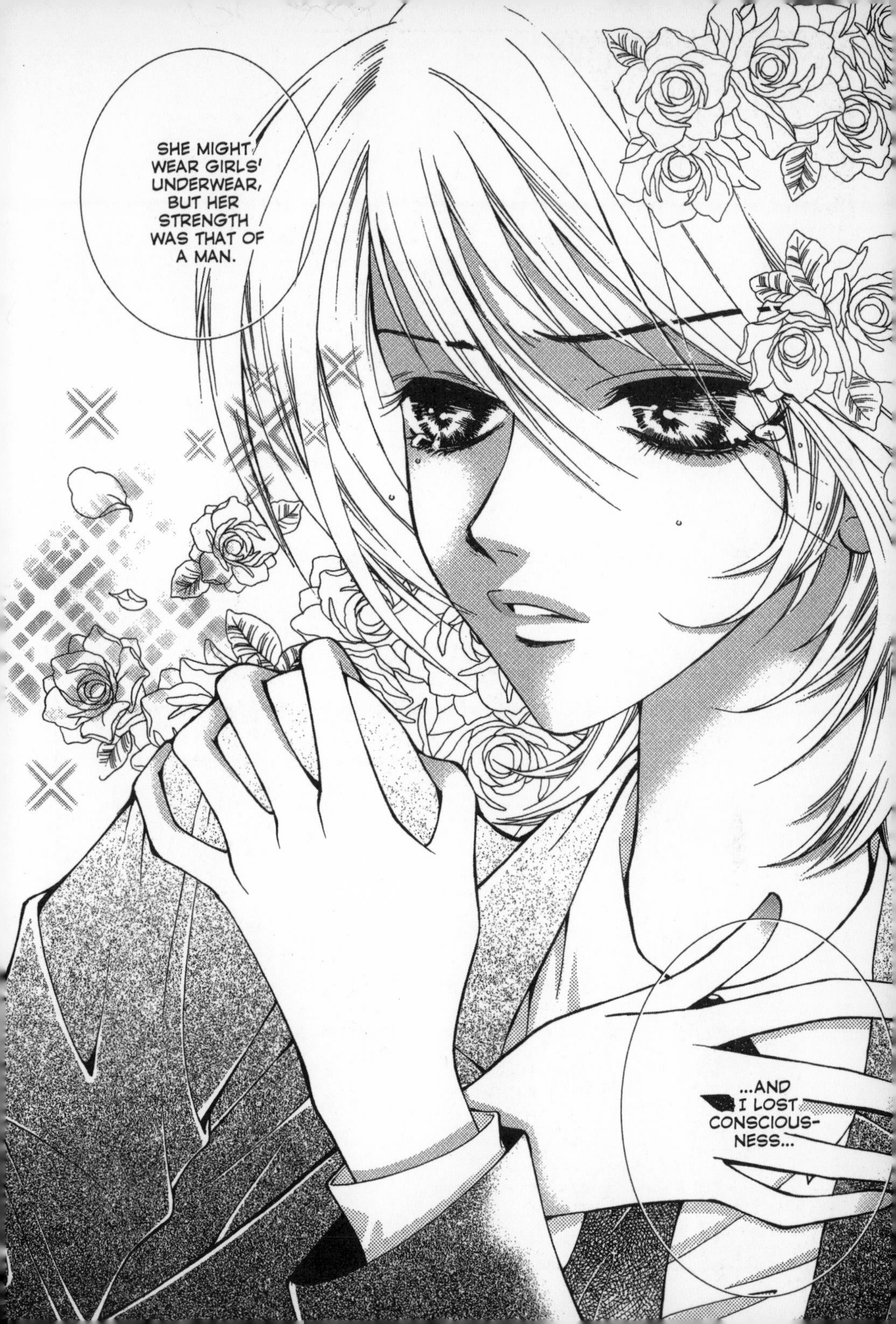
SHE MIGHT WEAR GIRLS' UNDERWEAR, BUT HER STRENGTH WAS THAT OF A MAN.
...AND I LOST CONSCIOUS-NESS...

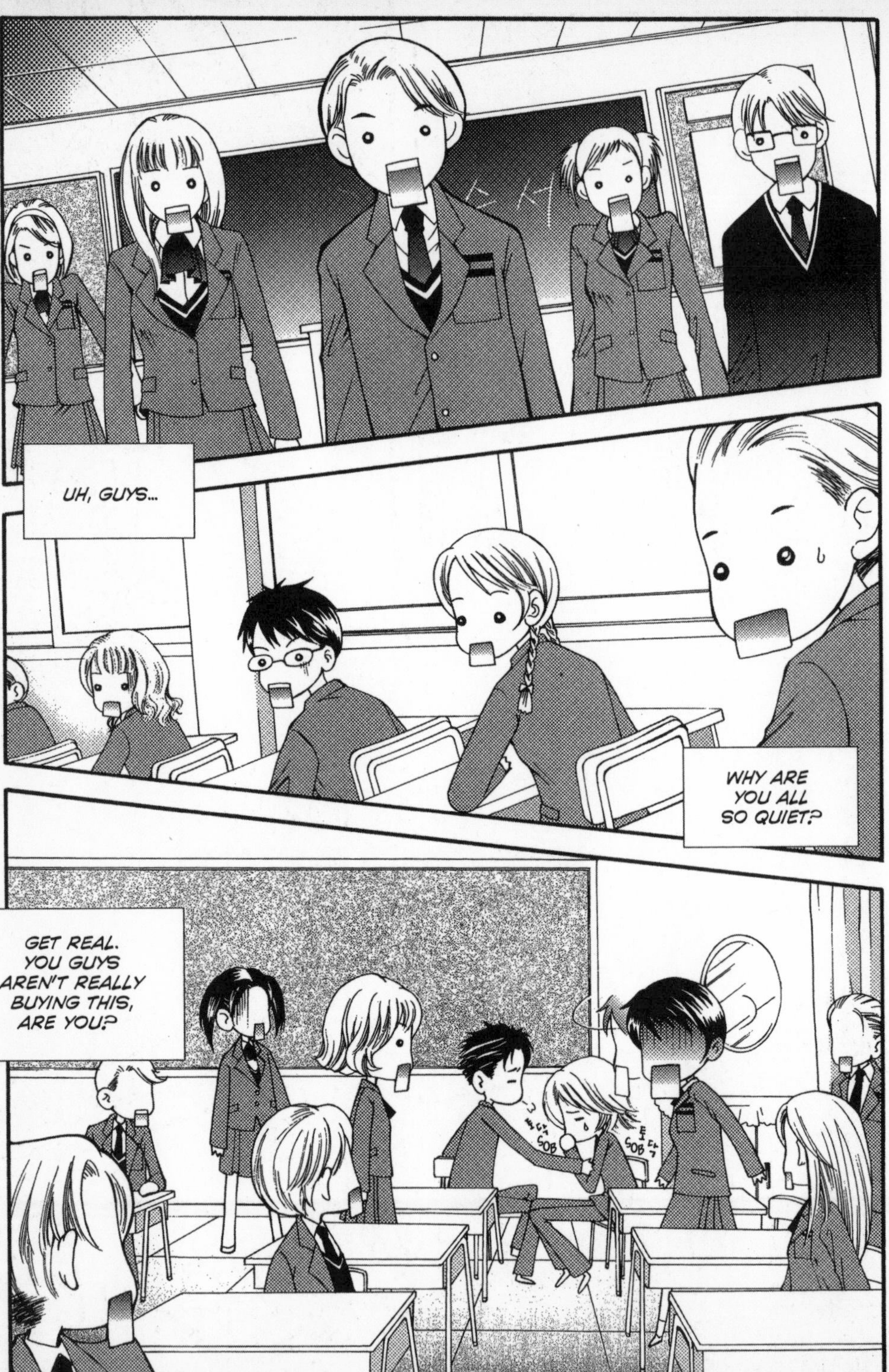
UH, GUYS...
WHY ARE YOU ALL SO QUIET?
GET REAL. YOU GUYS AREN'T REALLY BUYING THIS, ARE YOU?
SOB
SOB

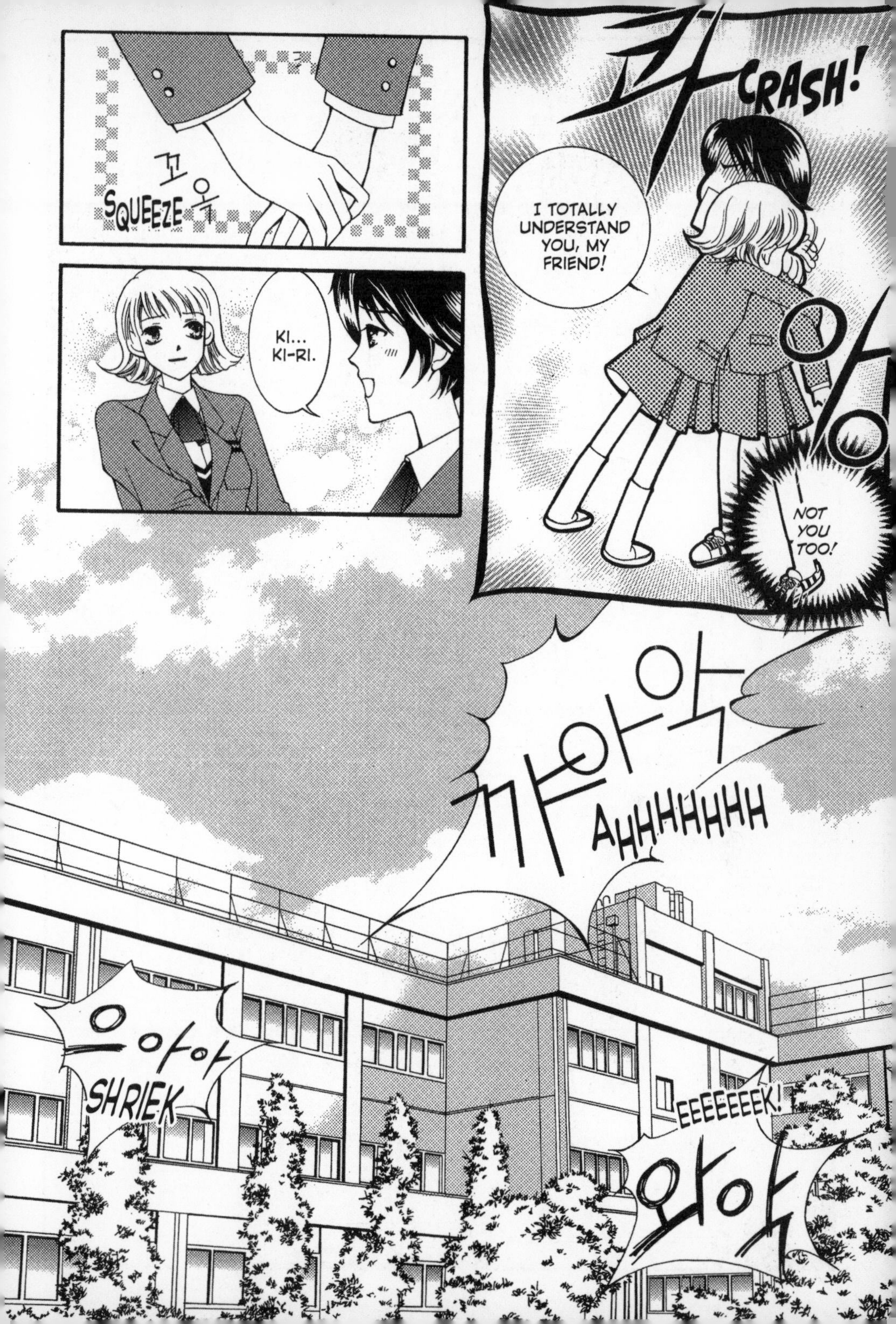
꼬옥
SQUEEZE
KI... KI-RI.
CRASH!
I TOTALLY UNDERSTAND YOU, MY FRIEND!
NOT YOU TOO!
AHHHHHHH
SHRIEK
EEEEEEEK!

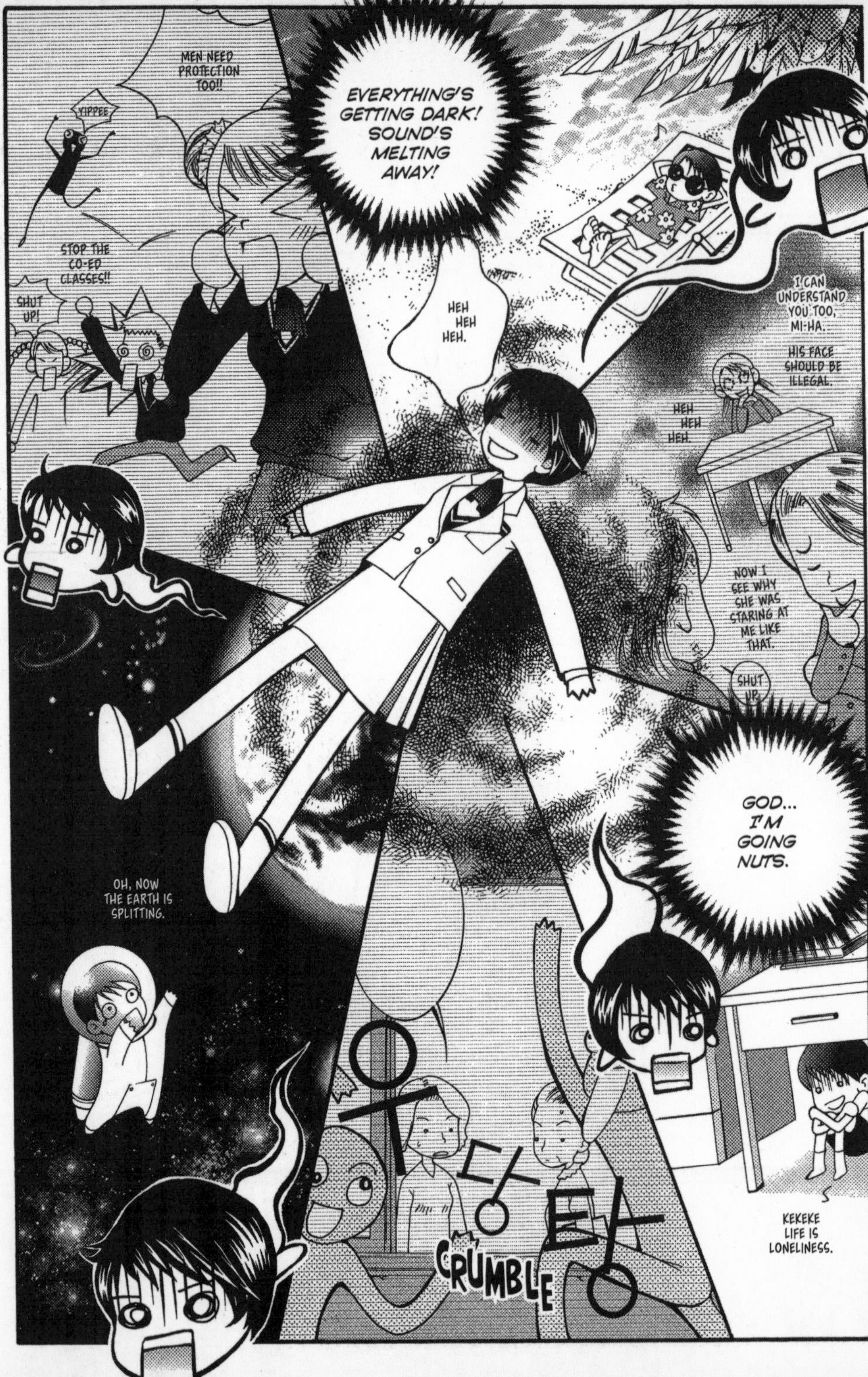
MEN NEED PROTECTION TOO!!
YIPPEE
EVERYTHING'S GETTING DARK! SOUND'S MELTING AWAY!
STOP THE CO-ED CLASSES!!
SHUT UP!
HEH HEH HEH.
I CAN UNDERSTAND YOU TOO, MI-HA.
HIS FACE SHOULD BE ILLEGAL.
HEH HEH HEH.
NOW I SEE WHY SHE WAS STARING AT ME LIKE THAT.
SHUT UP
GOD... I'M GOING NUTS.
OH, NOW THE EARTH IS SPLITTING.
CRUMBLE
KEKEKE LIFE IS LONELINESS.

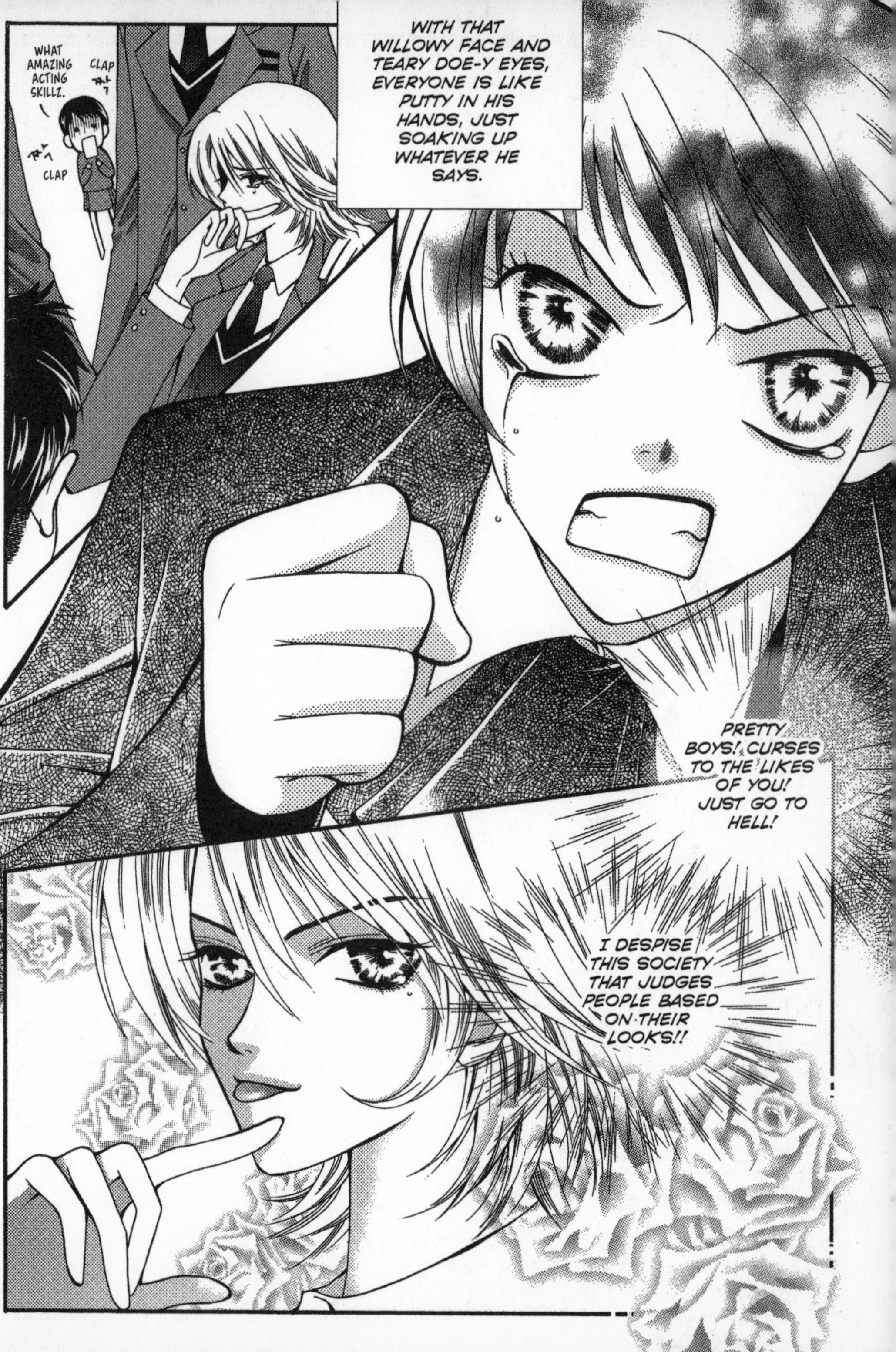
WHAT AMAZING ACTING SKILLZ.
CLAP
CLAP
WITH THAT WILLOWY FACE AND TEARY DOE-Y EYES, EVERYONE IS LIKE PUTTY IN HIS HANDS, JUST SOAKING UP WHATEVER HE SAYS.
PRETTY BOYS! CURSES TO THE LIKES OF YOU! JUST GO TO HELL!
I DESPISE THIS SOCIETY THAT JUDGES PEOPLE BASED ON THEIR LOOKS!!

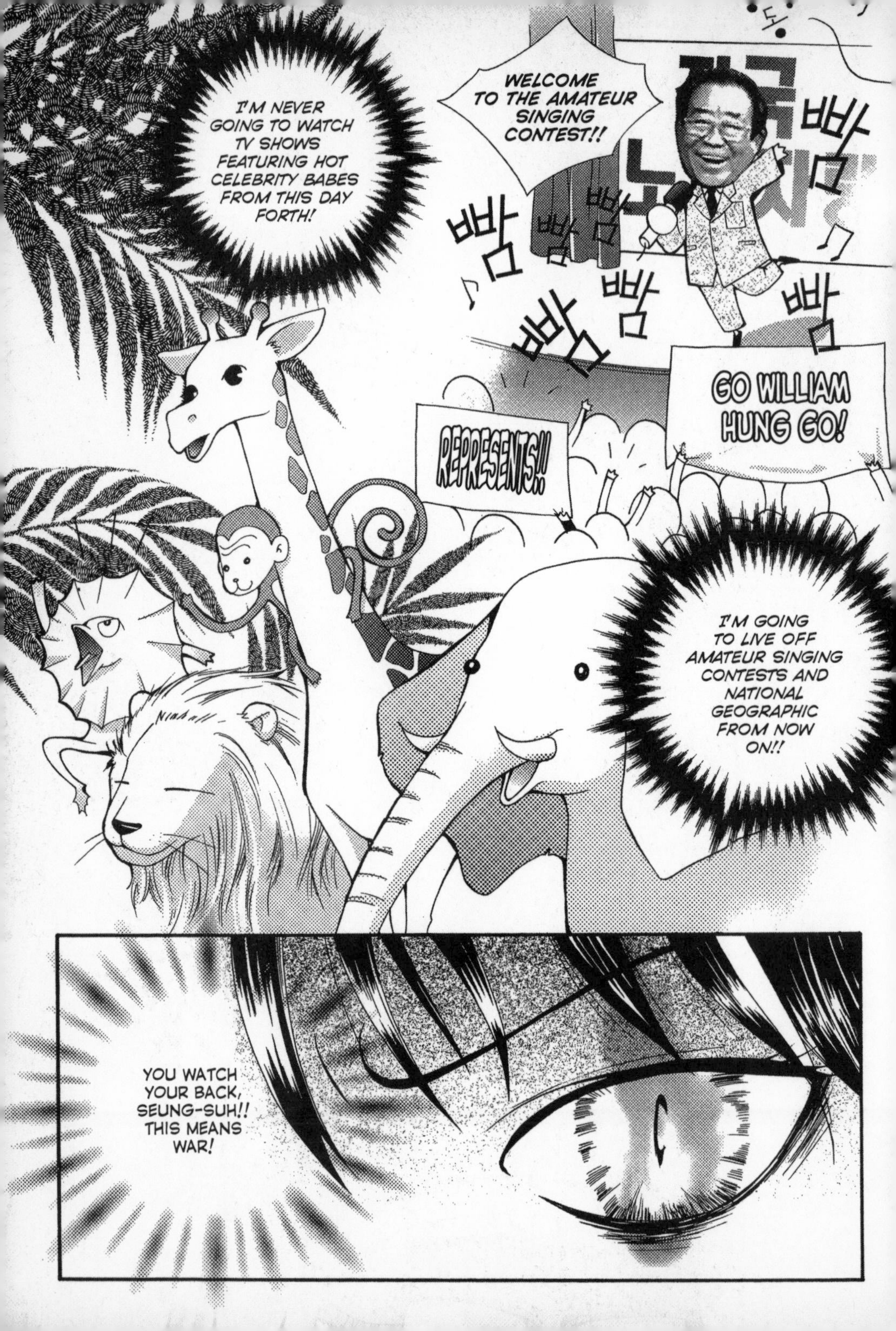
I'M NEVER GOING TO WATCH TV SHOWS FEATURING HOT CELEBRITY BABES FROM THIS DAY FORTH!
WELCOME TO THE AMATEUR SINGING CONTEST!!
빰 빰 빰 빰 빰 빰 빰
REPRESENTS!!
GO WILLIAM HUNG GO!
I'M GOING TO LIVE OFF AMATEUR SINGING CONTESTS AND NATIONAL GEOGRAPHIC FROM NOW ON!!
YOU WATCH YOUR BACK, SEUNG-SUH!! THIS MEANS WAR!

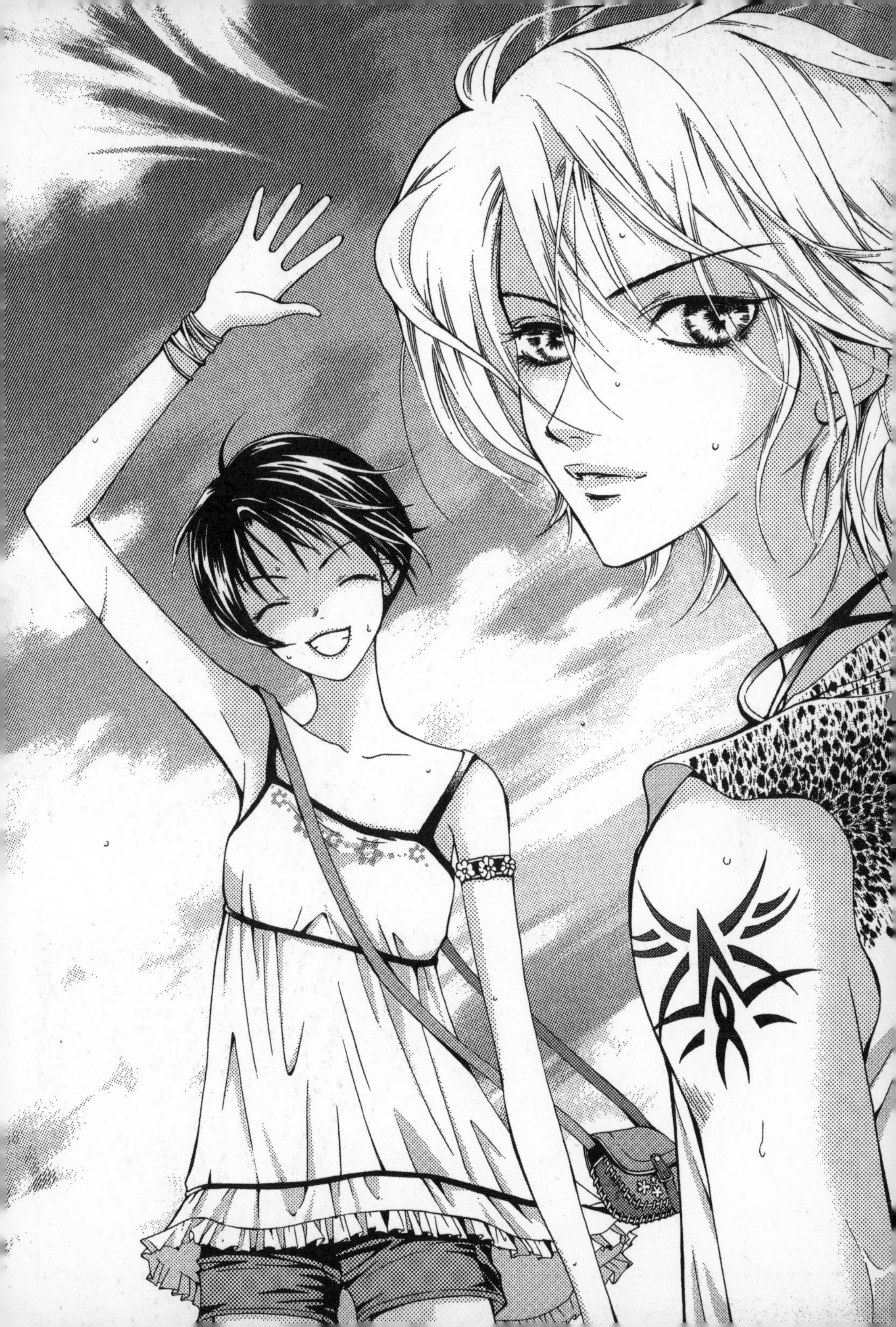

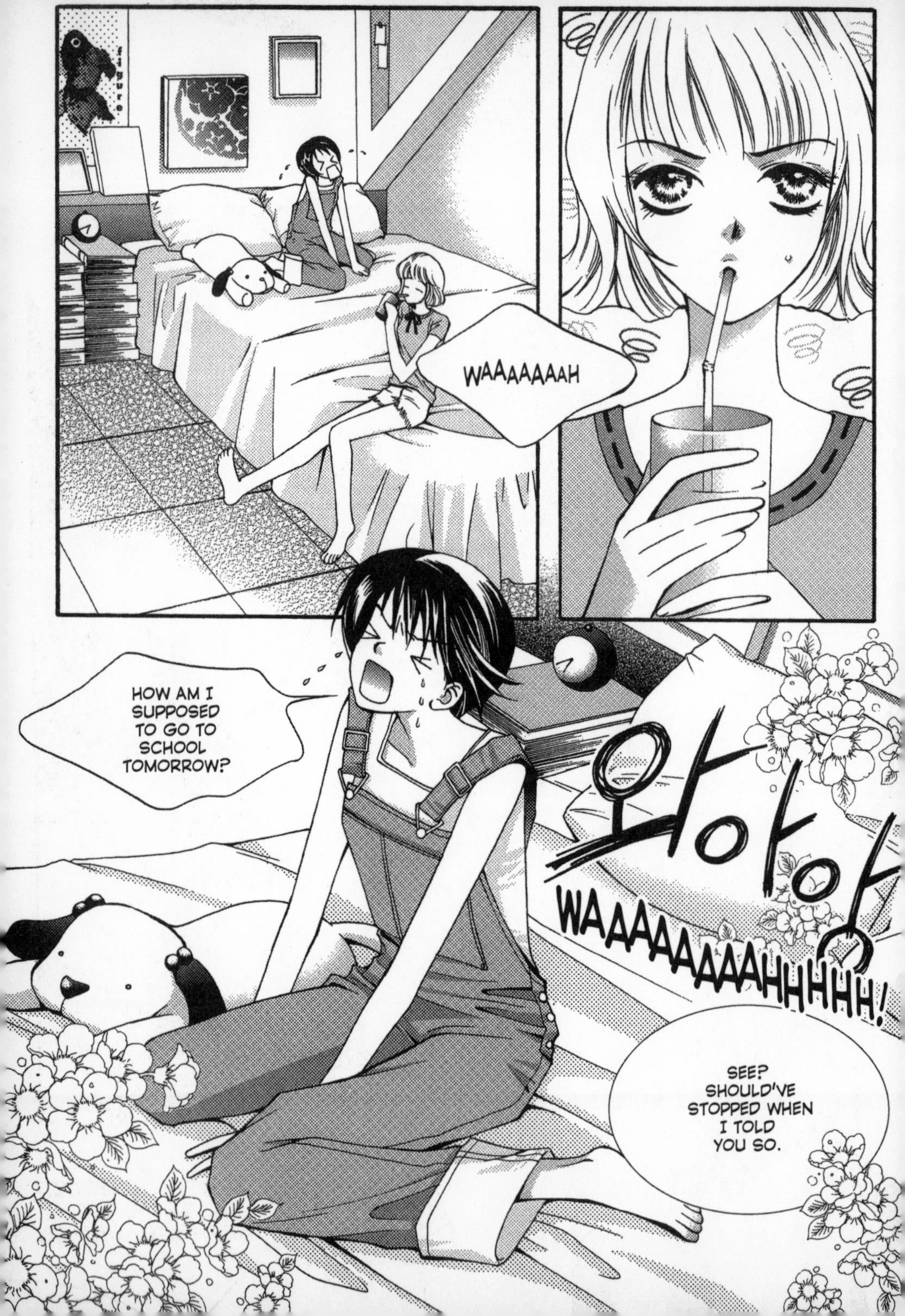
WAAAAAAAH
HOW AM I SUPPOSED TO GO TO SCHOOL TOMORROW?
으아아앙
WAAAAAAAAAAHHHHH!
SEE? SHOULD'VE STOPPED WHEN I TOLD YOU SO.

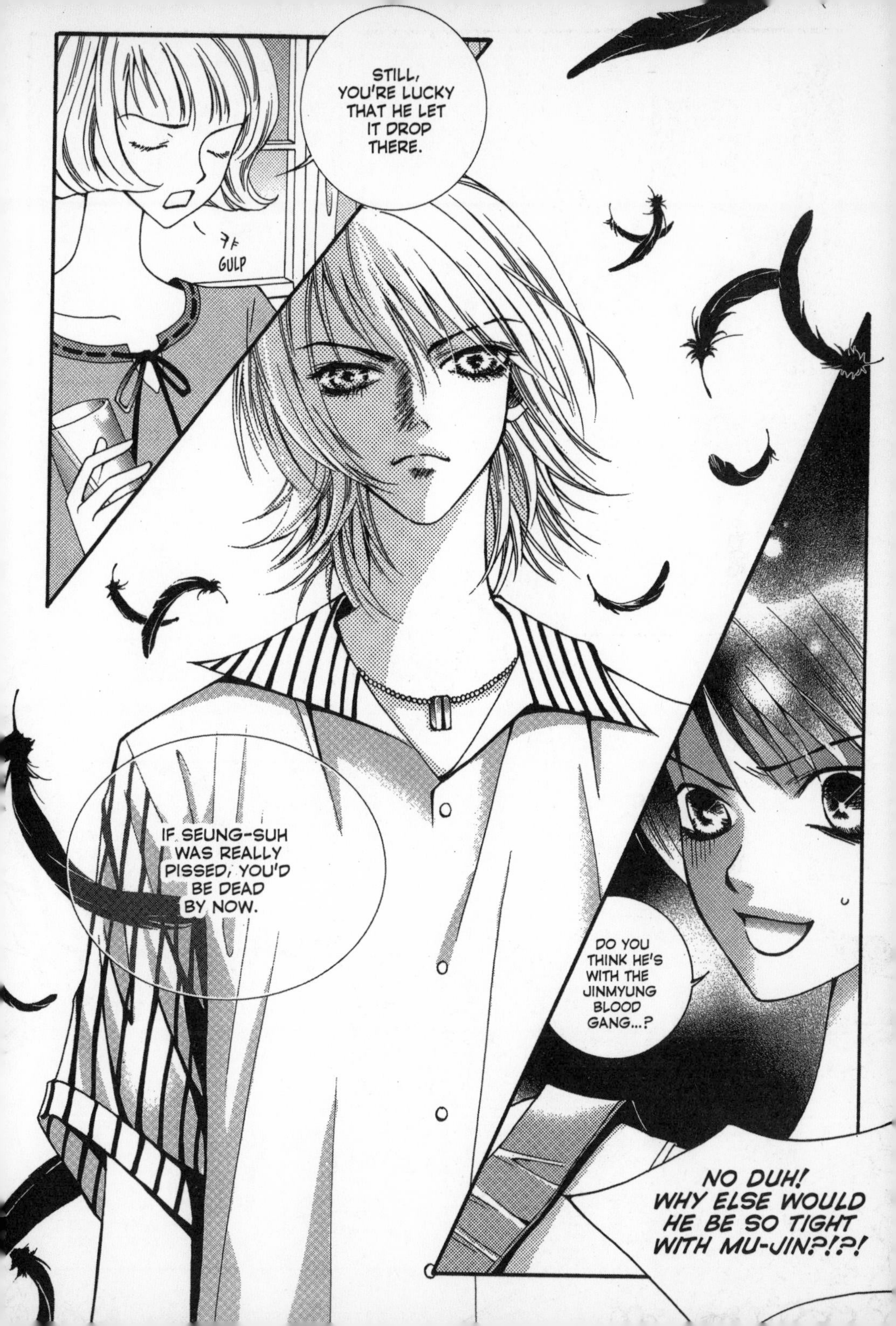

STILL, YOU'RE LUCKY THAT HE LET IT DROP THERE.
꿀꺽
GULP
IF SEUNG-SUH WAS REALLY PISSED, YOU'D BE DEAD BY NOW.
DO YOU THINK HE'S WITH THE JINMYUNG BLOOD GANG...?
NO DUH! WHY ELSE WOULD HE BE SO TIGHT WITH MU-JIN?!?!

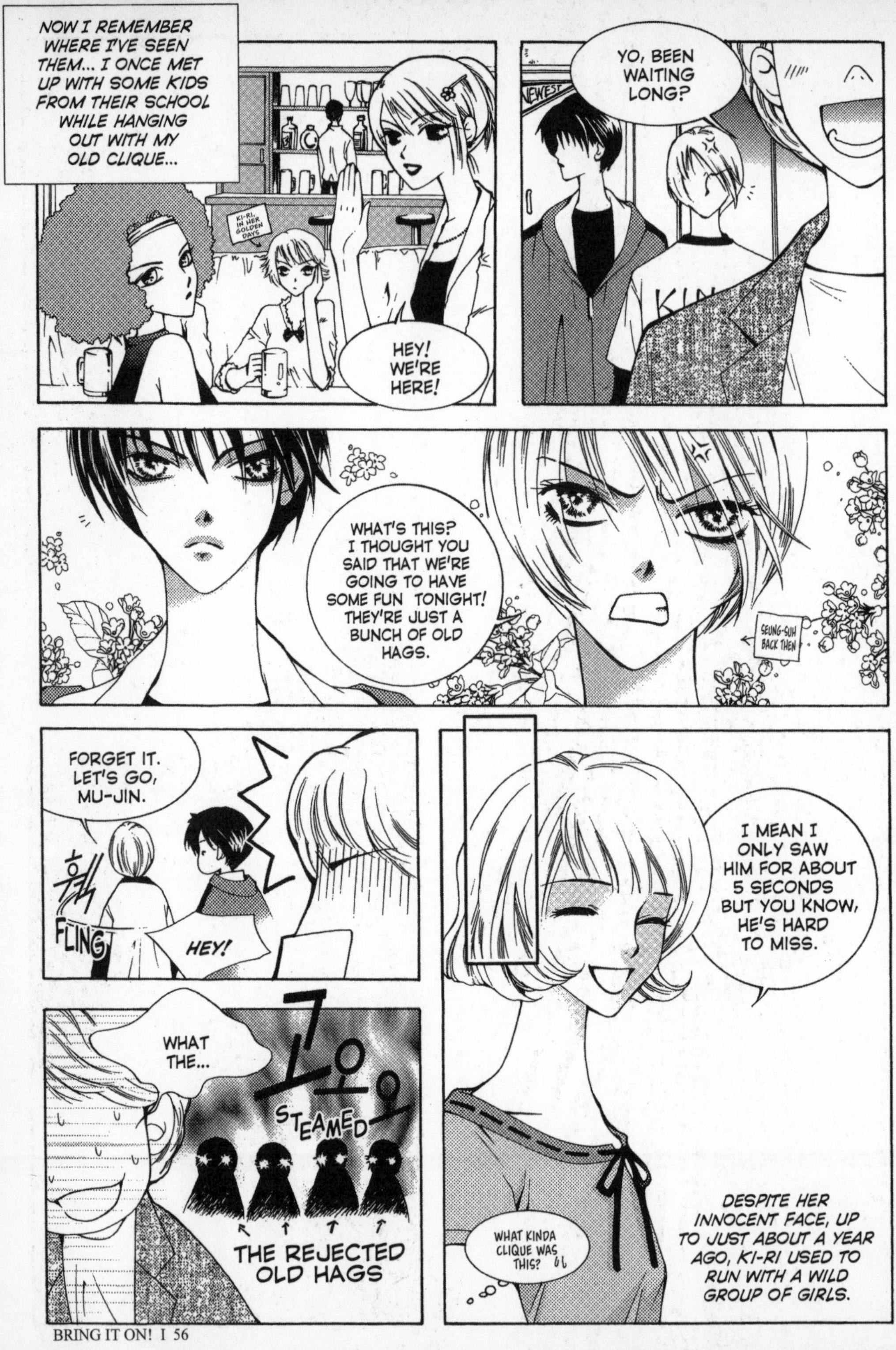
NOW I REMEMBER WHERE I'VE SEEN THEM... I ONCE MET UP WITH SOME KIDS FROM THEIR SCHOOL WHILE HANGING OUT WITH MY OLD CLIQUE...
KI-RI, IN HER GOLDEN DAYS
HEY! WE'RE HERE!
NEWEST
YO, BEEN WAITING LONG?
KIN
WHAT'S THIS? I THOUGHT YOU SAID THAT WE'RE GOING TO HAVE SOME FUN TONIGHT! THEY'RE JUST A BUNCH OF OLD HAGS.
SEUNG-SUH BACK THEN
FORGET IT. LET'S GO, MU-JIN.
FLING
HEY!
WHAT THE...
STEAMED
THE REJECTED OLD HAGS
I MEAN I ONLY SAW HIM FOR ABOUT 5 SECONDS BUT YOU KNOW, HE'S HARD TO MISS.
WHAT KINDA CLIQUE WAS THIS?
DESPITE HER INNOCENT FACE, UP TO JUST ABOUT A YEAR AGO, KI-RI USED TO RUN WITH A WILD GROUP OF GIRLS.

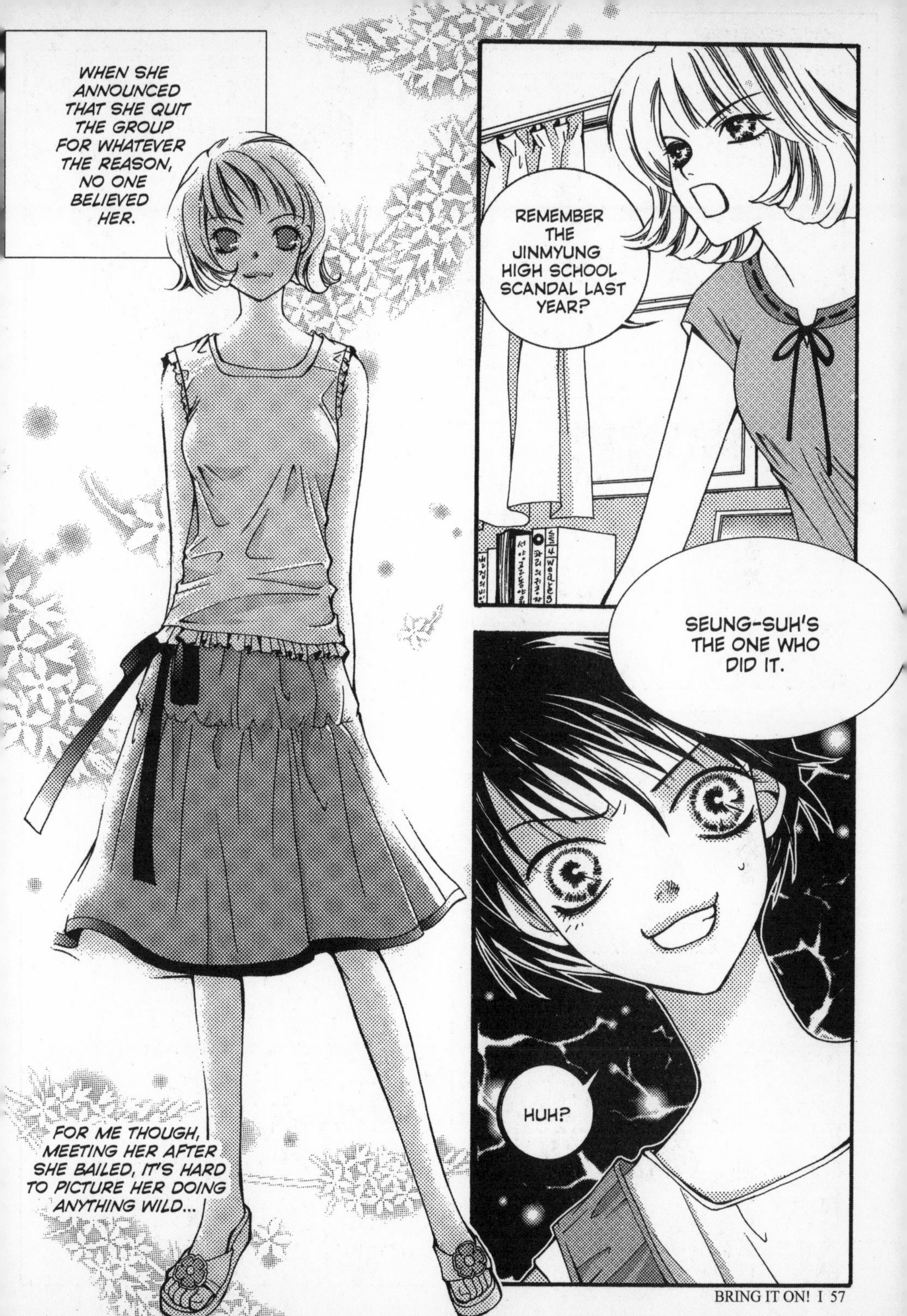
WHEN SHE ANNOUNCED THAT SHE QUIT THE GROUP FOR WHATEVER THE REASON, NO ONE BELIEVED HER.
FOR ME THOUGH, MEETING HER AFTER SHE BAILED, IT'S HARD TO PICTURE HER DOING ANYTHING WILD...
REMEMBER THE JINMYUNG HIGH SCHOOL SCANDAL LAST YEAR?
SEUNG-SUH'S THE ONE WHO DID IT.
HUH?

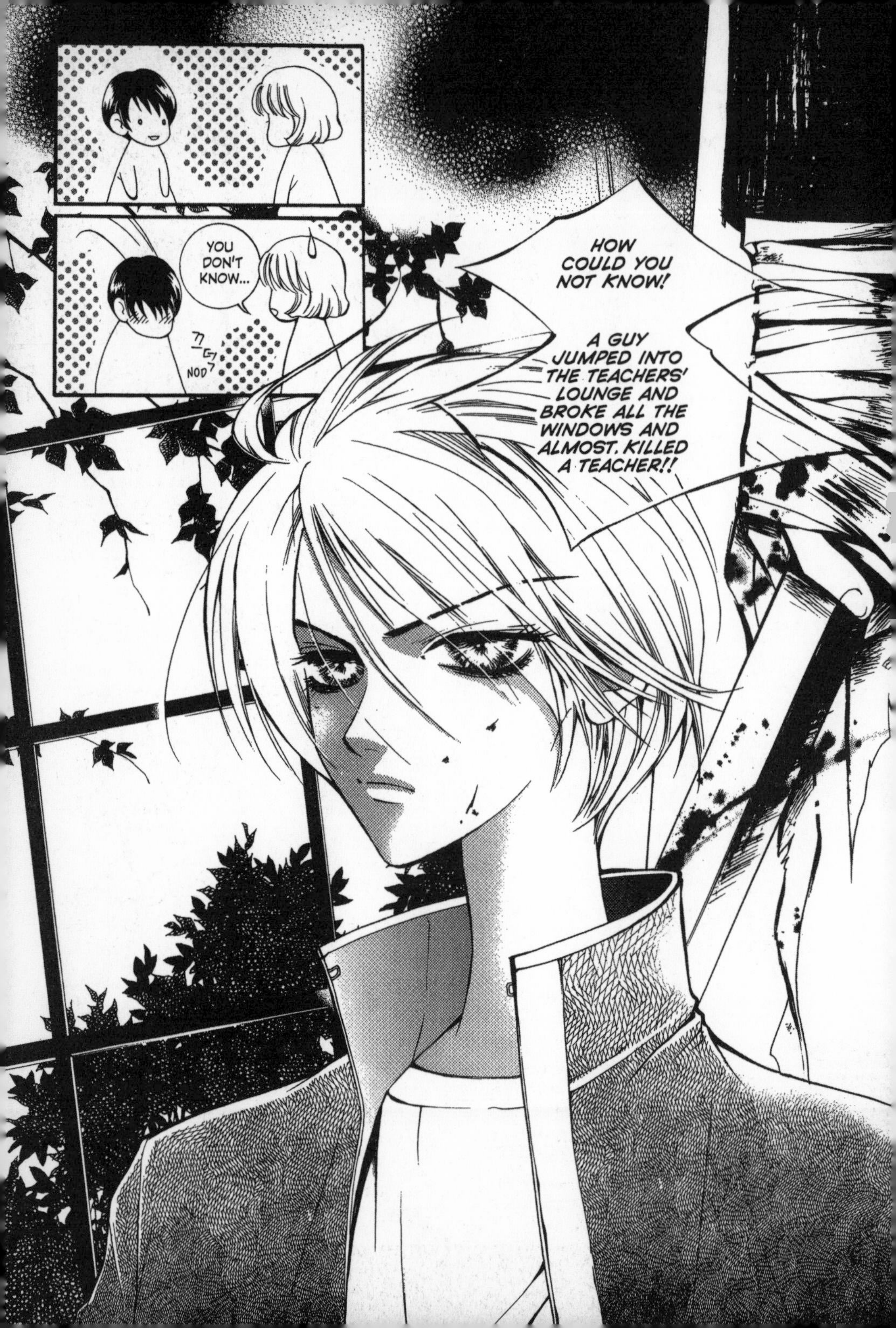

YOU DON'T KNOW...
NOD
HOW COULD YOU NOT KNOW!
A GUY JUMPED INTO THE TEACHERS' LOUNGE AND BROKE ALL THE WINDOWS AND ALMOST KILLED A TEACHER!!

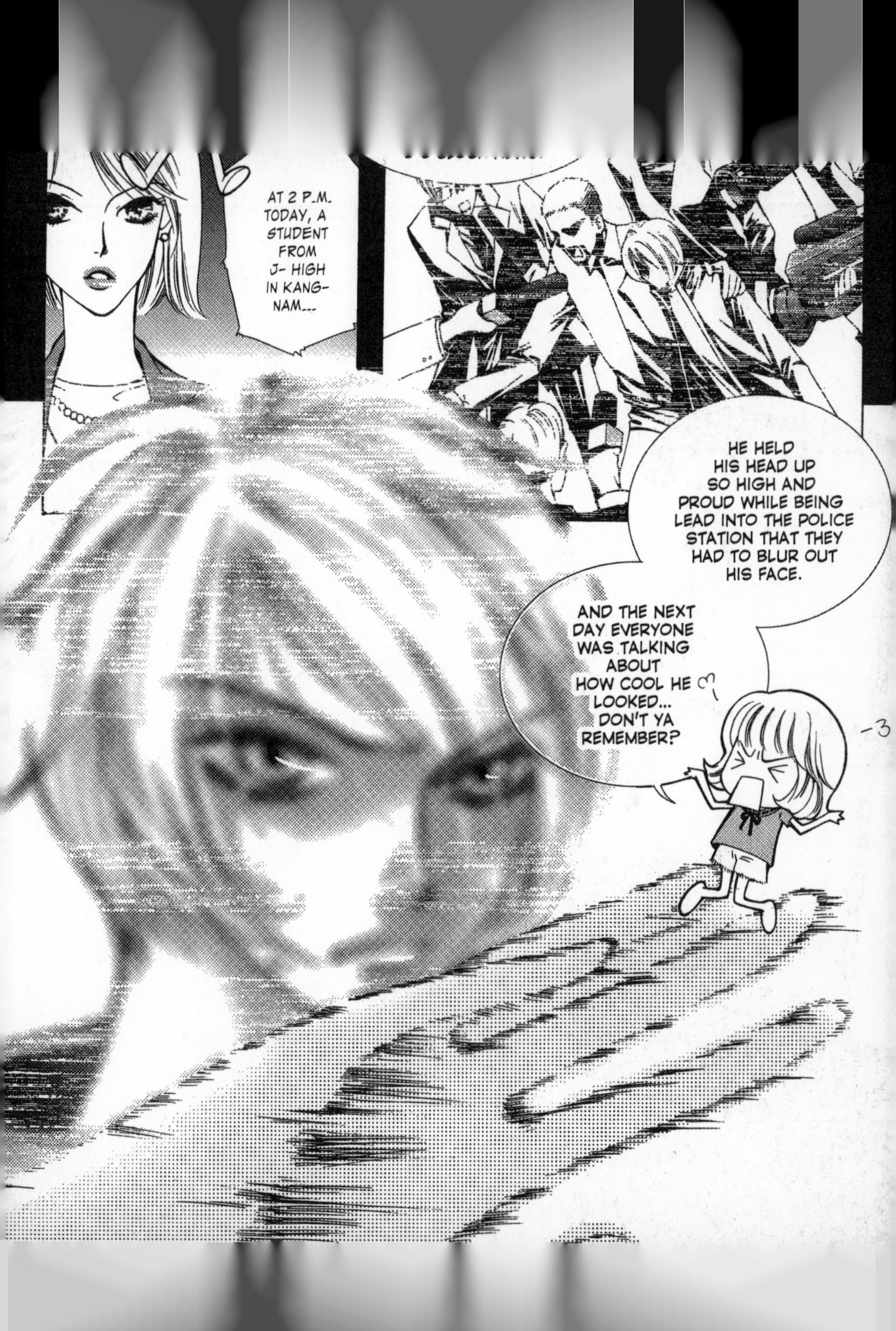
AT 2 P.M. TODAY, A STUDENT FROM J- HIGH IN KANG-NAM...
HE HELD HIS HEAD UP SO HIGH AND PROUD WHILE BEING LEAD INTO THE POLICE STATION THAT THEY HAD TO BLUR OUT HIS FACE.
AND THE NEXT DAY EVERYONE WAS TALKING ABOUT HOW COOL HE LOOKED... DON'T YA REMEMBER?

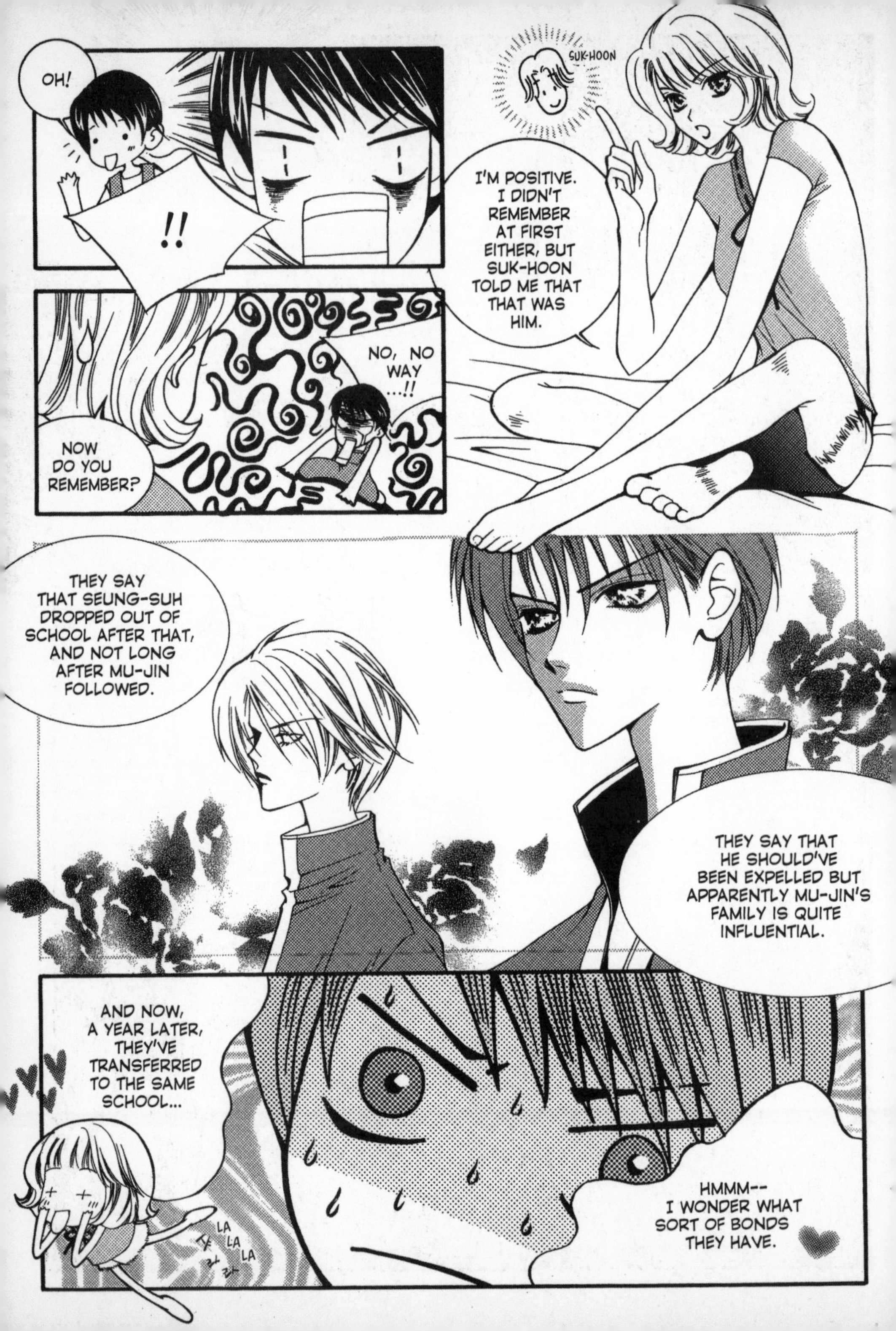
OH!
!!
SUK-HOON
I'M POSITIVE. I DIDN'T REMEMBER AT FIRST EITHER, BUT SUK-HOON TOLD ME THAT THAT WAS HIM.
NO, NO WAY ...!!
NOW DO YOU REMEMBER?
THEY SAY THAT SEUNG-SUH DROPPED OUT OF SCHOOL AFTER THAT, AND NOT LONG AFTER MU-JIN FOLLOWED.
THEY SAY THAT HE SHOULD'VE BEEN EXPELLED BUT APPARENTLY MU-JIN'S FAMILY IS QUITE INFLUENTIAL.
AND NOW, A YEAR LATER, THEY'VE TRANSFERRED TO THE SAME SCHOOL...
HMMM-- I WONDER WHAT SORT OF BONDS THEY HAVE.
LA LA LA

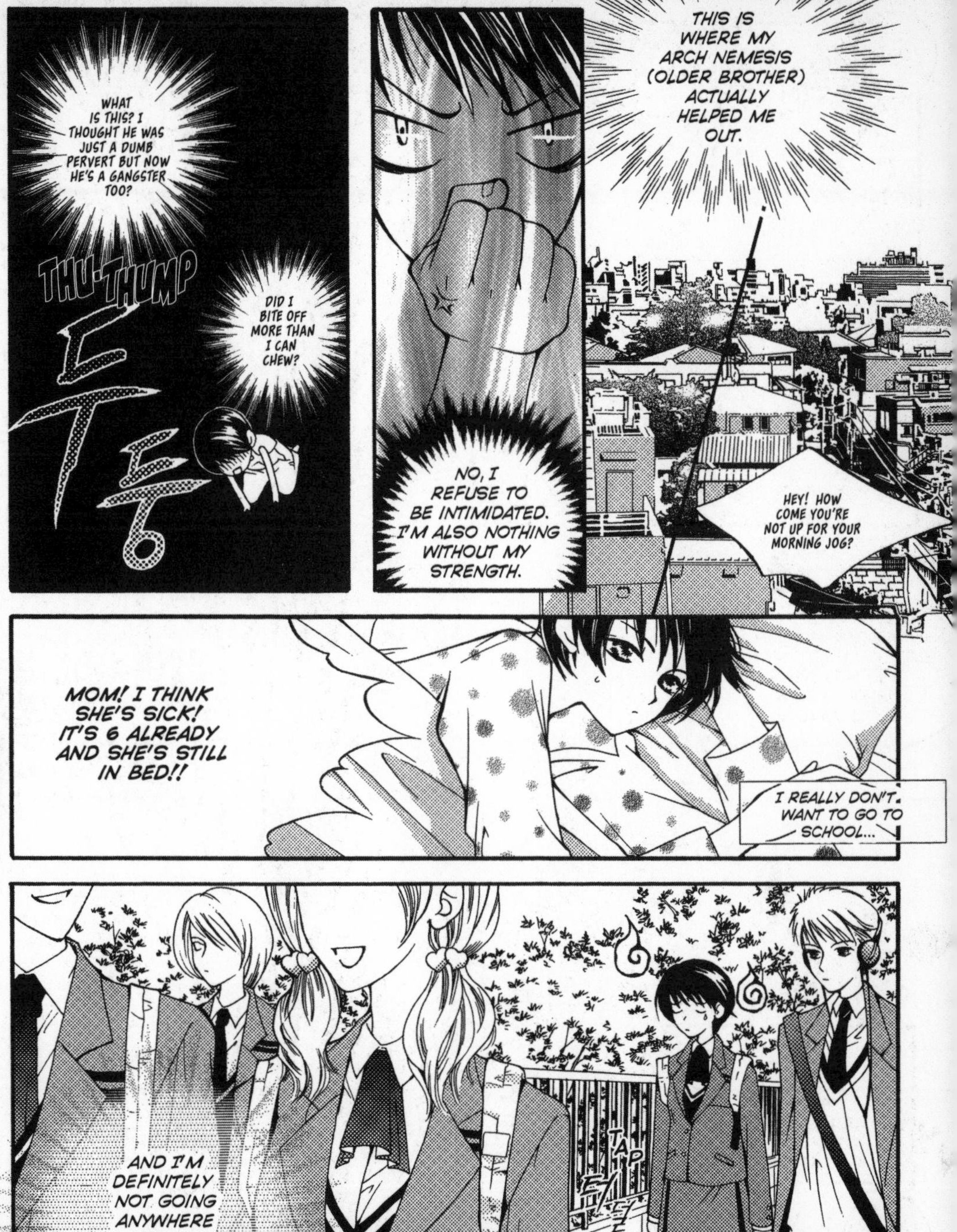
WHAT IS THIS? I THOUGHT HE WAS JUST A DUMB PERVERT BUT NOW HE'S A GANGSTER TOO?
THU-THUMP
DID I BITE OFF MORE THAN I CAN CHEW?
NO, I REFUSE TO BE INTIMIDATED. I'M ALSO NOTHING WITHOUT MY STRENGTH.
THIS IS WHERE MY ARCH NEMESIS (OLDER BROTHER) ACTUALLY HELPED ME OUT.
HEY! HOW COME YOU'RE NOT UP FOR YOUR MORNING JOG?
MOM! I THINK SHE'S SICK! IT'S 6 ALREADY AND SHE'S STILL IN BED!!
I REALLY DON'T WANT TO GO TO SCHOOL...
TAP
TAP
AND I'M DEFINITELY NOT GOING ANYWHERE NEAR THE SHOWER ROOM FOR A WHILE!

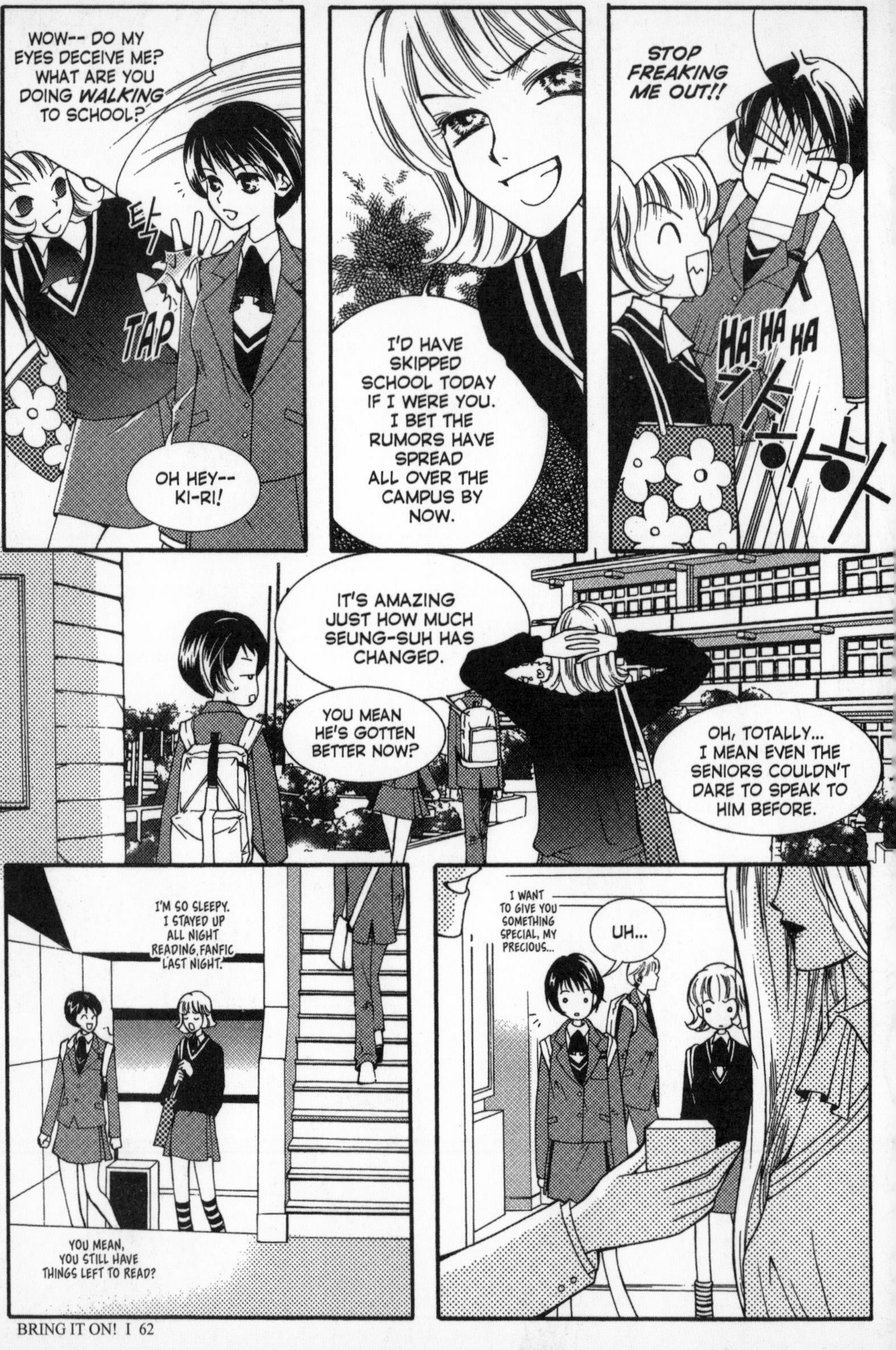
WOW-- DO MY EYES DECEIVE ME? WHAT ARE YOU DOING *WALKING* TO SCHOOL?
TAP
OH HEY-- KI-RI!
I'D HAVE SKIPPED SCHOOL TODAY IF I WERE YOU. I BET THE RUMORS HAVE SPREAD ALL OVER THE CAMPUS BY NOW.
STOP FREAKING ME OUT!!
HA HA HA
IT'S AMAZING JUST HOW MUCH SEUNG-SUH HAS CHANGED.
YOU MEAN HE'S GOTTEN BETTER NOW?
OH, TOTALLY... I MEAN EVEN THE SENIORS COULDN'T DARE TO SPEAK TO HIM BEFORE.
I'M SO SLEEPY. I STAYED UP ALL NIGHT READING FANFIC LAST NIGHT.
YOU MEAN, YOU STILL HAVE THINGS LEFT TO READ?
I WANT TO GIVE YOU SOMETHING SPECIAL, MY PRECIOUS...
UH...

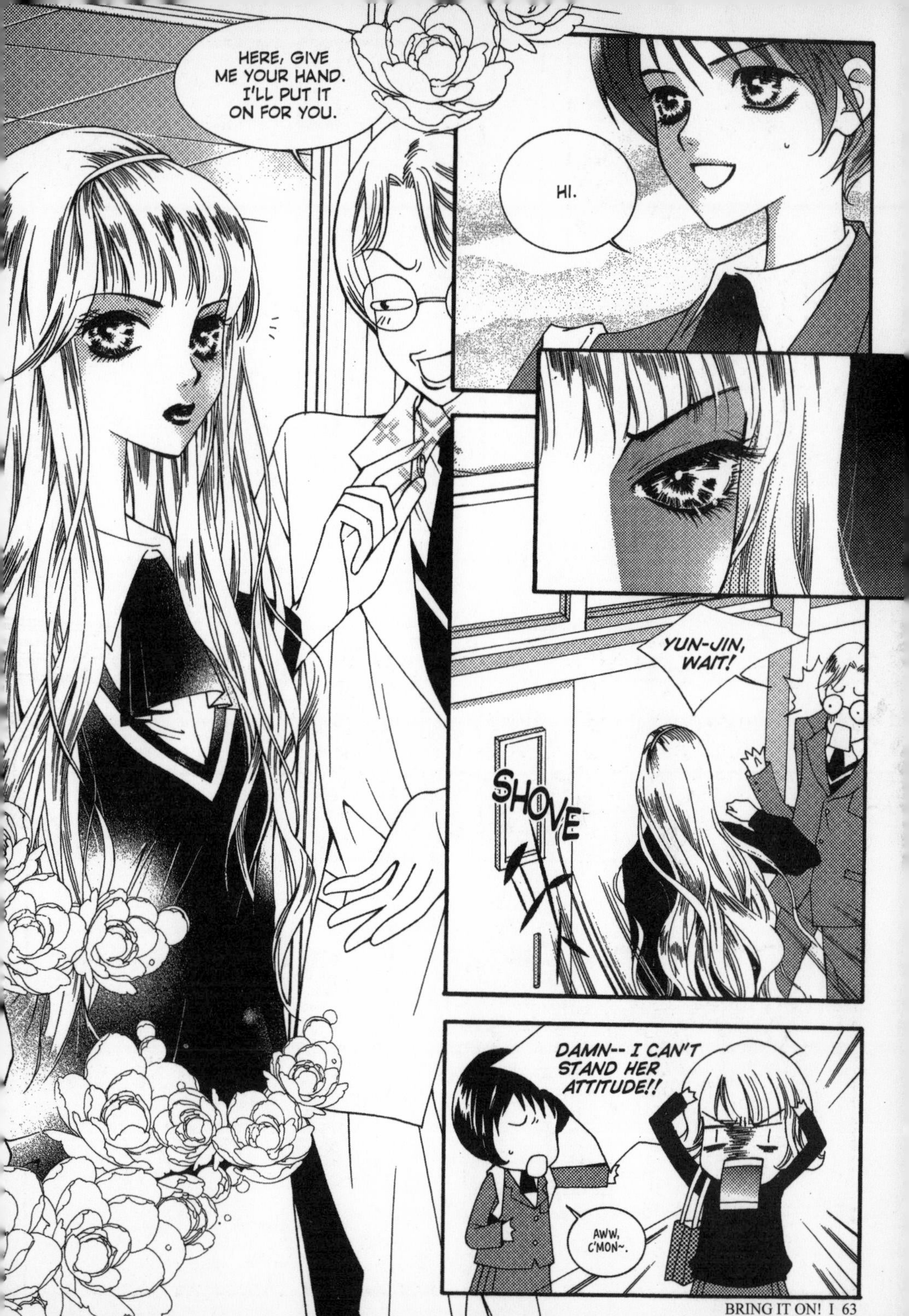
HERE, GIVE ME YOUR HAND. I'LL PUT IT ON FOR YOU.
HI.
YUN-JIN, WAIT!
SHOVE
DAMN-- I CAN'T STAND HER ATTITUDE!!
AWW, C'MON~.

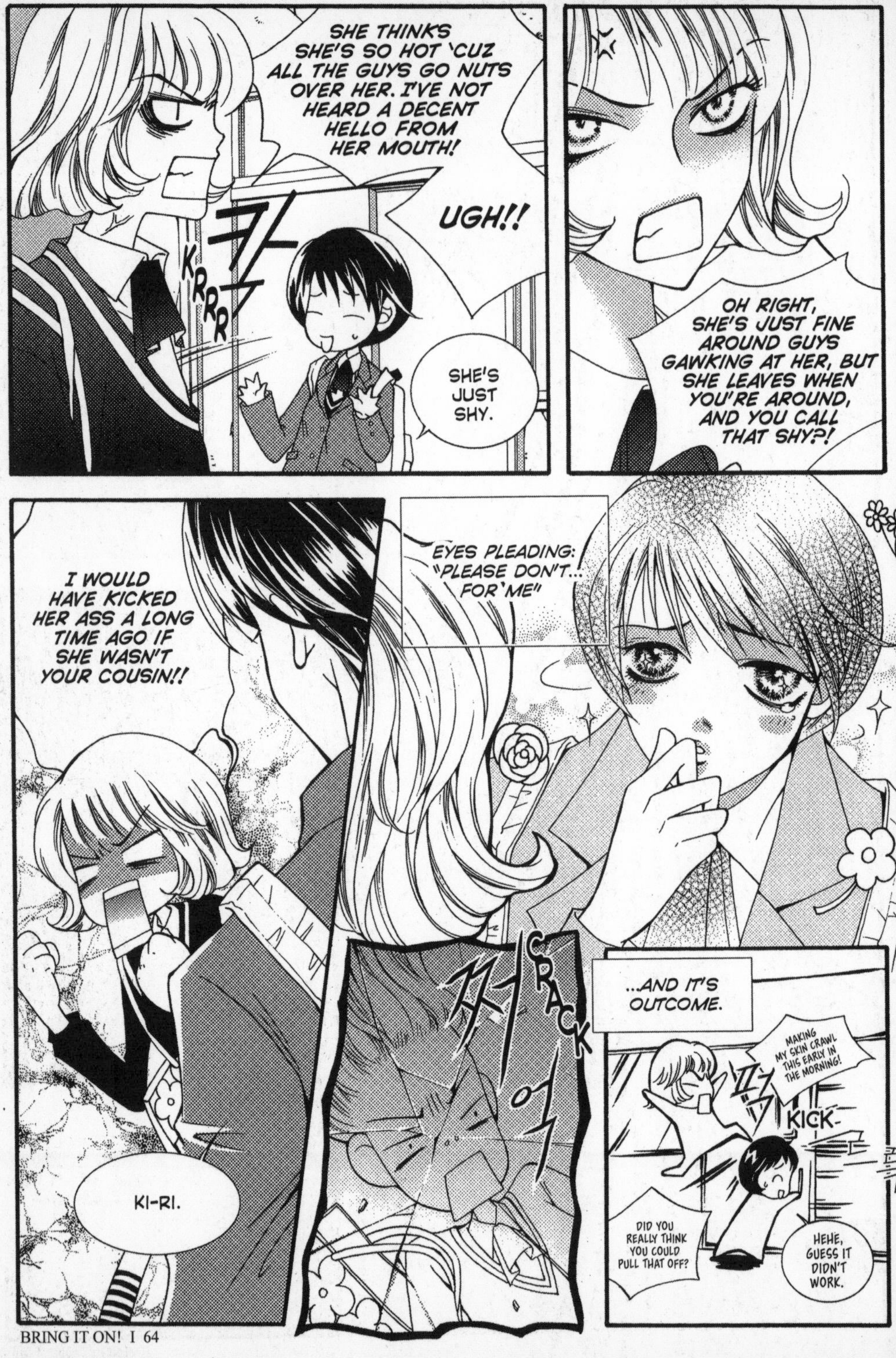
SHE THINKS SHE'S SO HOT 'CUZ ALL THE GUYS GO NUTS OVER HER. I'VE NOT HEARD A DECENT HELLO FROM HER MOUTH!
KRRR
UGH!!
SHE'S JUST SHY.
OH RIGHT, SHE'S JUST FINE AROUND GUYS GAWKING AT HER, BUT SHE LEAVES WHEN YOU'RE AROUND, AND YOU CALL THAT SHY?!
I WOULD HAVE KICKED HER ASS A LONG TIME AGO IF SHE WASN'T YOUR COUSIN!!
EYES PLEADING: "PLEASE DON'T... FOR 'ME"
KI-RI.
CRACK
...AND IT'S OUTCOME.
MAKING MY SKIN CRAWL THIS EARLY IN THE MORNING!
KICK
DID YOU REALLY THINK YOU COULD PULL THAT OFF?
HEHE, GUESS IT DIDN'T WORK.

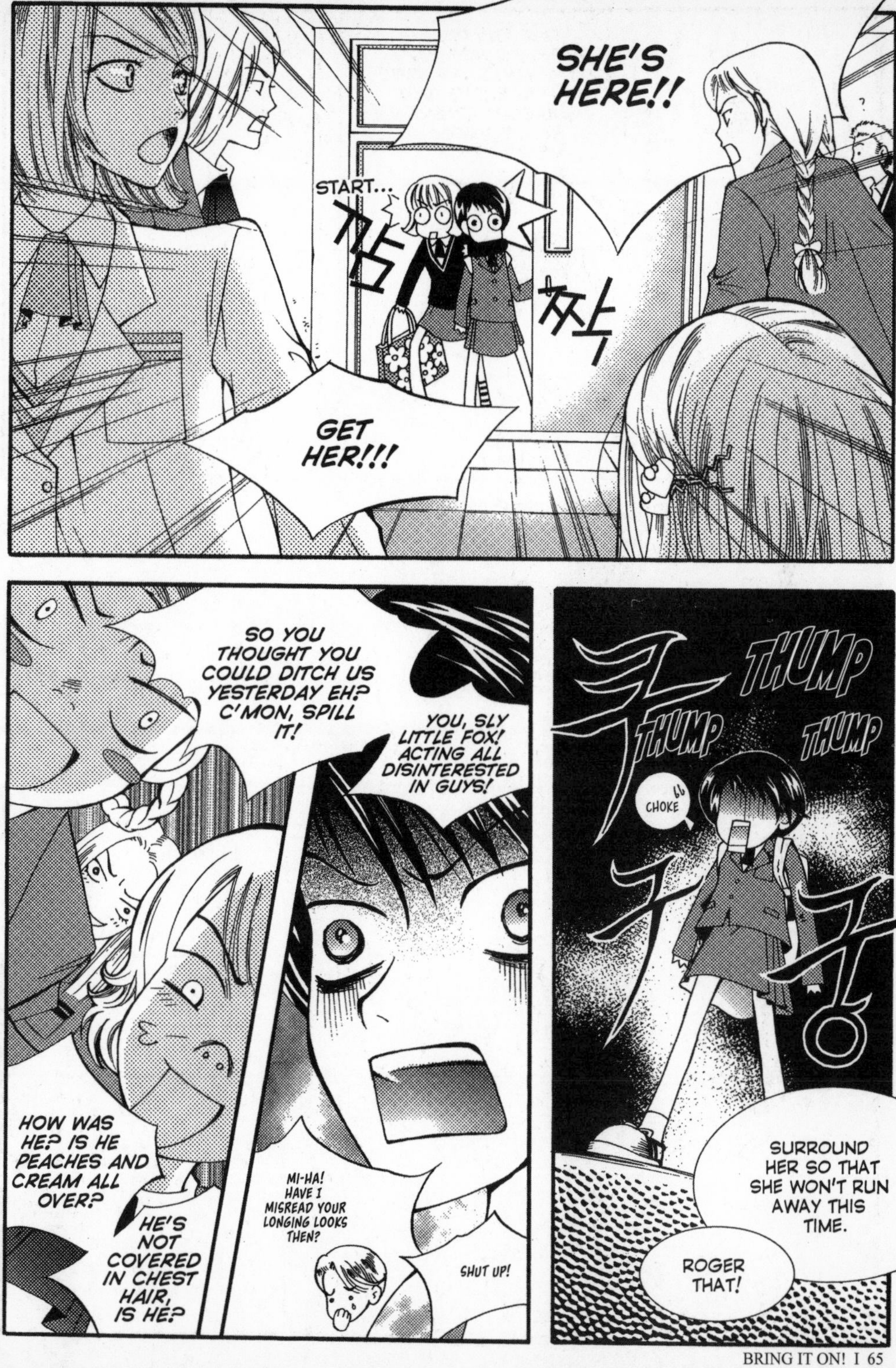
SHE'S HERE!!
START...
GET HER!!!
SO YOU THOUGHT YOU COULD DITCH US YESTERDAY EH? C'MON, SPILL IT!
YOU, SLY LITTLE FOX! ACTING ALL DISINTERESTED IN GUYS!
HOW WAS HE? IS HE PEACHES AND CREAM ALL OVER?
HE'S NOT COVERED IN CHEST HAIR, IS HE?
MI-HA! HAVE I MISREAD YOUR LONGING LOOKS THEN?
SHUT UP!
THUMP
THUMP
THUMP
CHOKE
SURROUND HER SO THAT SHE WON'T RUN AWAY THIS TIME.
ROGER THAT!

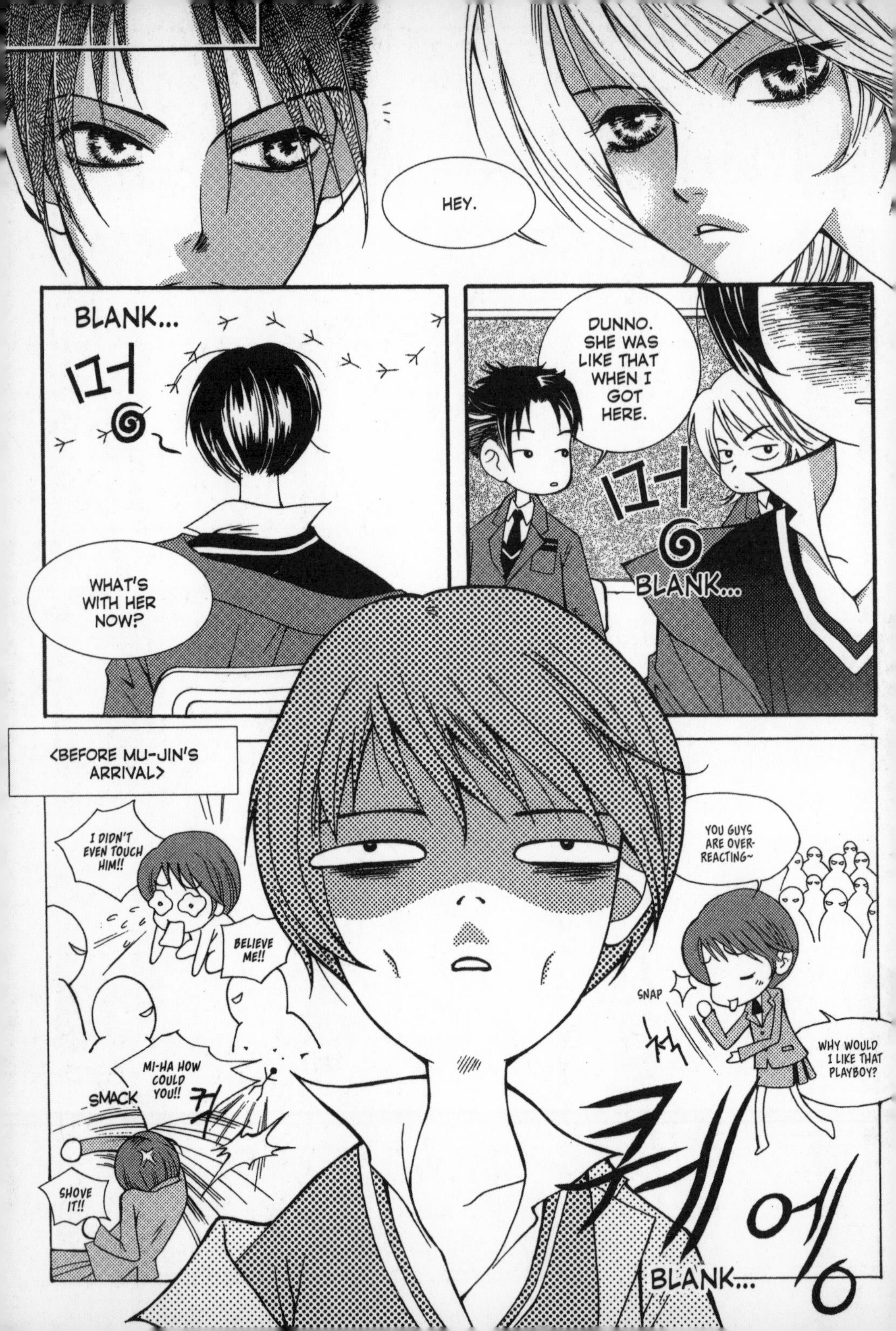

HEY.
BLANK...
WHAT'S WITH HER NOW?
DUNNO. SHE WAS LIKE THAT WHEN I GOT HERE.
BLANK...
<BEFORE MU-JIN'S ARRIVAL>
I DIDN'T EVEN TOUCH HIM!!
BELIEVE ME!!
MI-HA HOW COULD YOU!!
SMACK
SHOVE IT!!
YOU GUYS ARE OVER-REACTING~
SNAP
WHY WOULD I LIKE THAT PLAYBOY?
BLANK...

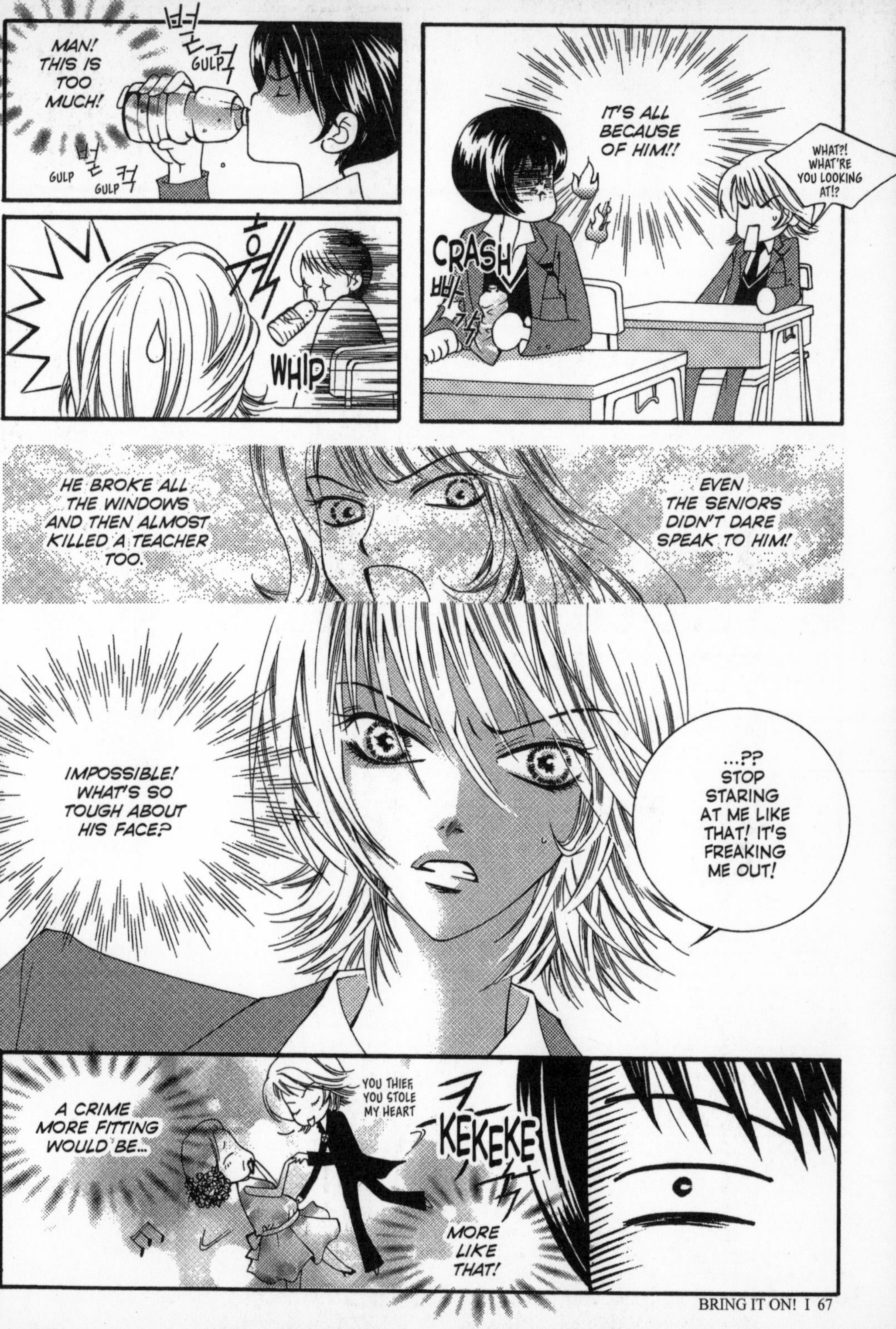
MAN! THIS IS TOO MUCH!
GULP
GULP
GULP
WHIP
IT'S ALL BECAUSE OF HIM!!
WHAT?! WHAT'RE YOU LOOKING AT!?
CRASH
HE BROKE ALL THE WINDOWS AND THEN ALMOST KILLED A TEACHER TOO.
EVEN THE SENIORS DIDN'T DARE SPEAK TO HIM!
IMPOSSIBLE! WHAT'S SO TOUGH ABOUT HIS FACE?
...?? STOP STARING AT ME LIKE THAT! IT'S FREAKING ME OUT!
A CRIME MORE FITTING WOULD BE...
YOU THIEF. YOU STOLE MY HEART
KEKEKE
MORE LIKE THAT!

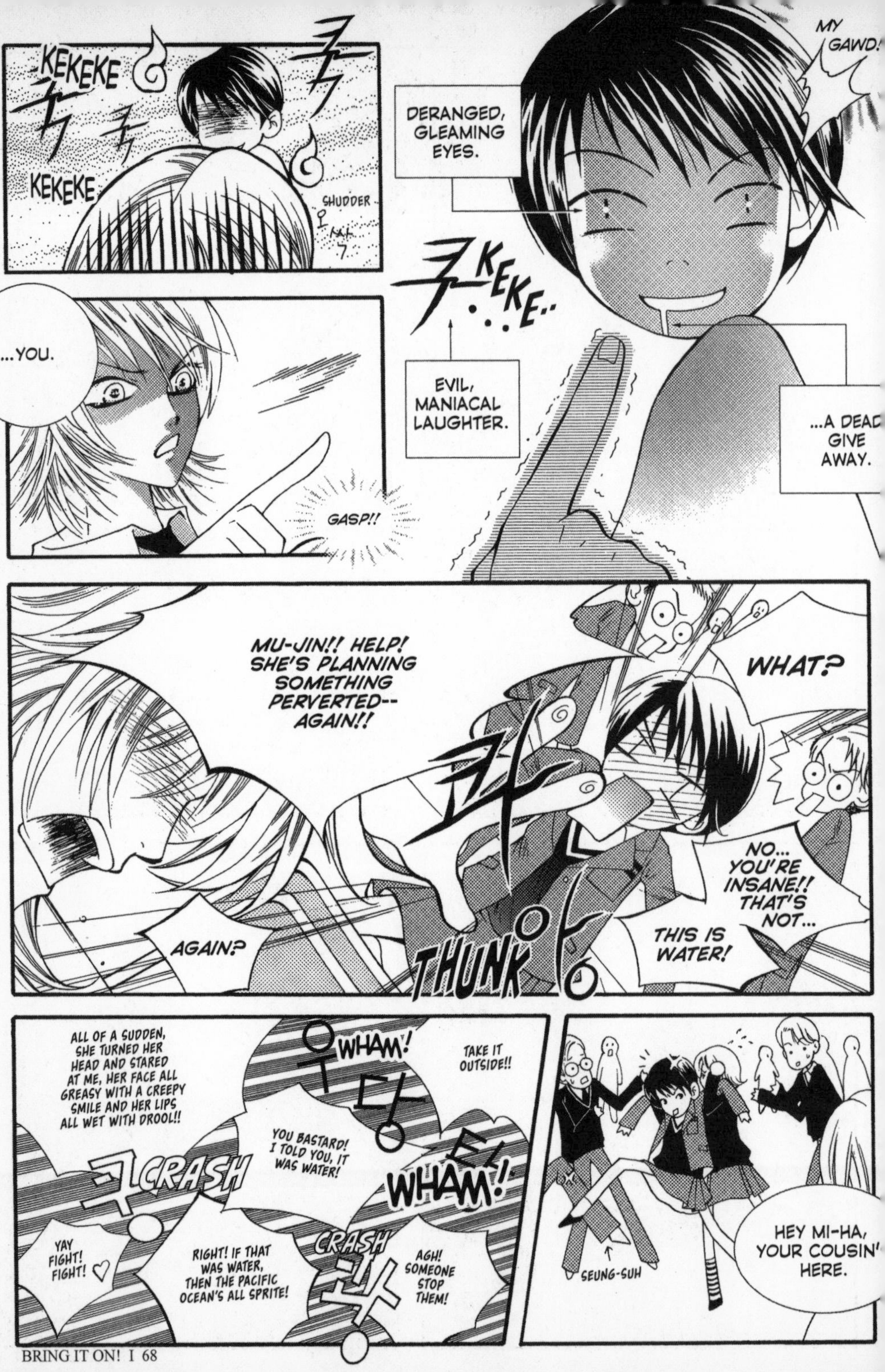
KEKEKE
KEKEKE
SHUDDER
MY GAWD!
DERANGED, GLEAMING EYES.
KEKE...
EVIL, MANIACAL LAUGHTER.
...A DEAD GIVE AWAY.
...YOU.
GASP!!
MU-JIN!! HELP! SHE'S PLANNING SOMETHING PERVERTED-- AGAIN!!
WHAT?
AGAIN?
THUNK
THIS IS WATER!
NO... YOU'RE INSANE!! THAT'S NOT...
ALL OF A SUDDEN, SHE TURNED HER HEAD AND STARED AT ME, HER FACE ALL GREASY WITH A CREEPY SMILE AND HER LIPS ALL WET WITH DROOL!!
WHAM!
TAKE IT OUTSIDE!!
YOU BASTARD! I TOLD YOU, IT WAS WATER!
CRASH
WHAM!
YAY FIGHT! FIGHT! ♡
RIGHT! IF THAT WAS WATER, THEN THE PACIFIC OCEAN'S ALL SPRITE!
CRASH
AGH! SOMEONE STOP THEM!
SEUNG-SUH
HEY MI-HA, YOUR COUSIN' HERE.

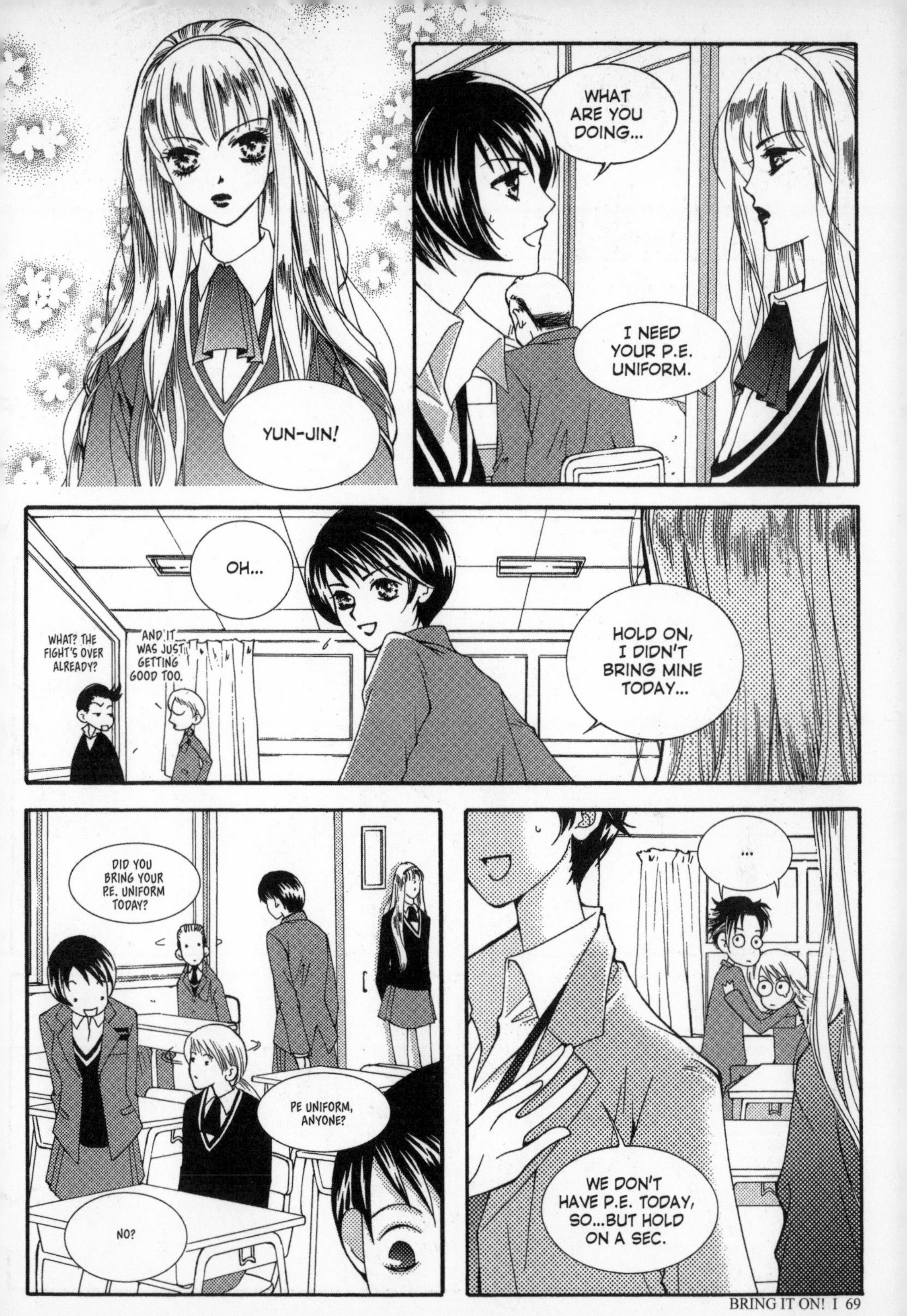
YUN-JIN!
WHAT ARE YOU DOING...
I NEED YOUR P.E. UNIFORM.
OH...
HOLD ON, I DIDN'T BRING MINE TODAY...
WHAT? THE FIGHT'S OVER ALREADY?
AND IT WAS JUST GETTING GOOD TOO.
DID YOU BRING YOUR P.E. UNIFORM TODAY?
PE UNIFORM, ANYONE?
NO?
...
WE DON'T HAVE P.E. TODAY, SO...BUT HOLD ON A SEC.

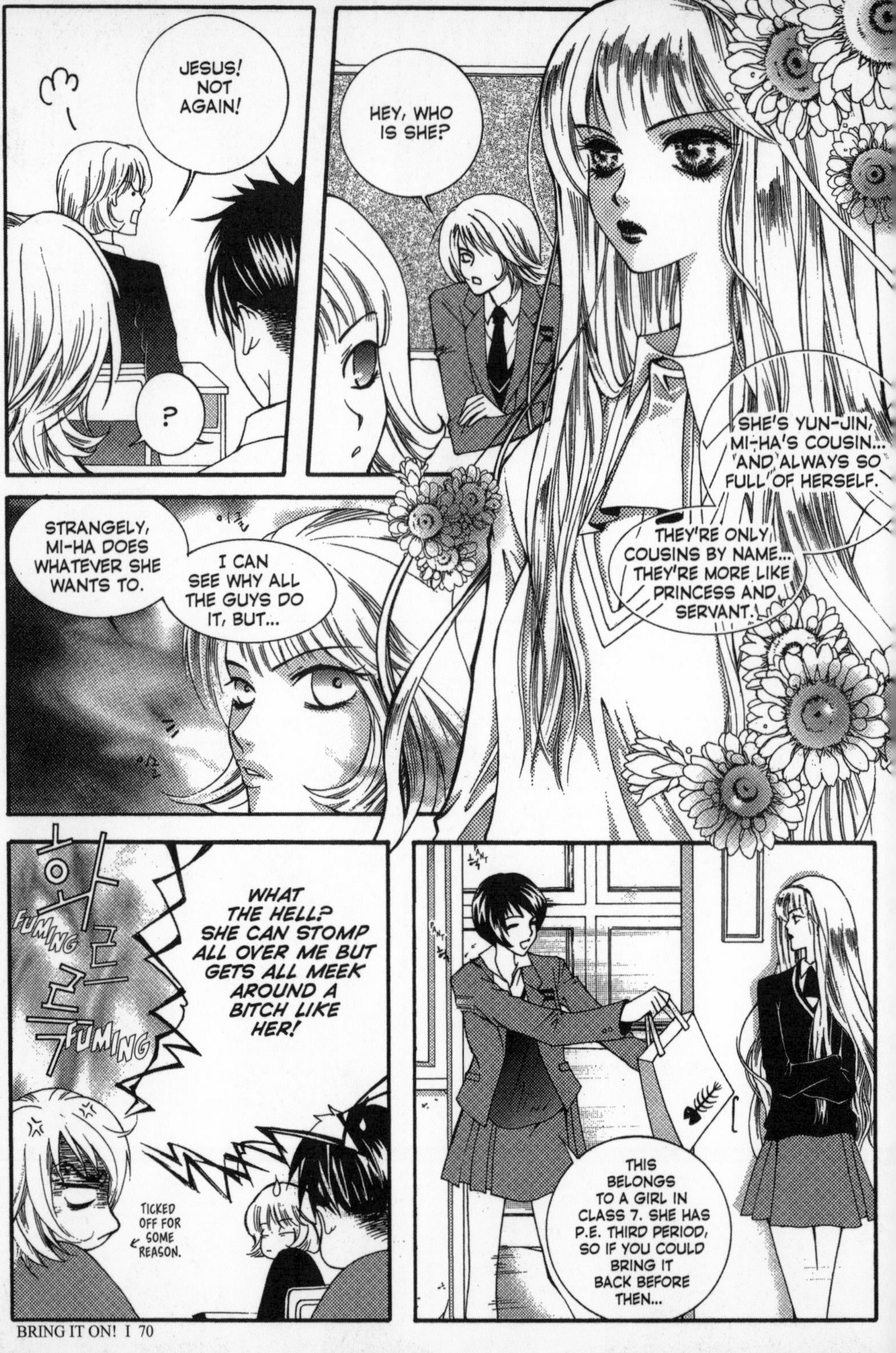
JESUS! NOT AGAIN!
?
HEY, WHO IS SHE?
SHE'S YUN-JIN, MI-HA'S COUSIN... AND ALWAYS SO FULL OF HERSELF.
THEY'RE ONLY COUSINS BY NAME... THEY'RE MORE LIKE PRINCESS AND SERVANT.
STRANGELY, MI-HA DOES WHATEVER SHE WANTS TO.
I CAN SEE WHY ALL THE GUYS DO IT, BUT...
FUMING
WHAT THE HELL? SHE CAN STOMP ALL OVER ME BUT GETS ALL MEEK AROUND A BITCH LIKE HER!
FUMING
TICKED OFF FOR SOME REASON.
PANT
PANT
THIS BELONGS TO A GIRL IN CLASS 7. SHE HAS P.E. THIRD PERIOD, SO IF YOU COULD BRING IT BACK BEFORE THEN...

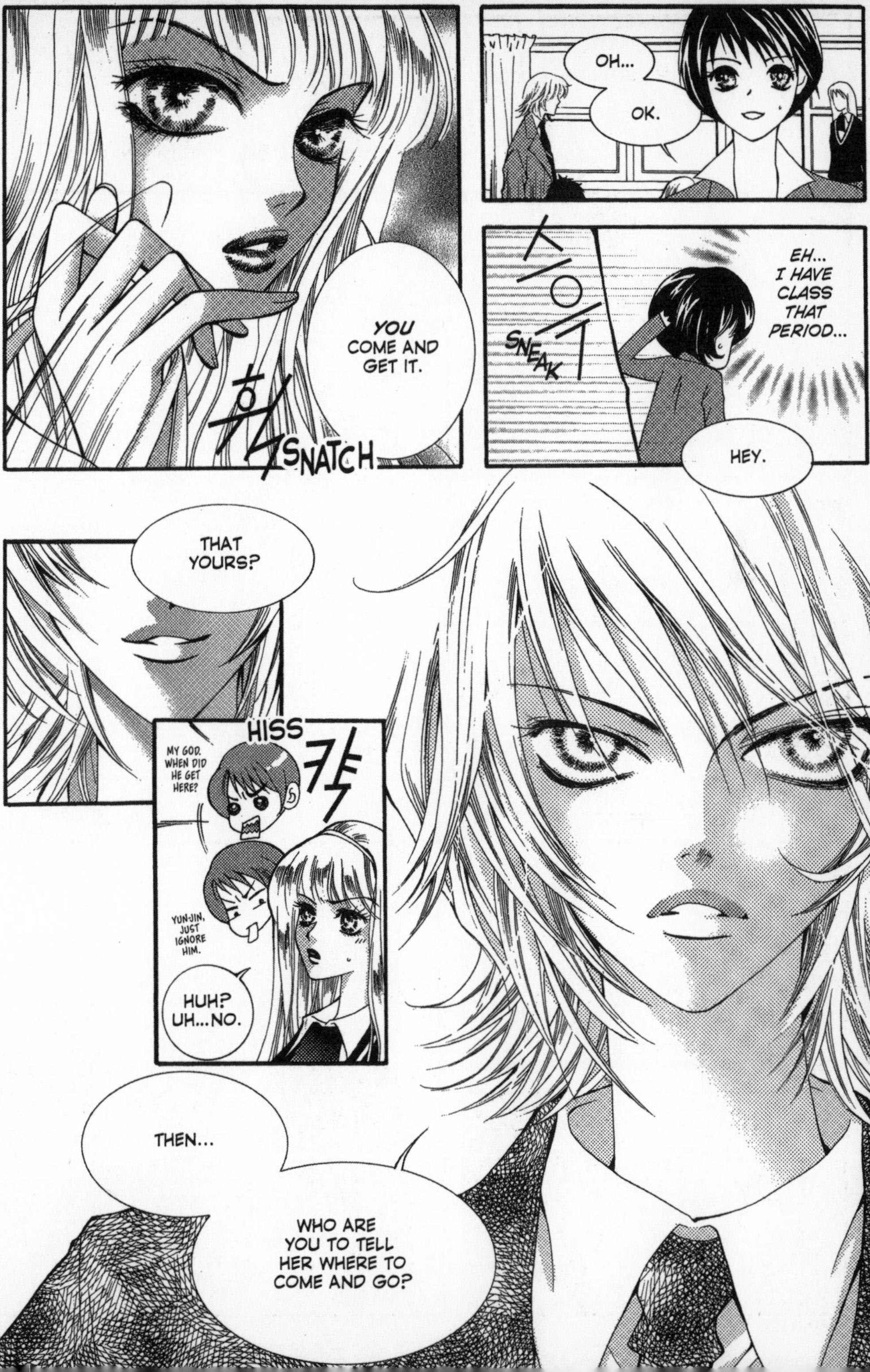

YOU COME AND GET IT.
SNATCH
OH...
OK.
SNEAK
EH... I HAVE CLASS THAT PERIOD...
HEY.
THAT YOURS?
HISS
MY GOD. WHEN DID HE GET HERE?
YUN-JIN, JUST IGNORE HIM.
HUH? UH...NO.
THEN...
WHO ARE YOU TO TELL HER WHERE TO COME AND GO?

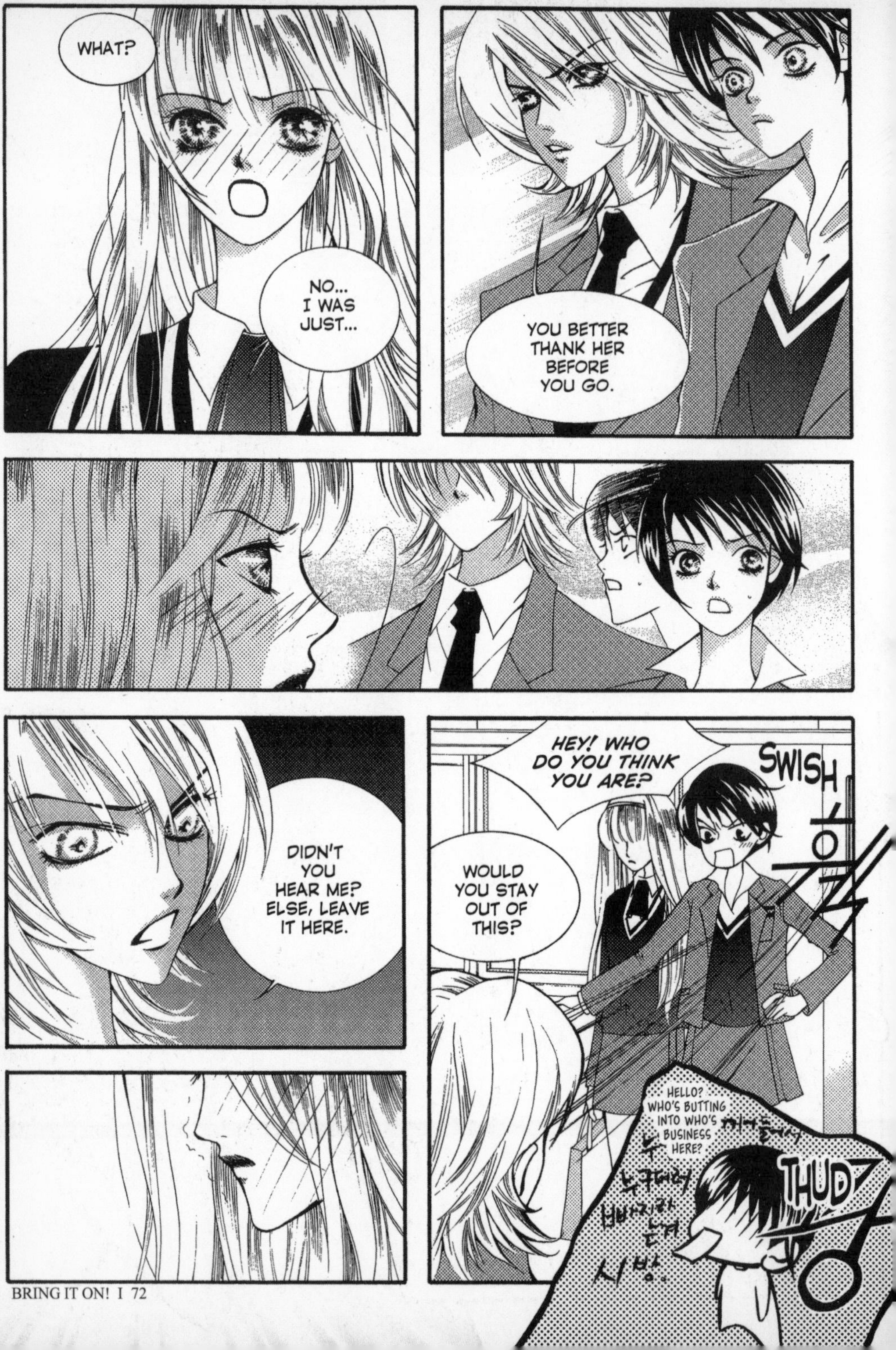
WHAT?
NO... I WAS JUST...
YOU BETTER THANK HER BEFORE YOU GO.
DIDN'T YOU HEAR ME? ELSE, LEAVE IT HERE.
HEY! WHO DO YOU THINK YOU ARE?
SWISH
WOULD YOU STAY OUT OF THIS?
HELLO? WHO'S BUTTING INTO WHO'S BUSINESS HERE?
THUD

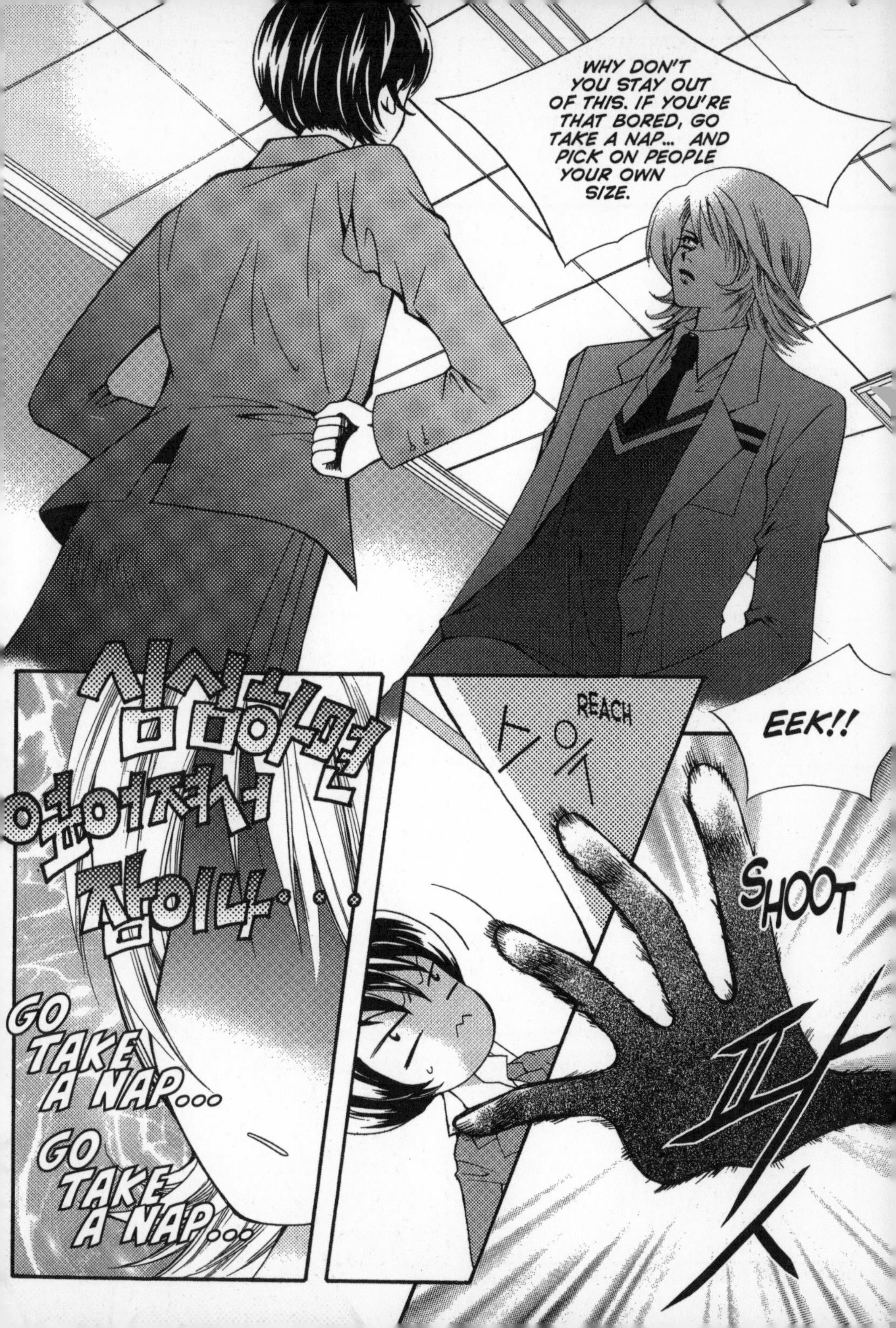

WHY DON'T YOU STAY OUT OF THIS. IF YOU'RE THAT BORED, GO TAKE A NAP... AND PICK ON PEOPLE YOUR OWN SIZE.
EEK!!
REACH
SHOOT
GO TAKE A NAP...
GO TAKE A NAP...

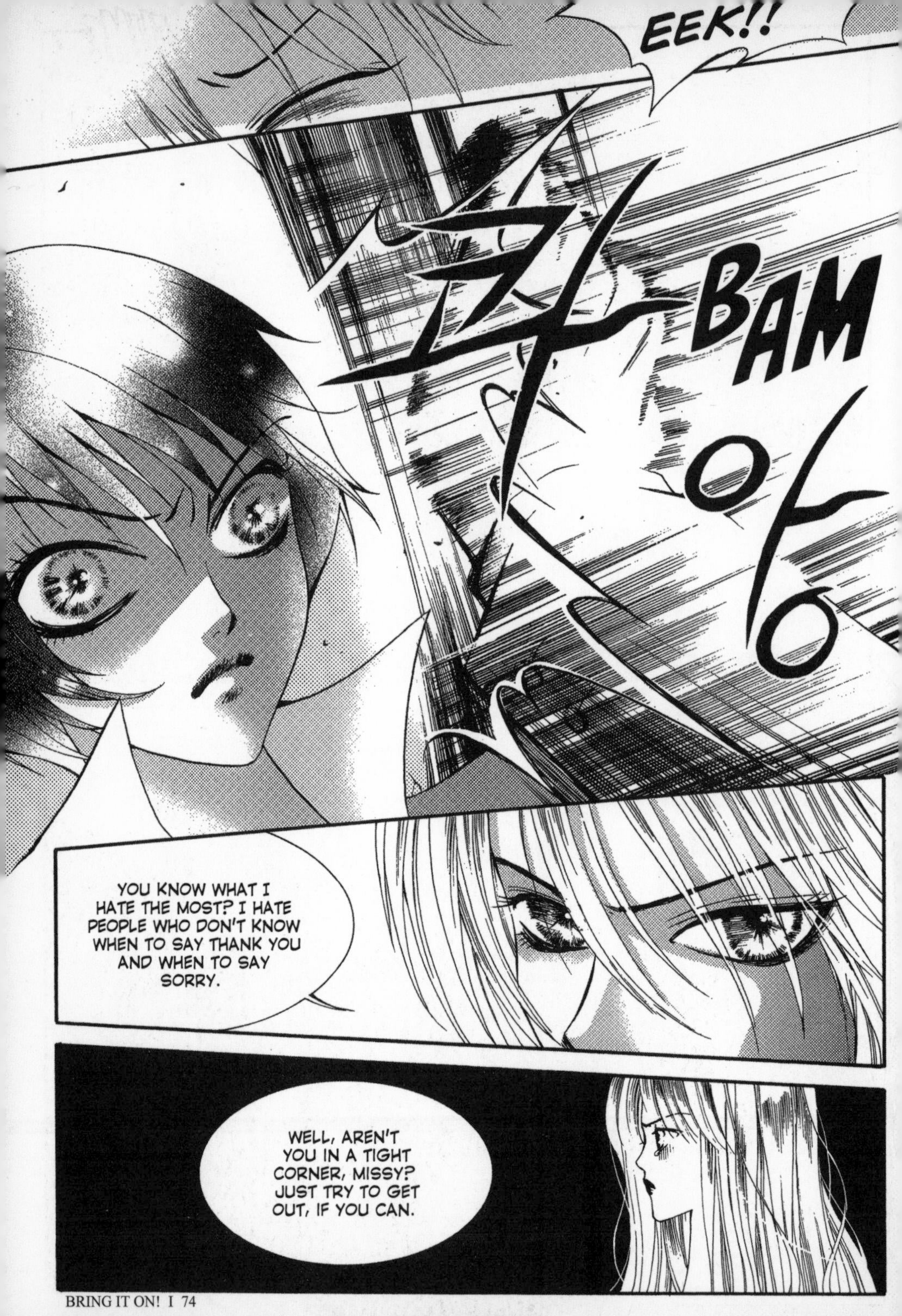
EEK!!
BAM
YOU KNOW WHAT I HATE THE MOST? I HATE PEOPLE WHO DON'T KNOW WHEN TO SAY THANK YOU AND WHEN TO SAY SORRY.
WELL, AREN'T YOU IN A TIGHT CORNER, MISSY? JUST TRY TO GET OUT, IF YOU CAN.

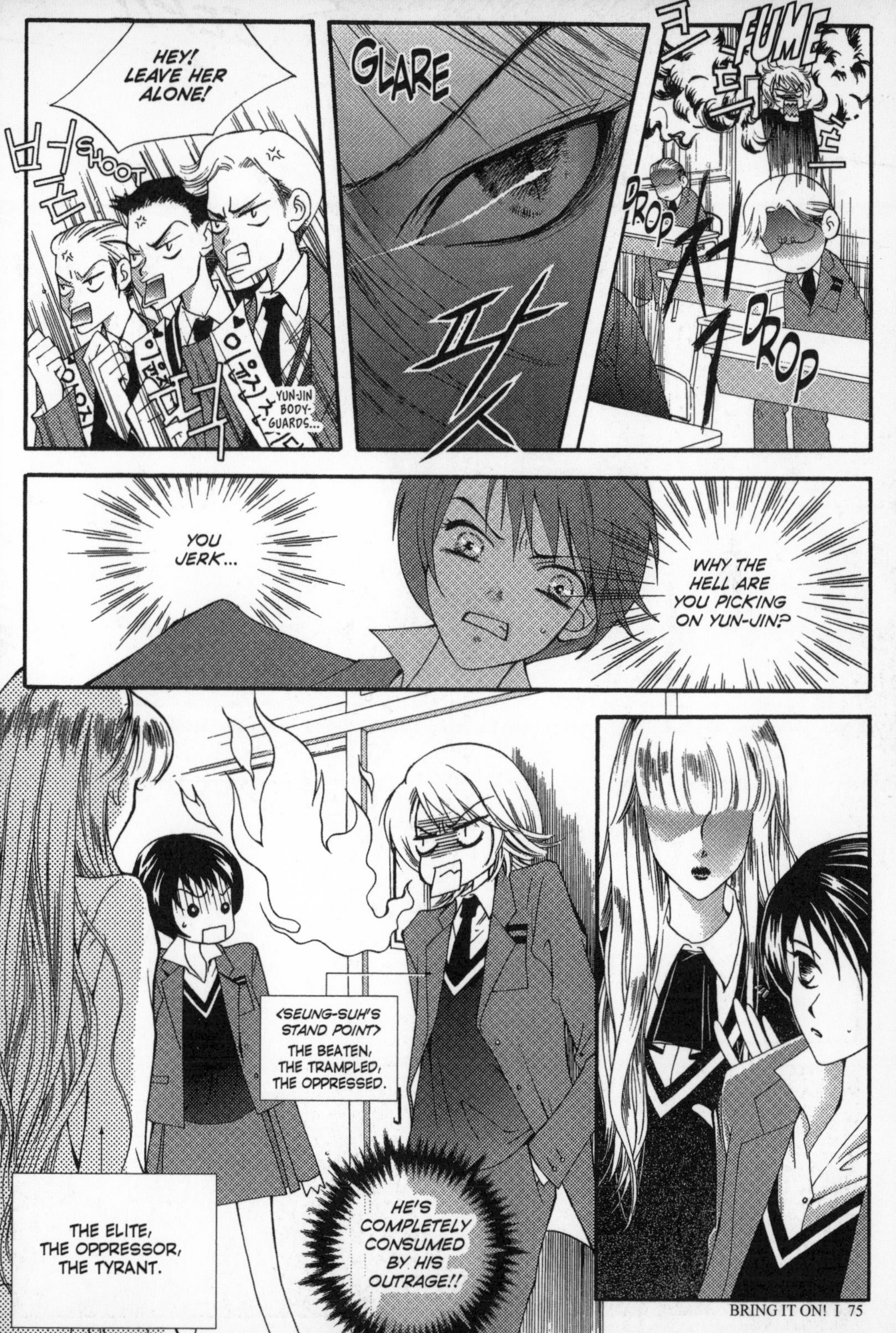
HEY! LEAVE HER ALONE!
SHOOT
YUN-JIN BODY-GUARDS...
GLARE
FUME
DROP
DROP
YOU JERK...
WHY THE HELL ARE YOU PICKING ON YUN-JIN?
<SEUNG-SUH'S STAND POINT> THE BEATEN, THE TRAMPLED, THE OPPRESSED.
THE ELITE, THE OPPRESSOR, THE TYRANT.
HE'S COMPLETELY CONSUMED BY HIS OUTRAGE!!

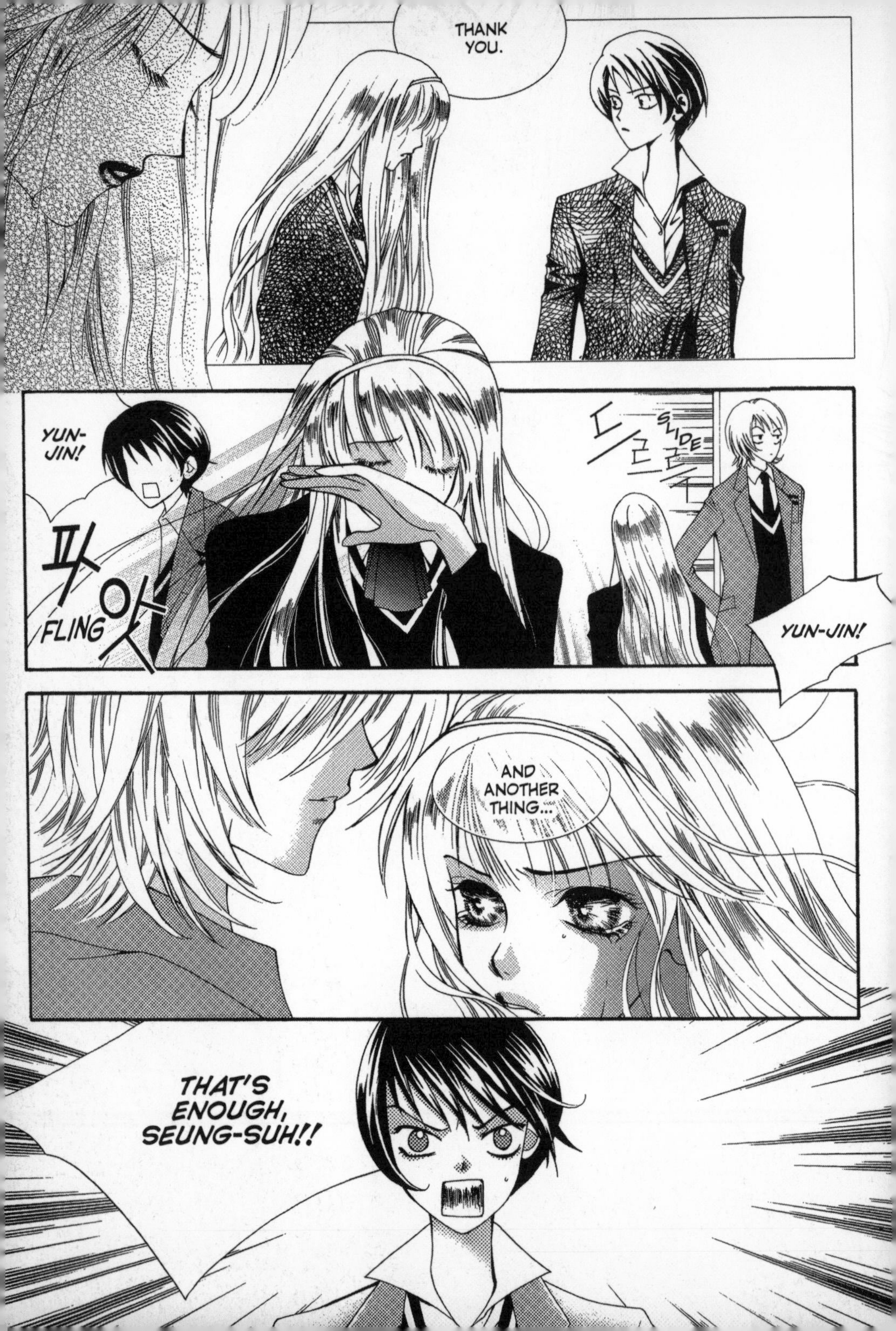
THANK YOU.
YUN-JIN!
파앗
FLING
드르륵
SLIDE
YUN-JIN!
AND ANOTHER THING...
THAT'S ENOUGH, SEUNG-SUH!!

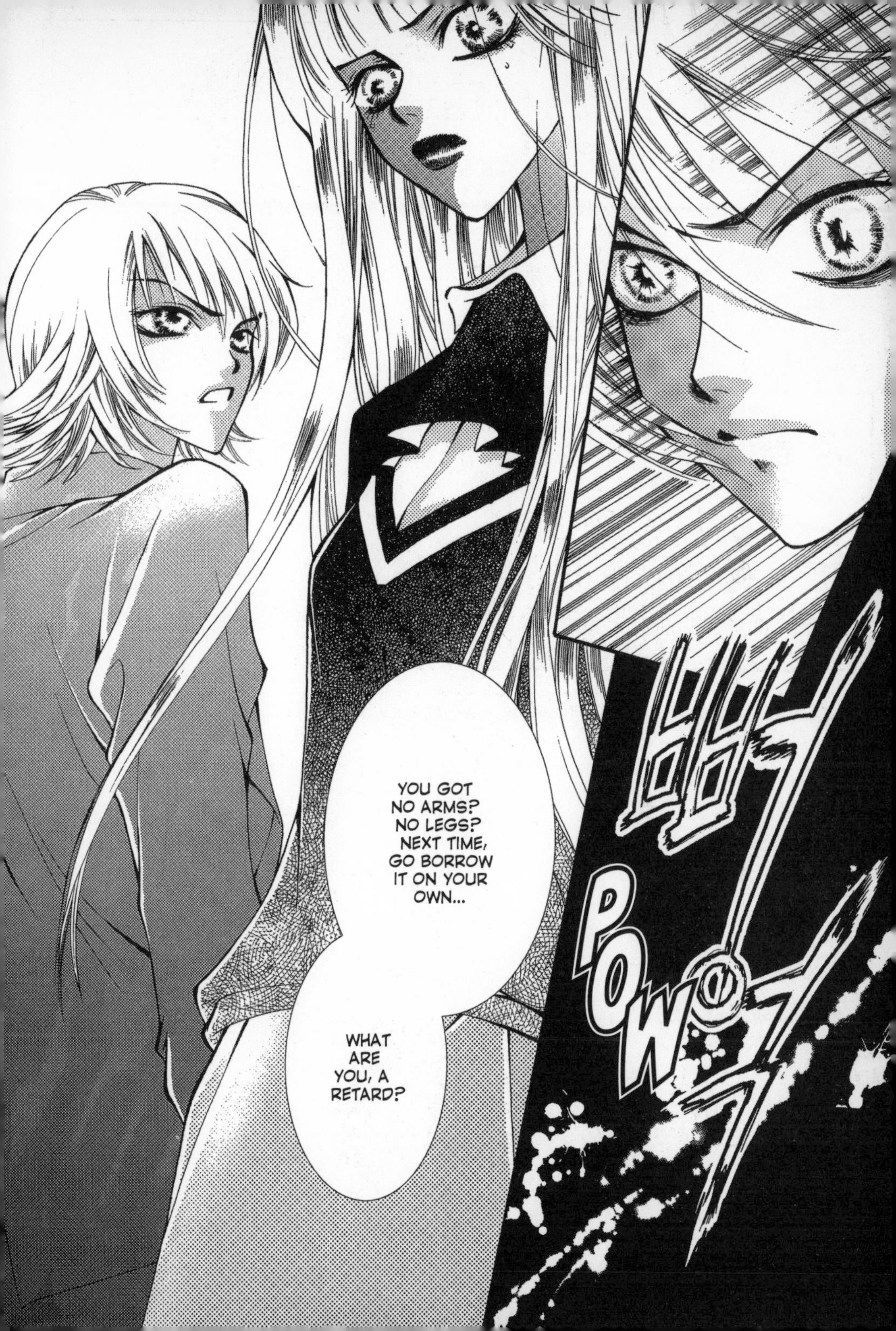
YOU GOT NO ARMS? NO LEGS? NEXT TIME, GO BORROW IT ON YOUR OWN...
WHAT ARE YOU, A RETARD?
POW

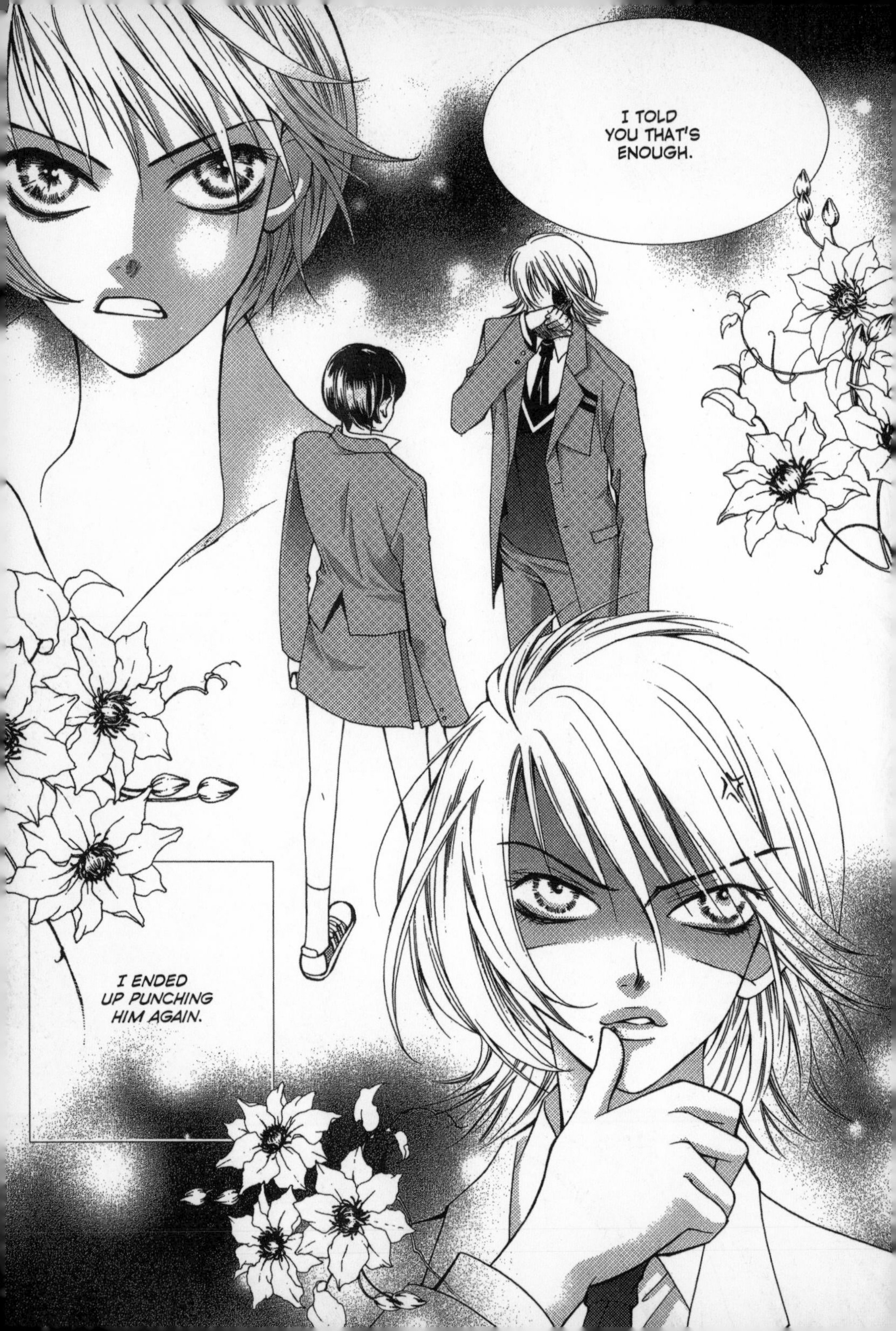
I TOLD YOU THAT'S ENOUGH.
I ENDED UP PUNCHING HIM AGAIN.

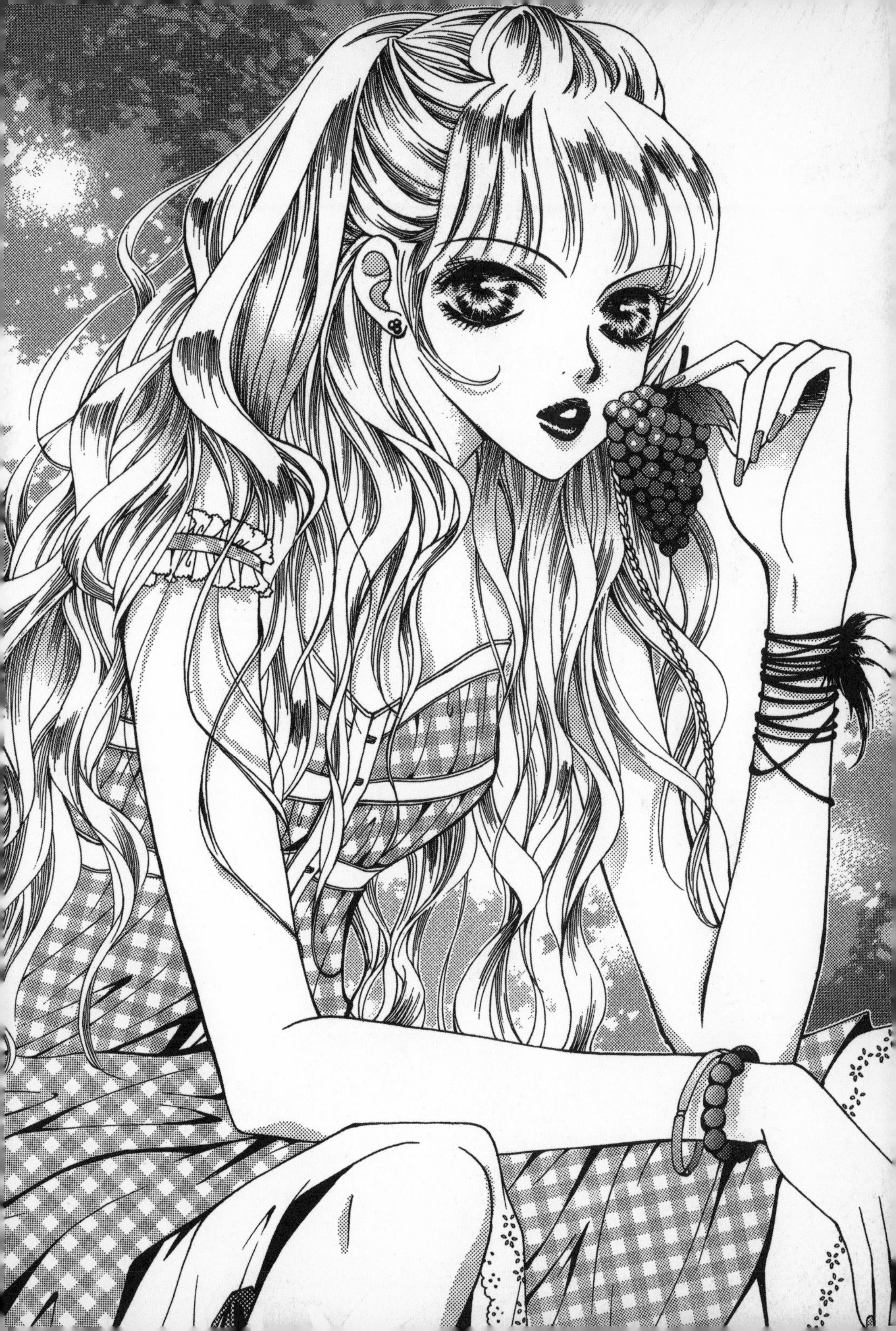

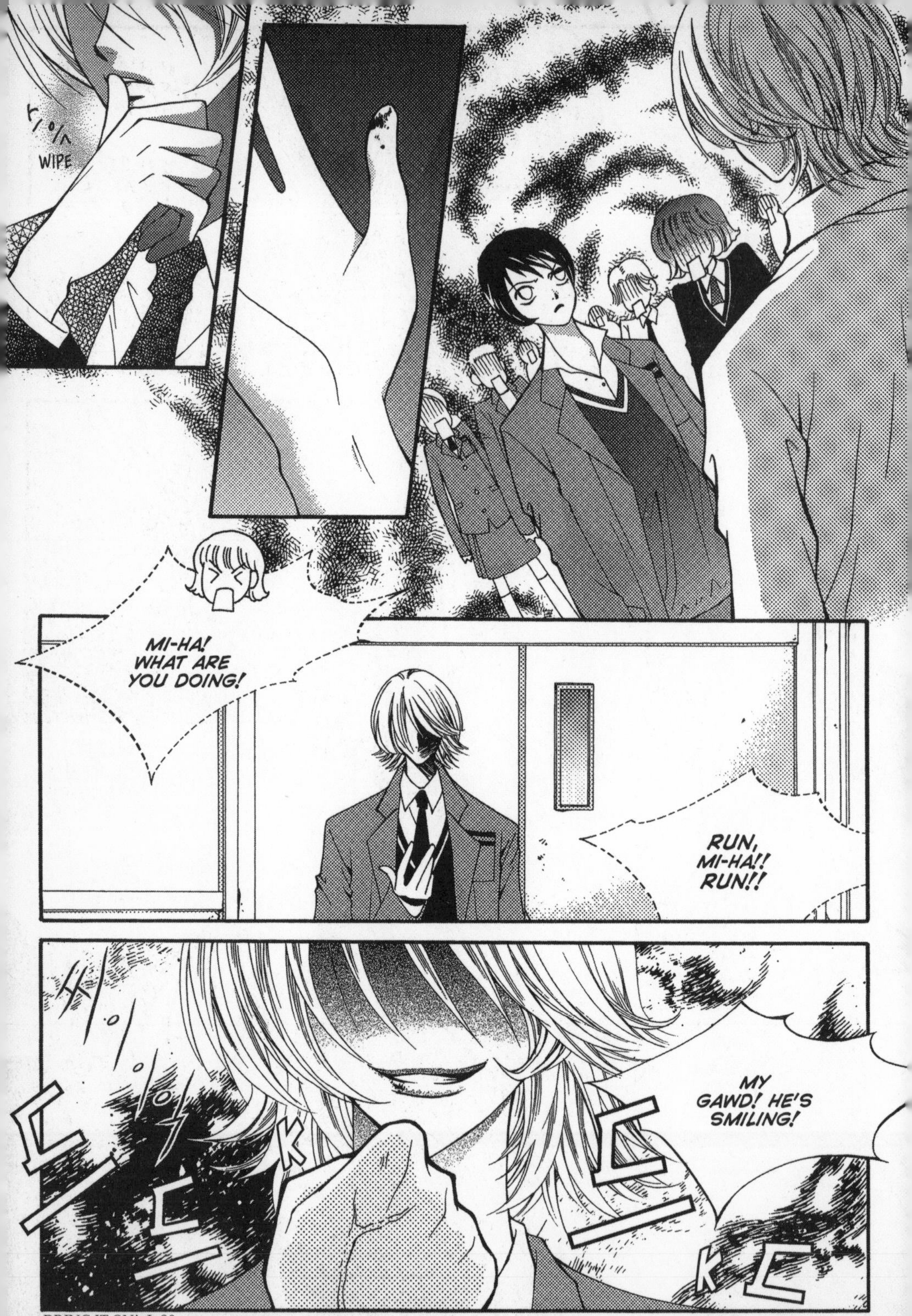
WIPE
MI-HA! WHAT ARE YOU DOING!
RUN, MI-HA!! RUN!!
K
MY GAWD! HE'S SMILING!
K

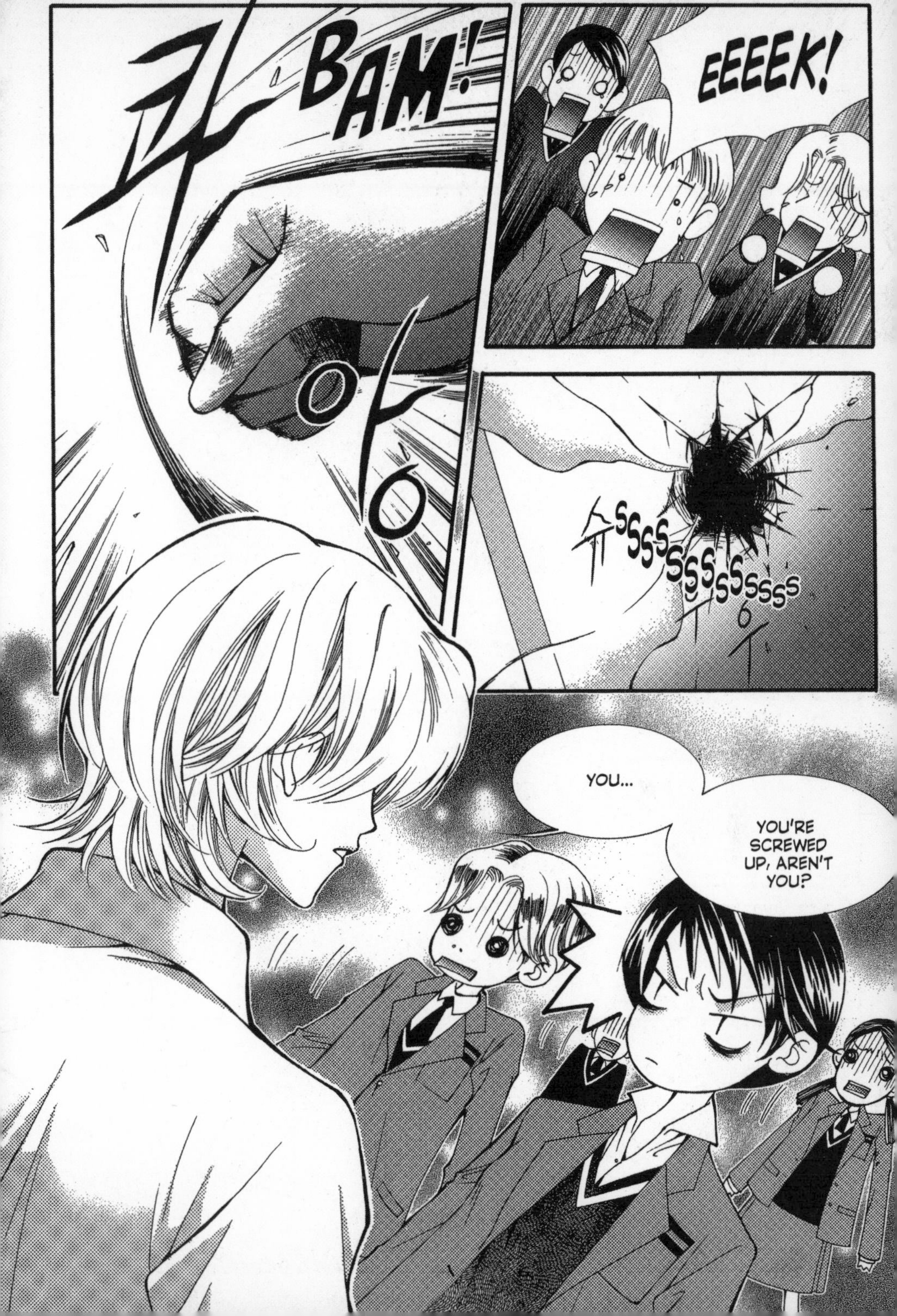
BAM!
EEEEK!
SSSSSSSSSSSSS
YOU...
YOU'RE SCREWED UP, AREN'T YOU?

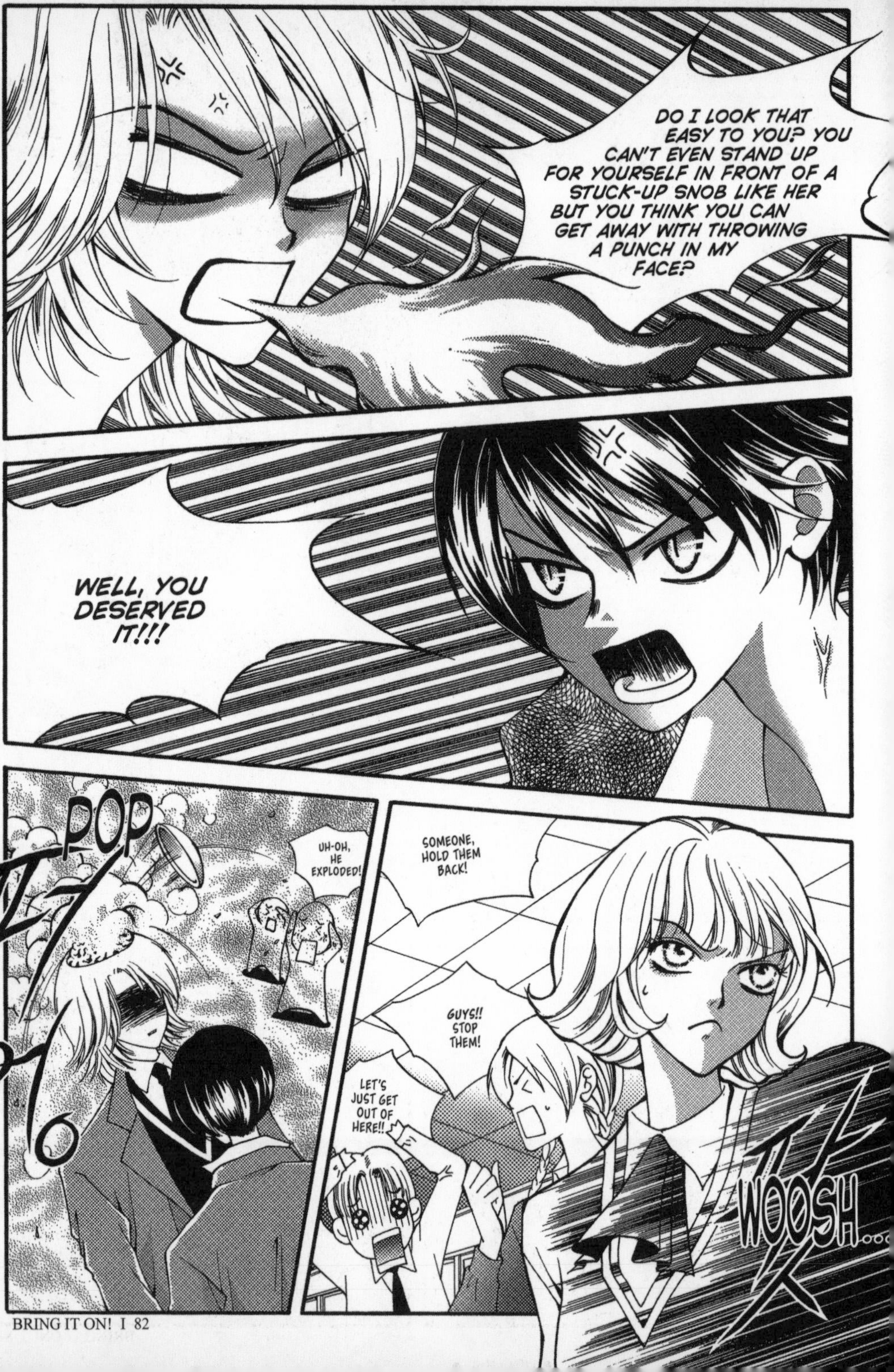
DO I LOOK THAT EASY TO YOU? YOU CAN'T EVEN STAND UP FOR YOURSELF IN FRONT OF A STUCK-UP SNOB LIKE HER BUT YOU THINK YOU CAN GET AWAY WITH THROWING A PUNCH IN MY FACE?
WELL, YOU DESERVED IT!!!
POP
UH-OH, HE EXPLODED!
SOMEONE, HOLD THEM BACK!
GUYS!! STOP THEM!
LET'S JUST GET OUT OF HERE!!
WOOSH...

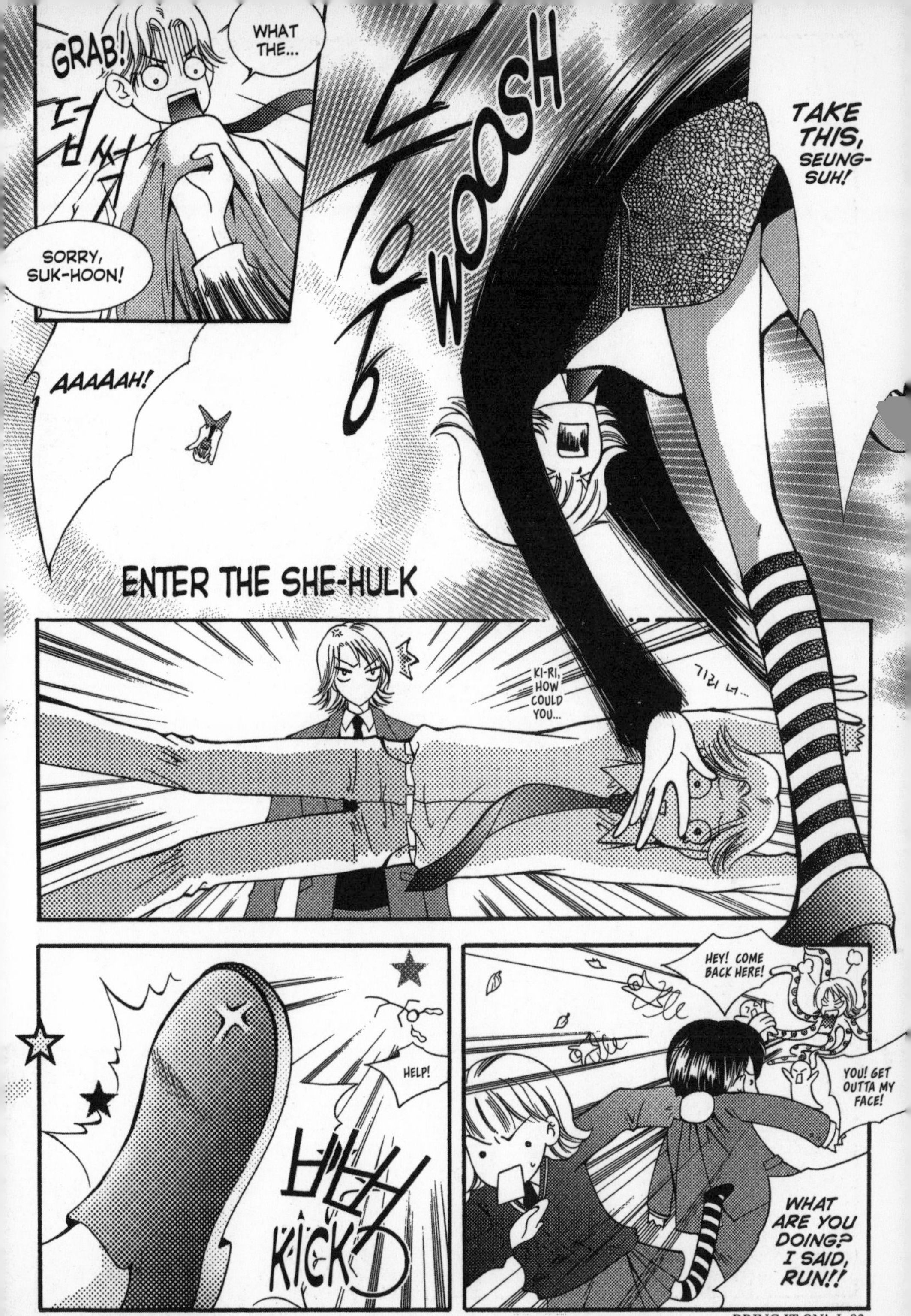
GRAB!
WHAT THE...
SORRY, SUK-HOON!
WOOSH
TAKE THIS, SEUNG-SUH!
AAAAAH!
ENTER THE SHE-HULK
KI-RI, HOW COULD YOU...
기리 너...
HELP!
KICK
HEY! COME BACK HERE!
YOU! GET OUTTA MY FACE!
WHAT ARE YOU DOING? I SAID, RUN!!

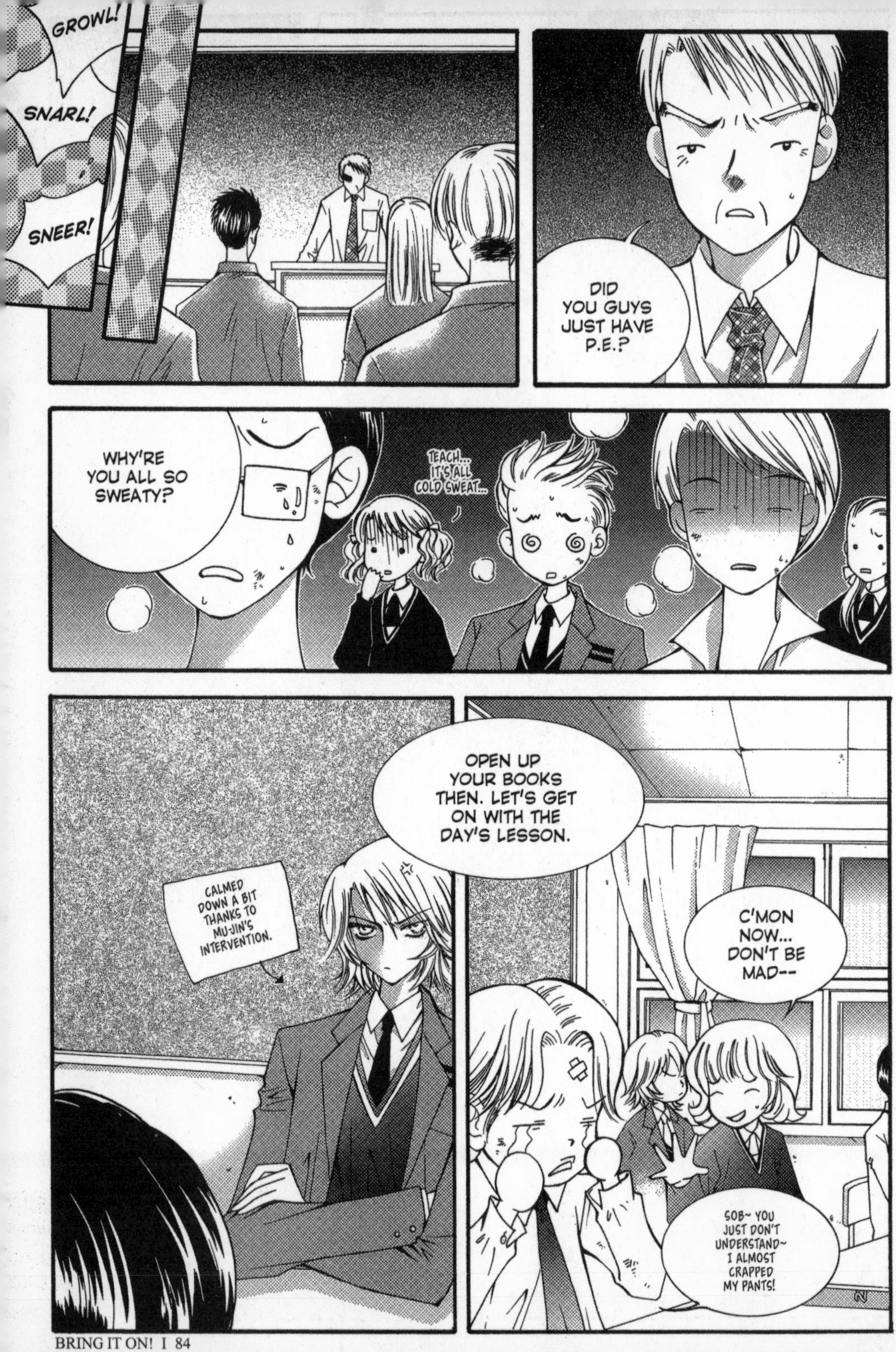
GROWL!
SNARL!
SNEER!
DID YOU GUYS JUST HAVE P.E.?
WHY'RE YOU ALL SO SWEATY?
TEACH... IT'S ALL COLD SWEAT...
OPEN UP YOUR BOOKS THEN. LET'S GET ON WITH THE DAY'S LESSON.
CALMED DOWN A BIT THANKS TO MU-JIN'S INTERVENTION.
C'MON NOW... DON'T BE MAD--
SOB~ YOU JUST DON'T UNDERSTAND~ I ALMOST CRAPPED MY PANTS!

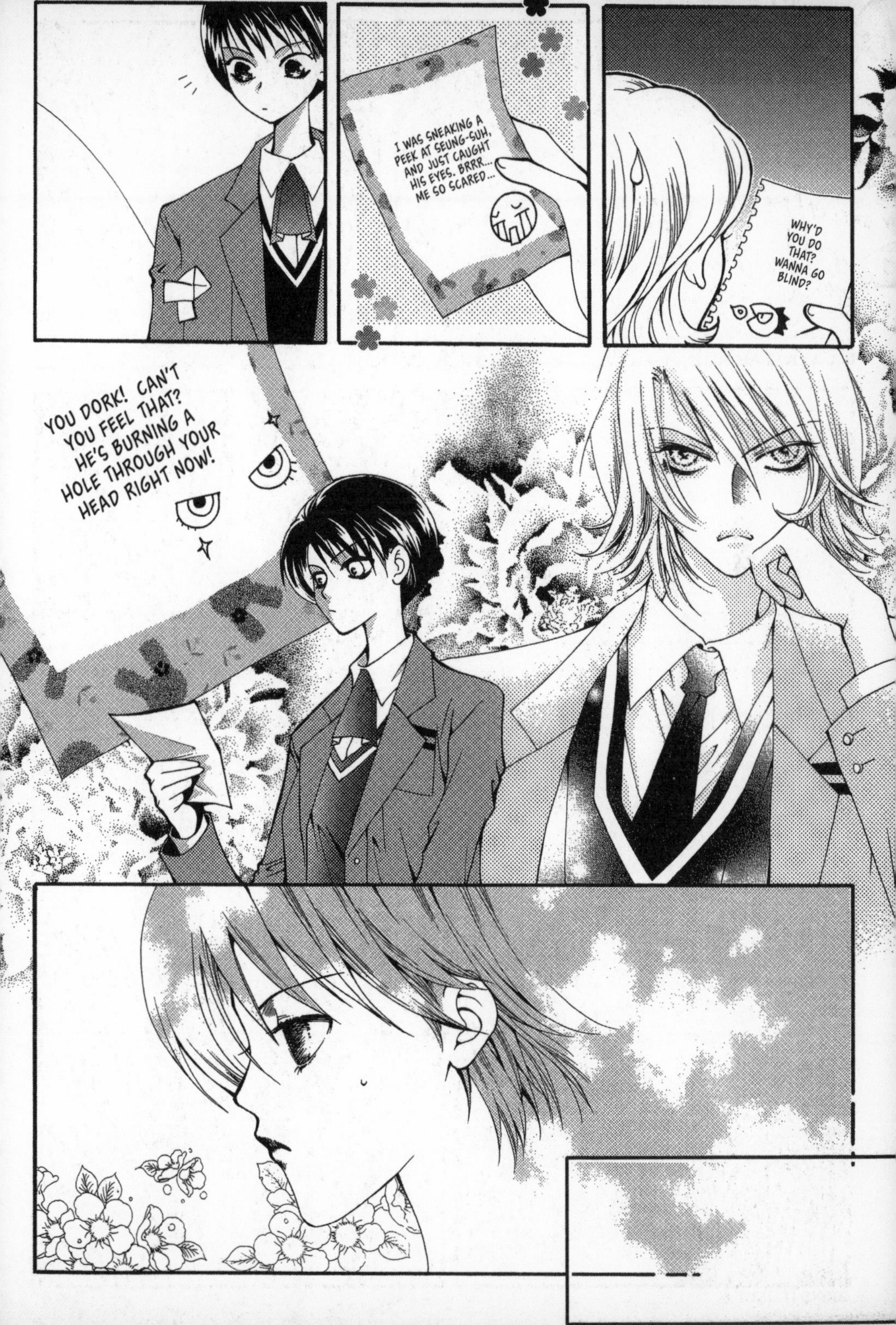
I WAS SNEAKING A PEEK AT SEUNG-SUH, AND JUST CAUGHT HIS EYES. BRRR... ME SO SCARED...
WHY'D YOU DO THAT? WANNA GO BLIND?
YOU DORK! CAN'T YOU FEEL THAT? HE'S BURNING A HOLE THROUGH YOUR HEAD RIGHT NOW!

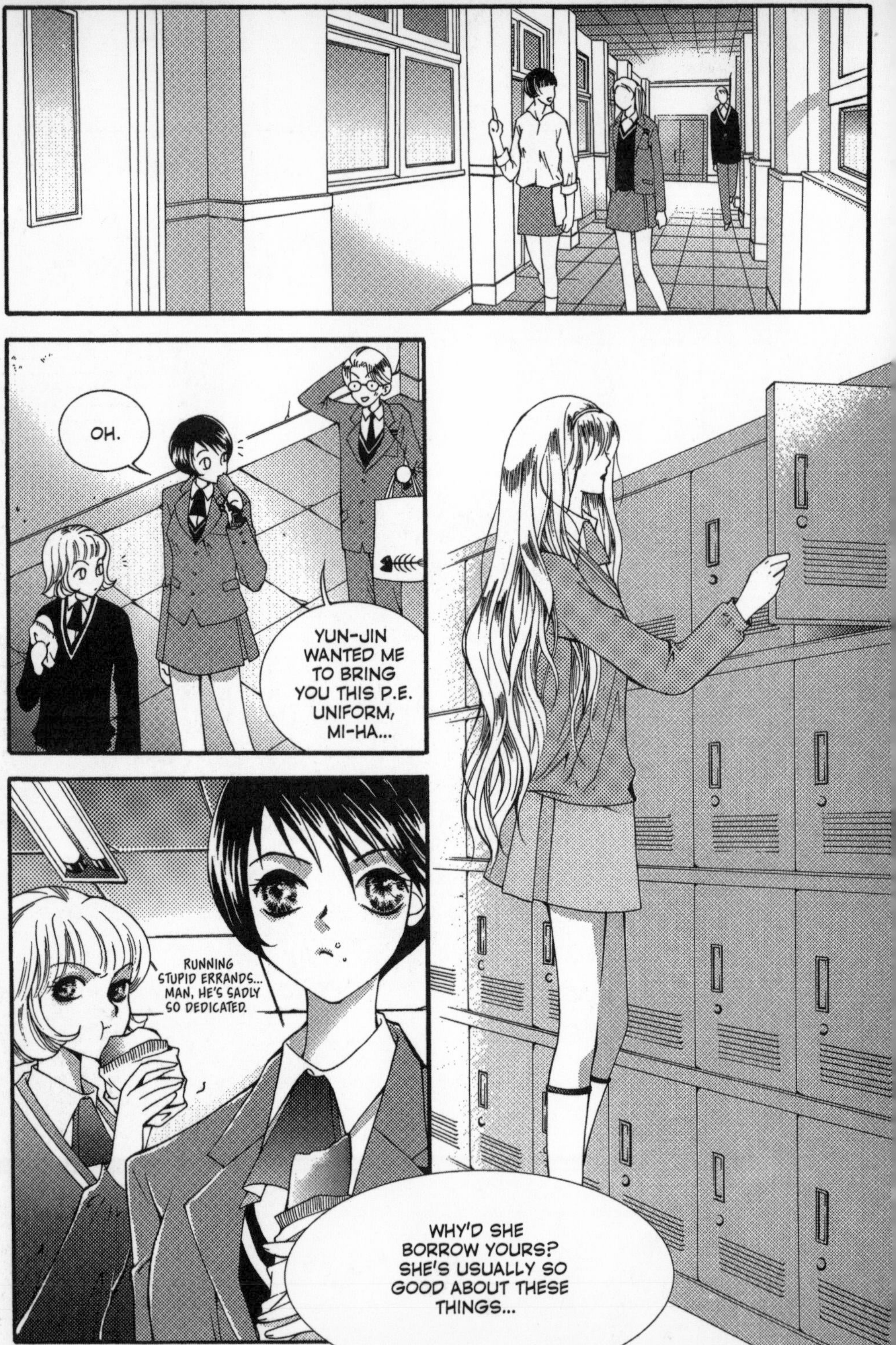
OH.
YUN-JIN WANTED ME TO BRING YOU THIS P.E. UNIFORM, MI-HA...
RUNNING STUPID ERRANDS... MAN, HE'S SADLY SO DEDICATED.
WHY'D SHE BORROW YOURS? SHE'S USUALLY SO GOOD ABOUT THESE THINGS...

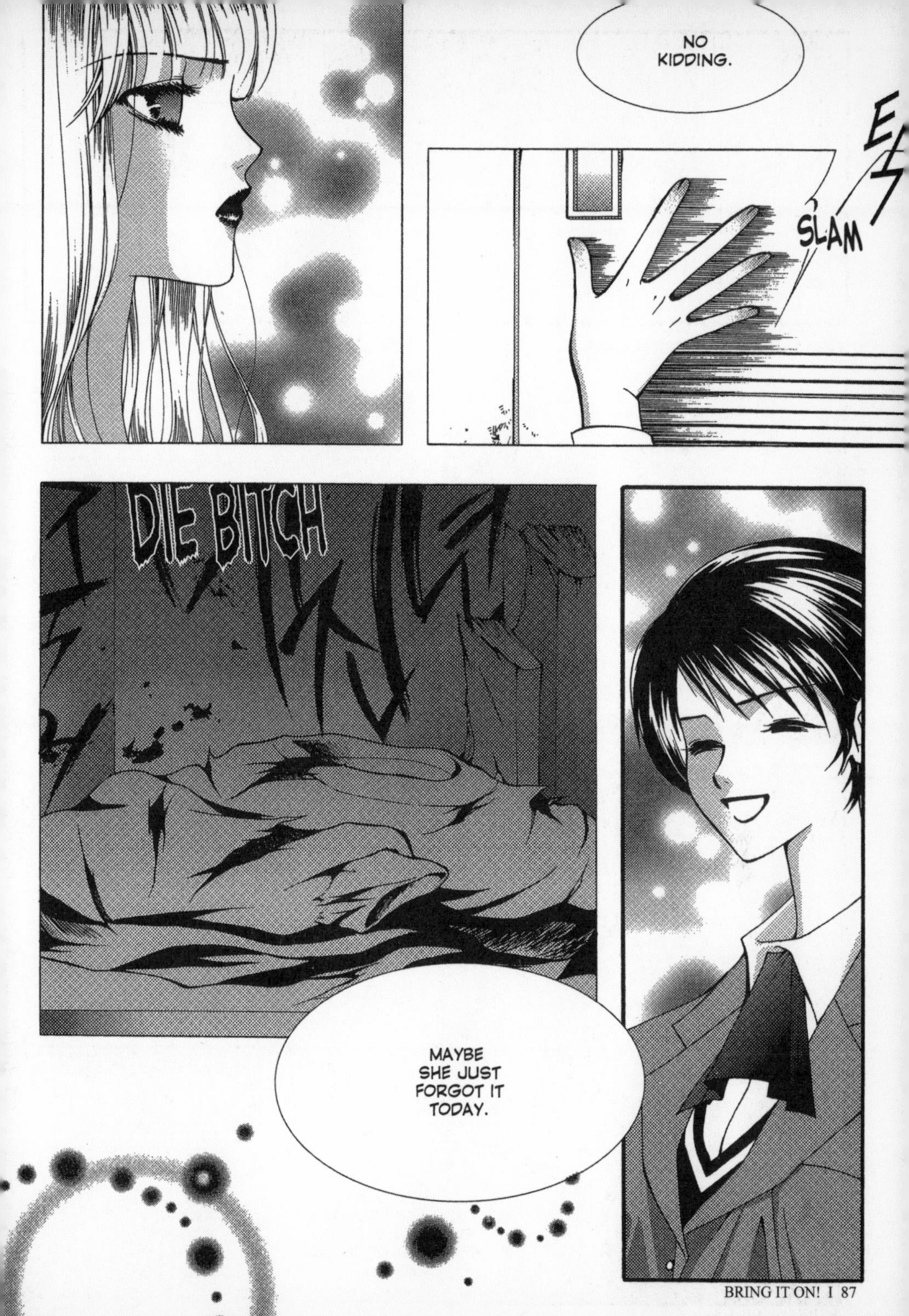
NO KIDDING.
SLAM
MAYBE SHE JUST FORGOT IT TODAY.
DIE BITCH

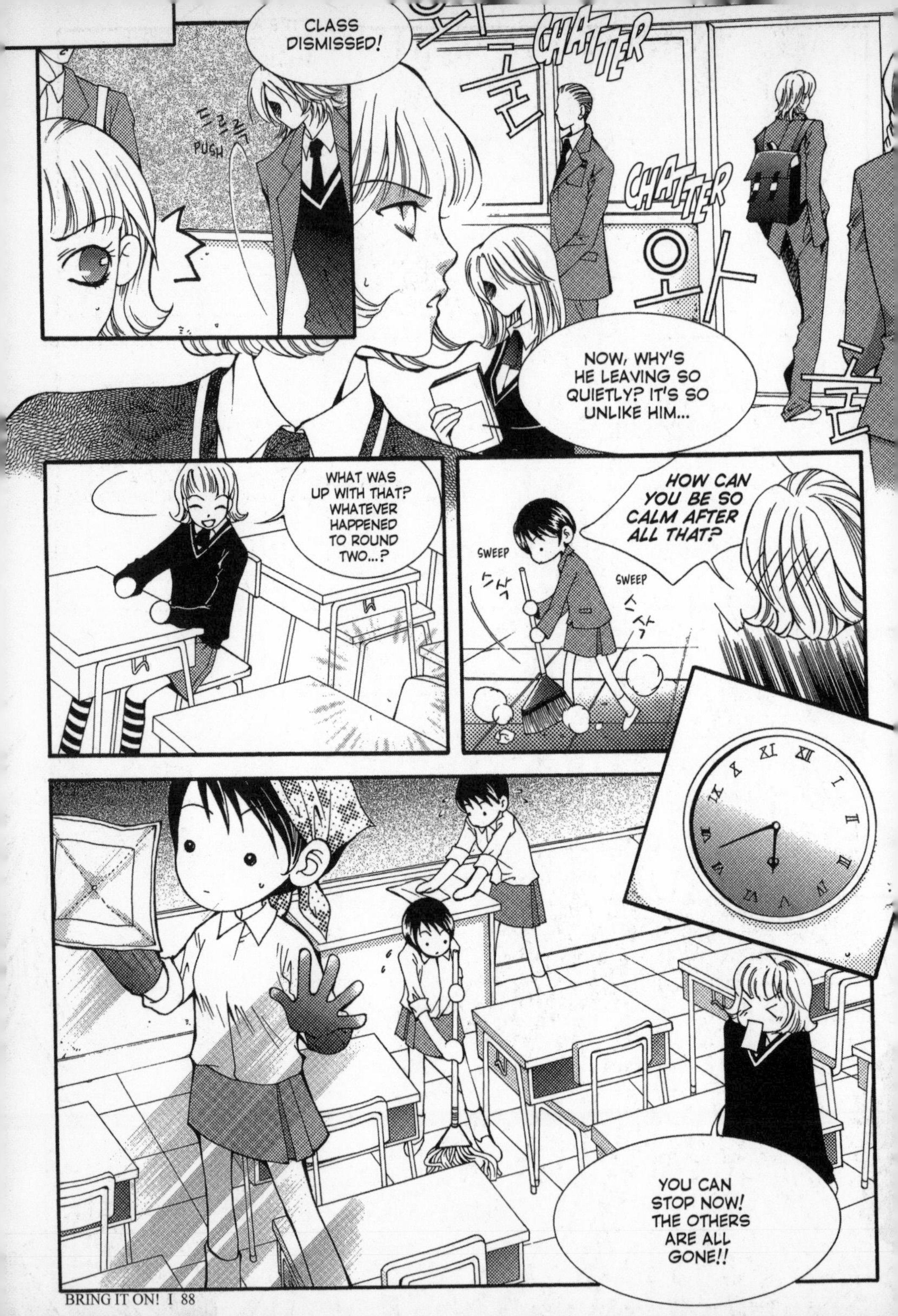
CLASS DISMISSED!
드르륵
PUSH
CHATTER
CHATTER
NOW, WHY'S HE LEAVING SO QUIETLY? IT'S SO UNLIKE HIM...
WHAT WAS UP WITH THAT? WHATEVER HAPPENED TO ROUND TWO...?
HOW CAN YOU BE SO CALM AFTER ALL THAT?
SWEEP
SWEEP
YOU CAN STOP NOW! THE OTHERS ARE ALL GONE!!

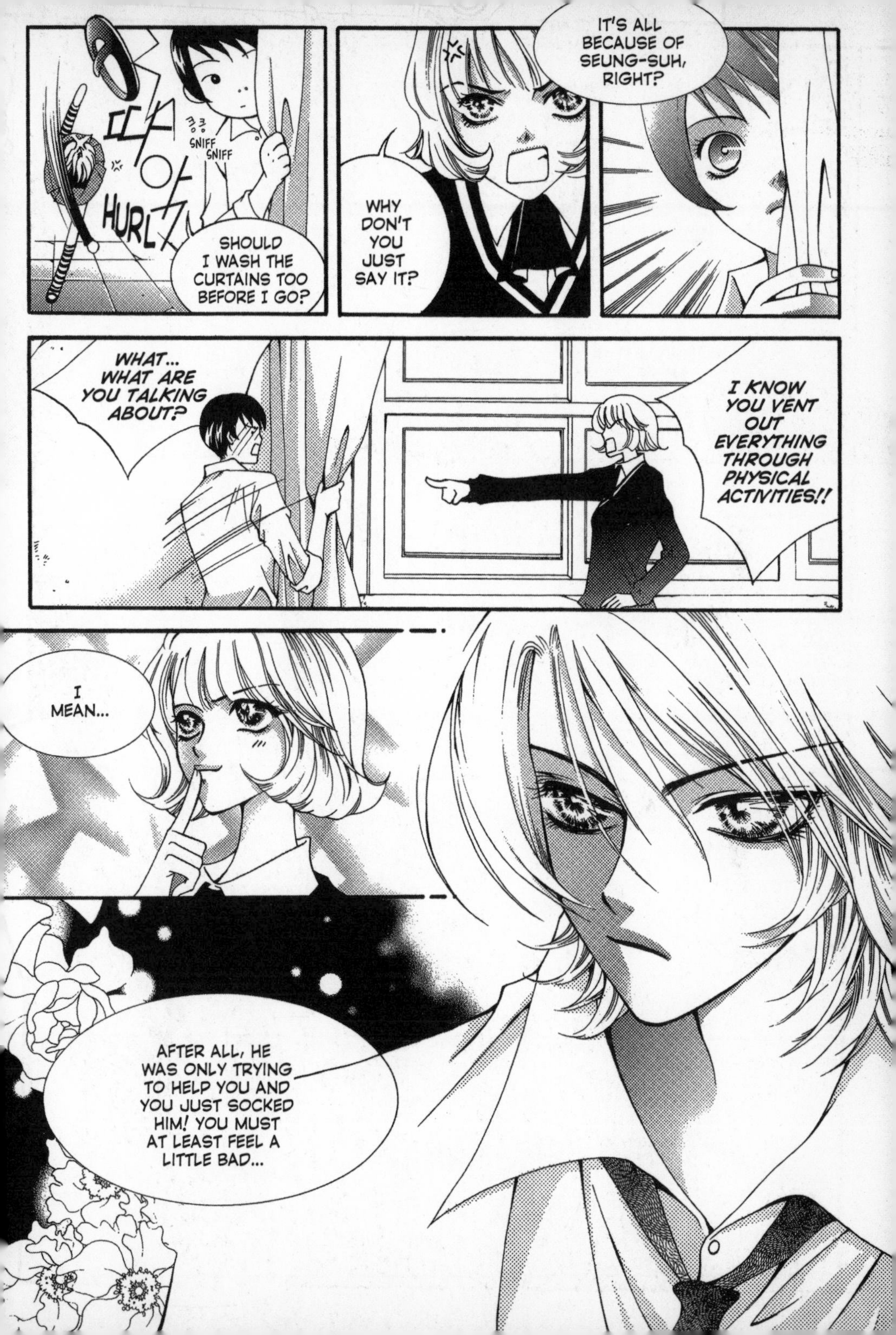
SNIFF SNIFF
HURL
SHOULD I WASH THE CURTAINS TOO BEFORE I GO?
WHY DON'T YOU JUST SAY IT?
IT'S ALL BECAUSE OF SEUNG-SUH, RIGHT?
WHAT... WHAT ARE YOU TALKING ABOUT?
I KNOW YOU VENT OUT EVERYTHING THROUGH PHYSICAL ACTIVITIES!!
I MEAN...
AFTER ALL, HE WAS ONLY TRYING TO HELP YOU AND YOU JUST SOCKED HIM! YOU MUST AT LEAST FEEL A LITTLE BAD...

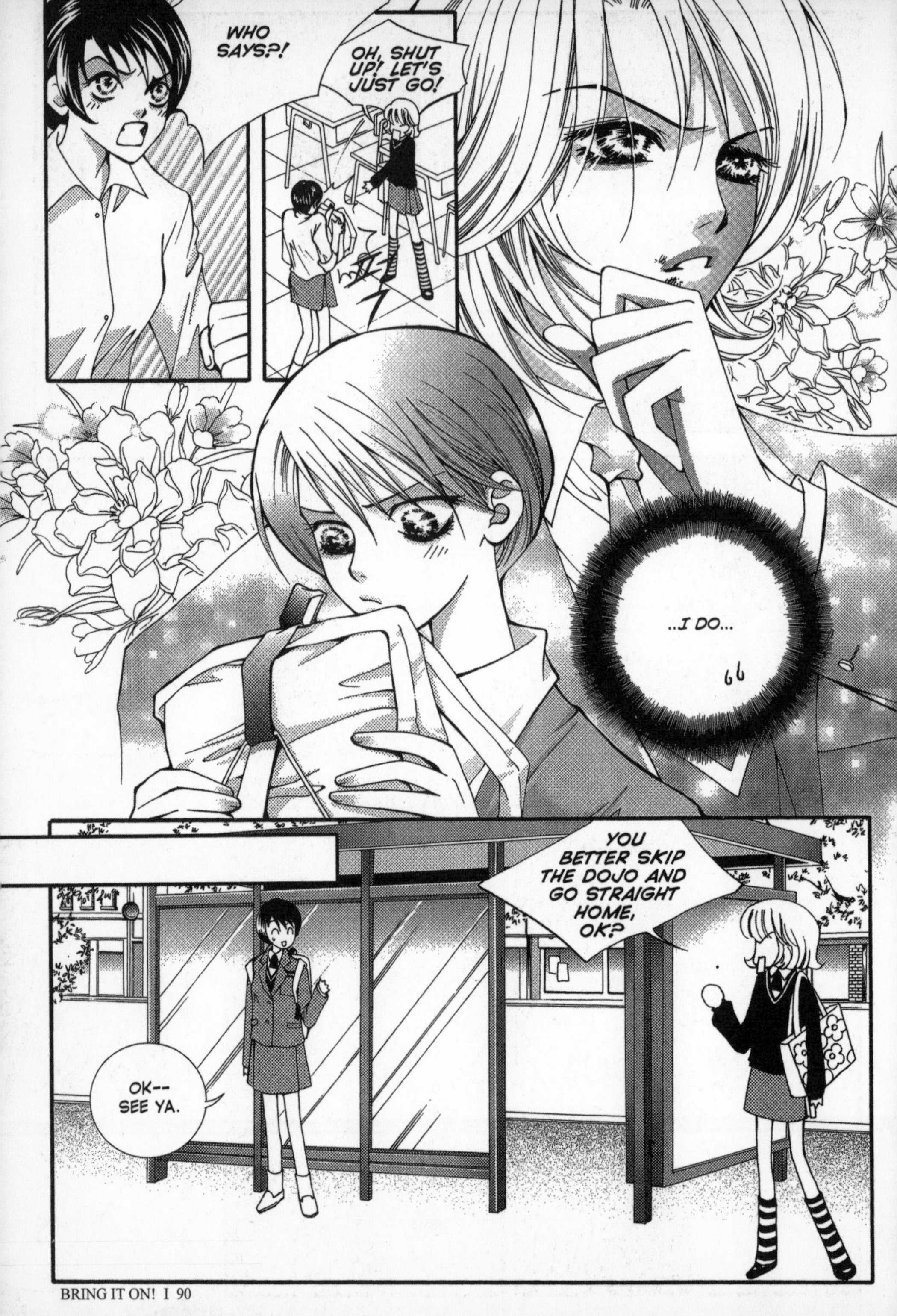
WHO SAYS?!
OH, SHUT UP! LET'S JUST GO!
...I DO...
YOU BETTER SKIP THE DOJO AND GO STRAIGHT HOME, OK?
OK-- SEE YA.

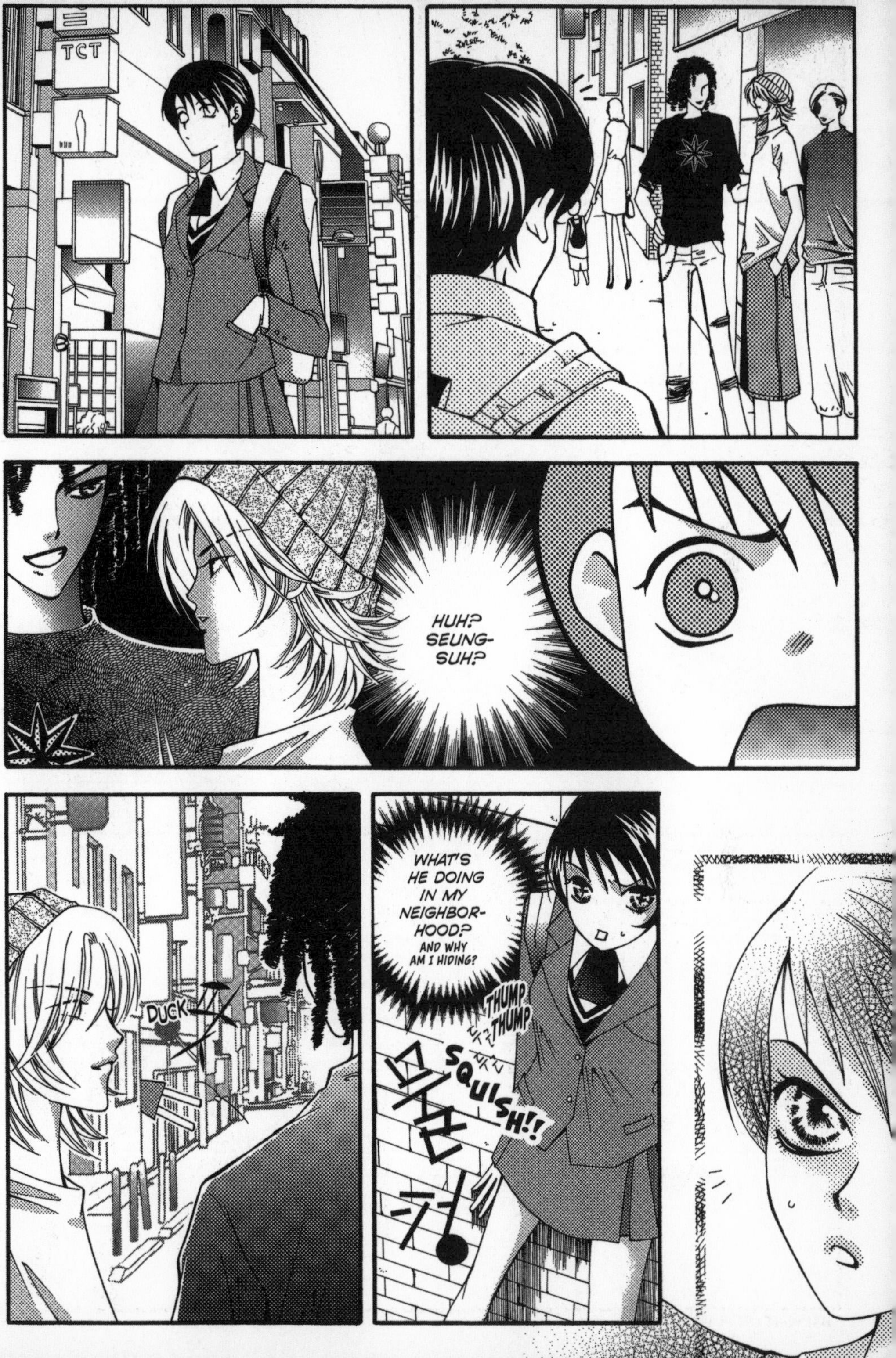
HUH? SEUNG-SUH?
DUCK
WHAT'S HE DOING IN MY NEIGHBORHOOD?
AND WHY AM I HIDING?
THUMP THUMP
SQUISH!!

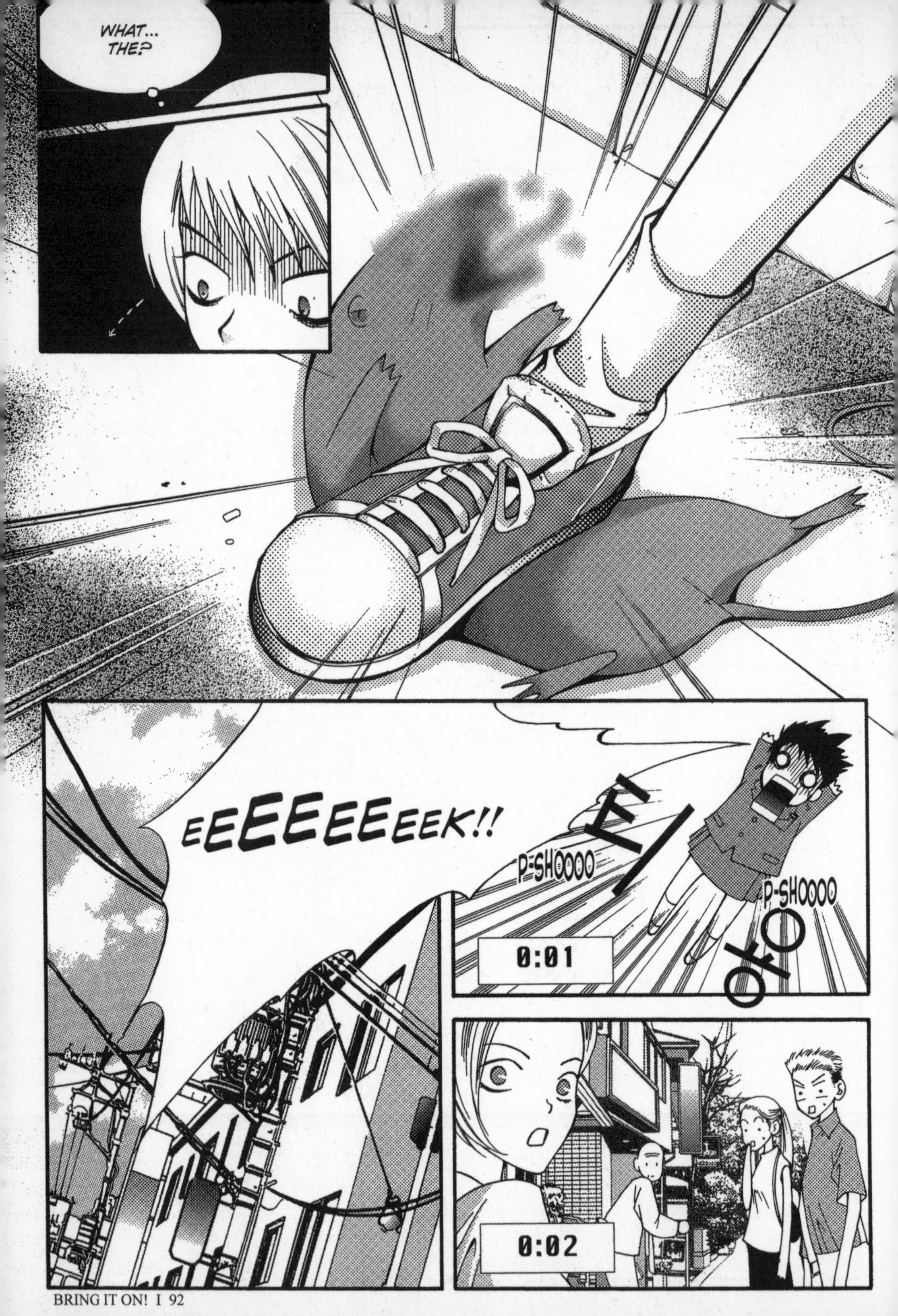
WHAT... THE?
EEEEEEEEEK!!
P-SHOOOO
P-SHOOOO
0:01
0:02

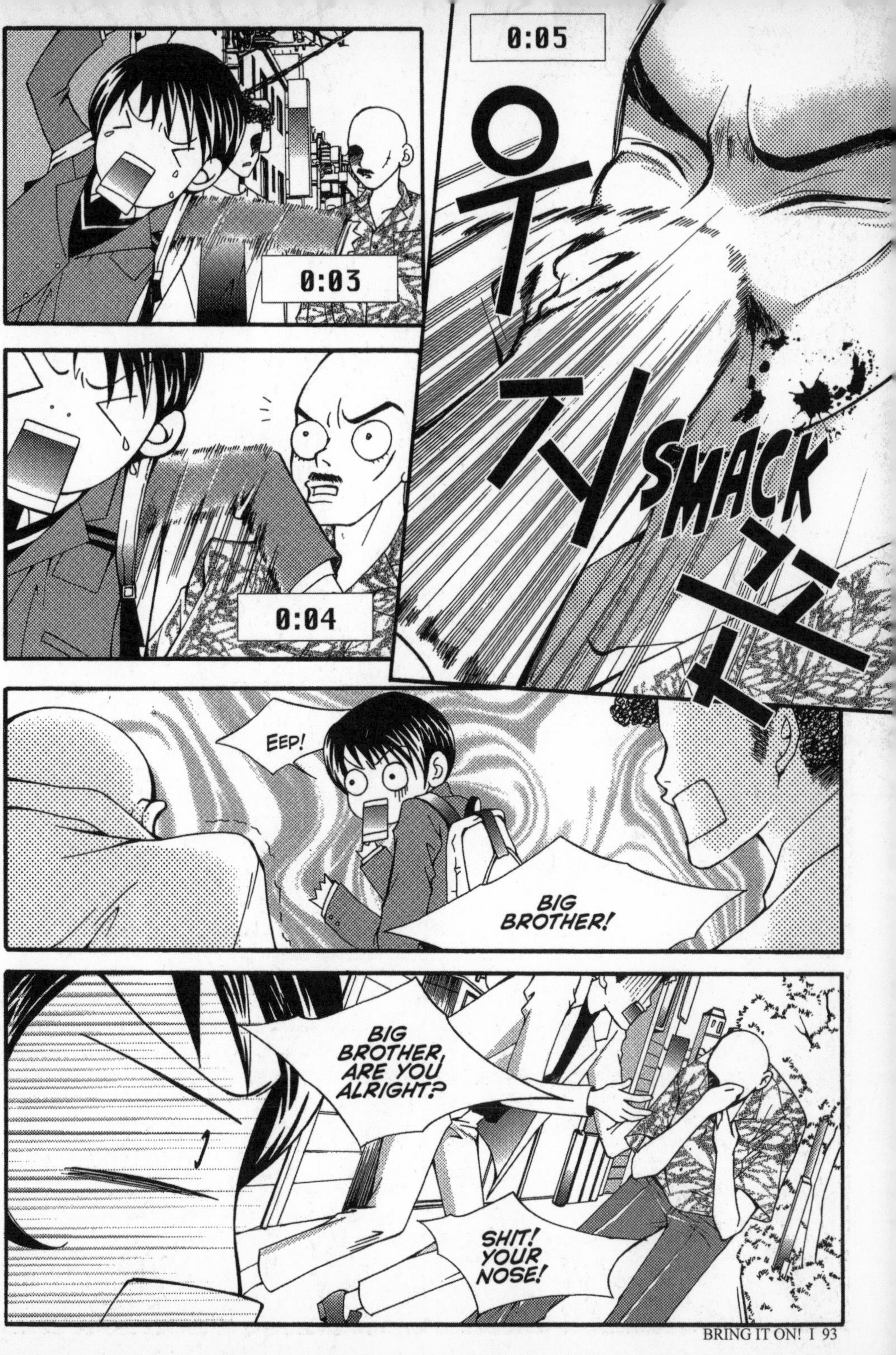
0:03
0:04
0:05
SMACK
EEP!
BIG BROTHER!
BIG BROTHER, ARE YOU ALRIGHT?
SHIT! YOUR NOSE!

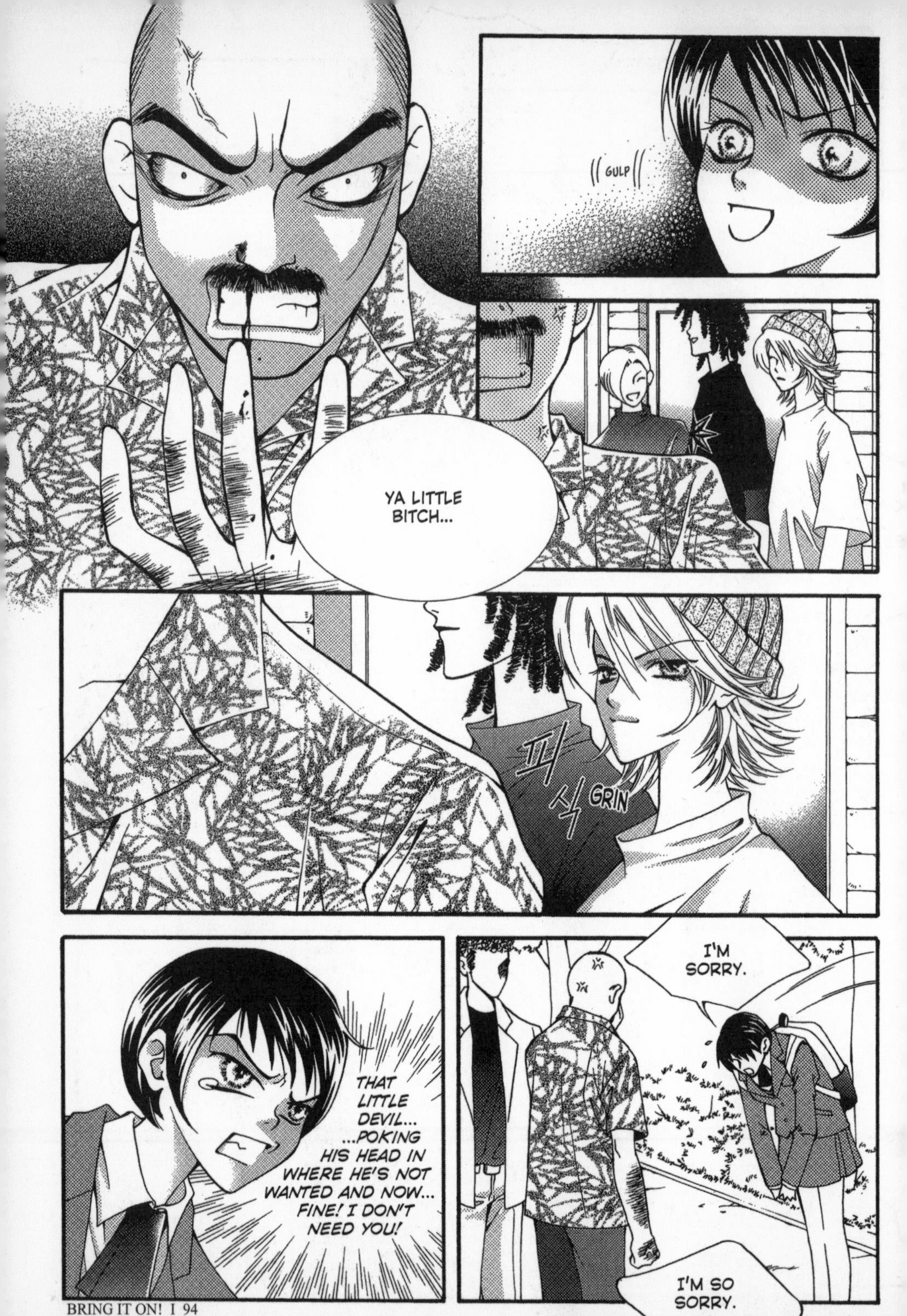
GULP
YA LITTLE BITCH...
파삭
GRIN
THAT LITTLE DEVIL... ...POKING HIS HEAD IN WHERE HE'S NOT WANTED AND NOW... FINE! I DON'T NEED YOU!
I'M SORRY.
I'M SO SORRY.

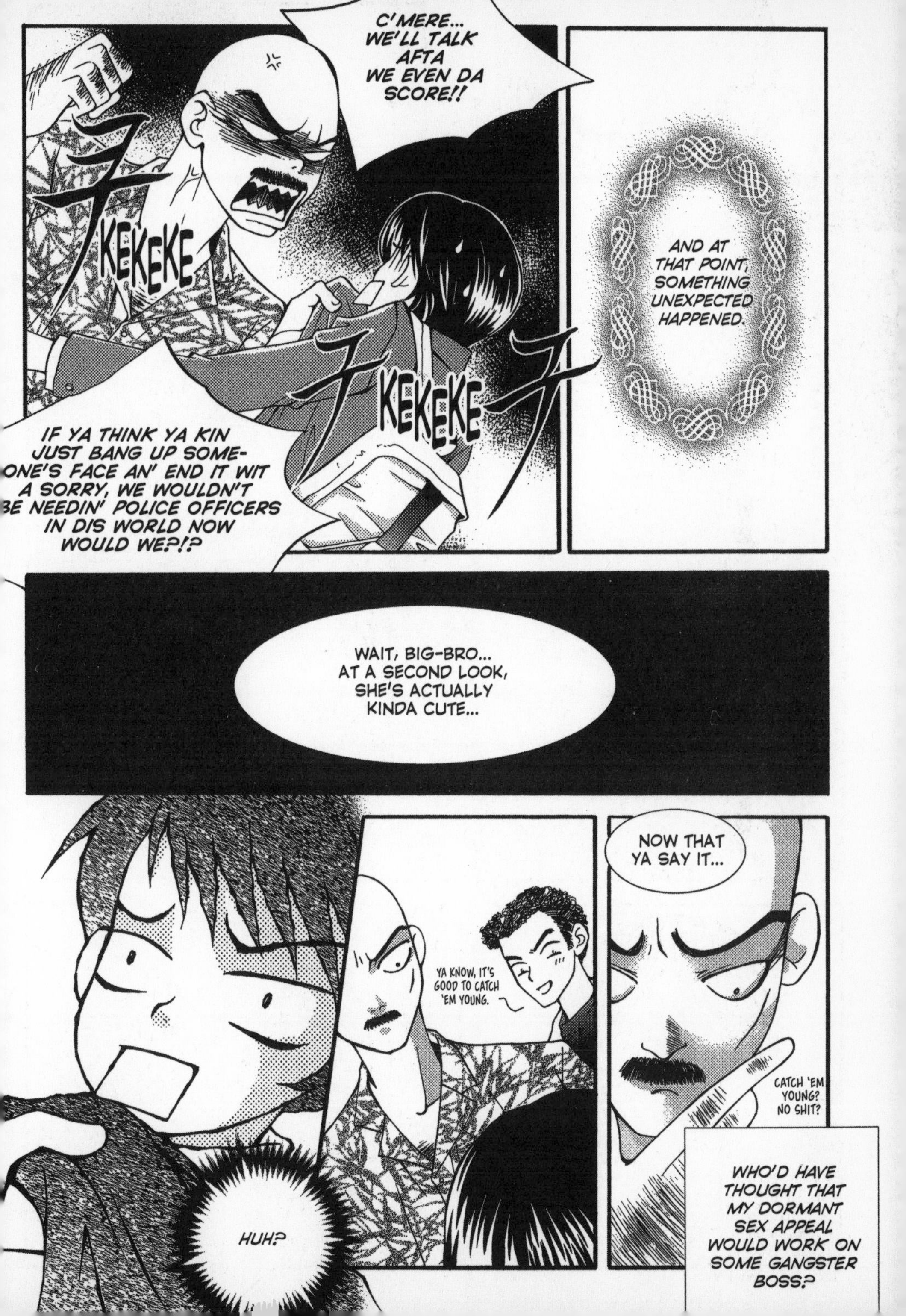
C'MERE... WE'LL TALK AFTA WE EVEN DA SCORE!!
KEKEKE
KEKEKE
IF YA THINK YA KIN JUST BANG UP SOME-ONE'S FACE AN' END IT WIT A SORRY, WE WOULDN'T BE NEEDIN' POLICE OFFICERS IN DIS WORLD NOW WOULD WE?!?
AND AT THAT POINT, SOMETHING UNEXPECTED HAPPENED.
WAIT, BIG-BRO... AT A SECOND LOOK, SHE'S ACTUALLY KINDA CUTE...
HUH?
YA KNOW, IT'S GOOD TO CATCH 'EM YOUNG.
NOW THAT YA SAY IT...
CATCH 'EM YOUNG? NO SHIT?
WHO'D HAVE THOUGHT THAT MY DORMANT SEX APPEAL WOULD WORK ON SOME GANGSTER BOSS?

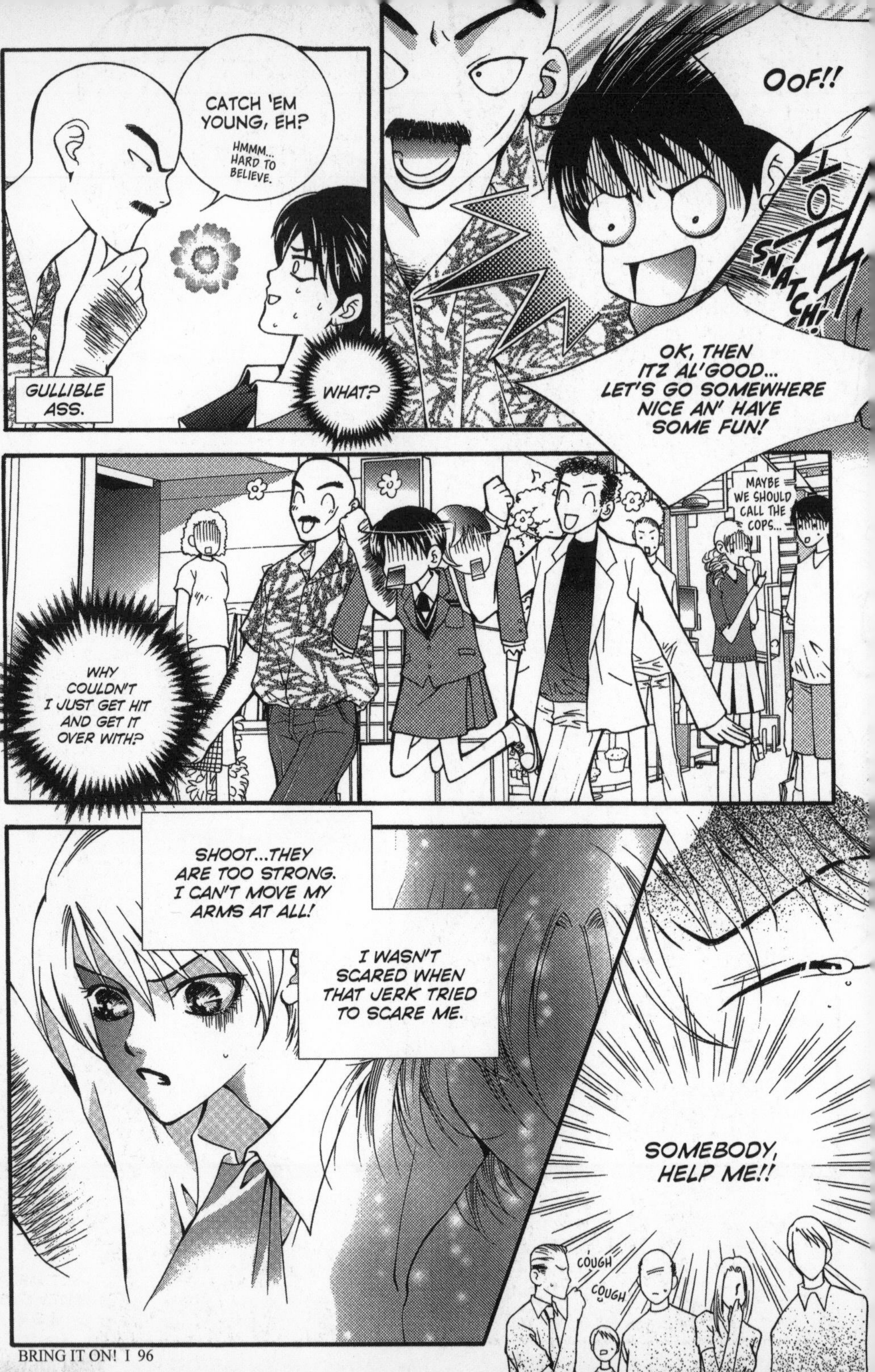
CATCH 'EM YOUNG, EH?
HMMM... HARD TO BELIEVE.
GULLIBLE ASS.
WHAT?
OOF!!
SNATCH!
OK, THEN ITZ AL'GOOD... LET'S GO SOMEWHERE NICE AN' HAVE SOME FUN!
WHY COULDN'T I JUST GET HIT AND GET IT OVER WITH?
MAYBE WE SHOULD CALL THE COPS...
SHOOT...THEY ARE TOO STRONG. I CAN'T MOVE MY ARMS AT ALL!
I WASN'T SCARED WHEN THAT JERK TRIED TO SCARE ME.
SOMEBODY, HELP ME!!
COUGH
COUGH

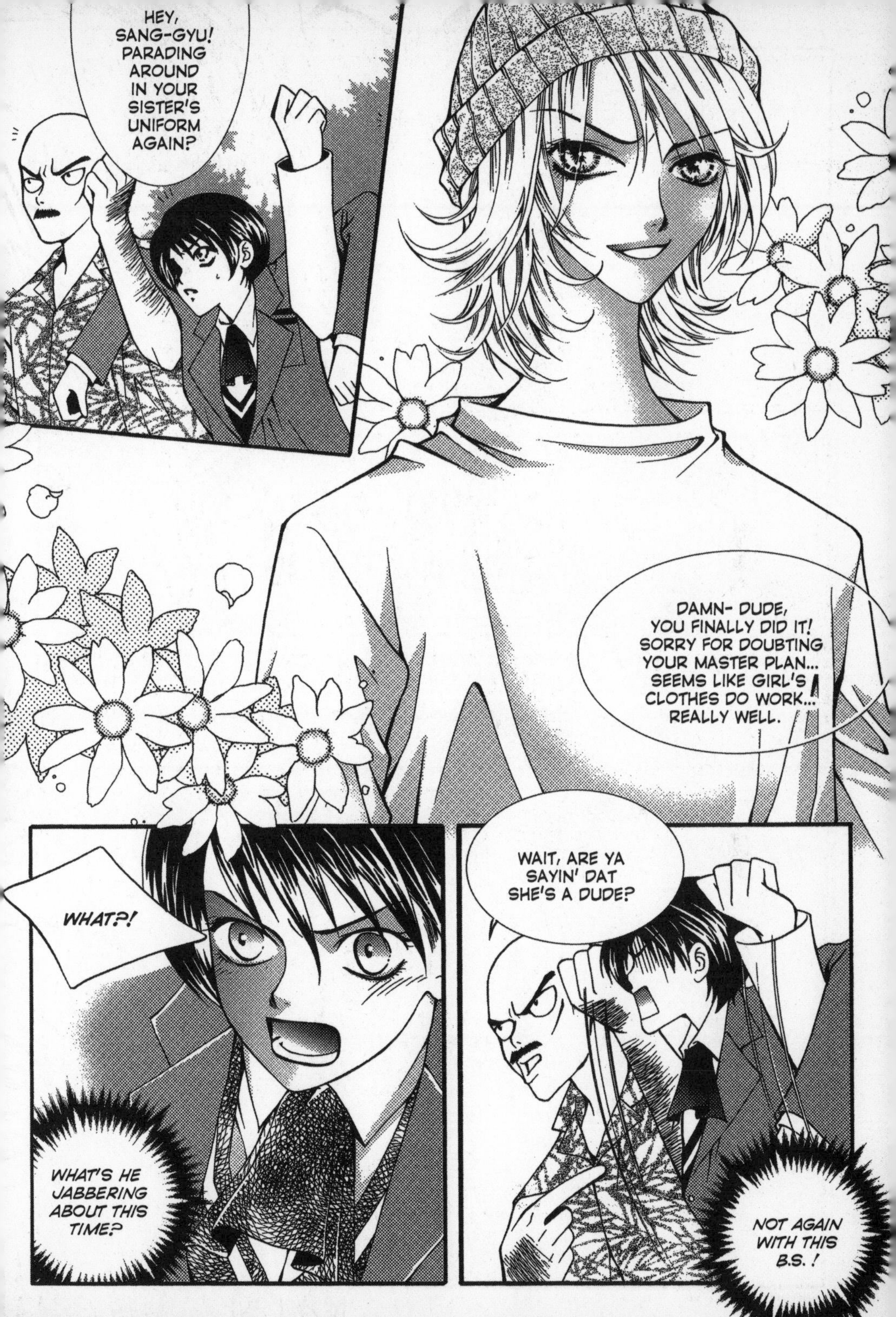
HEY, SANG-GYU! PARADING AROUND IN YOUR SISTER'S UNIFORM AGAIN?
DAMN- DUDE, YOU FINALLY DID IT! SORRY FOR DOUBTING YOUR MASTER PLAN... SEEMS LIKE GIRL'S CLOTHES DO WORK... REALLY WELL.
WHAT?!
WHAT'S HE JABBERING ABOUT THIS TIME?
WAIT, ARE YA SAYIN' DAT SHE'S A DUDE?
NOT AGAIN WITH THIS B.S.!

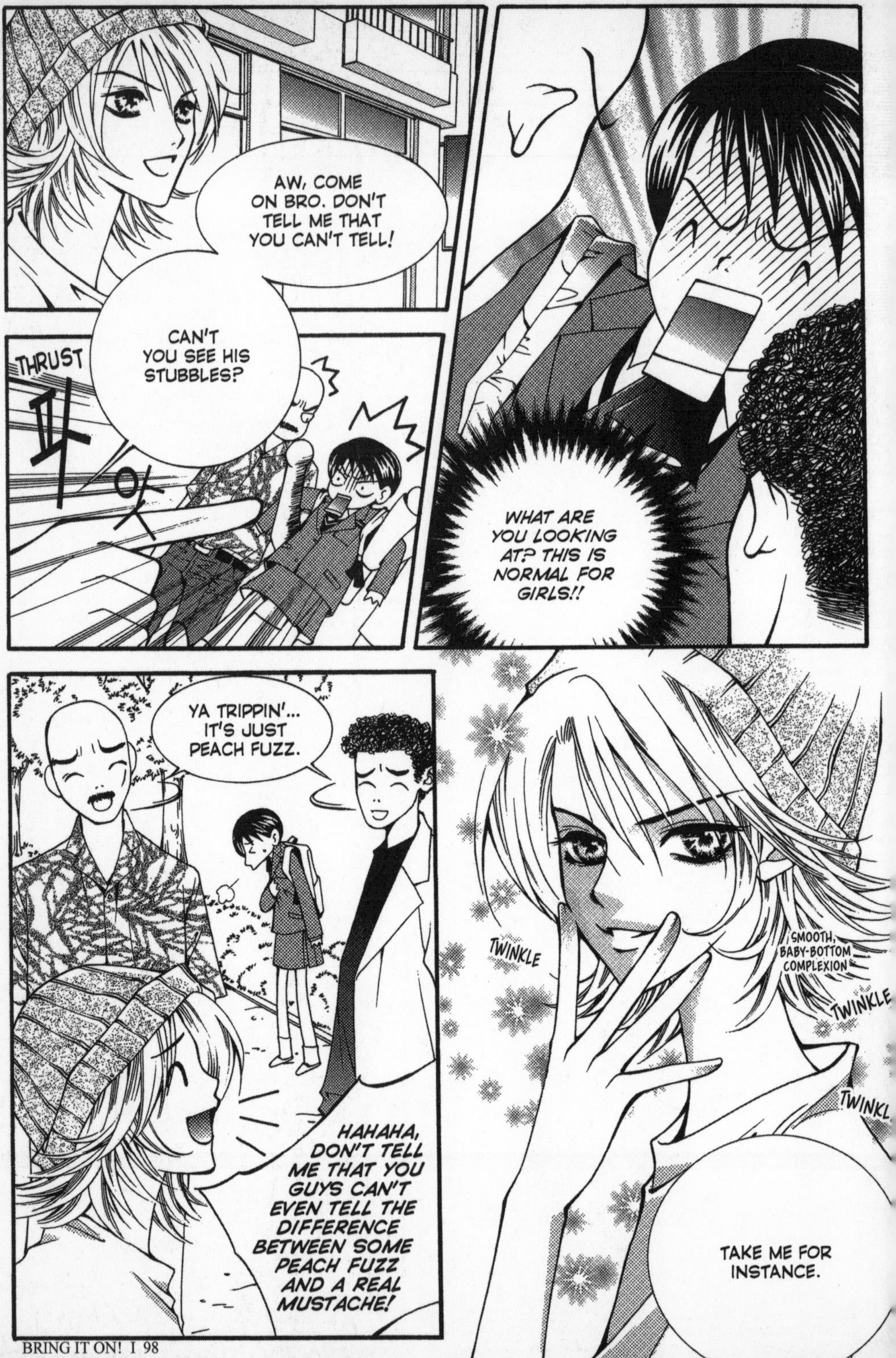
AW, COME ON BRO. DON'T TELL ME THAT YOU CAN'T TELL!
CAN'T YOU SEE HIS STUBBLES?
THRUST
WHAT ARE YOU LOOKING AT? THIS IS NORMAL FOR GIRLS!!
YA TRIPPIN'... IT'S JUST PEACH FUZZ.
HAHAHA, DON'T TELL ME THAT YOU GUYS CAN'T EVEN TELL THE DIFFERENCE BETWEEN SOME PEACH FUZZ AND A REAL MUSTACHE!
TWINKLE
SMOOTH, BABY-BOTTOM COMPLEXION
TWINKLE
TWINKL
TAKE ME FOR INSTANCE.

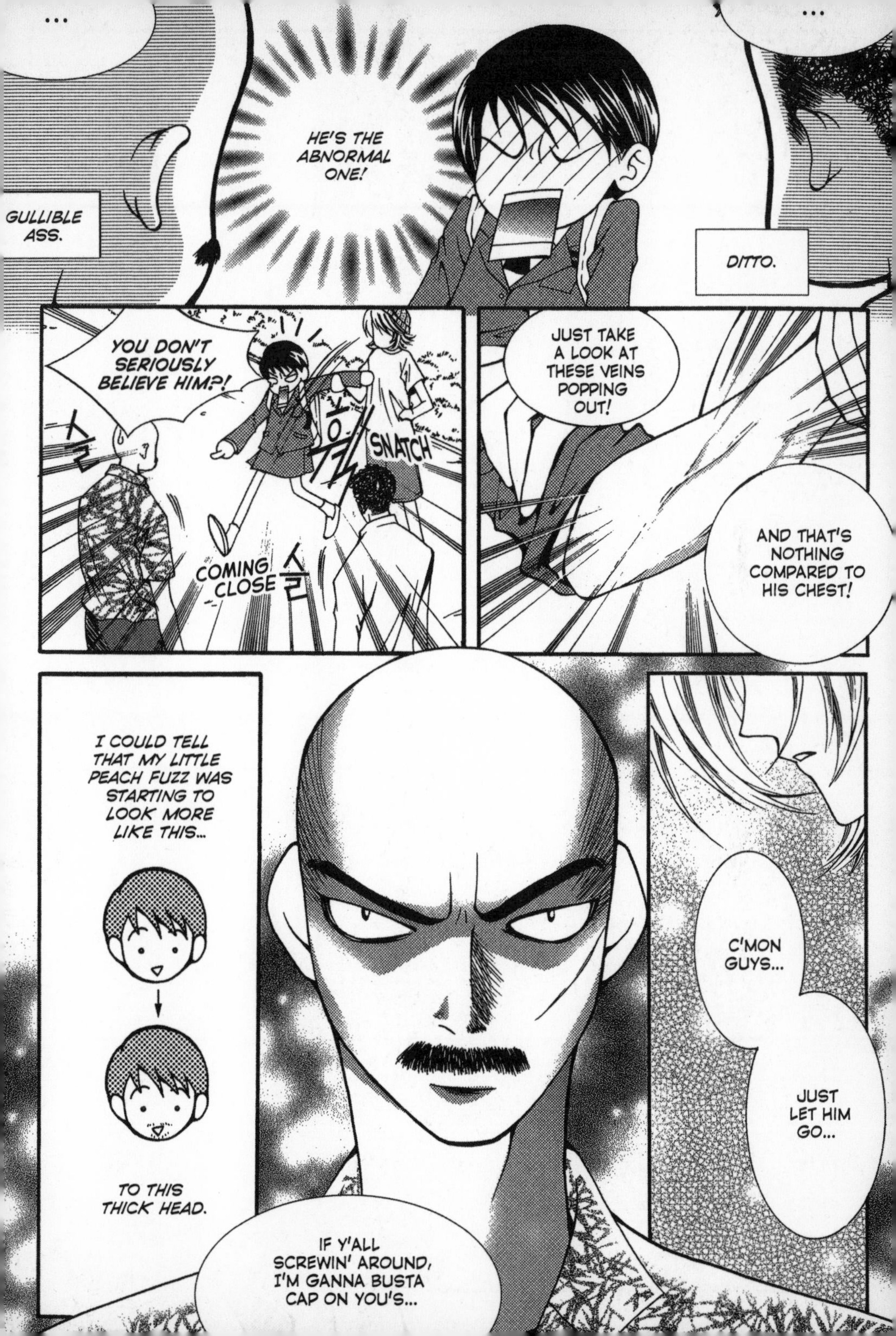
...
GULLIBLE ASS.
HE'S THE ABNORMAL ONE!
DITTO.
...
YOU DON'T SERIOUSLY BELIEVE HIM?!
SNATCH
COMING CLOSE
JUST TAKE A LOOK AT THESE VEINS POPPING OUT!
AND THAT'S NOTHING COMPARED TO HIS CHEST!
I COULD TELL THAT MY LITTLE PEACH FUZZ WAS STARTING TO LOOK MORE LIKE THIS...
TO THIS THICK HEAD.
IF Y'ALL SCREWIN' AROUND, I'M GANNA BUSTA CAP ON YOU'S...
C'MON GUYS...
JUST LET HIM GO...

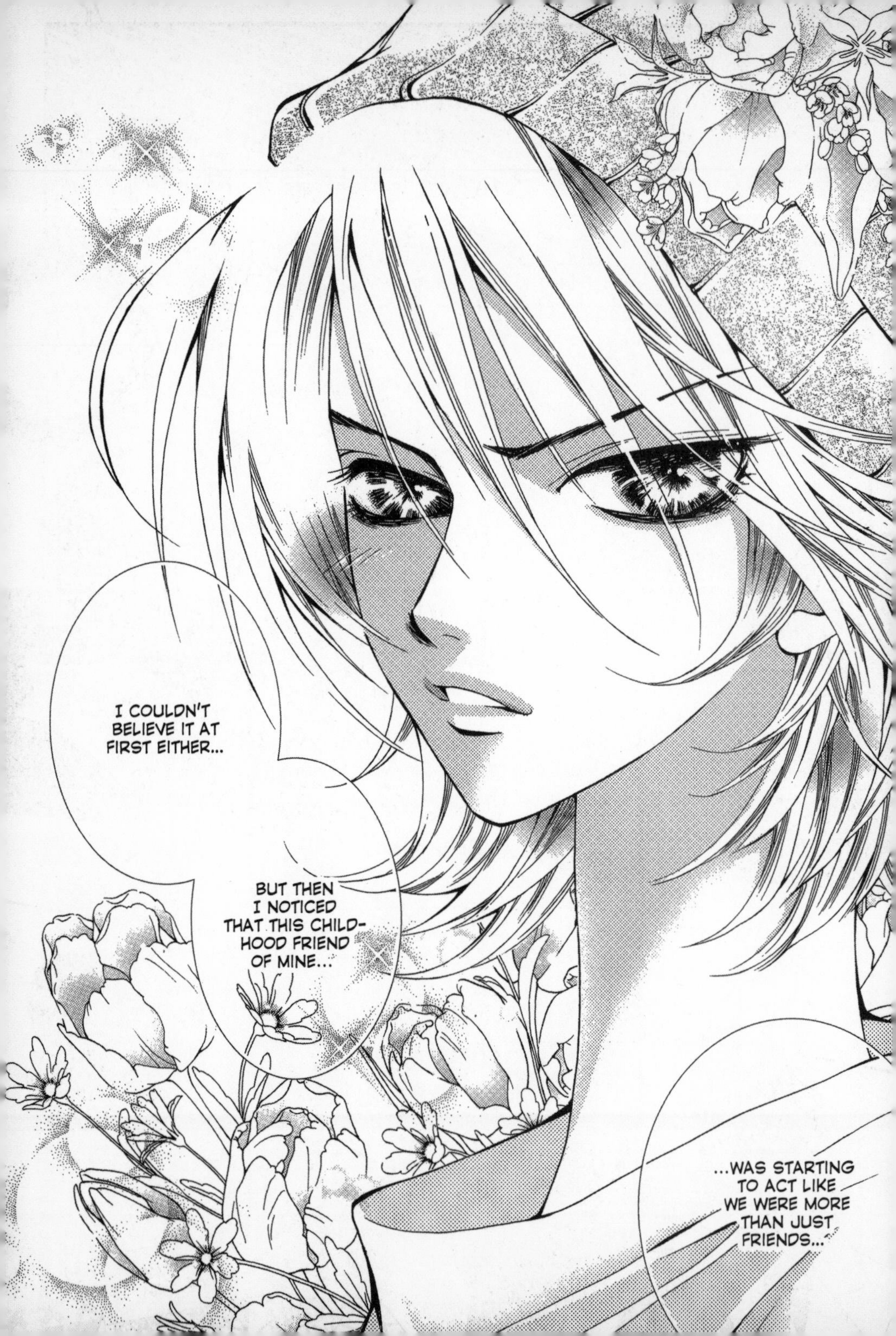
I COULDN'T BELIEVE IT AT FIRST EITHER...
BUT THEN I NOTICED THAT THIS CHILD-HOOD FRIEND OF MINE...
...WAS STARTING TO ACT LIKE WE WERE MORE THAN JUST FRIENDS...

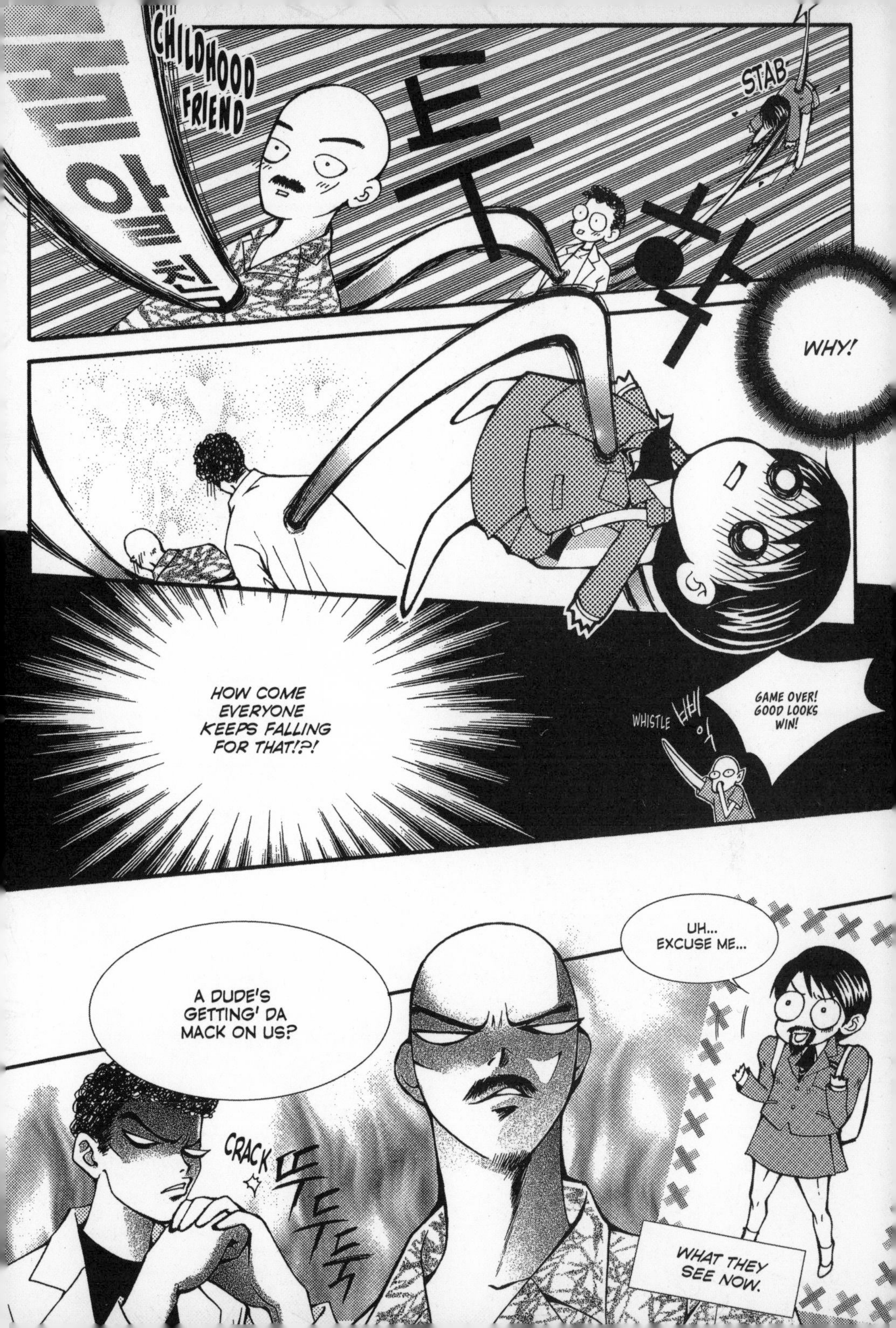
CHILDHOOD FRIEND
STAB
WHY!
HOW COME EVERYONE KEEPS FALLING FOR THAT!?!
WHISTLE
GAME OVER! GOOD LOOKS WIN!
A DUDE'S GETTING' DA MACK ON US?
UH... EXCUSE ME...
CRACK
WHAT THEY SEE NOW.

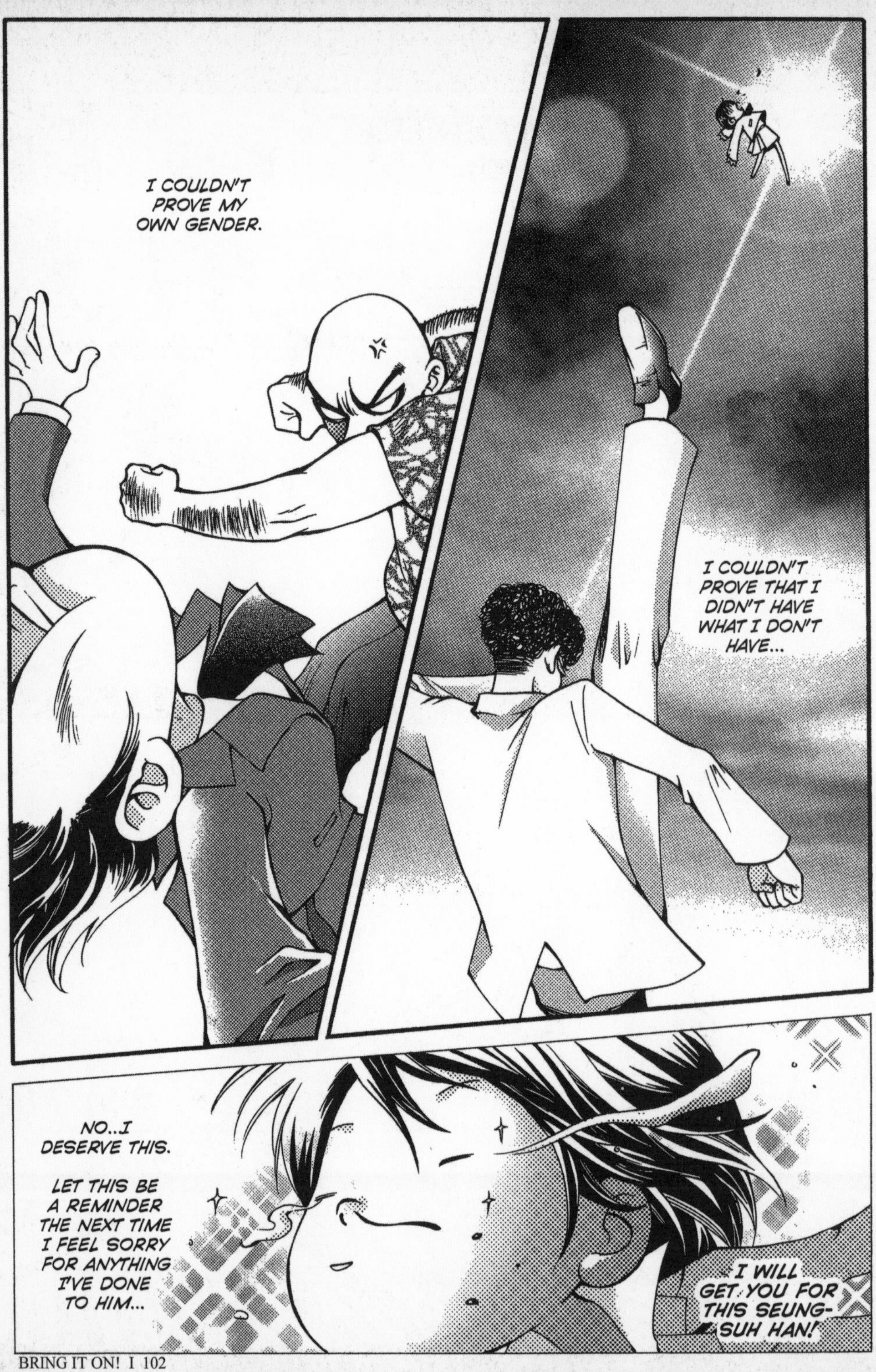
I COULDN'T PROVE MY OWN GENDER.
I COULDN'T PROVE THAT I DIDN'T HAVE WHAT I DON'T HAVE...
NO...I DESERVE THIS.
LET THIS BE A REMINDER THE NEXT TIME I FEEL SORRY FOR ANYTHING I'VE DONE TO HIM...
I WILL GET YOU FOR THIS SEUNG-SUH HAN!

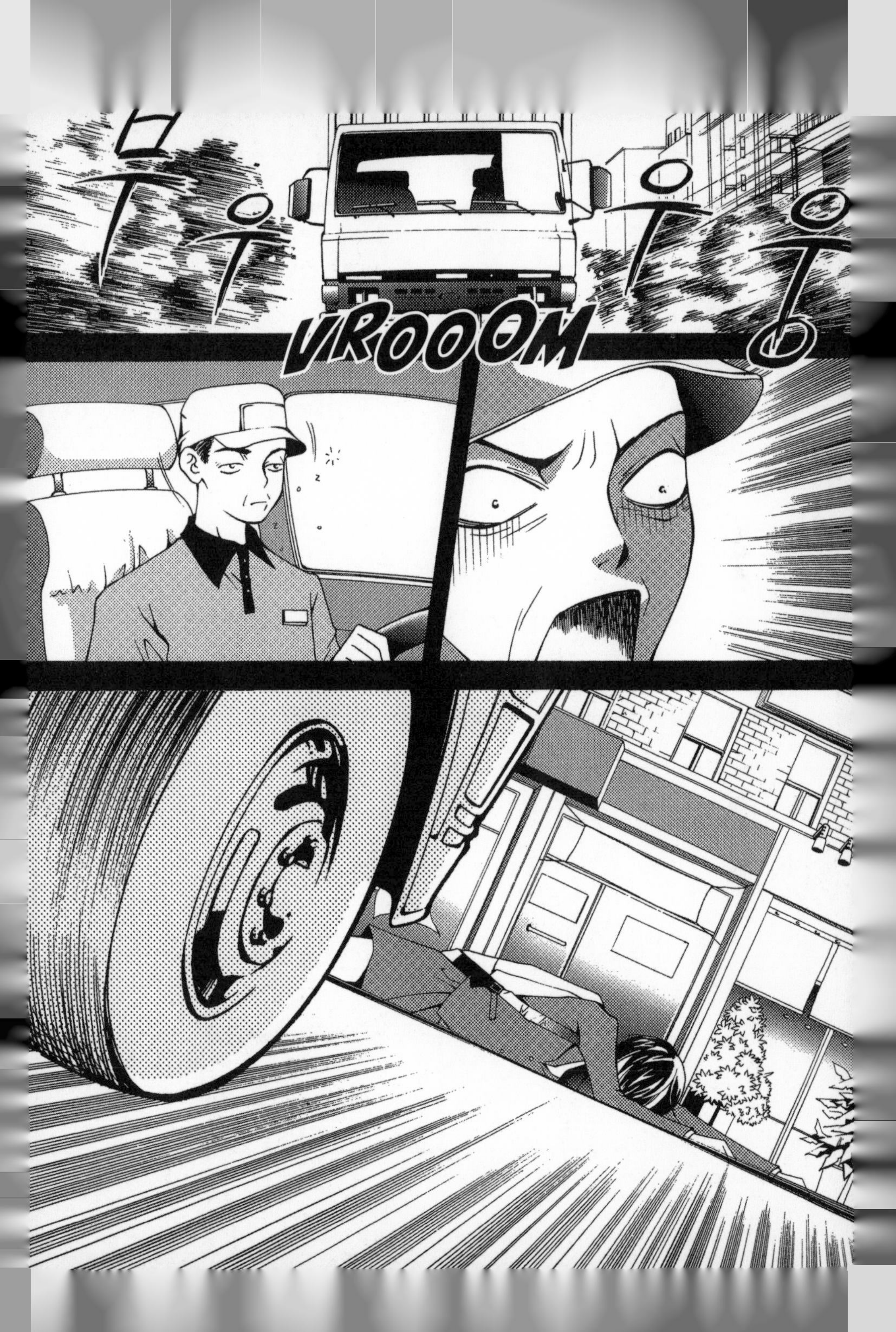
VROOOM

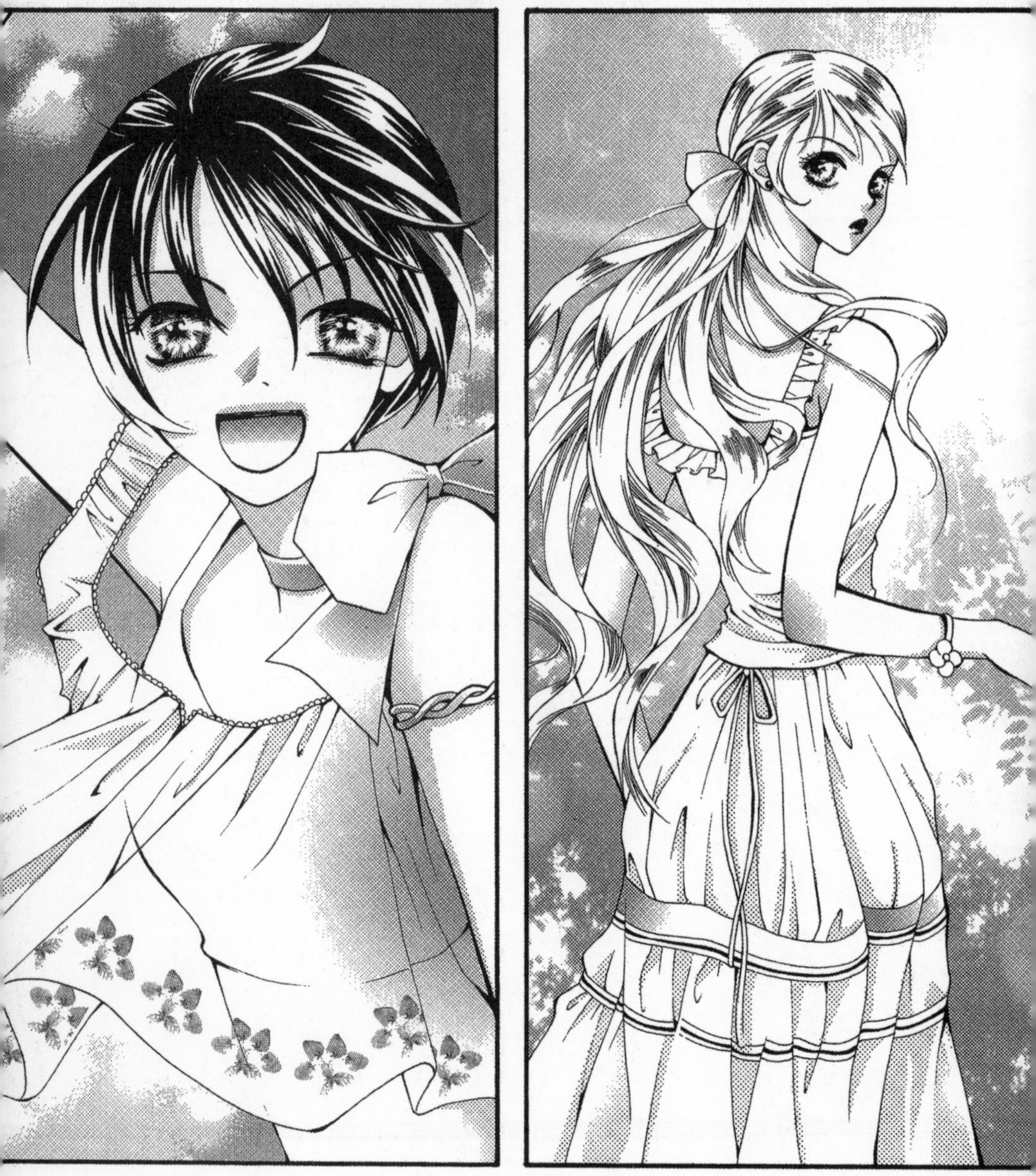

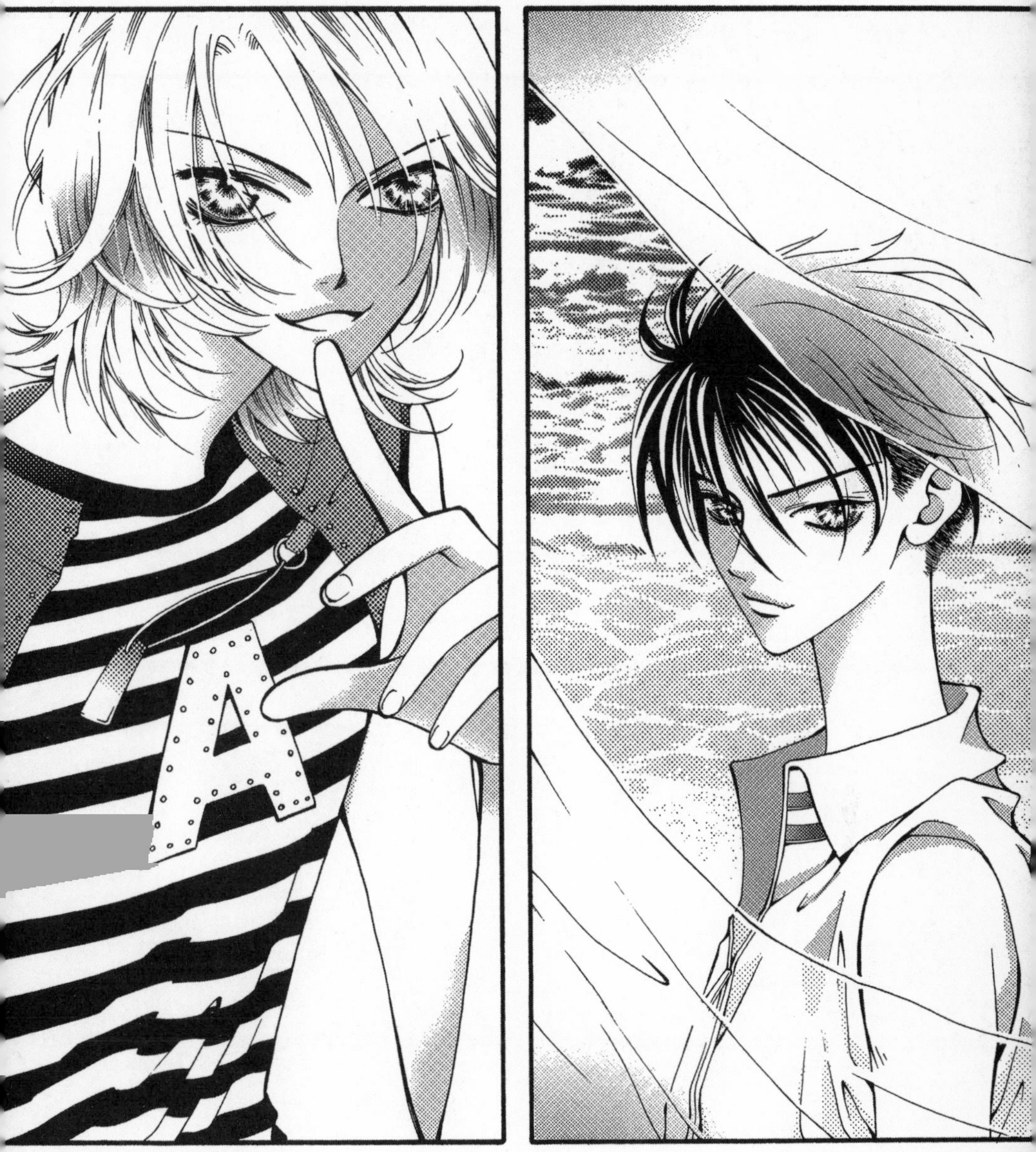

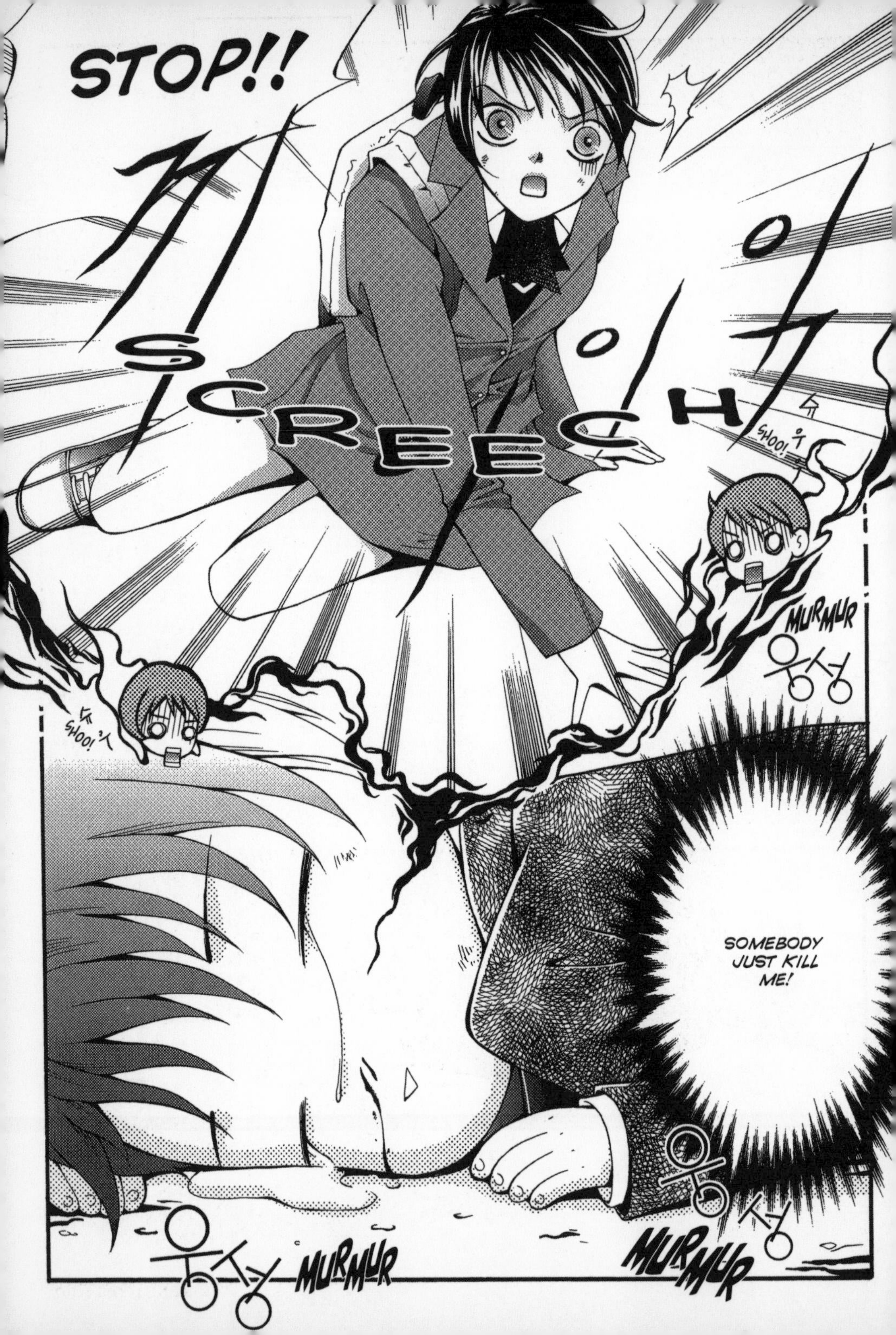
STOP!!
SCREECH
SHOO!
MURMUR
SHOO!
SOMEBODY JUST KILL ME!
MURMUR
MURMUR

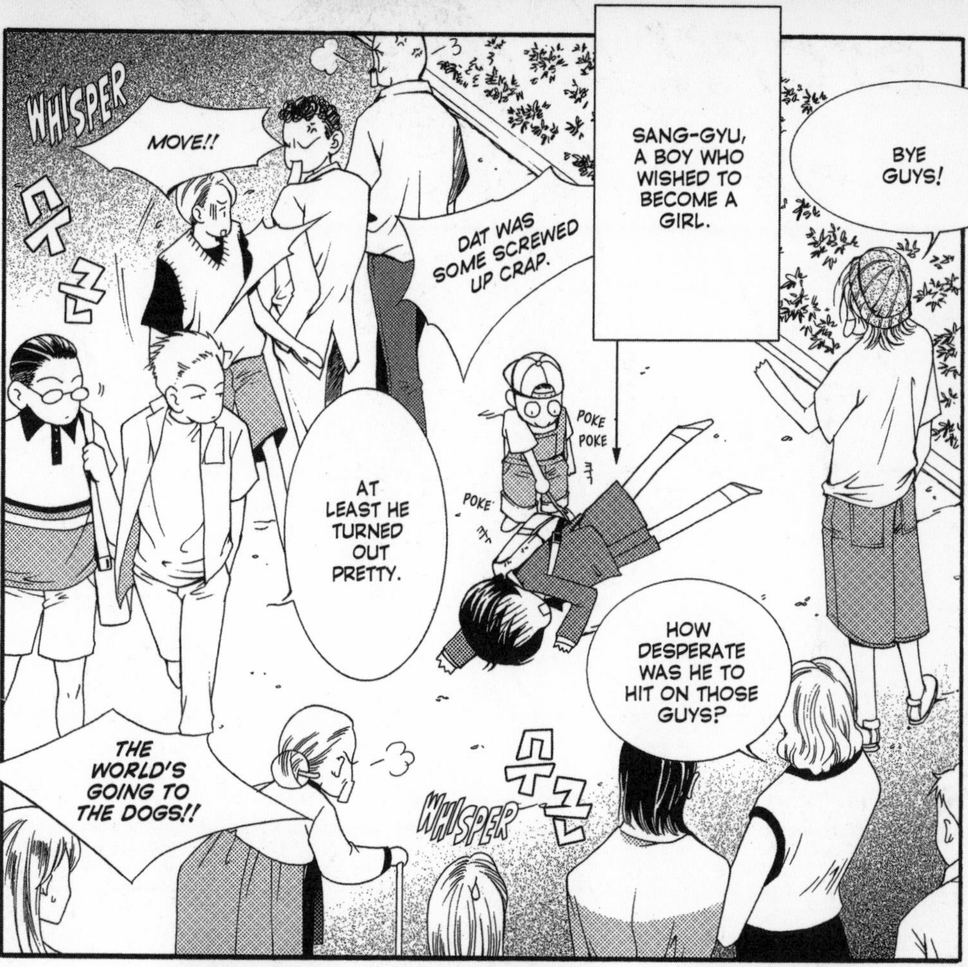
WHISPER
MOVE!!
DAT WAS SOME SCREWED UP CRAP.
SANG-GYU, A BOY WHO WISHED TO BECOME A GIRL.
BYE GUYS!
POKE POKE
AT LEAST HE TURNED OUT PRETTY.
POKE
HOW DESPERATE WAS HE TO HIT ON THOSE GUYS?
THE WORLD'S GOING TO THE DOGS!!
WHISPER
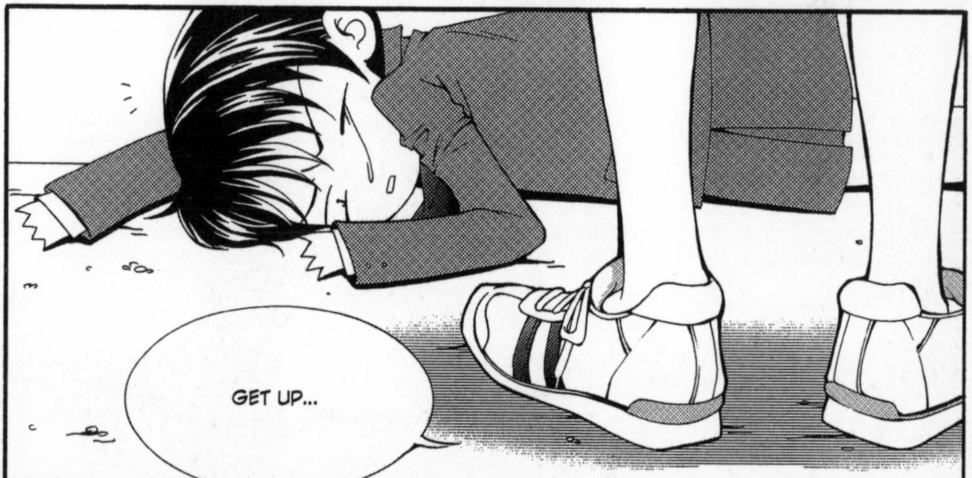
GET UP...

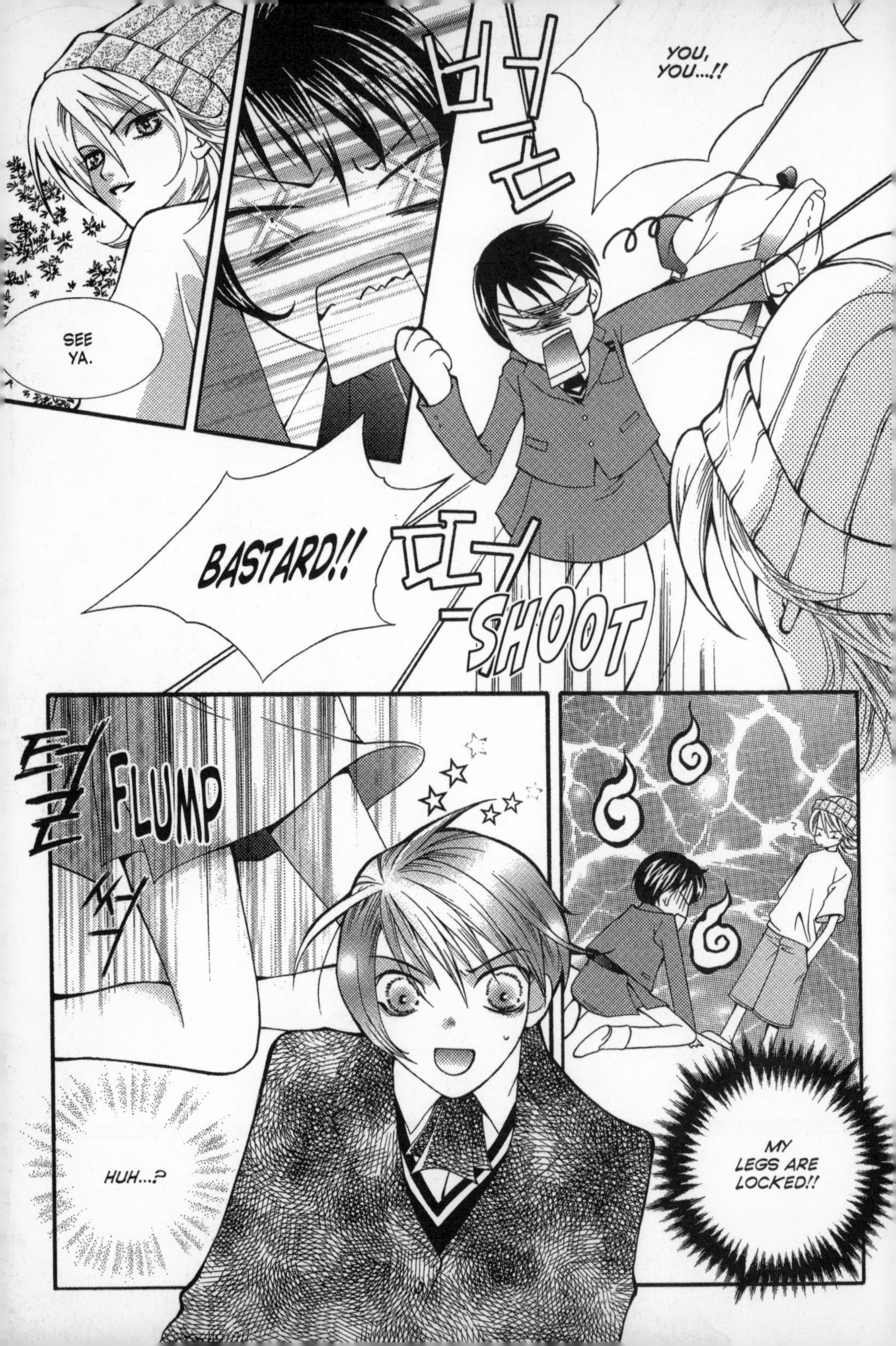
SEE YA.
YOU, YOU...!!
BASTARD!!
SHOOT
FLUMP
HUH...?
MY LEGS ARE LOCKED!!

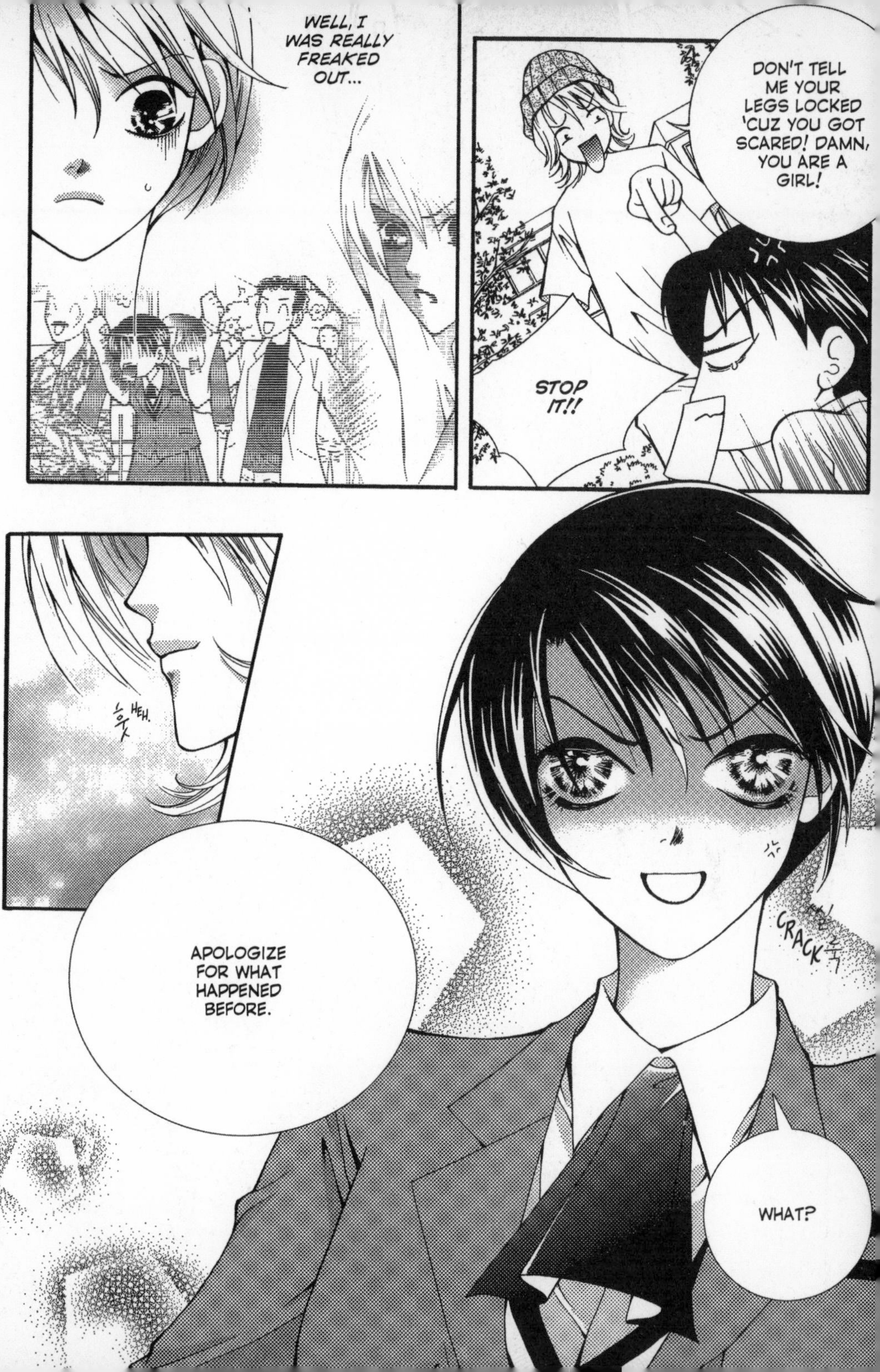
WELL, I WAS REALLY FREAKED OUT...
DON'T TELL ME YOUR LEGS LOCKED 'CUZ YOU GOT SCARED! DAMN, YOU ARE A GIRL!
STOP IT!!
HEH.
APOLOGIZE FOR WHAT HAPPENED BEFORE.
CRACK
WHAT?

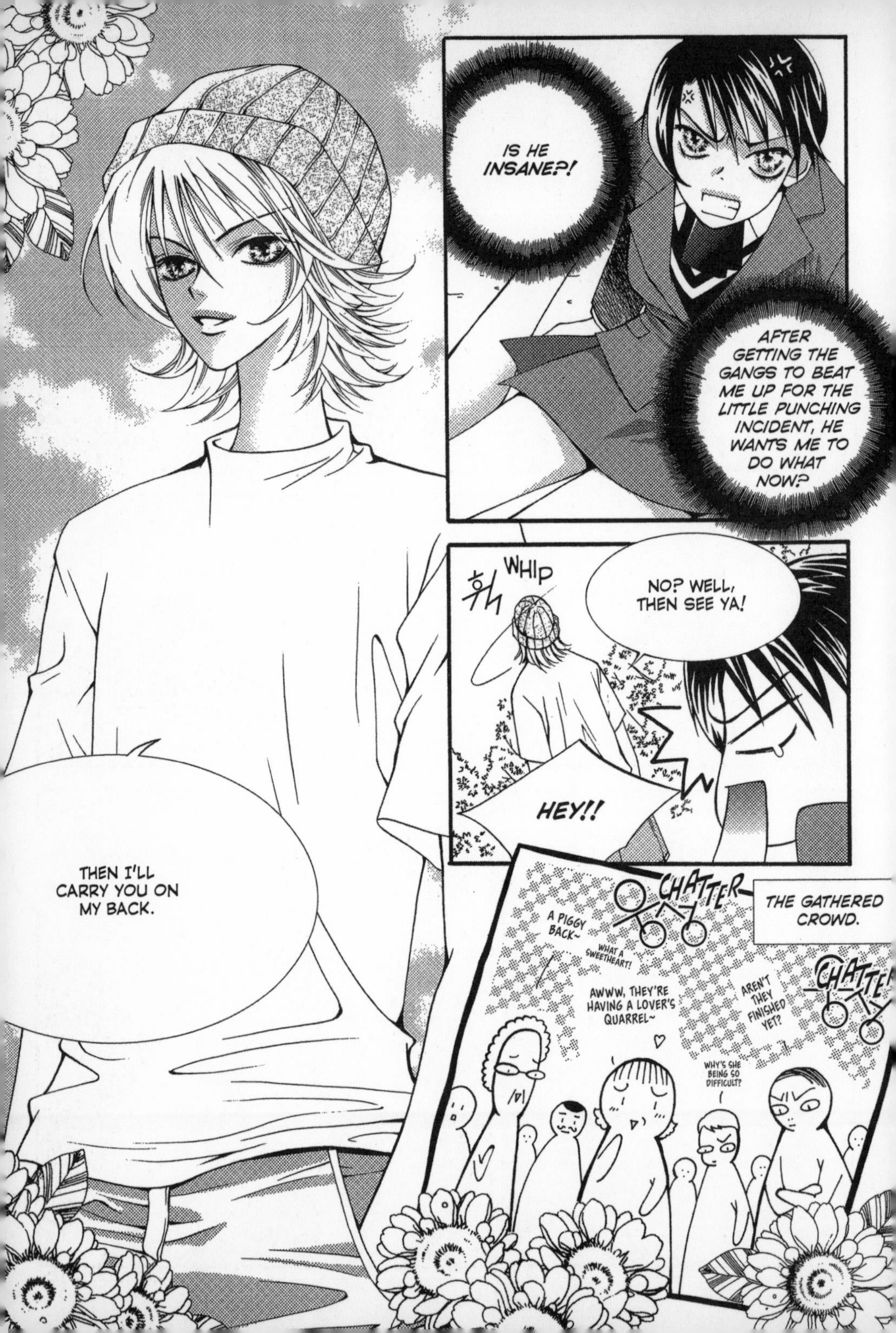
THEN I'LL CARRY YOU ON MY BACK.
IS HE INSANE?!
AFTER GETTING THE GANGS TO BEAT ME UP FOR THE LITTLE PUNCHING INCIDENT, HE WANTS ME TO DO WHAT NOW?
WHIP
NO? WELL, THEN SEE YA!
HEY!!
CHATTER
THE GATHERED CROWD.
A PIGGY BACK~
WHAT A SWEETHEART!
AWWW, THEY'RE HAVING A LOVER'S QUARREL~
AREN'T THEY FINISHED YET?
CHATTER
WHY'S SHE BEING SO DIFFICULT?

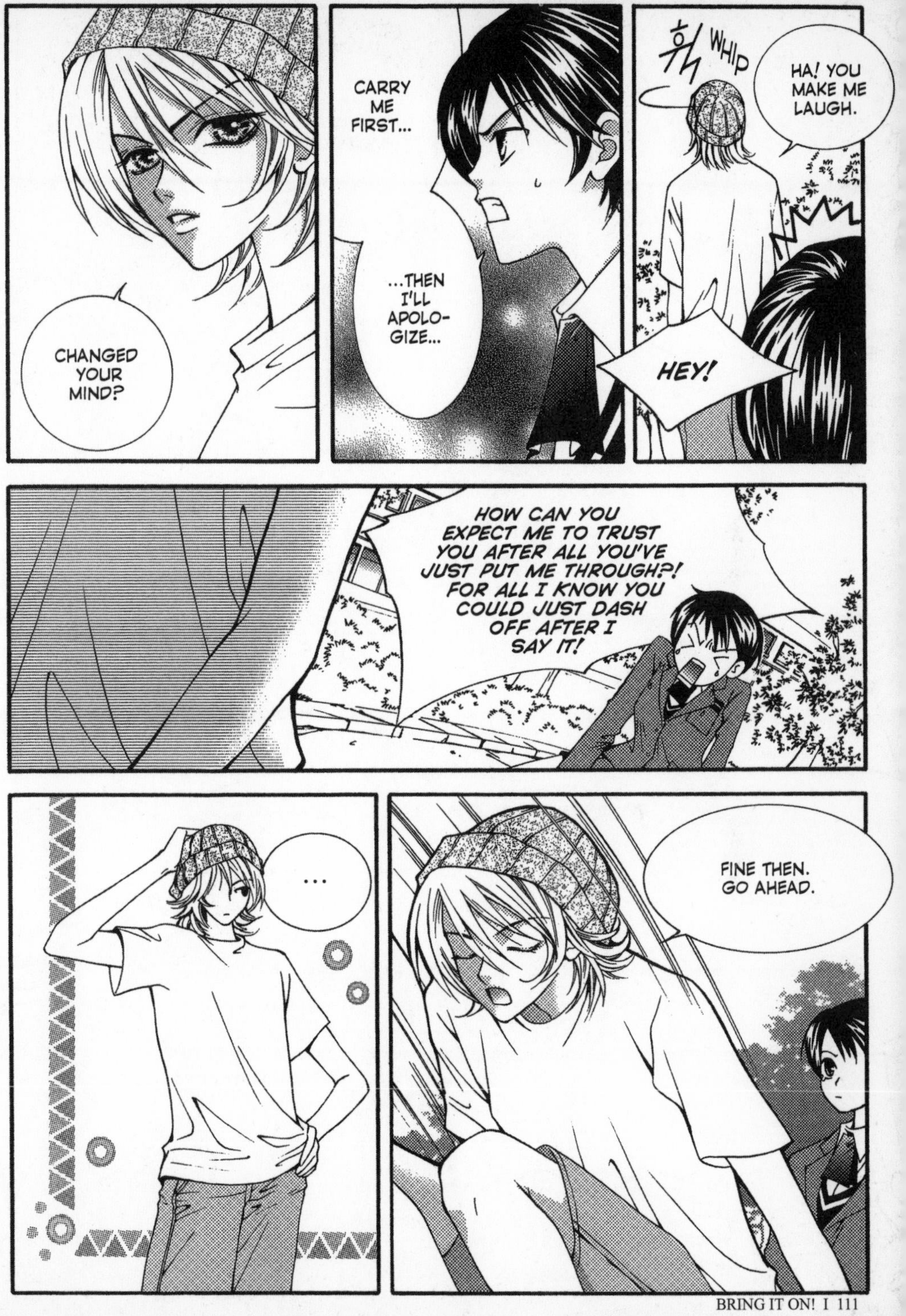
CHANGED YOUR MIND?
CARRY ME FIRST...
...THEN I'LL APOLOGIZE...
휙
WHIP
HA! YOU MAKE ME LAUGH.
HEY!
HOW CAN YOU EXPECT ME TO TRUST YOU AFTER ALL YOU'VE JUST PUT ME THROUGH?! FOR ALL I KNOW YOU COULD JUST DASH OFF AFTER I SAY IT!
...
FINE THEN. GO AHEAD.

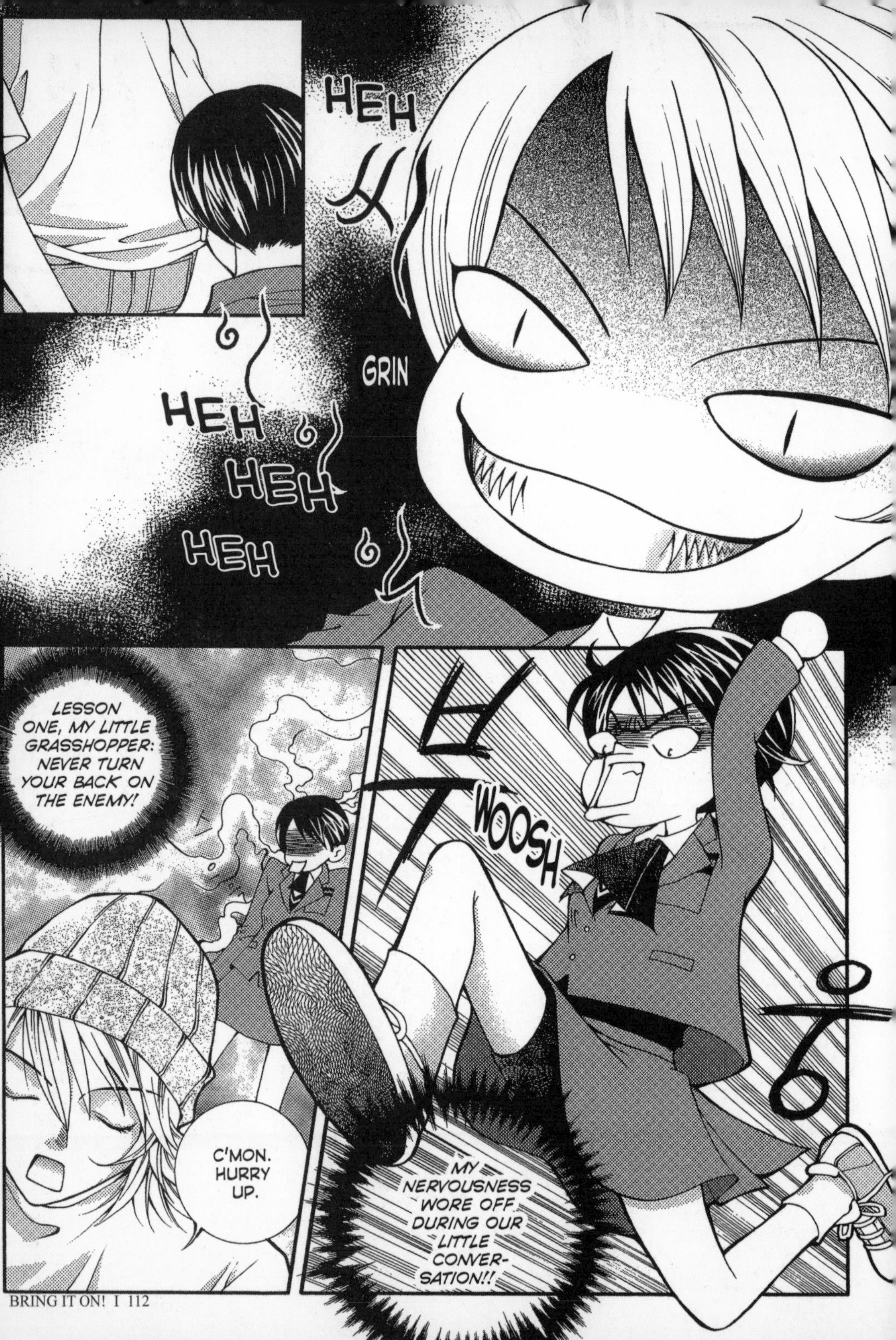
HEH
GRIN
HEH
HEH
HEH
LESSON ONE, MY LITTLE GRASSHOPPER: NEVER TURN YOUR BACK ON THE ENEMY!
C'MON. HURRY UP.
WOOSH
MY NERVOUSNESS WORE OFF DURING OUR LITTLE CONVER-SATION!!

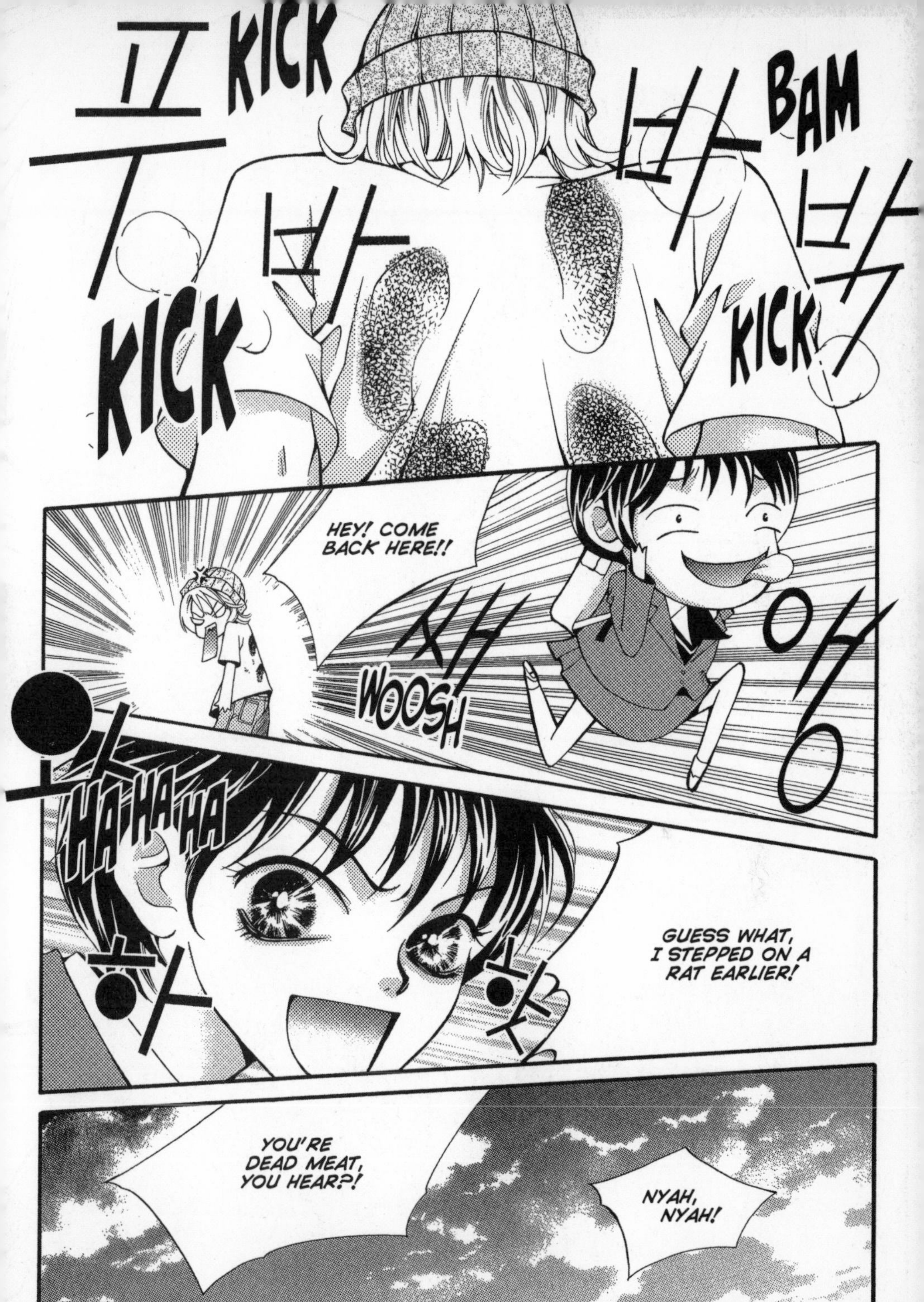
KICK
BAM
KICK
KICK
HEY! COME BACK HERE!!
WOOSH
HA-HA-HA
GUESS WHAT, I STEPPED ON A RAT EARLIER!
YOU'RE DEAD MEAT, YOU HEAR?!
NYAH, NYAH!

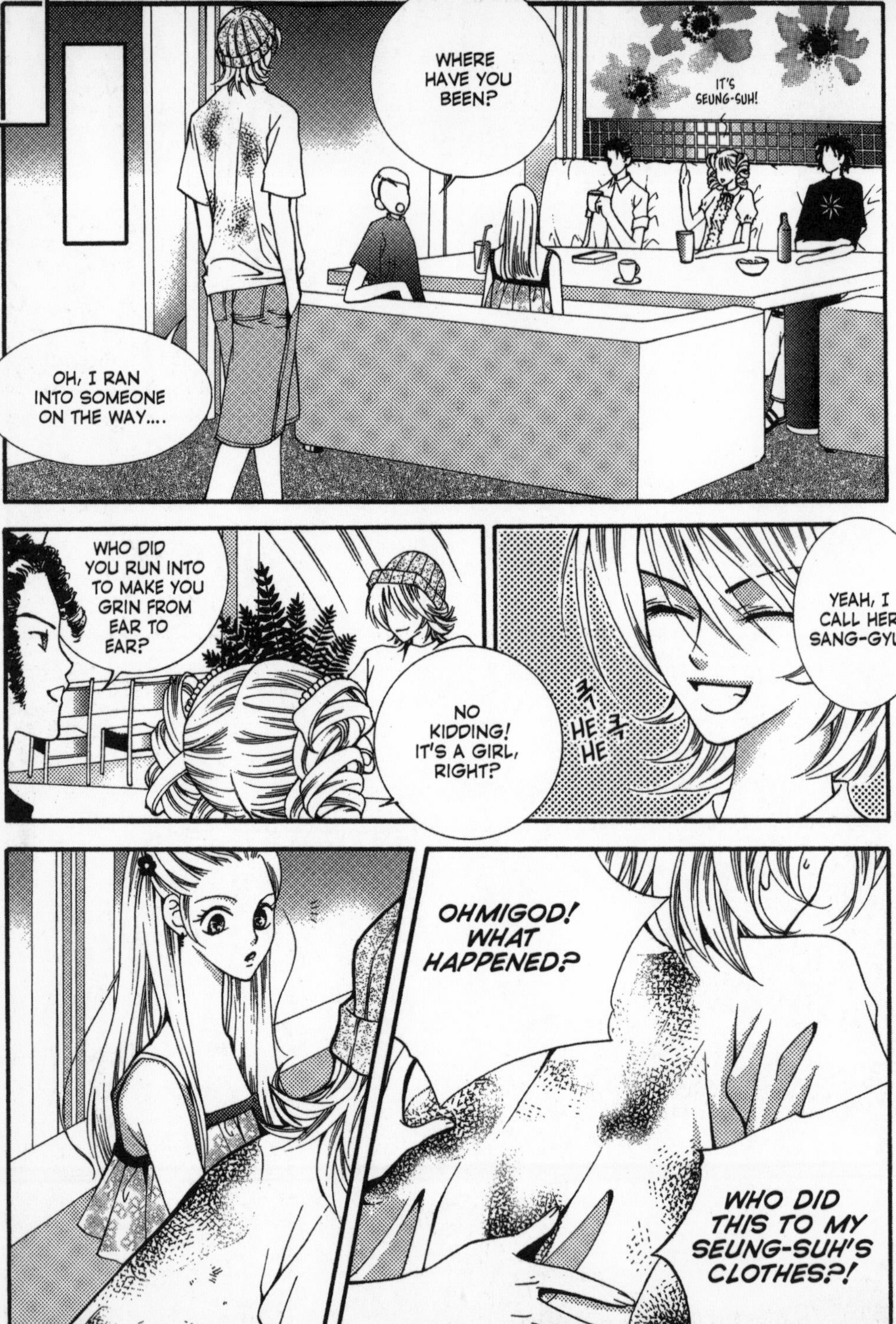
WHERE HAVE YOU BEEN?
IT'S SEUNG-SUH!
OH, I RAN INTO SOMEONE ON THE WAY....
WHO DID YOU RUN INTO TO MAKE YOU GRIN FROM EAR TO EAR?
NO KIDDING! IT'S A GIRL, RIGHT?
YEAH, I CALL HER SANG-GYU.
쿡 쿡
HE HE
OHMIGOD! WHAT HAPPENED?
WHO DID THIS TO MY SEUNG-SUH'S CLOTHES?!

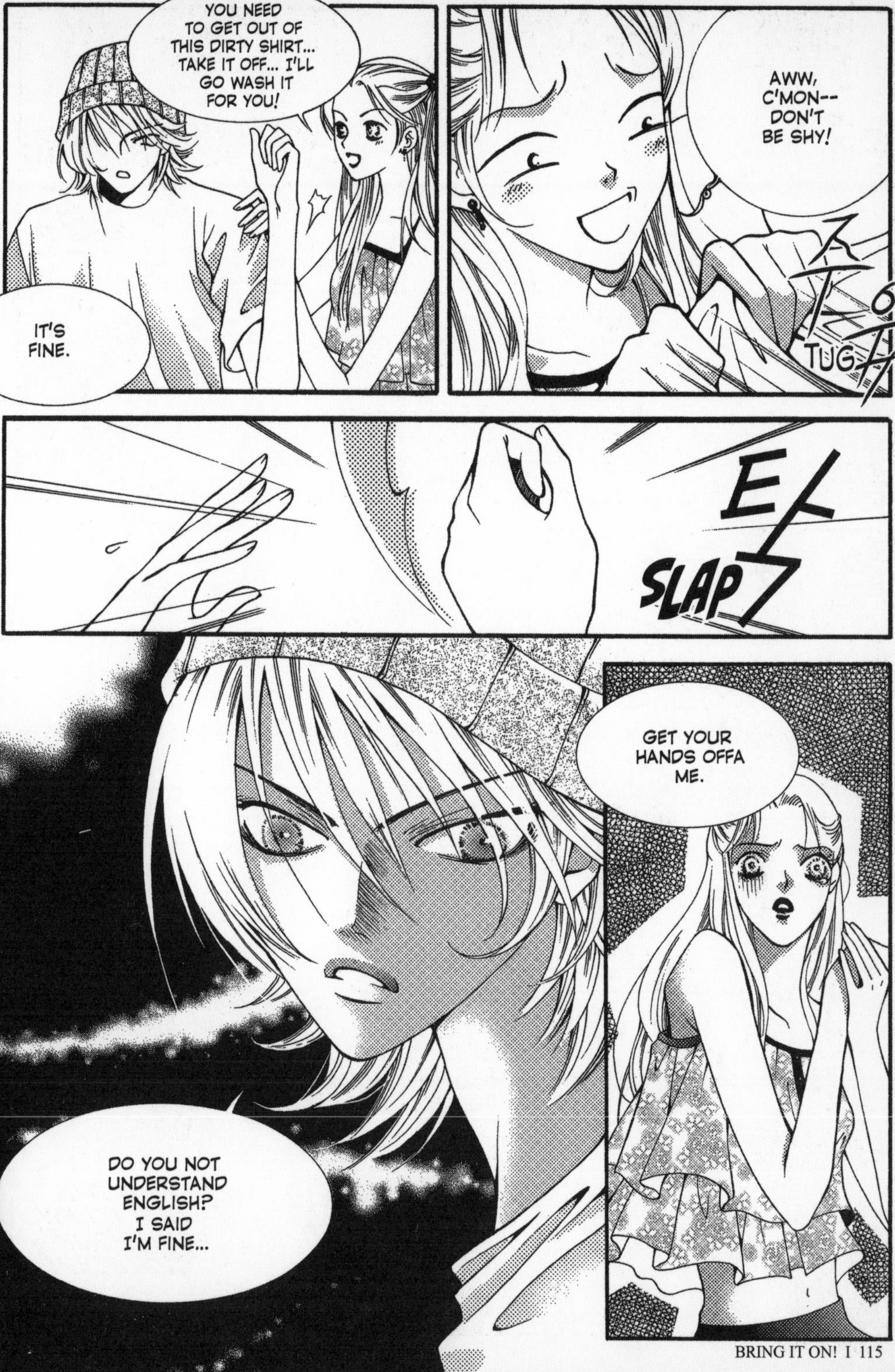
YOU NEED TO GET OUT OF THIS DIRTY SHIRT... TAKE IT OFF... I'LL GO WASH IT FOR YOU!
IT'S FINE.
AWW, C'MON-- DON'T BE SHY!
TUG
SLAP
GET YOUR HANDS OFFA ME.
DO YOU NOT UNDERSTAND ENGLISH? I SAID I'M FINE...

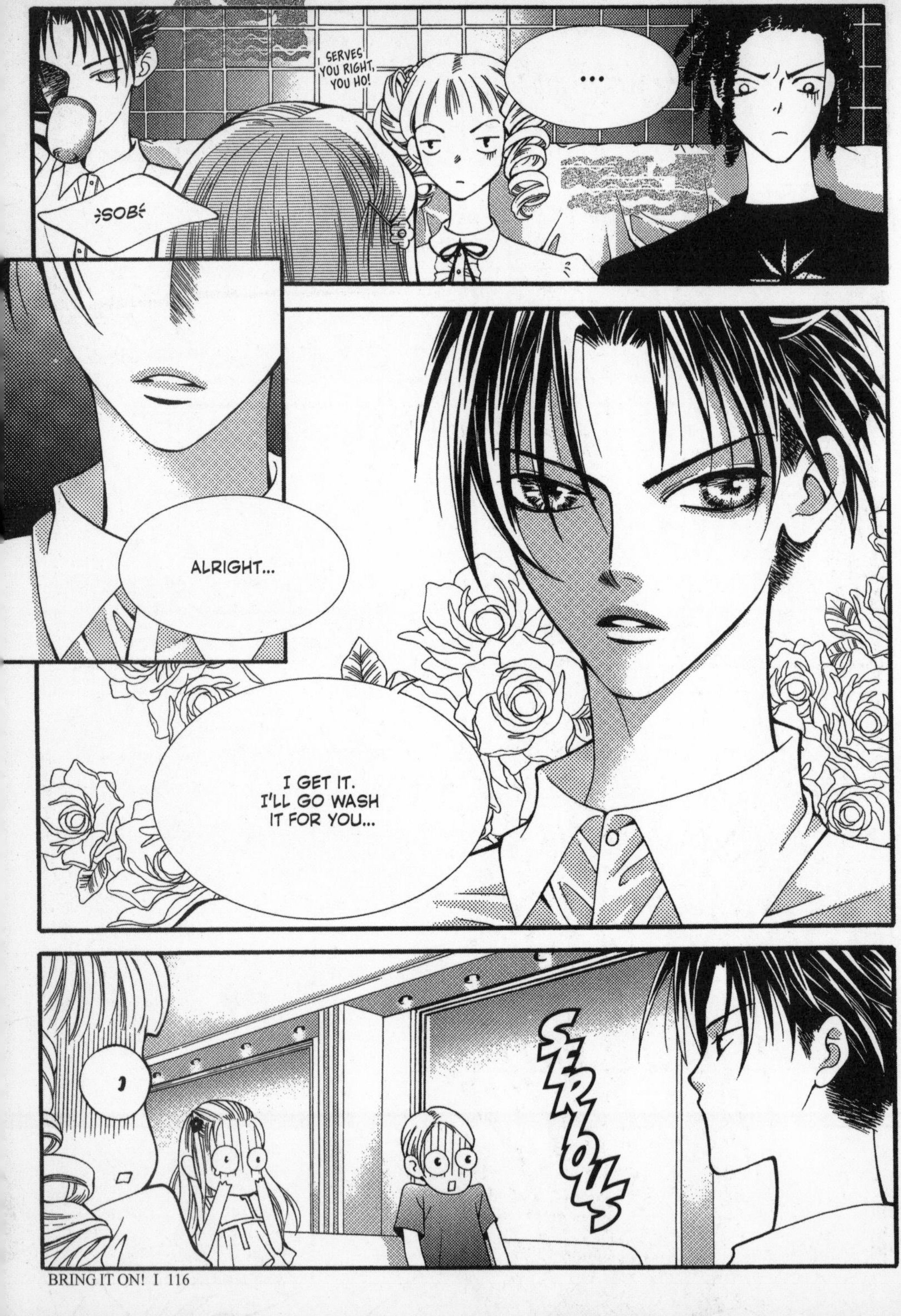
SERVES YOU RIGHT, YOU HO!
...
SOB
ALRIGHT...
I GET IT. I'LL GO WASH IT FOR YOU...
SERIOUS

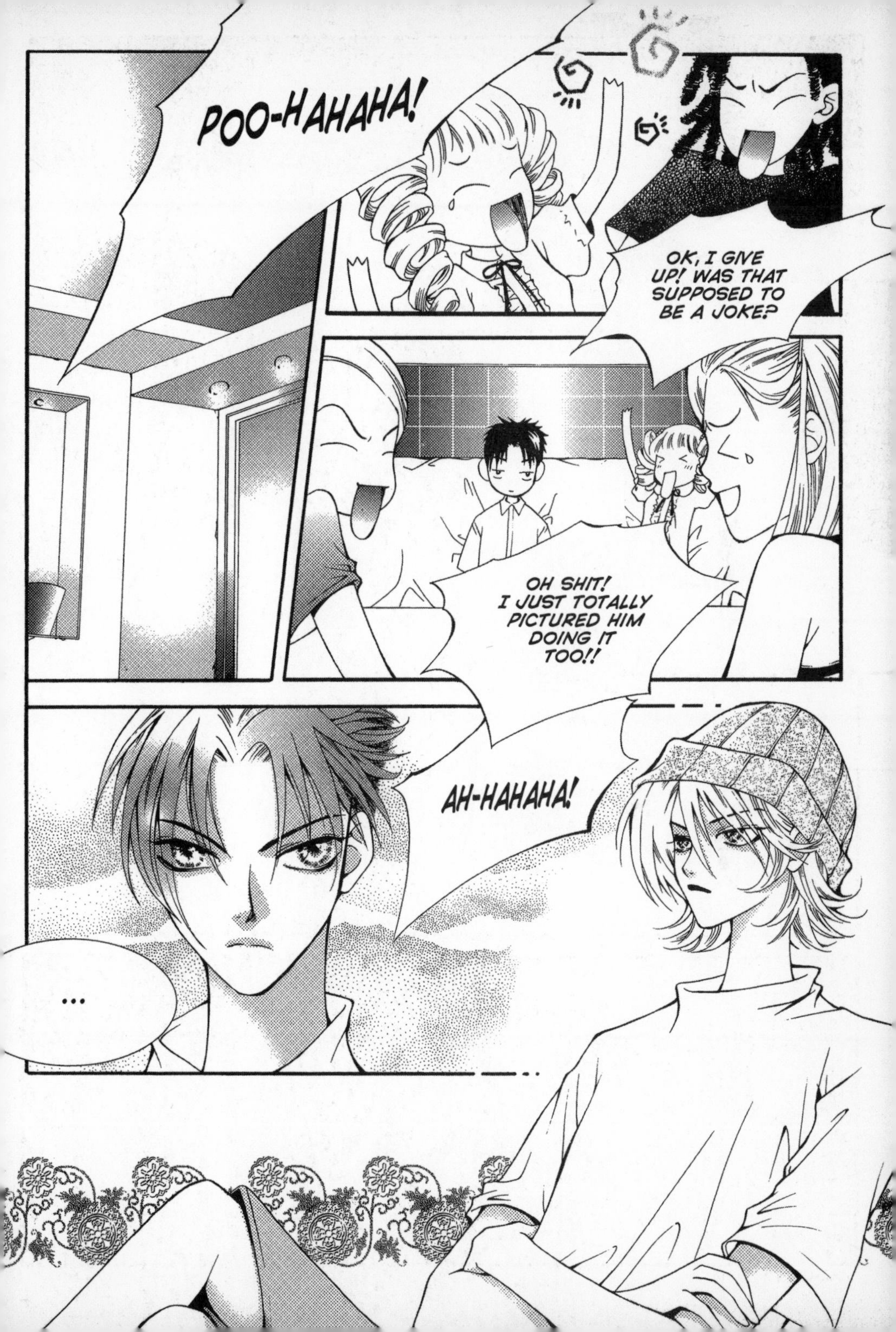
POO-HAHAHA!
OK, I GIVE UP! WAS THAT SUPPOSED TO BE A JOKE?
OH SHIT! I JUST TOTALLY PICTURED HIM DOING IT TOO!!
...
AH-HAHAHA!

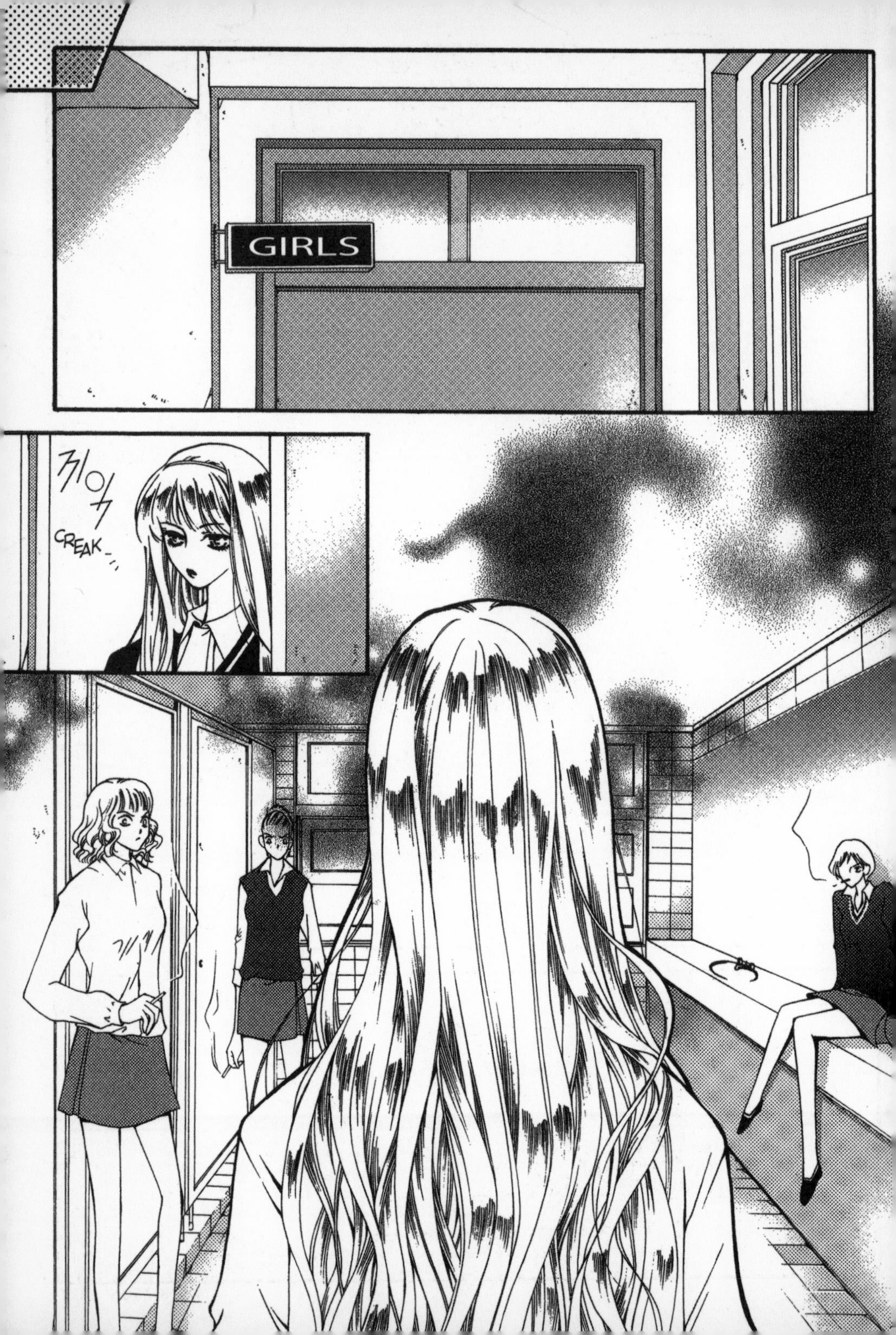
GIRLS
기익
CREAK...

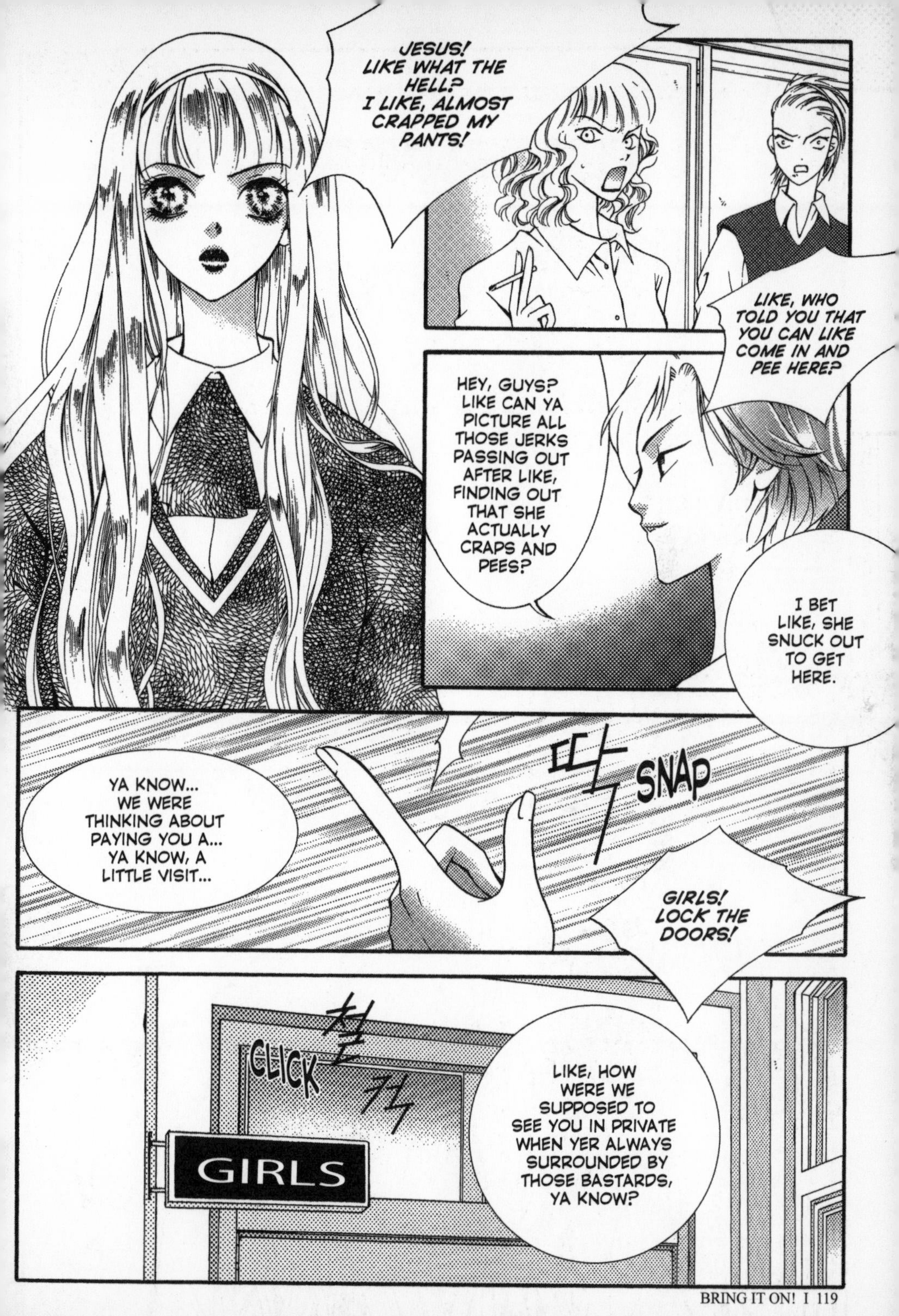
JESUS! LIKE WHAT THE HELL? I LIKE, ALMOST CRAPPED MY PANTS!
LIKE, WHO TOLD YOU THAT YOU CAN LIKE COME IN AND PEE HERE?
HEY, GUYS? LIKE CAN YA PICTURE ALL THOSE JERKS PASSING OUT AFTER LIKE, FINDING OUT THAT SHE ACTUALLY CRAPS AND PEES?
I BET LIKE, SHE SNUCK OUT TO GET HERE.
YA KNOW... WE WERE THINKING ABOUT PAYING YOU A... YA KNOW, A LITTLE VISIT...
SNAP
GIRLS! LOCK THE DOORS!
CLICK
GIRLS
LIKE, HOW WERE WE SUPPOSED TO SEE YOU IN PRIVATE WHEN YER ALWAYS SURROUNDED BY THOSE BASTARDS, YA KNOW?

DID YOU LIKE YOUR P.E. UNIFORM? YA THINK IT WAS WORTH OUR TIME PICKING YER LOCKER?

I MEAN, WHY DO YOU EVEN BOTHER BRINGING IT WHEN LIKE, YOU ALWAYS JUST CHILL OUT WITH SOME MYSTERIOUS ILLNESS ANYWAY?

YOU SHOULD'VE LIKE, JOINED US WHEN YOU HAD THE CHANCE... NOW IT'S JUST TOO LATE, GIRL...

PUSH

WHAT? YA GOT A PROBLEM? WANNA DIE?

LUNCH DOESN'T END FOR 10 MORE MINUTES. THAT GIVES US... LIKE WHAT? LIKE 15, RIGHT?

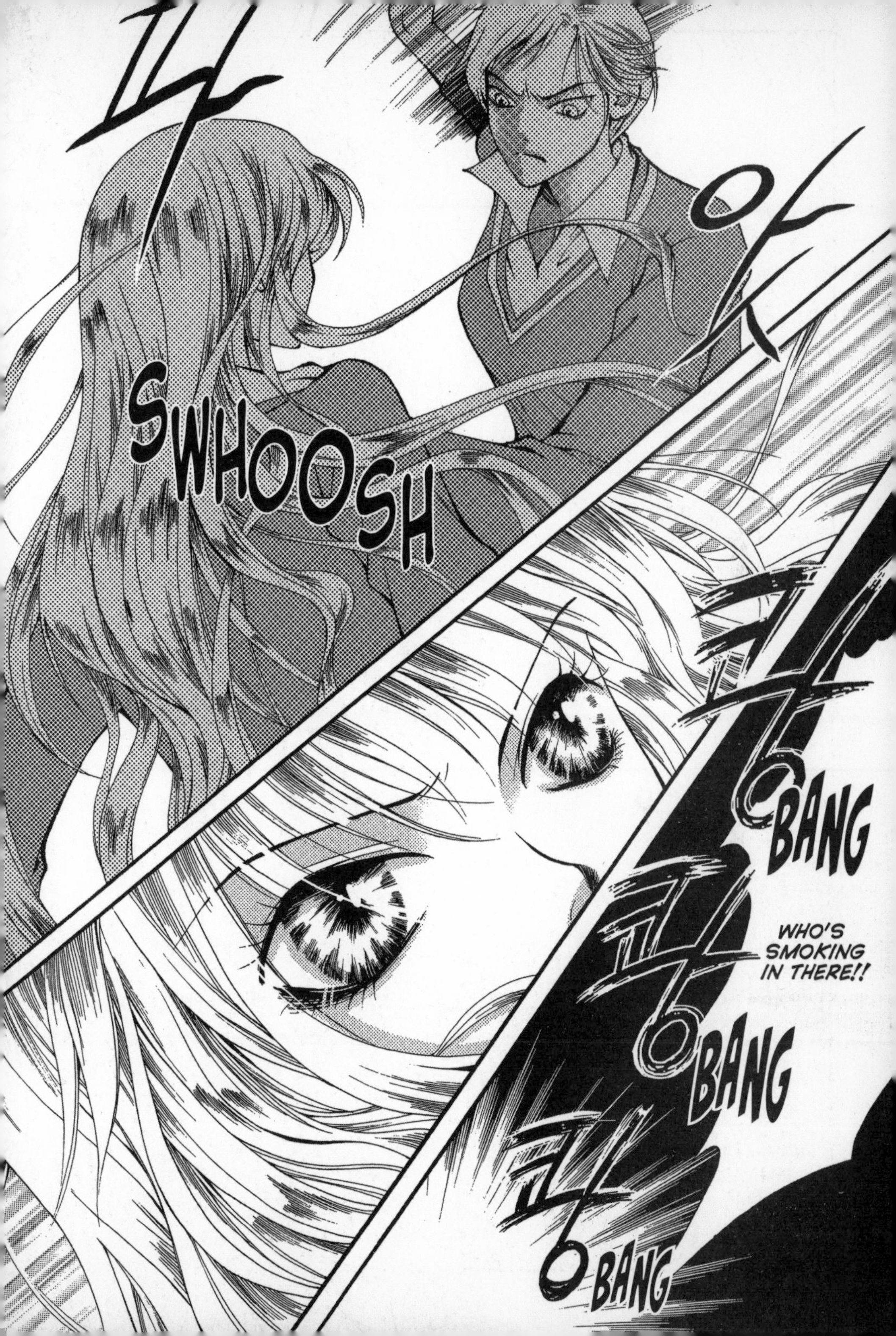
SWHOOSH
BANG
WHO'S SMOKING IN THERE!!
BANG
BANG

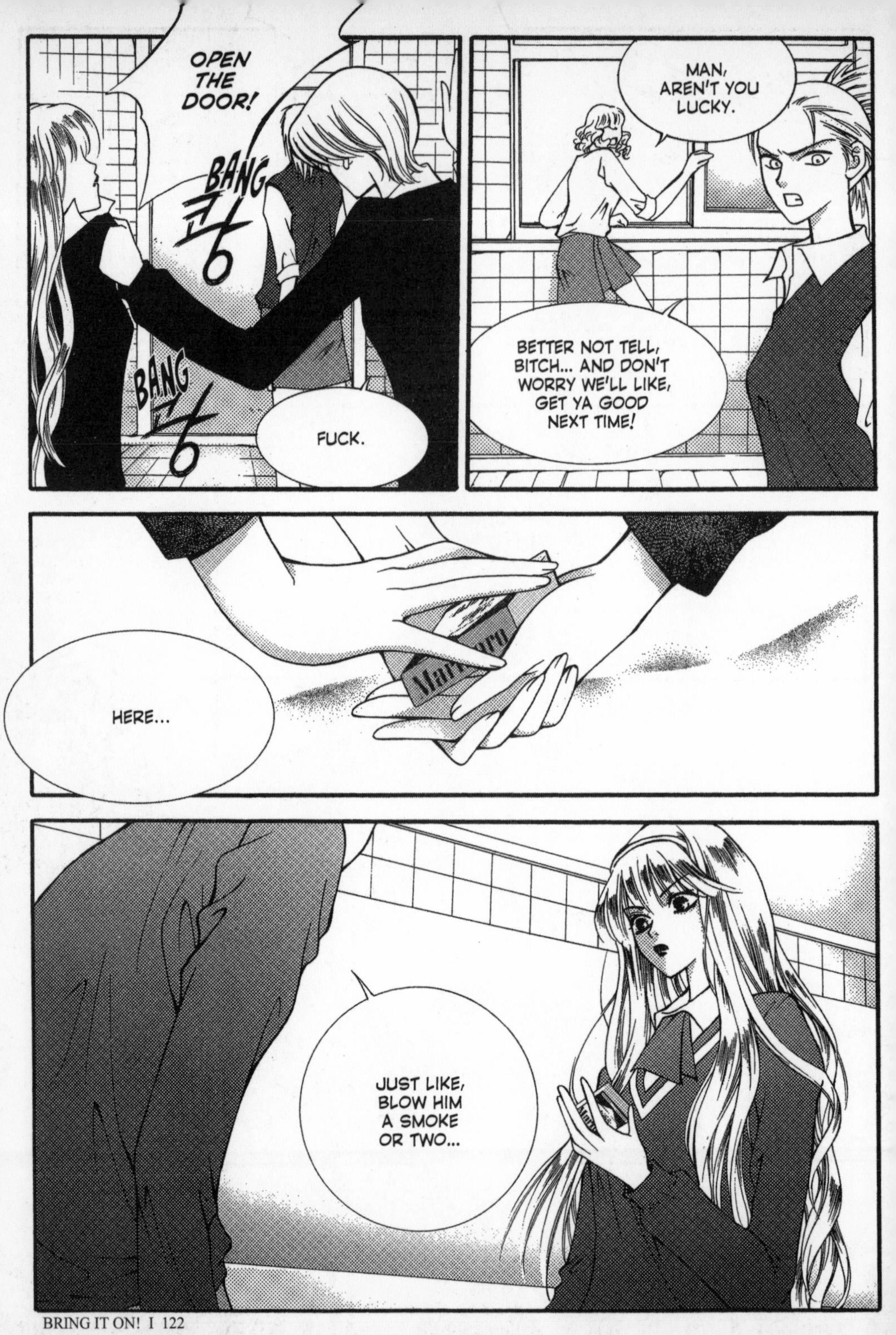
OPEN THE DOOR!
BANG
BANG
FUCK.
MAN, AREN'T YOU LUCKY.
BETTER NOT TELL, BITCH... AND DON'T WORRY WE'LL LIKE, GET YA GOOD NEXT TIME!
HERE...
JUST LIKE, BLOW HIM A SMOKE OR TWO...

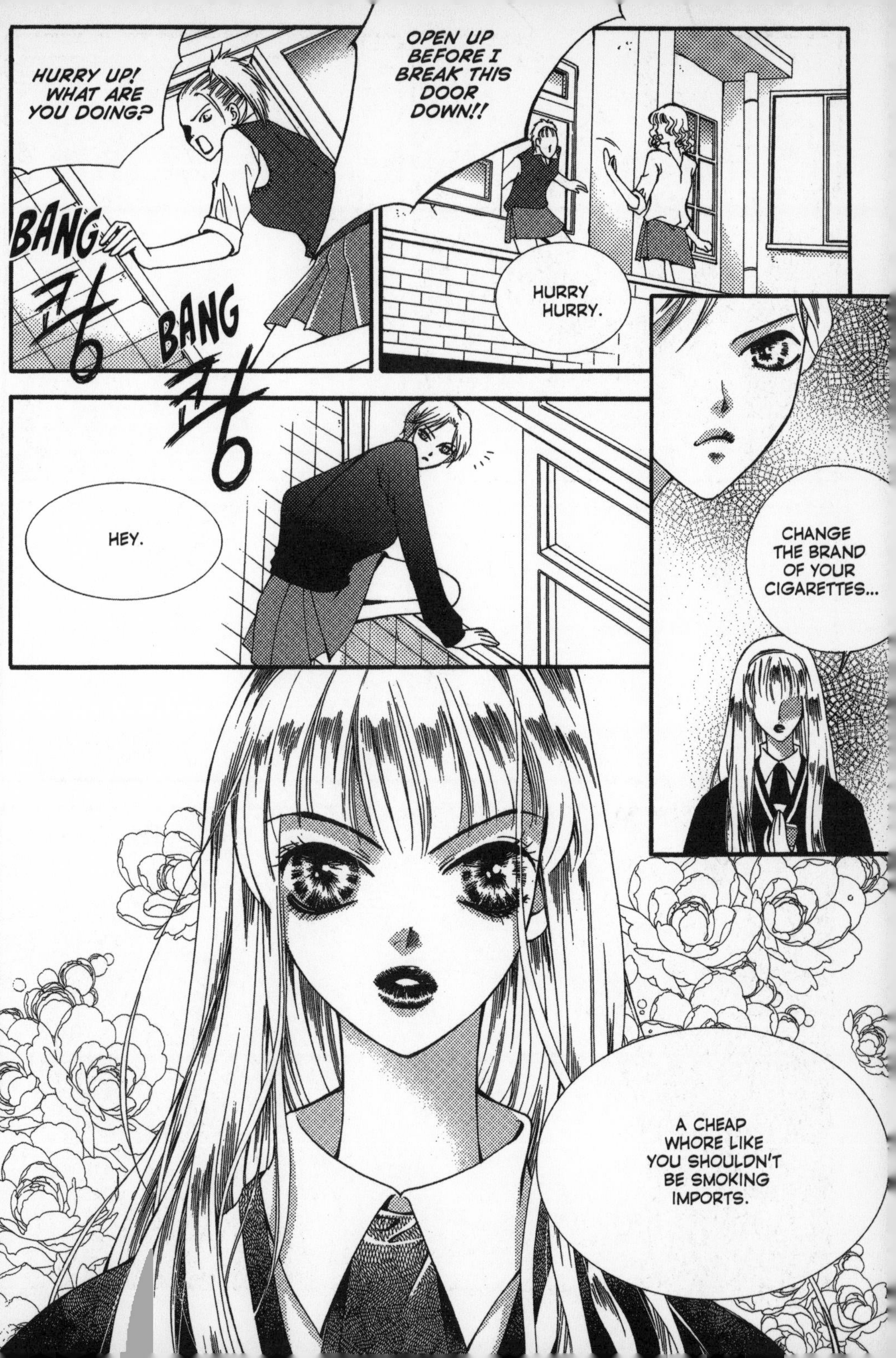

HURRY UP! WHAT ARE YOU DOING?
BANG
쾅
BANG
쾅
OPEN UP BEFORE I BREAK THIS DOOR DOWN!!
HURRY HURRY.
HEY.
CHANGE THE BRAND OF YOUR CIGARETTES...
A CHEAP WHORE LIKE YOU SHOULDN'T BE SMOKING IMPORTS.

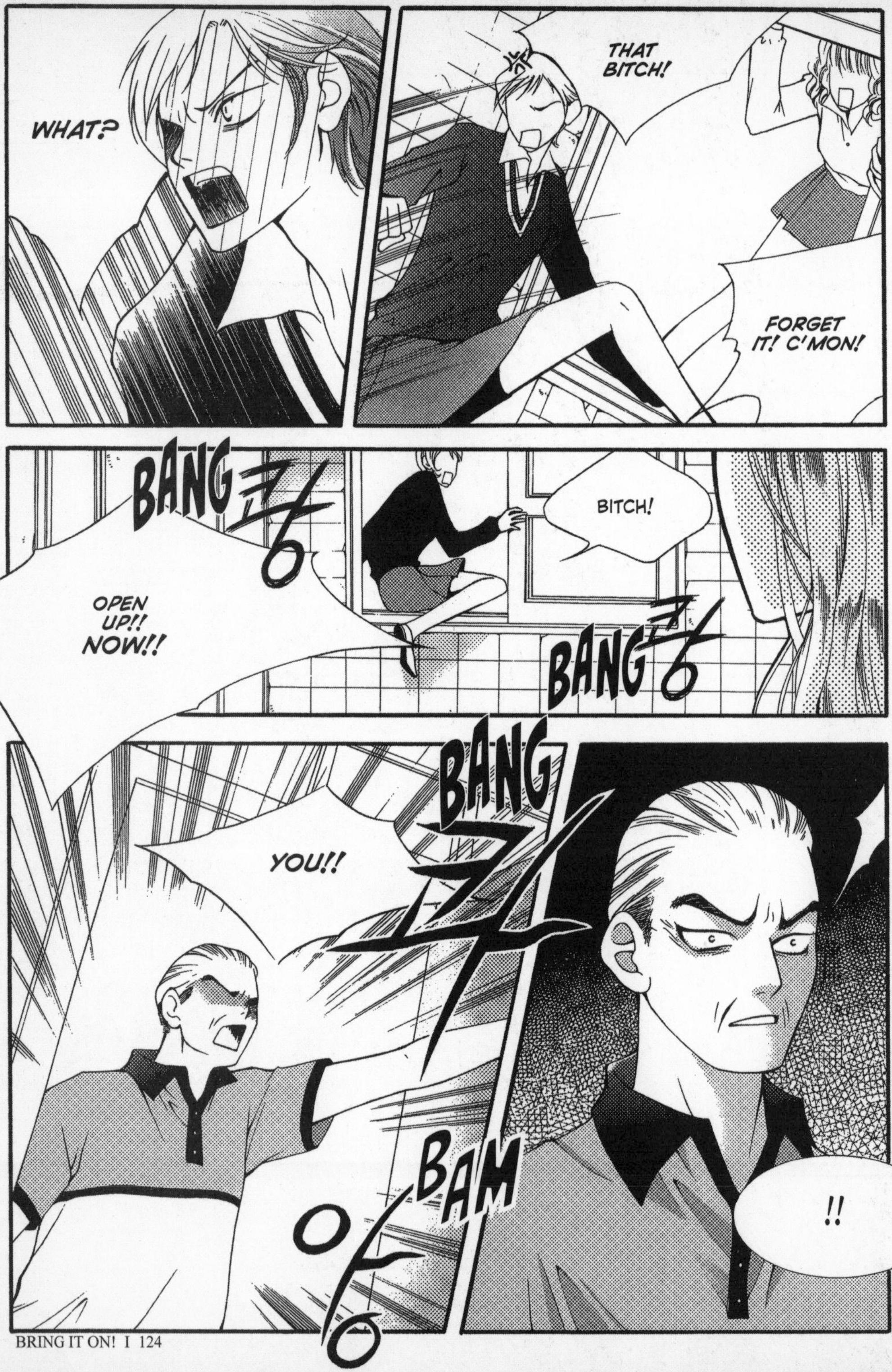
WHAT?
THAT BITCH!
FORGET IT! C'MON!
BANG
OPEN UP!! NOW!!
BITCH!
BANG
YOU!!
BANG
BAM
!!

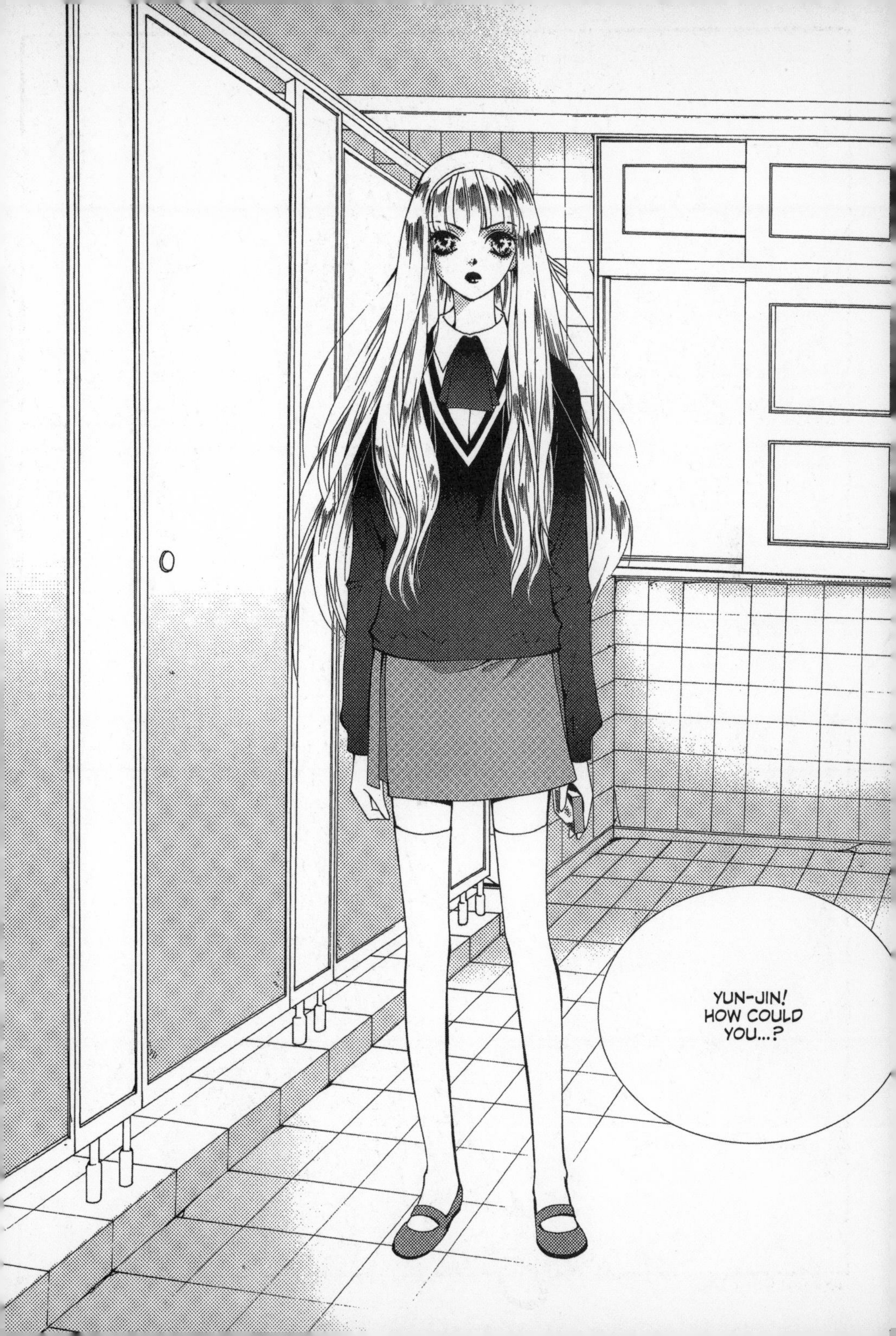
YUN-JIN! HOW COULD YOU...?

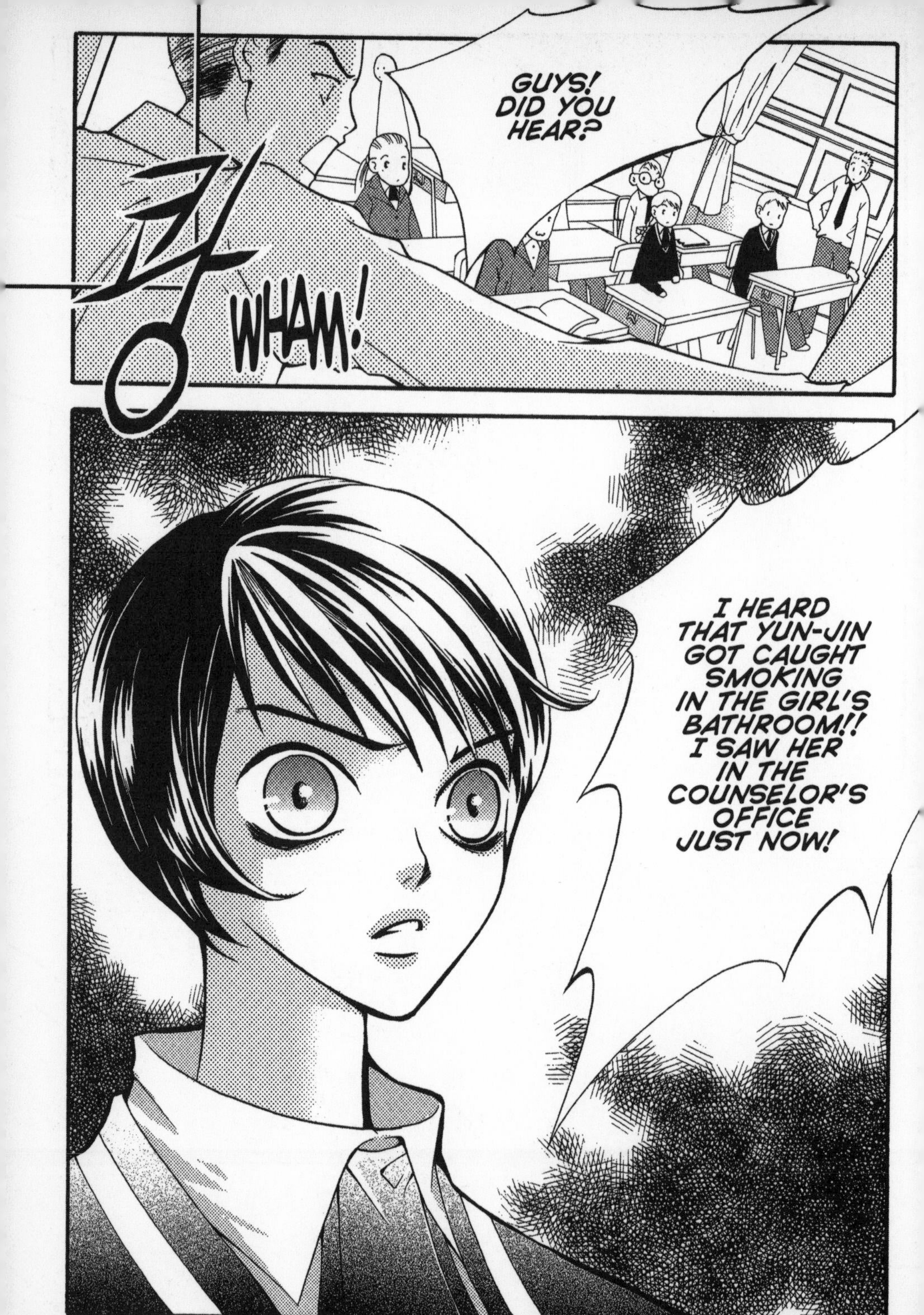
WHAM!
GUYS! DID YOU HEAR?
I HEARD THAT YUN-JIN GOT CAUGHT SMOKING IN THE GIRL'S BATHROOM!! I SAW HER IN THE COUNSELOR'S OFFICE JUST NOW!

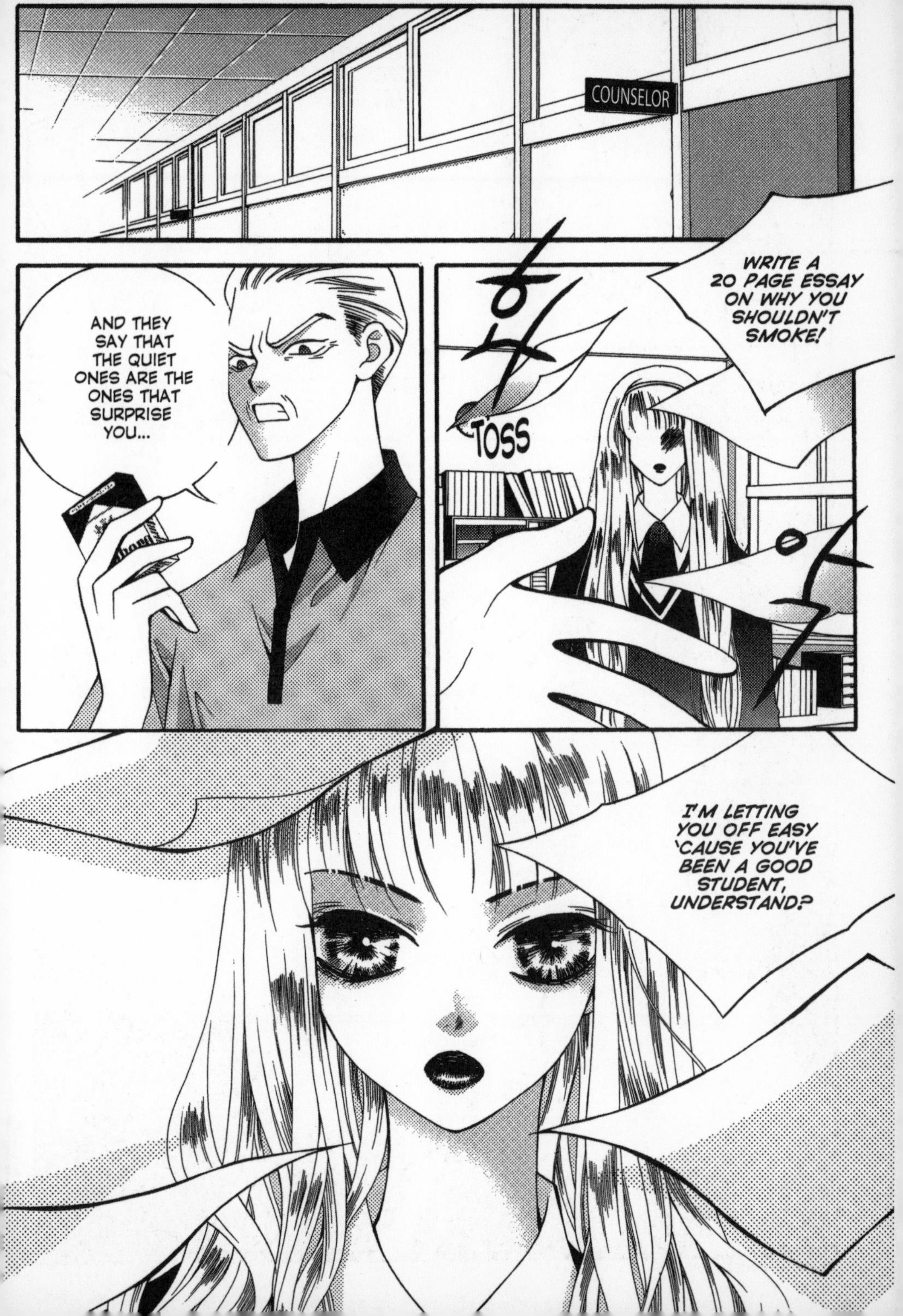
COUNSELOR
AND THEY SAY THAT THE QUIET ONES ARE THE ONES THAT SURPRISE YOU...
TOSS
WRITE A 20 PAGE ESSAY ON WHY YOU SHOULDN'T SMOKE!
I'M LETTING YOU OFF EASY 'CAUSE YOU'VE BEEN A GOOD STUDENT, UNDERSTAND?

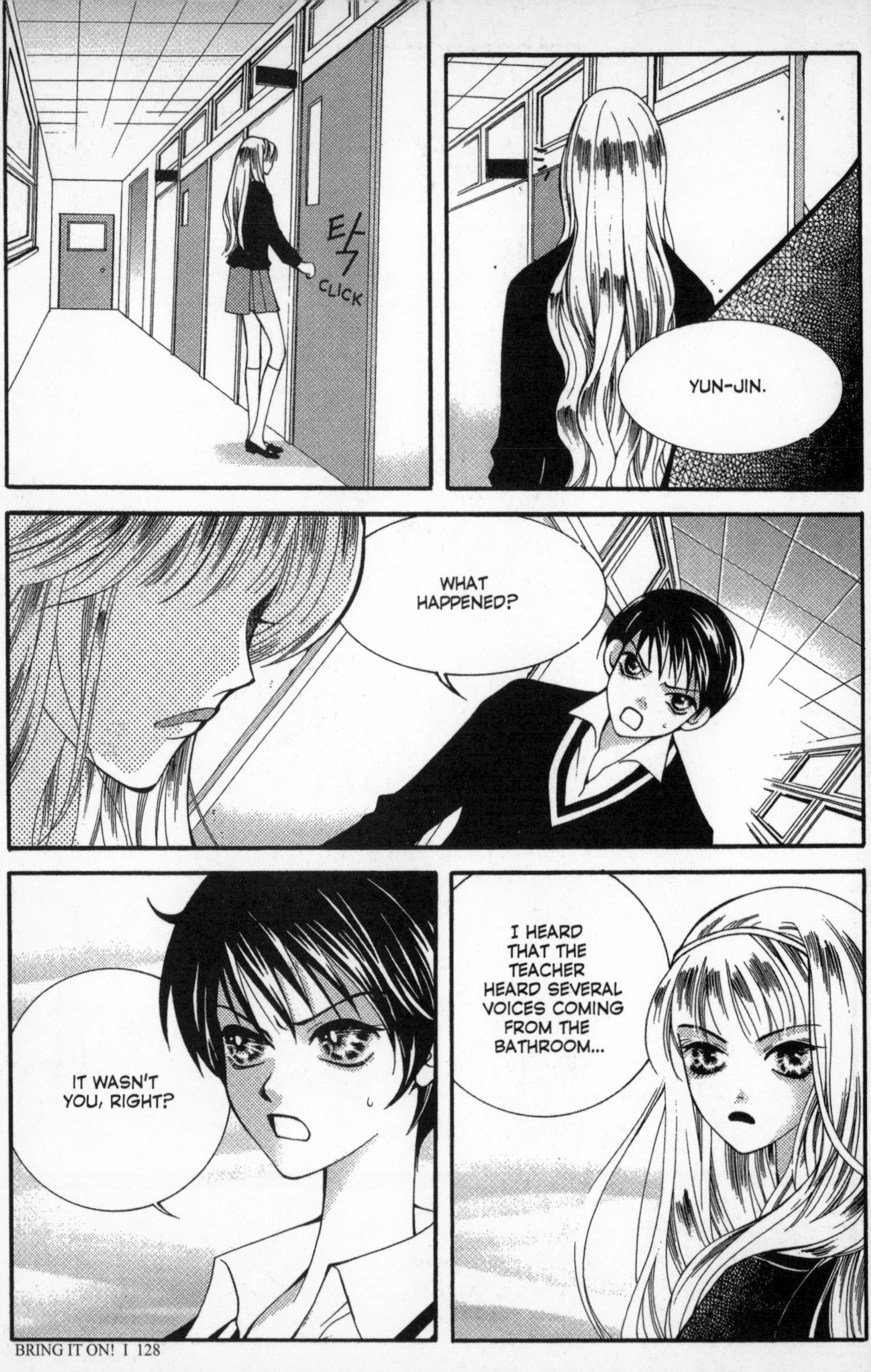
CLICK
YUN-JIN.
WHAT HAPPENED?
IT WASN'T YOU, RIGHT?
I HEARD THAT THE TEACHER HEARD SEVERAL VOICES COMING FROM THE BATHROOM...

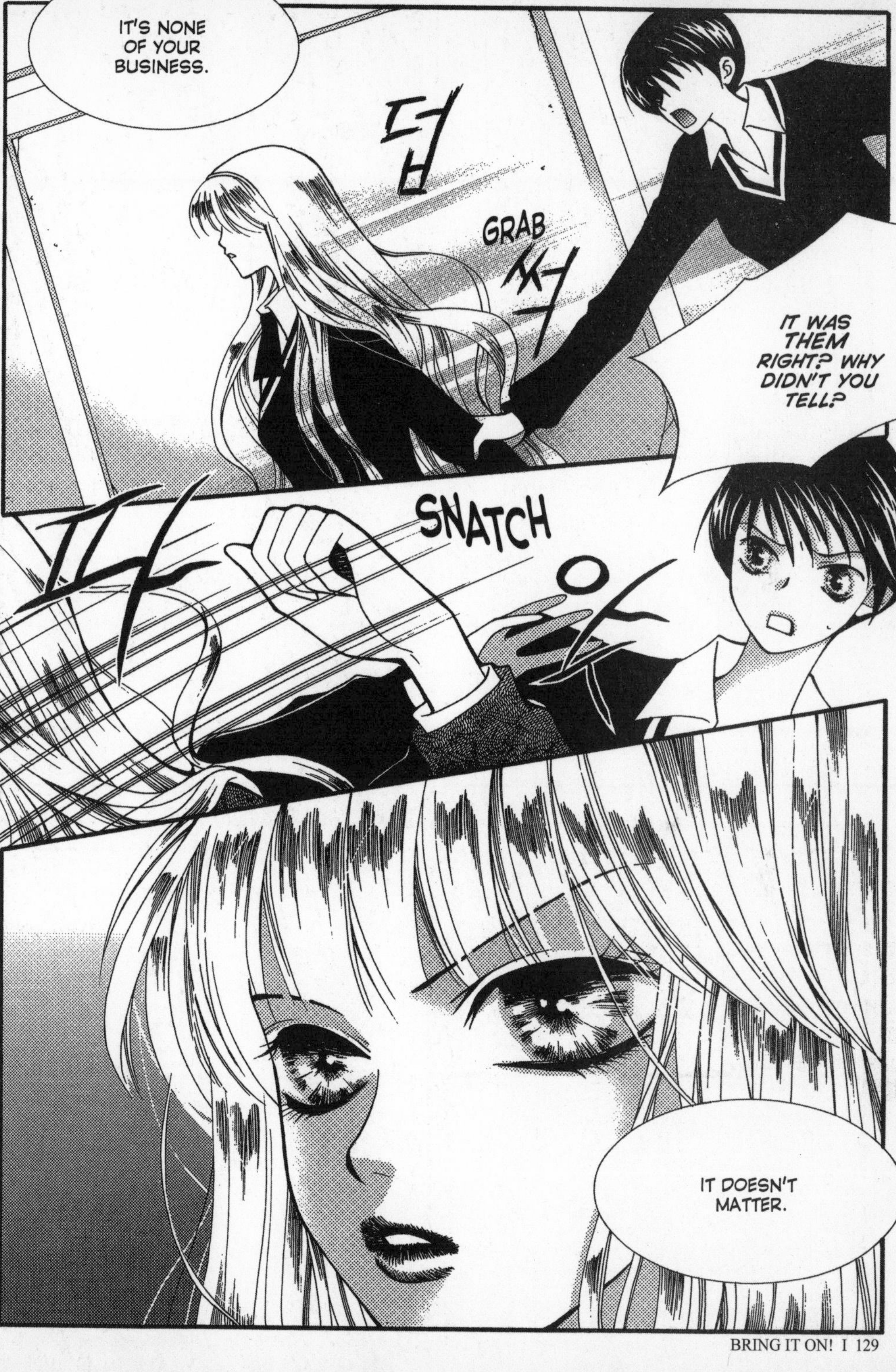
IT'S NONE OF YOUR BUSINESS.
GRAB
IT WAS THEM RIGHT? WHY DIDN'T YOU TELL?
SNATCH
IT DOESN'T MATTER.

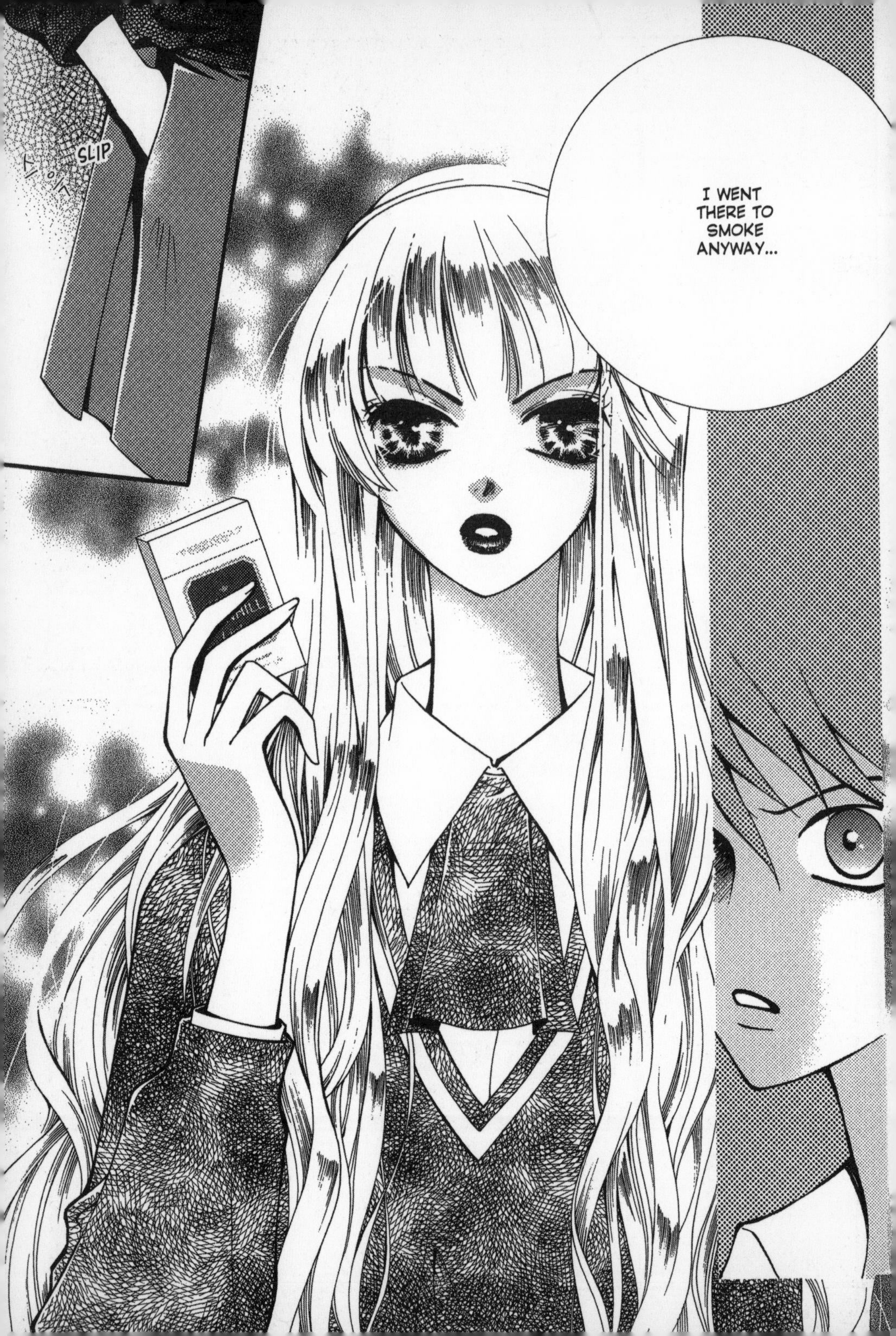
SLIP
I WENT THERE TO SMOKE ANYWAY...

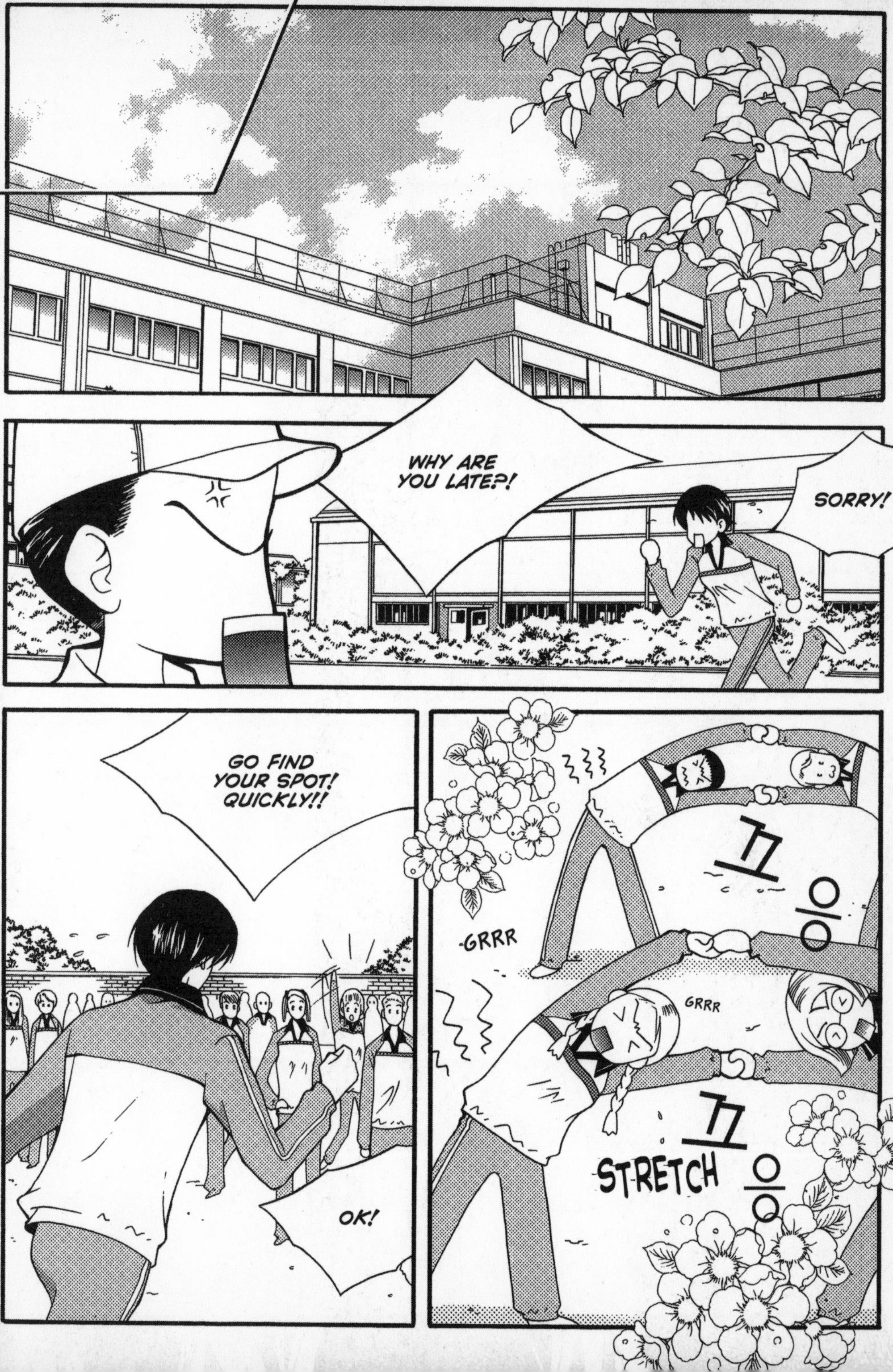
WHY ARE YOU LATE?!
SORRY!
GO FIND YOUR SPOT! QUICKLY!!
OK!
끄응
-GRRR
GRRR
끄응
STRETCH

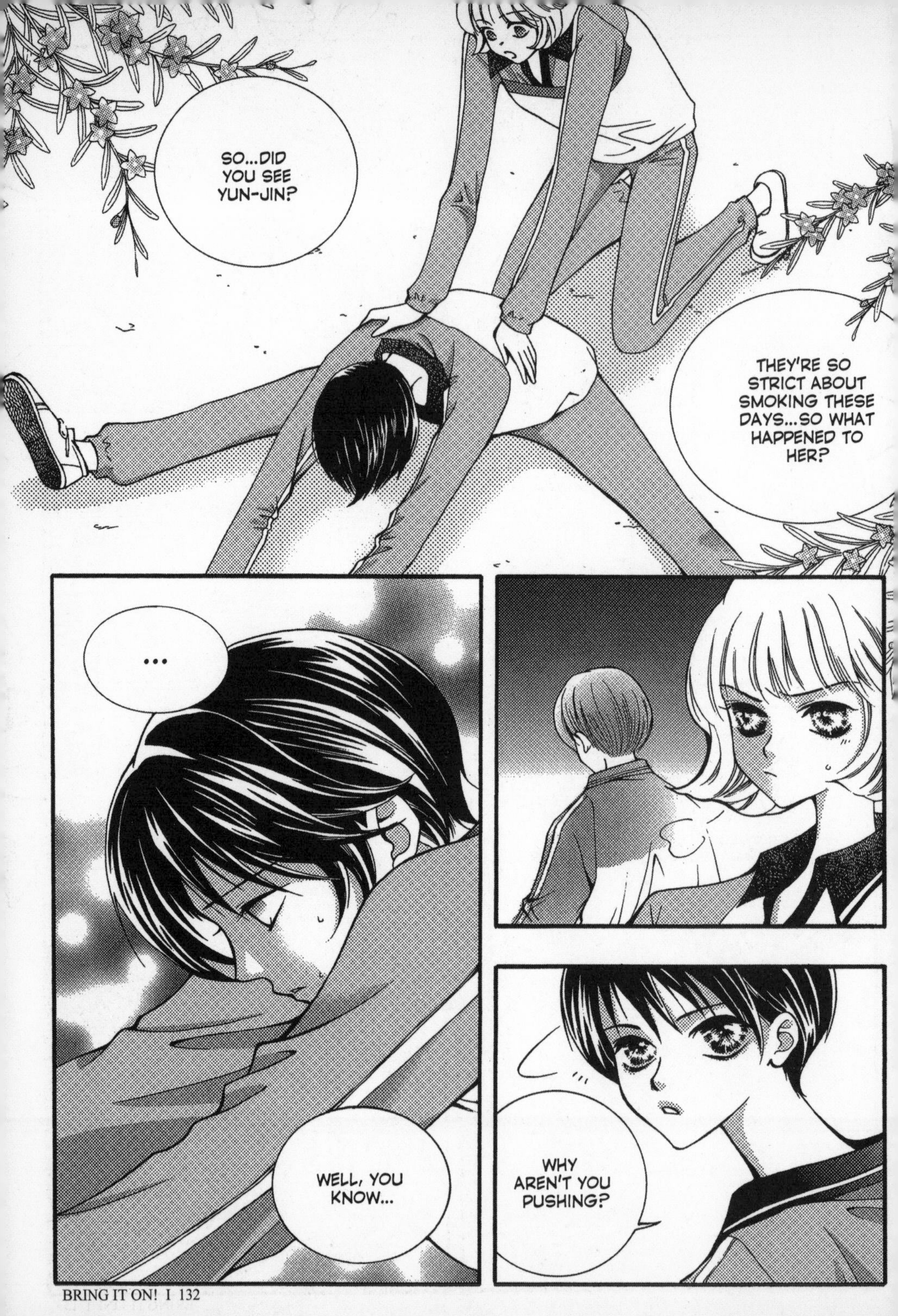
SO...DID YOU SEE YUN-JIN?
THEY'RE SO STRICT ABOUT SMOKING THESE DAYS...SO WHAT HAPPENED TO HER?
...
WELL, YOU KNOW...
WHY AREN'T YOU PUSHING?

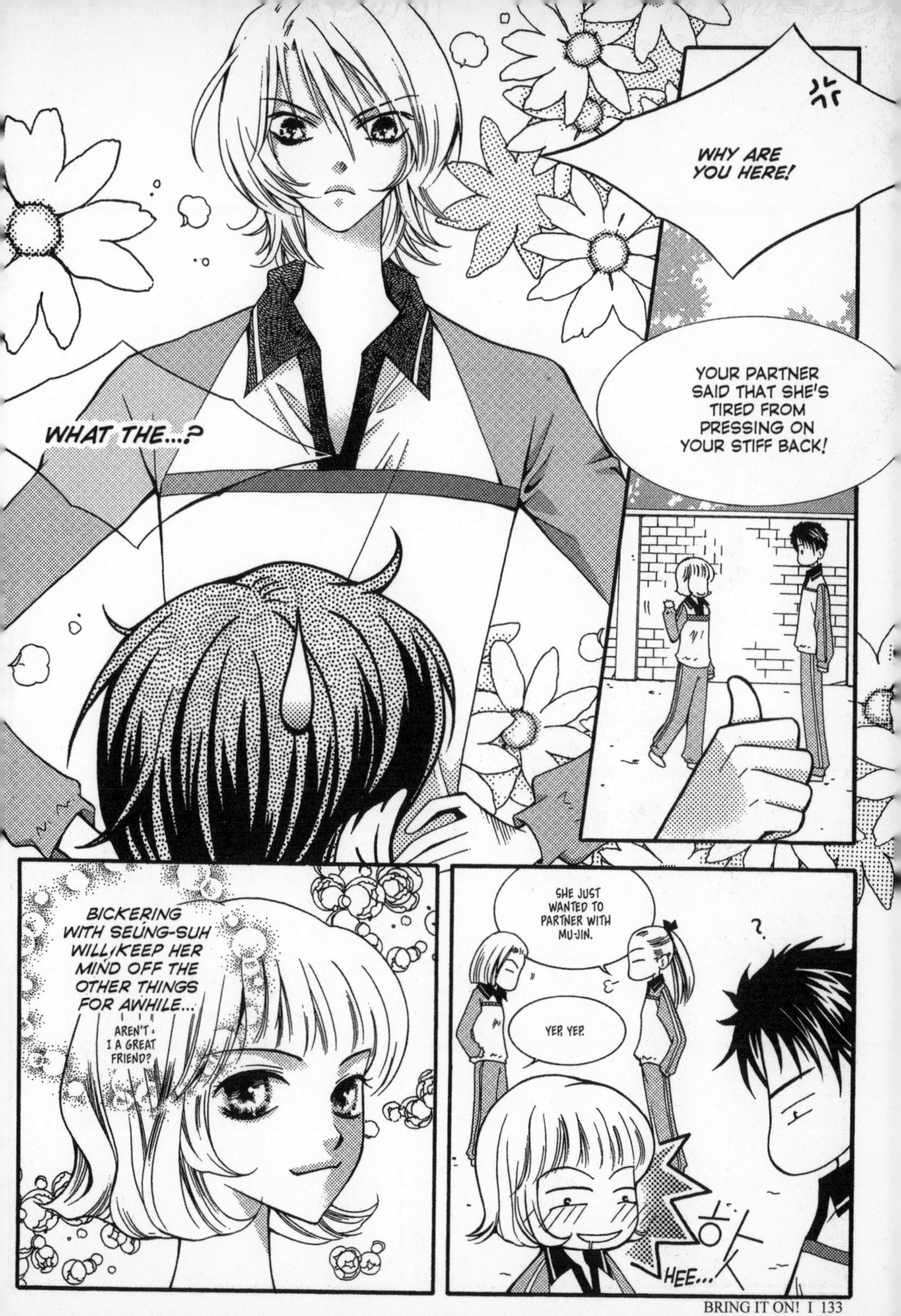
WHAT THE...?
WHY ARE YOU HERE!
YOUR PARTNER SAID THAT SHE'S TIRED FROM PRESSING ON YOUR STIFF BACK!
BICKERING WITH SEUNG-SUH WILL KEEP HER MIND OFF THE OTHER THINGS FOR AWHILE...
AREN'T I A GREAT FRIEND?
SHE JUST WANTED TO PARTNER WITH MU-JIN.
YEP, YEP.
HEE...

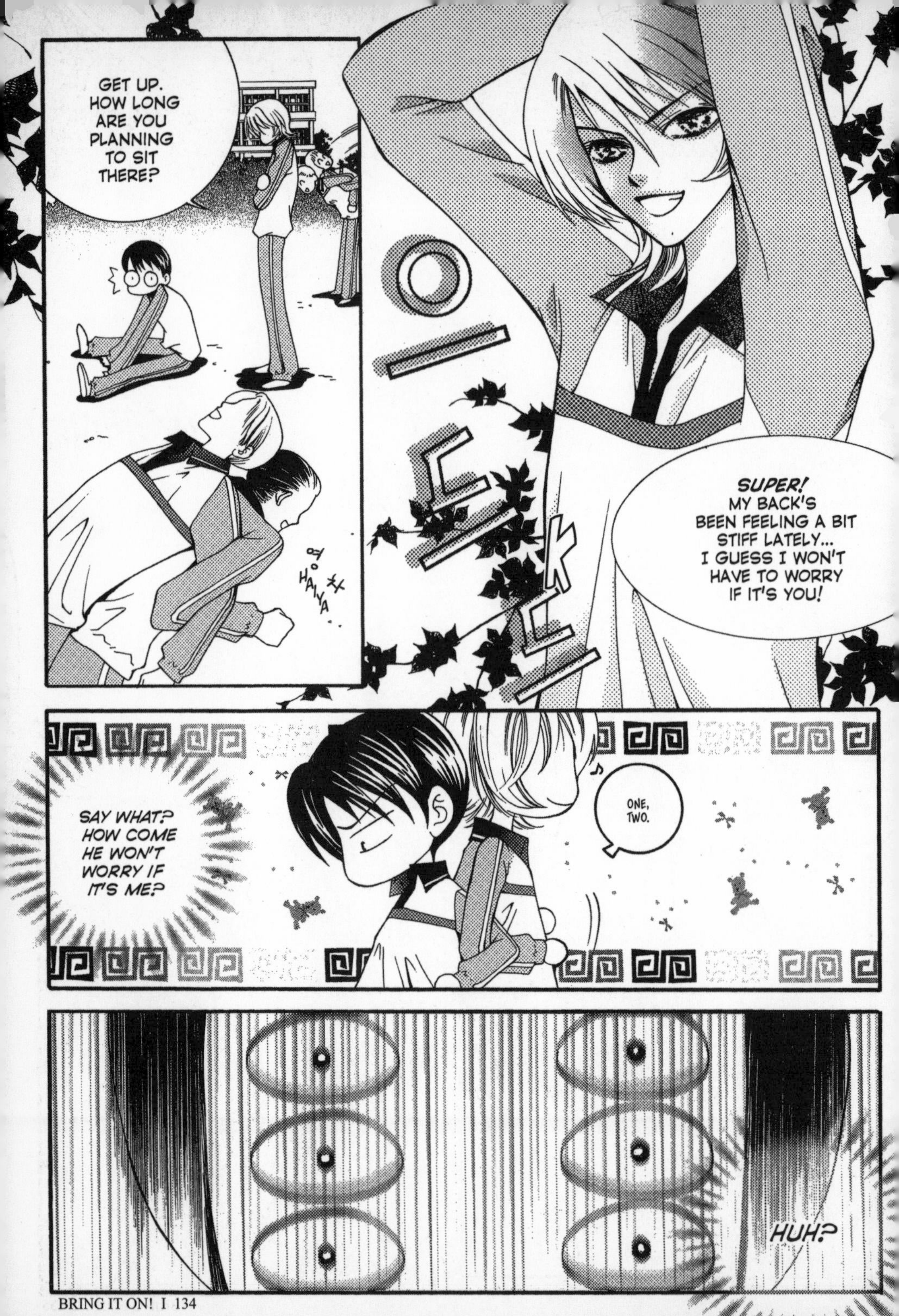
GET UP. HOW LONG ARE YOU PLANNING TO SIT THERE?
HAIYA..
SUPER! MY BACK'S BEEN FEELING A BIT STIFF LATELY... I GUESS I WON'T HAVE TO WORRY IF IT'S YOU!
SAY WHAT? HOW COME HE WON'T WORRY IF IT'S ME?
ONE, TWO.
HUH?

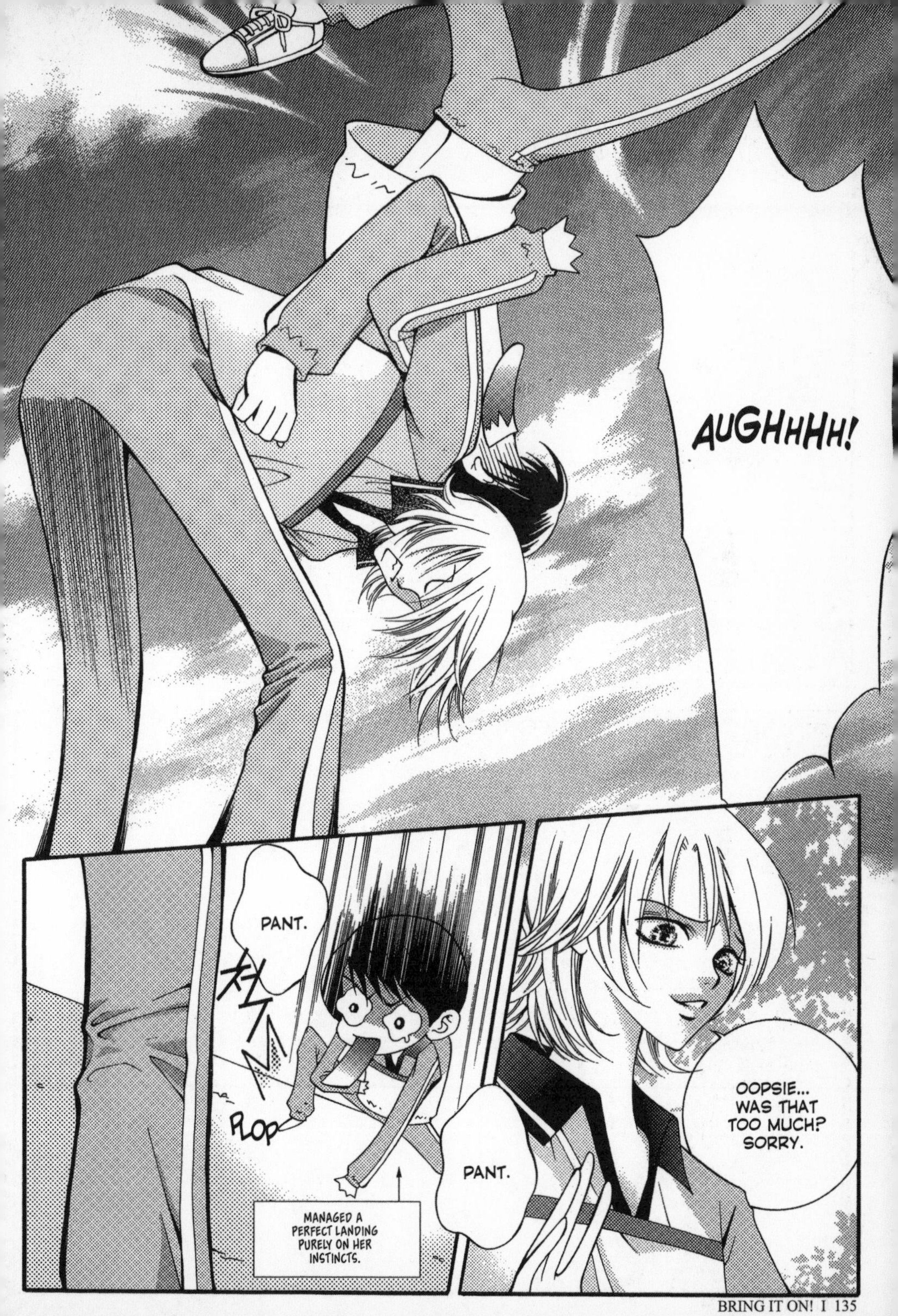
AUGHHHH!
PANT.
KLANG
PLOP
MANAGED A PERFECT LANDING PURELY ON HER INSTINCTS.
PANT.
OOPSIE... WAS THAT TOO MUCH? SORRY.

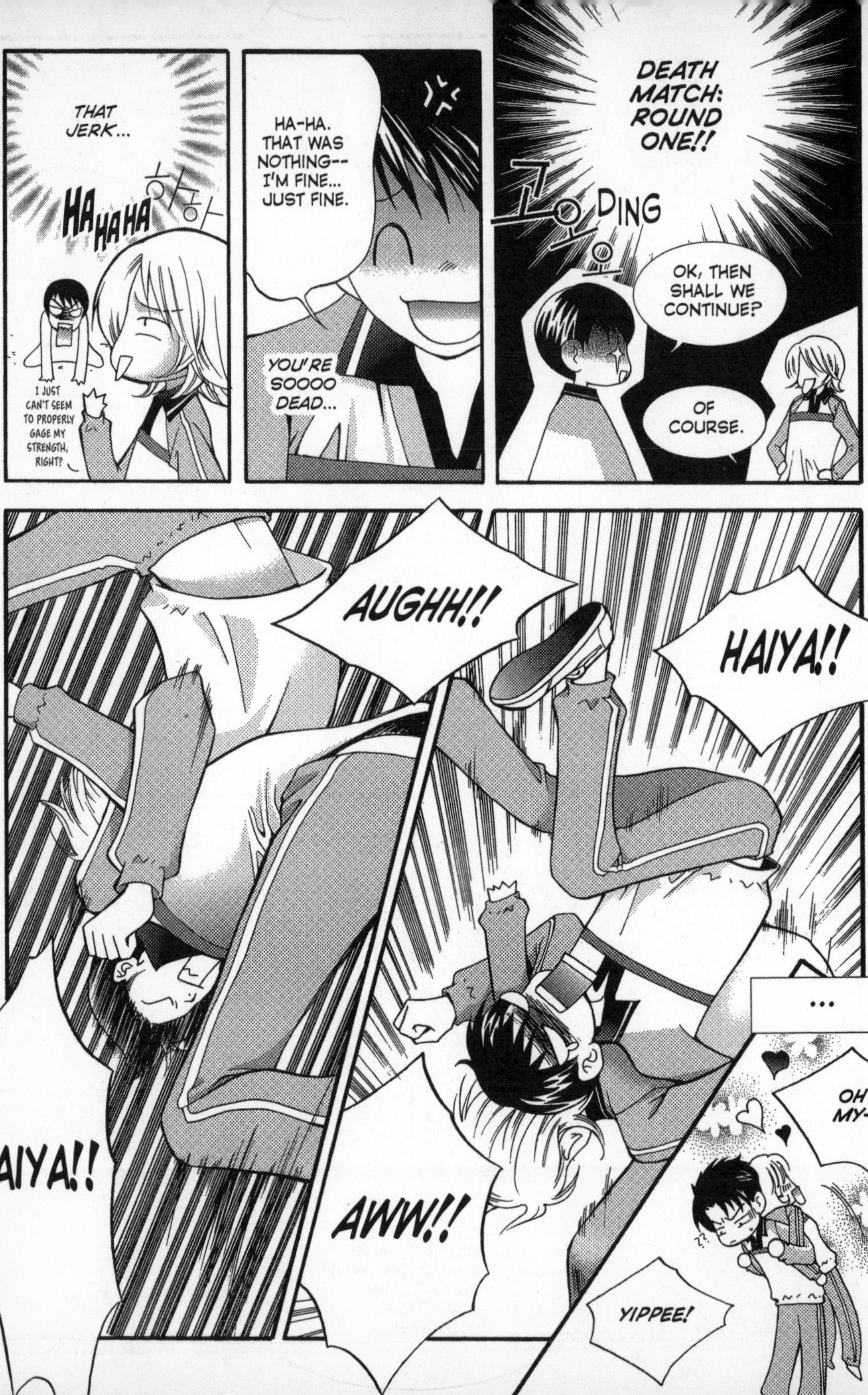
THAT JERK...
HAHAHA
I JUST CAN'T SEEM TO PROPERLY GAGE MY STRENGTH, RIGHT?
HA-HA. THAT WAS NOTHING-- I'M FINE... JUST FINE.
YOU'RE SOOOO DEAD...
DEATH MATCH: ROUND ONE!!
DING
OK, THEN SHALL WE CONTINUE?
OF COURSE.
AUGHH!!
AIYA!!
HAIYA!!
AWW!!
...
OH MY--
YIPPEE!

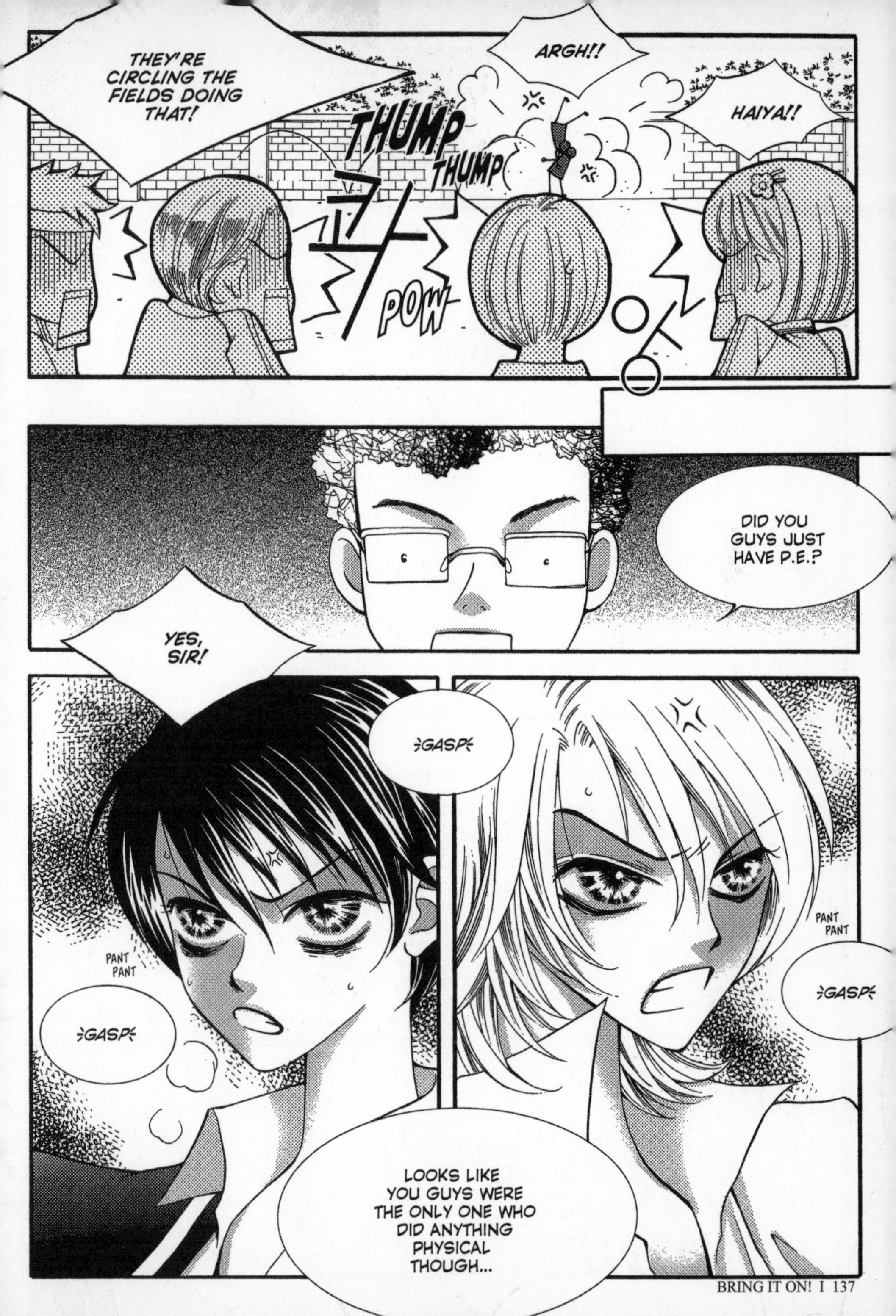
THEY'RE CIRCLING THE FIELDS DOING THAT!
THUMP
THUMP
ARGH!!
POW
HAIYA!!
DID YOU GUYS JUST HAVE P.E.?
YES, SIR!
GASP
PANT PANT
GASP
PANT PANT
GASP
LOOKS LIKE YOU GUYS WERE THE ONLY ONE WHO DID ANYTHING PHYSICAL THOUGH...

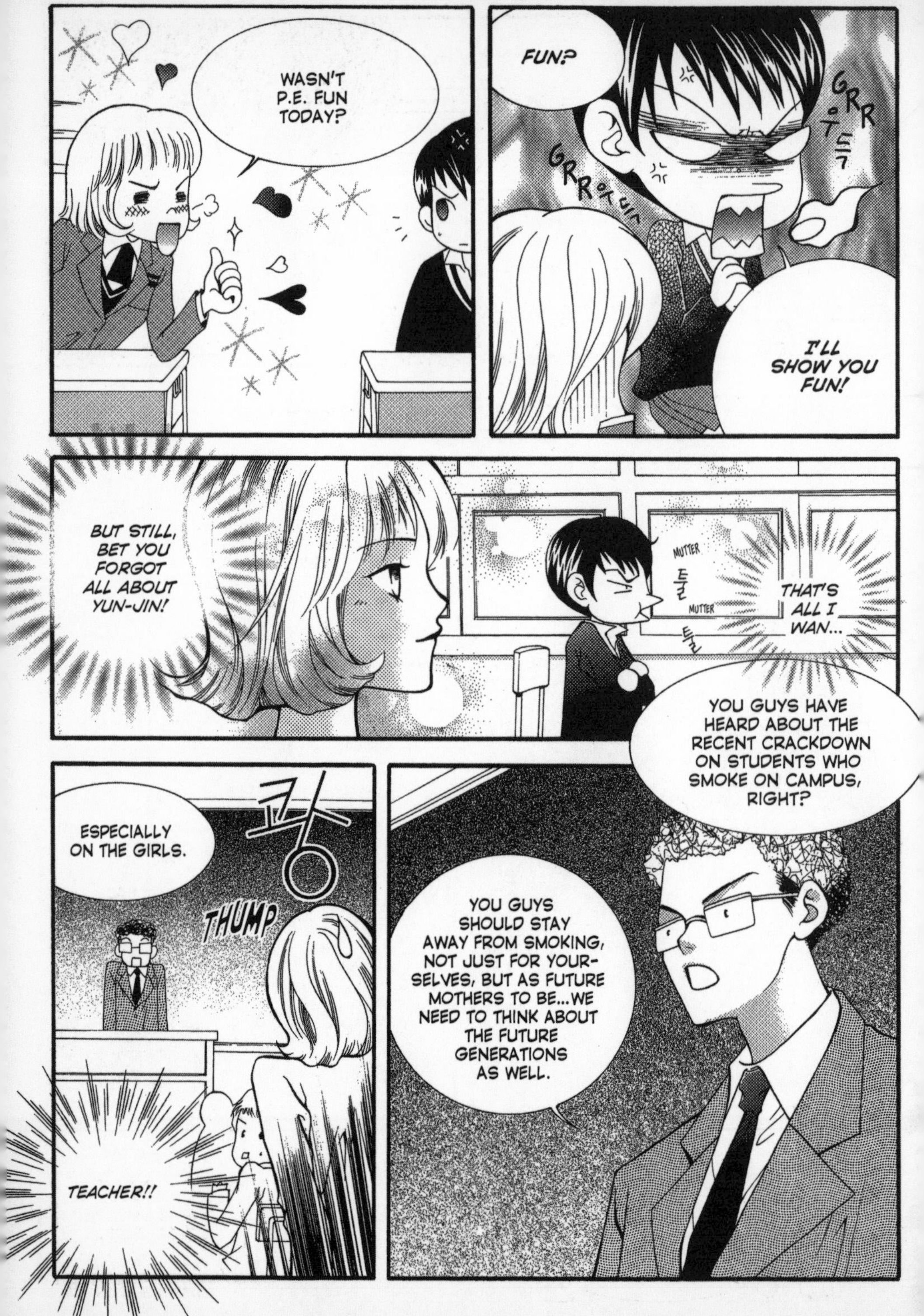
WASN'T P.E. FUN TODAY?
FUN?
GRR
GRR
I'LL SHOW YOU FUN!
BUT STILL, BET YOU FORGOT ALL ABOUT YUN-JIN!
MUTTER
MUTTER
THAT'S ALL I WAN...
ESPECIALLY ON THE GIRLS.
THUMP
TEACHER!!
YOU GUYS HAVE HEARD ABOUT THE RECENT CRACKDOWN ON STUDENTS WHO SMOKE ON CAMPUS, RIGHT?
YOU GUYS SHOULD STAY AWAY FROM SMOKING, NOT JUST FOR YOUR-SELVES, BUT AS FUTURE MOTHERS TO BE...WE NEED TO THINK ABOUT THE FUTURE GENERATIONS AS WELL.

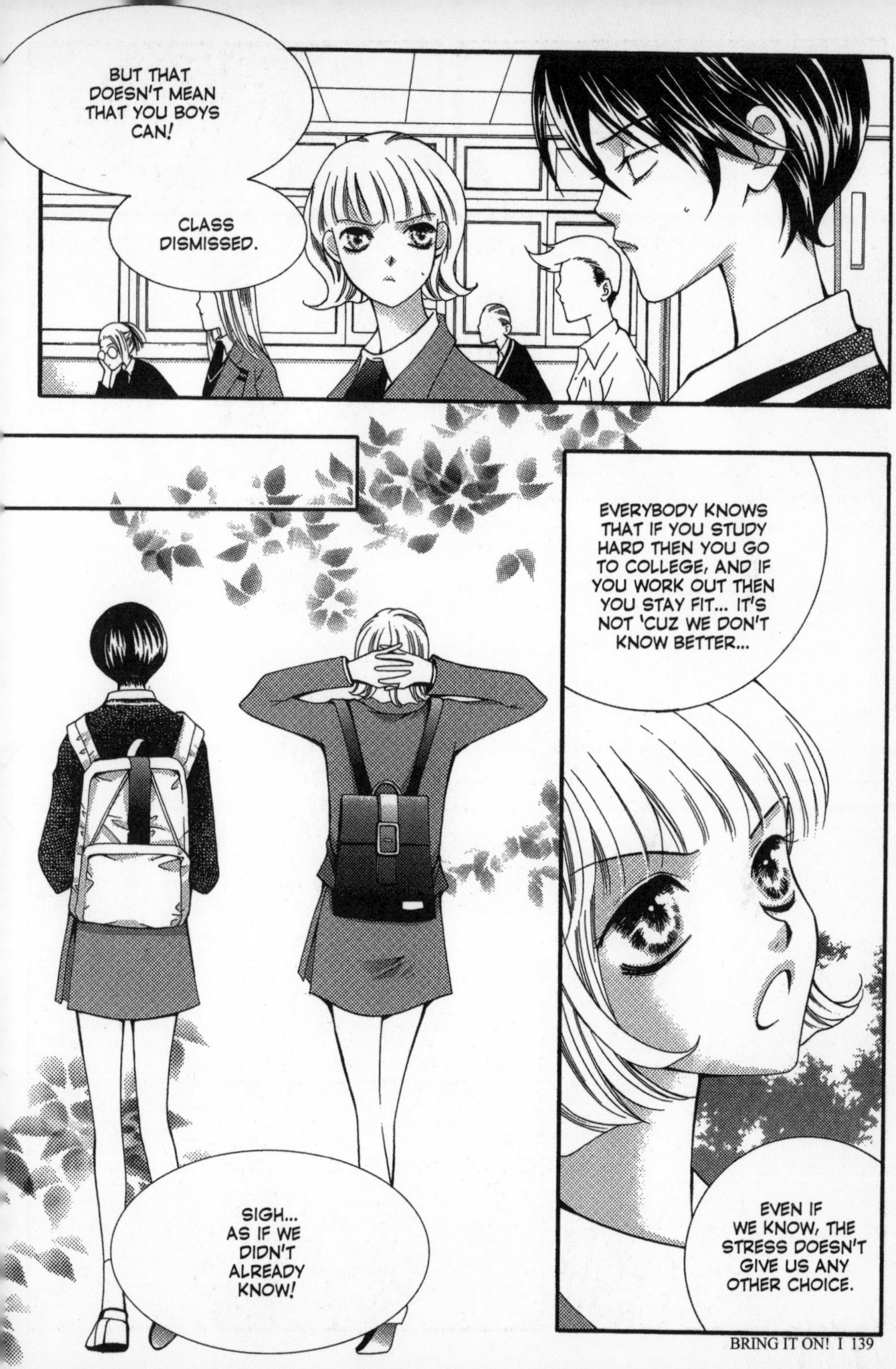
BUT THAT DOESN'T MEAN THAT YOU BOYS CAN!
CLASS DISMISSED.
SIGH... AS IF WE DIDN'T ALREADY KNOW!
EVERYBODY KNOWS THAT IF YOU STUDY HARD THEN YOU GO TO COLLEGE, AND IF YOU WORK OUT THEN YOU STAY FIT... IT'S NOT 'CUZ WE DON'T KNOW BETTER...
EVEN IF WE KNOW, THE STRESS DOESN'T GIVE US ANY OTHER CHOICE.

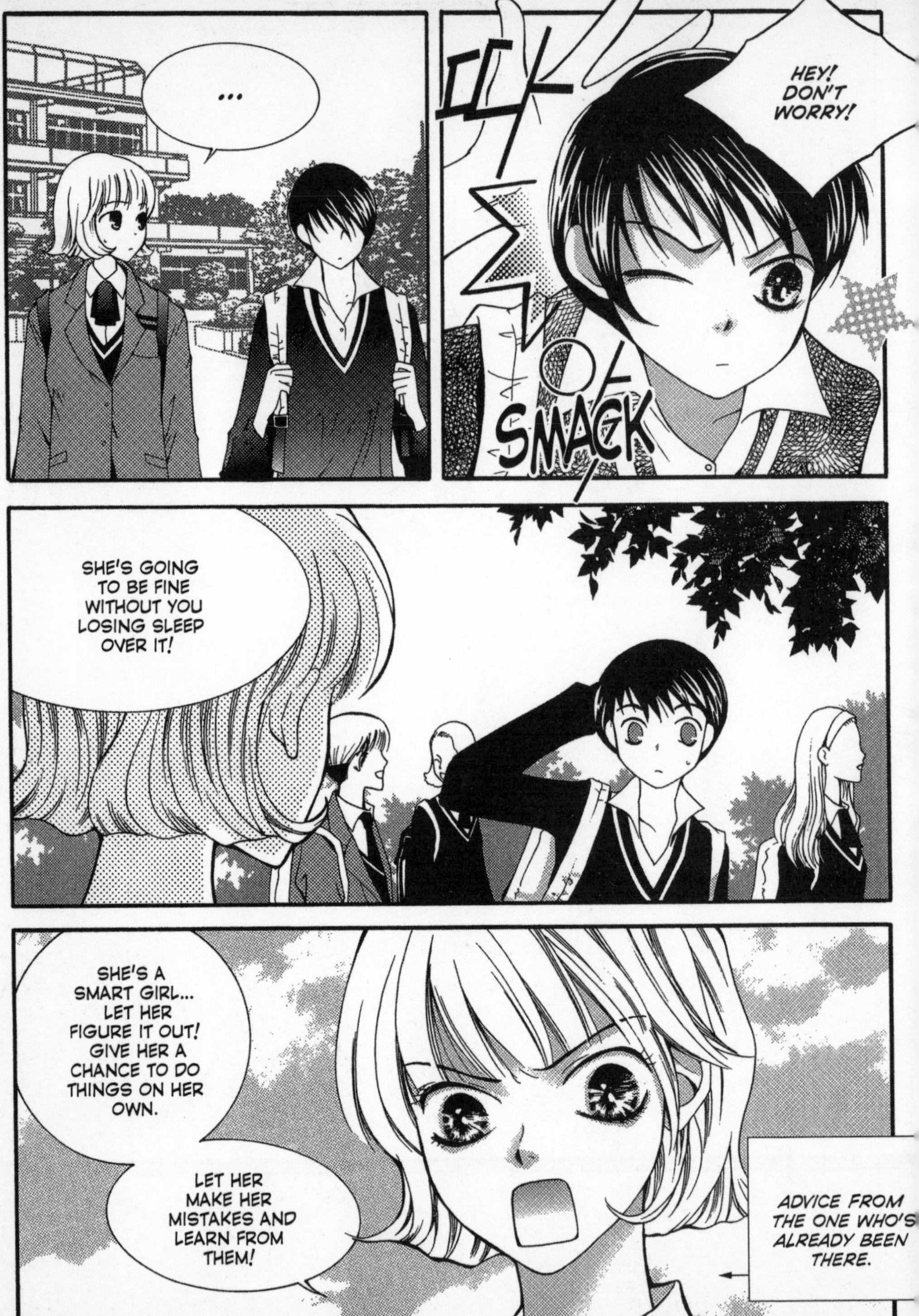
...
ICK
SMACK
HEY! DON'T WORRY!
SHE'S GOING TO BE FINE WITHOUT YOU LOSING SLEEP OVER IT!
SHE'S A SMART GIRL... LET HER FIGURE IT OUT! GIVE HER A CHANCE TO DO THINGS ON HER OWN.
LET HER MAKE HER MISTAKES AND LEARN FROM THEM!
ADVICE FROM THE ONE WHO'S ALREADY BEEN THERE.

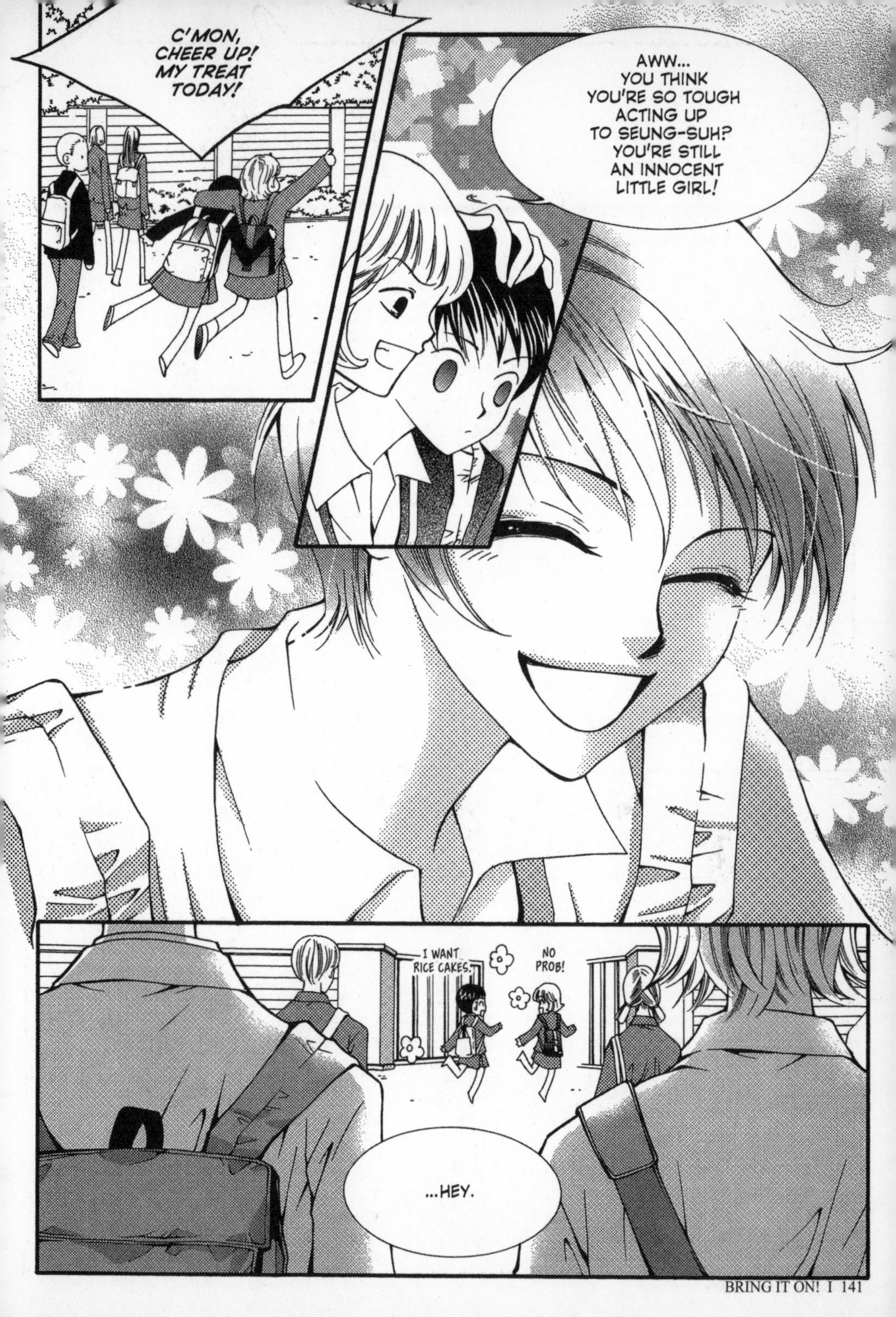
C'MON, CHEER UP! MY TREAT TODAY!
AWW... YOU THINK YOU'RE SO TOUGH ACTING UP TO SEUNG-SUH? YOU'RE STILL AN INNOCENT LITTLE GIRL!
I WANT RICE CAKES.
NO PROB!
...HEY.

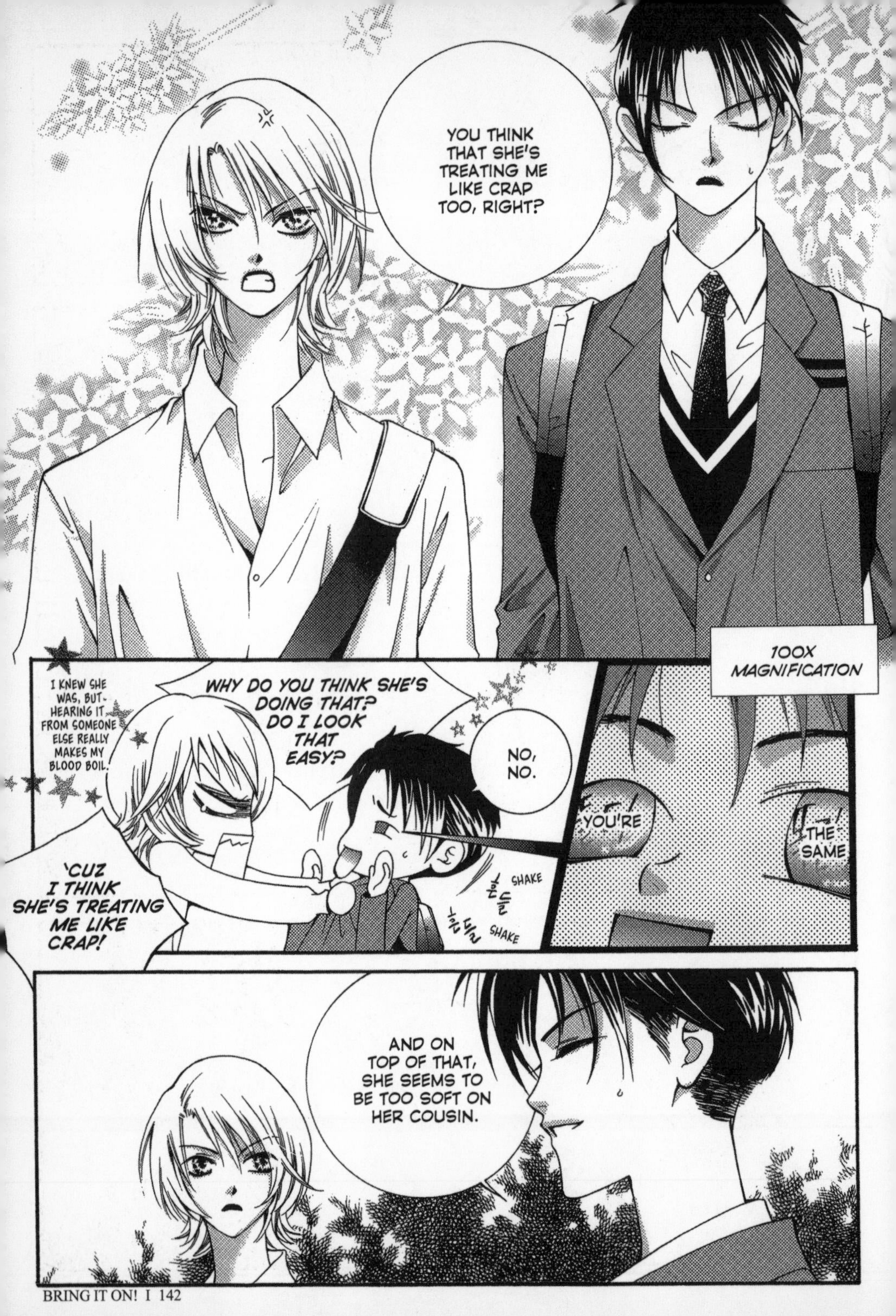
YOU THINK THAT SHE'S TREATING ME LIKE CRAP TOO, RIGHT?
I KNEW SHE WAS, BUT- HEARING IT FROM SOMEONE ELSE REALLY MAKES MY BLOOD BOIL.
WHY DO YOU THINK SHE'S DOING THAT? DO I LOOK THAT EASY?
'CUZ I THINK SHE'S TREATING ME LIKE CRAP!
NO, NO.
SHAKE
SHAKE
100X MAGNIFICATION
YOU'RE
THE SAME
AND ON TOP OF THAT, SHE SEEMS TO BE TOO SOFT ON HER COUSIN.

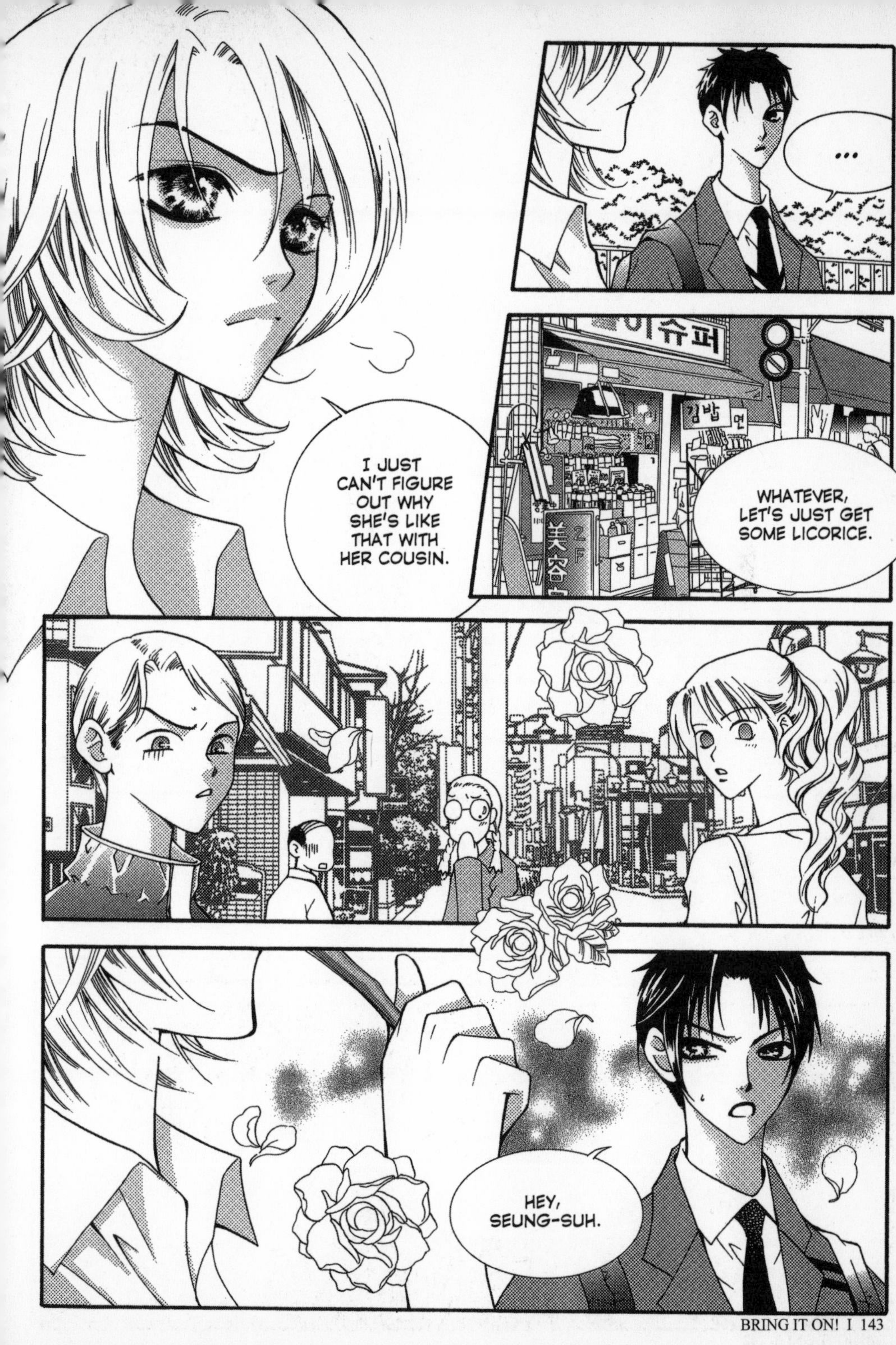

I JUST CAN'T FIGURE OUT WHY SHE'S LIKE THAT WITH HER COUSIN.
...
WHATEVER, LET'S JUST GET SOME LICORICE.
HEY, SEUNG-SUH.

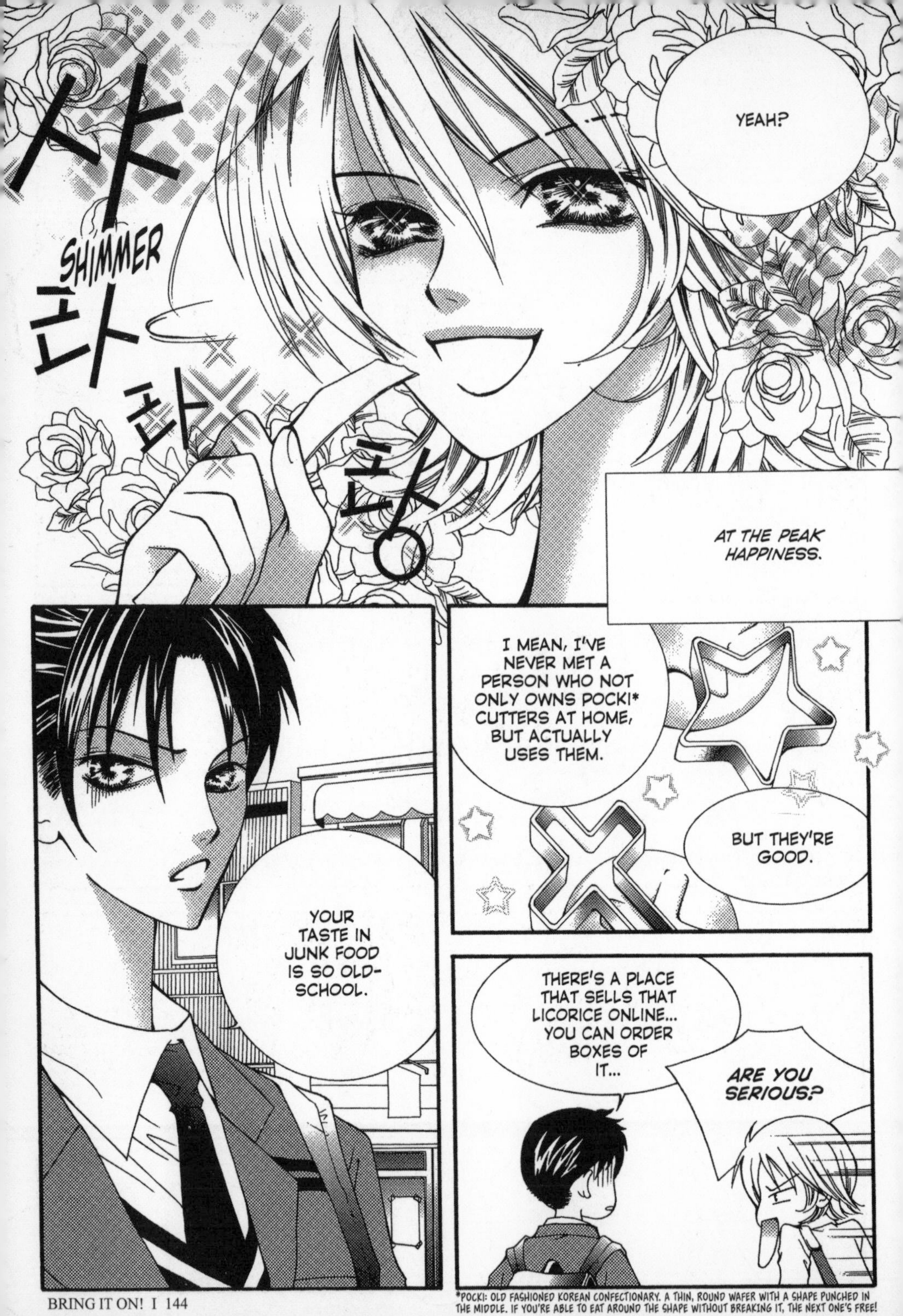
SHIMMER
YEAH?
AT THE PEAK HAPPINESS.
YOUR TASTE IN JUNK FOOD IS SO OLD-SCHOOL.
I MEAN, I'VE NEVER MET A PERSON WHO NOT ONLY OWNS POCKI* CUTTERS AT HOME, BUT ACTUALLY USES THEM.
BUT THEY'RE GOOD.
THERE'S A PLACE THAT SELLS THAT LICORICE ONLINE... YOU CAN ORDER BOXES OF IT...
ARE YOU SERIOUS?

*POCKI: OLD FASHIONED KOREAN CONFECTIONARY. A THIN, ROUND WAFER WITH A SHAPE PUNCHED IN THE MIDDLE. IF YOU'RE ABLE TO EAT AROUND THE SHAPE WITHOUT BREAKING IT, THE NEXT ONE'S FREE!

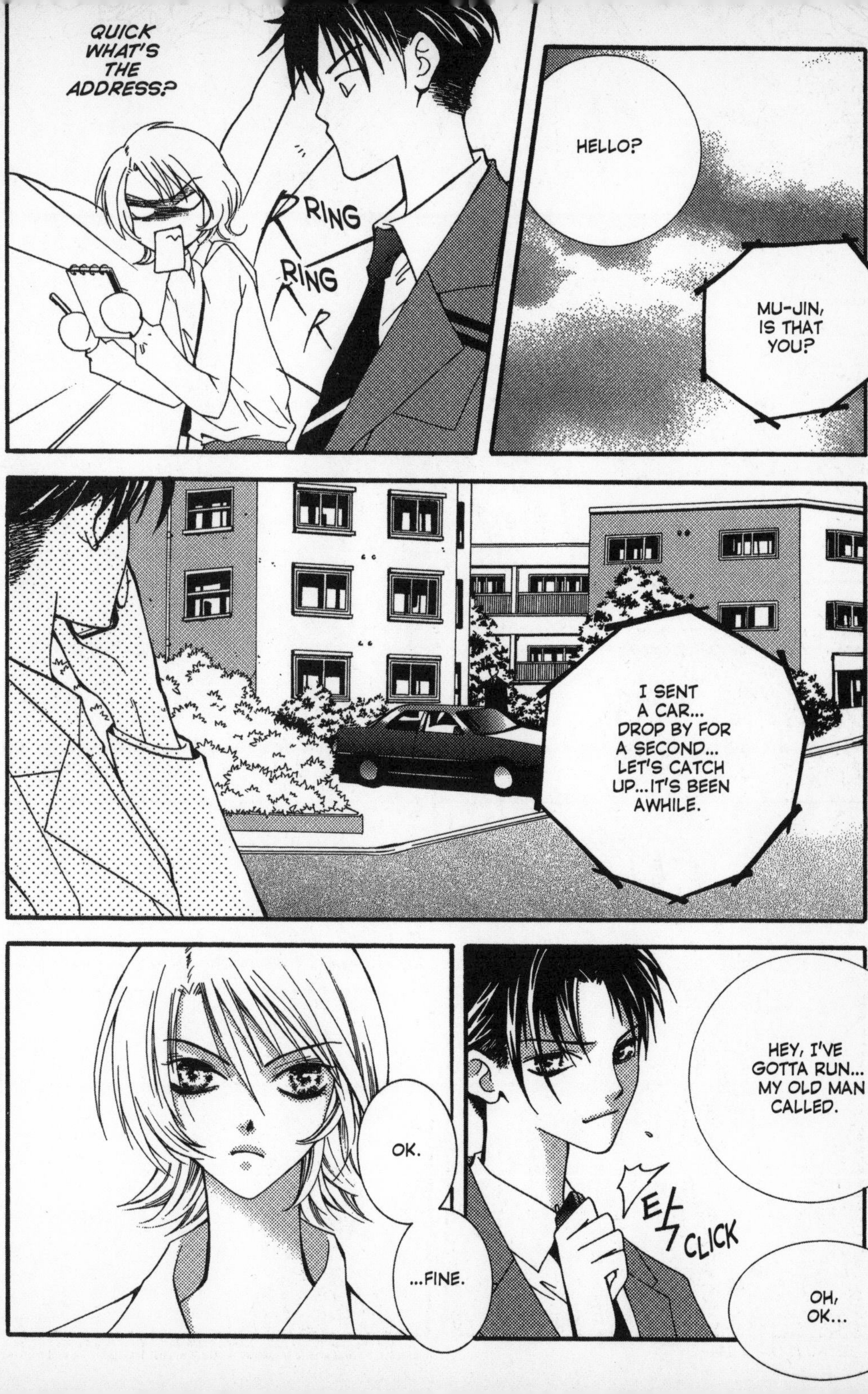
QUICK WHAT'S THE ADDRESS?
RRING
RRING
HELLO?
MU-JIN, IS THAT YOU?
I SENT A CAR... DROP BY FOR A SECOND... LET'S CATCH UP...IT'S BEEN AWHILE.
OK.
...FINE.
HEY, I'VE GOTTA RUN... MY OLD MAN CALLED.
CLICK
OH, OK...

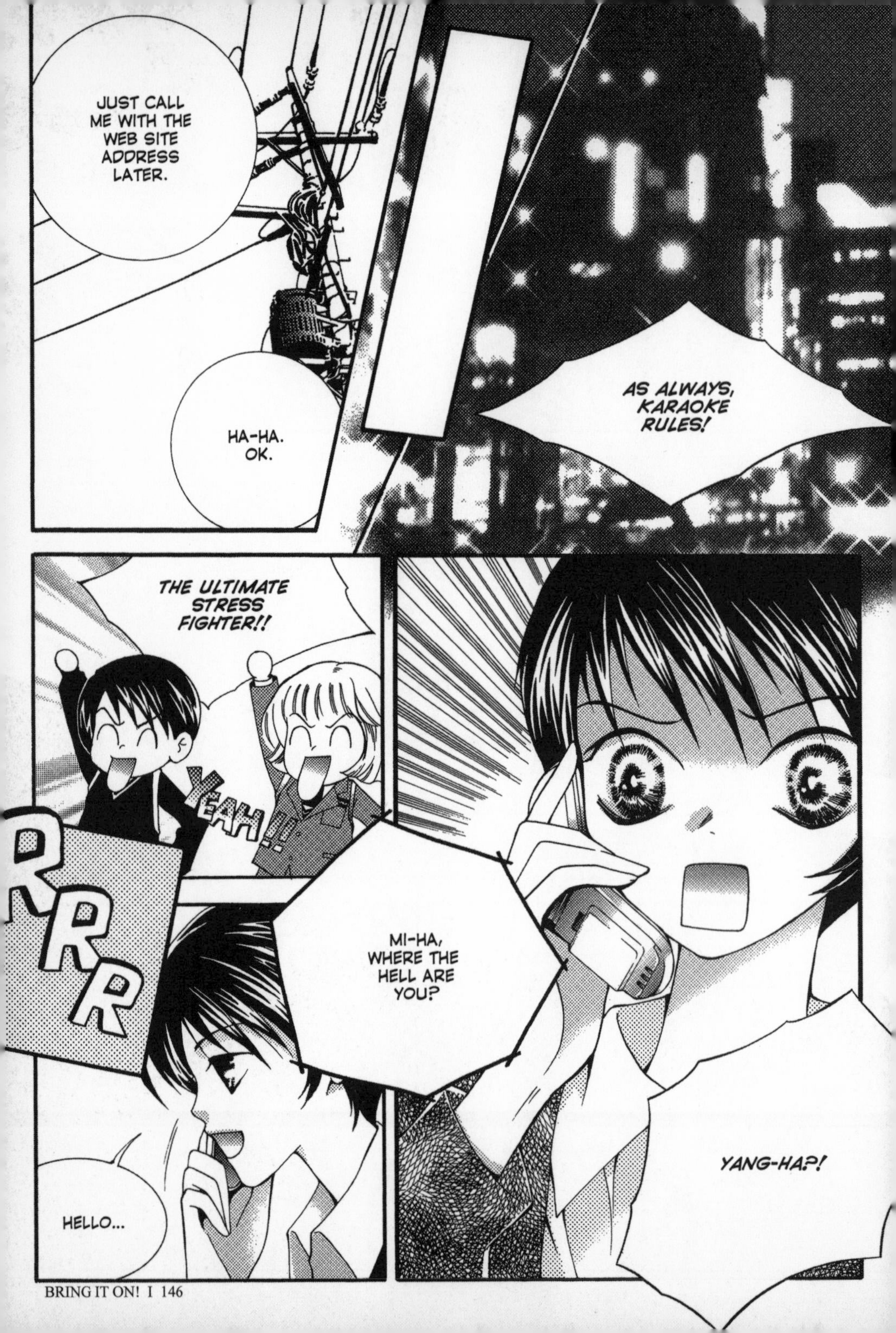
JUST CALL ME WITH THE WEB SITE ADDRESS LATER.
HA-HA. OK.
AS ALWAYS, KARAOKE RULES!
THE ULTIMATE STRESS FIGHTER!!
YEAH!!
RRR
HELLO...
MI-HA, WHERE THE HELL ARE YOU?
YANG-HA?!

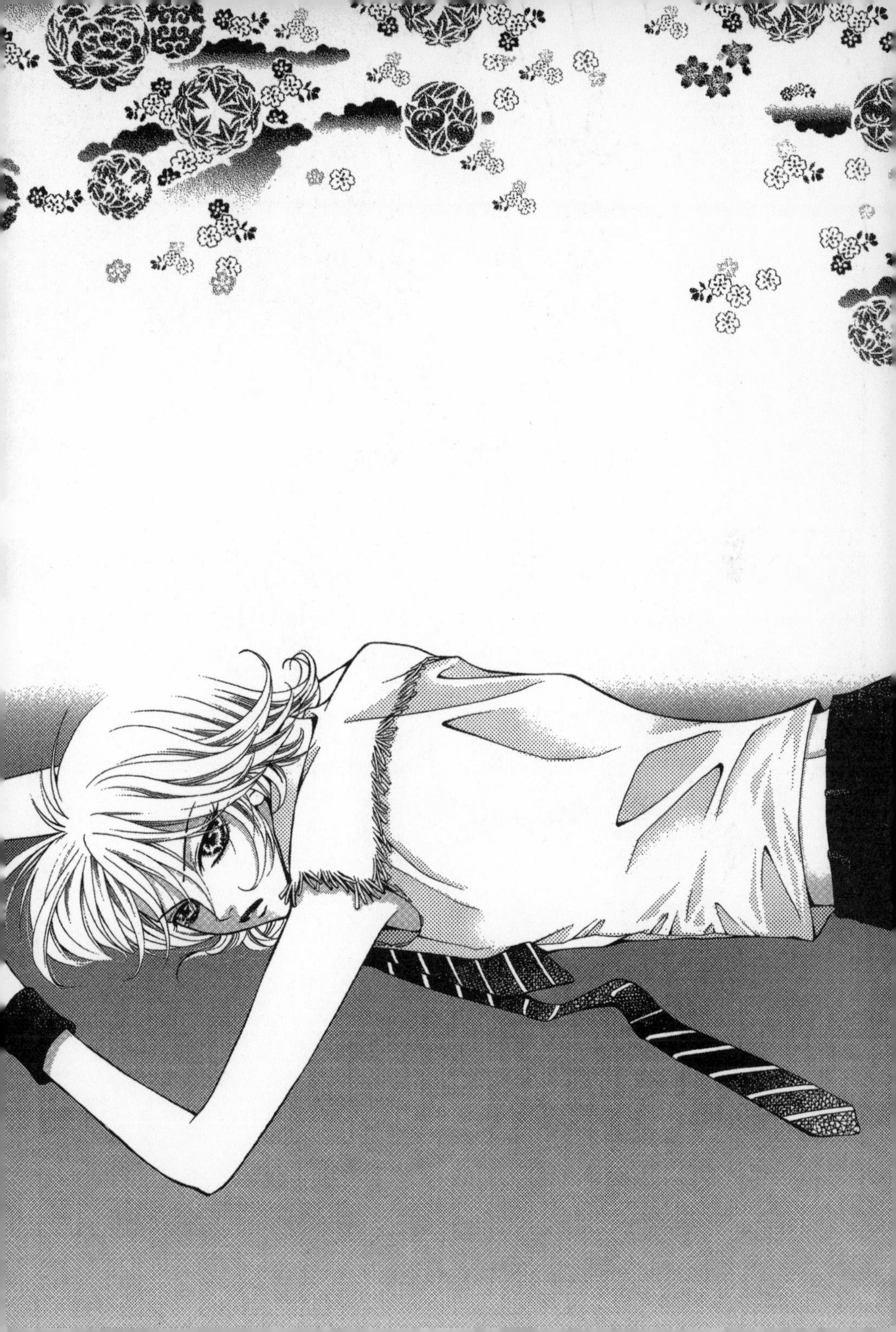

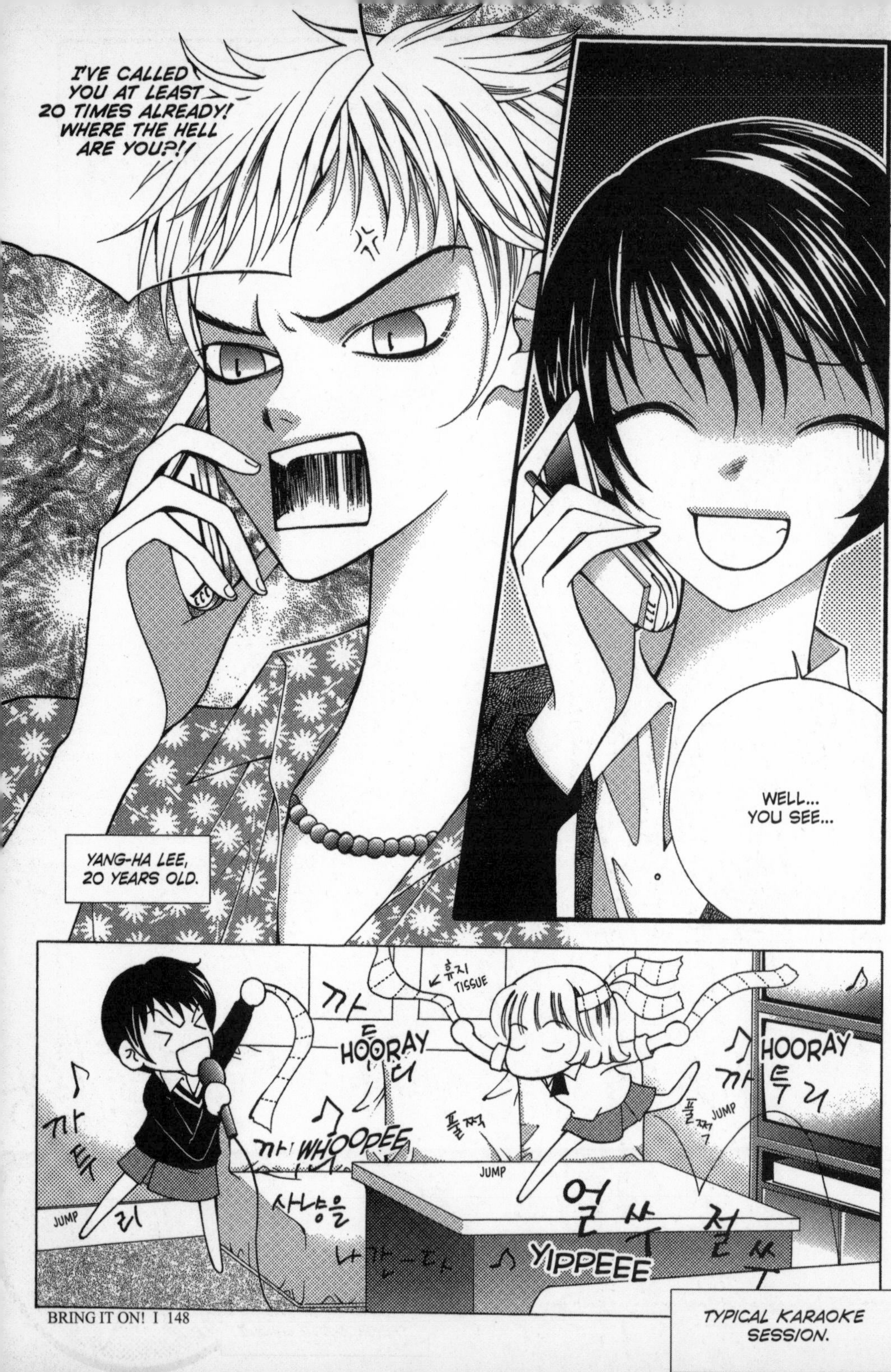
I'VE CALLED YOU AT LEAST 20 TIMES ALREADY! WHERE THE HELL ARE YOU?!!
YANG-HA LEE, 20 YEARS OLD.
WELL... YOU SEE...
까뚜리
휴지 TISSUE
까뚜리 HOORAY
HOORAY
까뚜리
까뚜리 WHOOPEE
폴짝
폴짝 JUMP
JUMP
JUMP
사냥을 나간다
얼쑤 절쑤
YIPPEEE
TYPICAL KARAOKE SESSION.

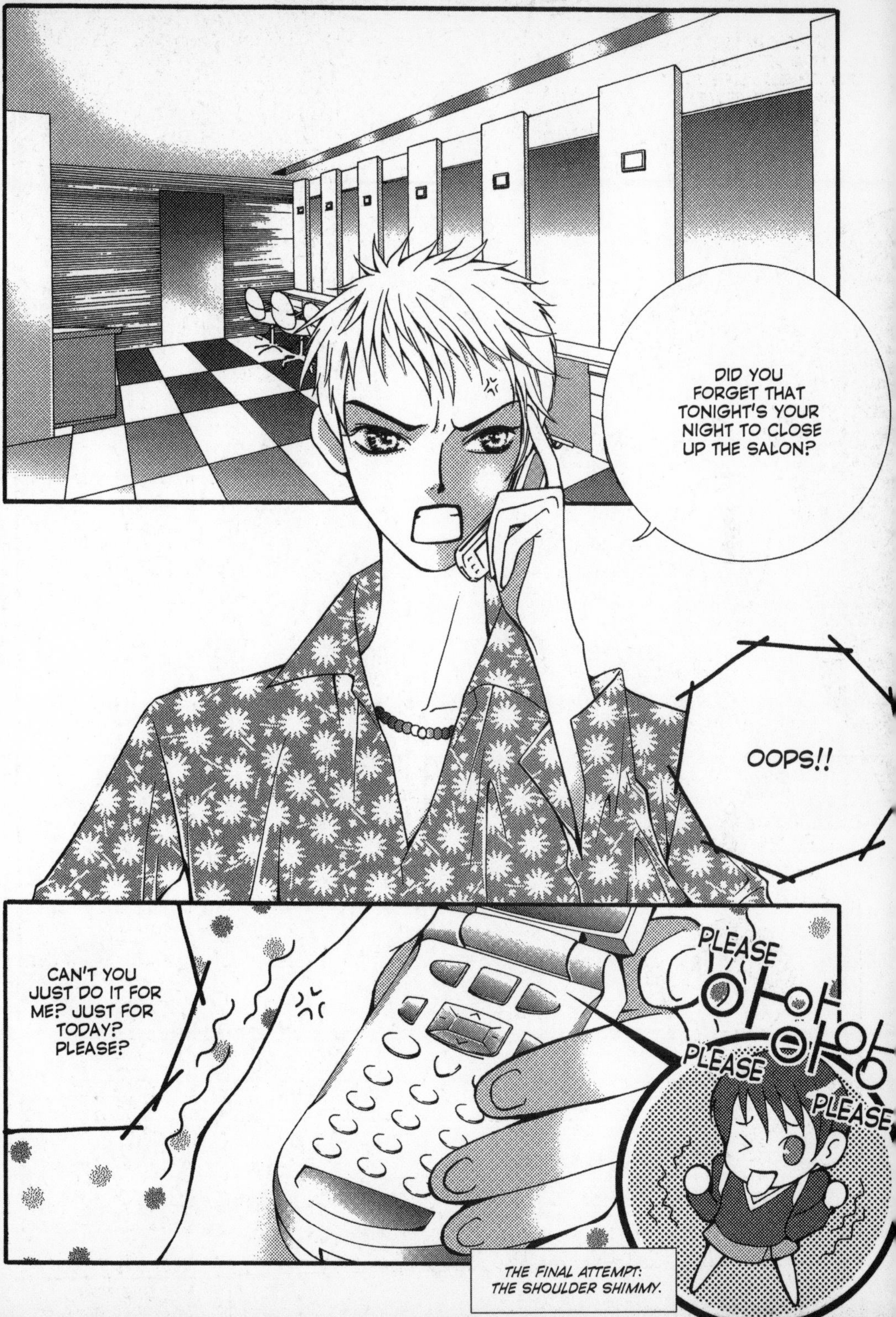

DID YOU FORGET THAT TONIGHT'S YOUR NIGHT TO CLOSE UP THE SALON?
OOPS!!
CAN'T YOU JUST DO IT FOR ME? JUST FOR TODAY? PLEASE?
PLEASE
PLEASE
PLEASE
THE FINAL ATTEMPT: THE SHOULDER SHIMMY.

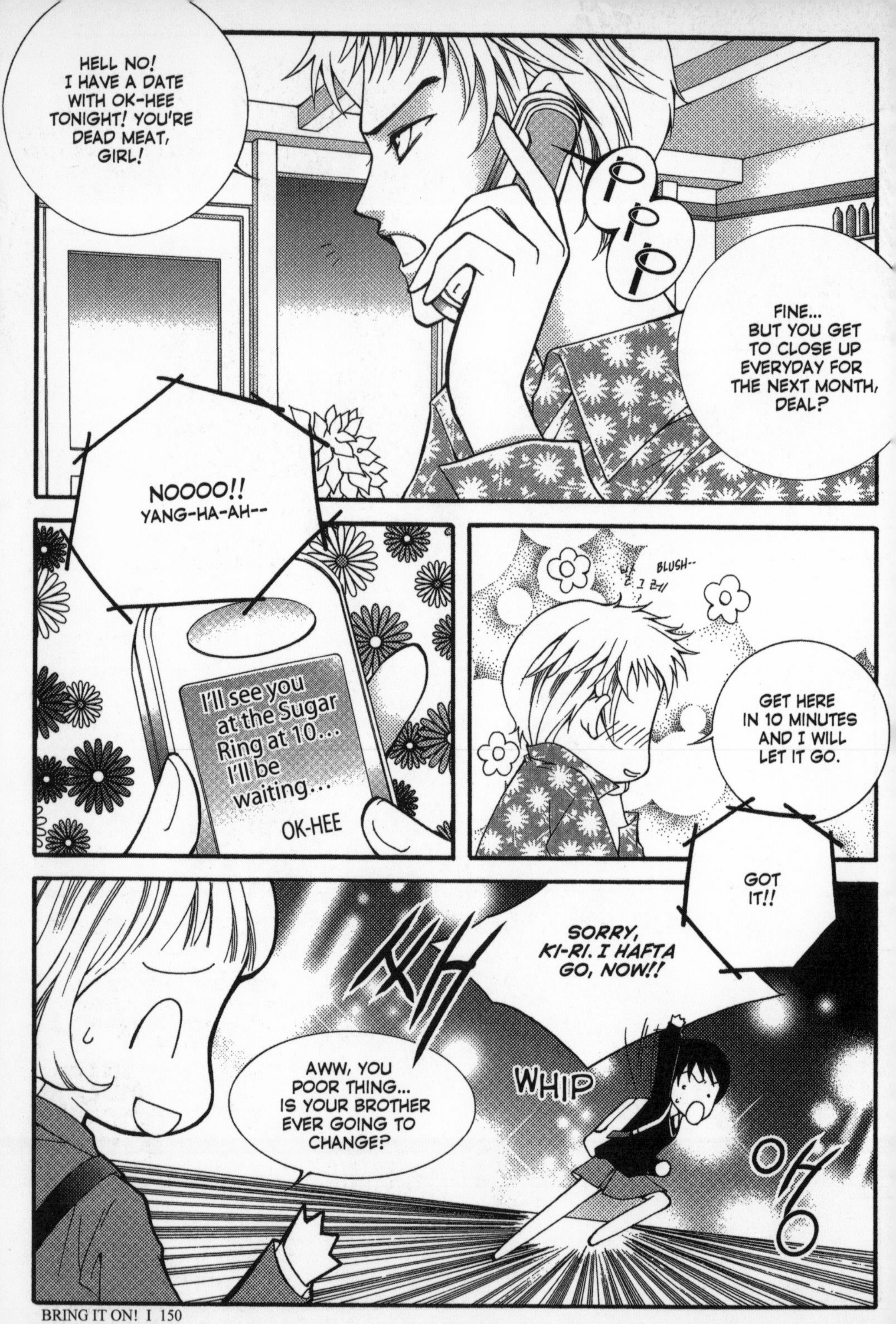
HELL NO! I HAVE A DATE WITH OK-HEE TONIGHT! YOU'RE DEAD MEAT, GIRL!
FINE... BUT YOU GET TO CLOSE UP EVERYDAY FOR THE NEXT MONTH, DEAL?
NOOOO!! YANG-HA-AH--
I'll see you at the Sugar Ring at 10... I'll be waiting...
OK-HEE
BLUSH--
GET HERE IN 10 MINUTES AND I WILL LET IT GO.
GOT IT!!
SORRY, KI-RI. I HAFTA GO, NOW!!
AWW, YOU POOR THING... IS YOUR BROTHER EVER GOING TO CHANGE?
WHIP

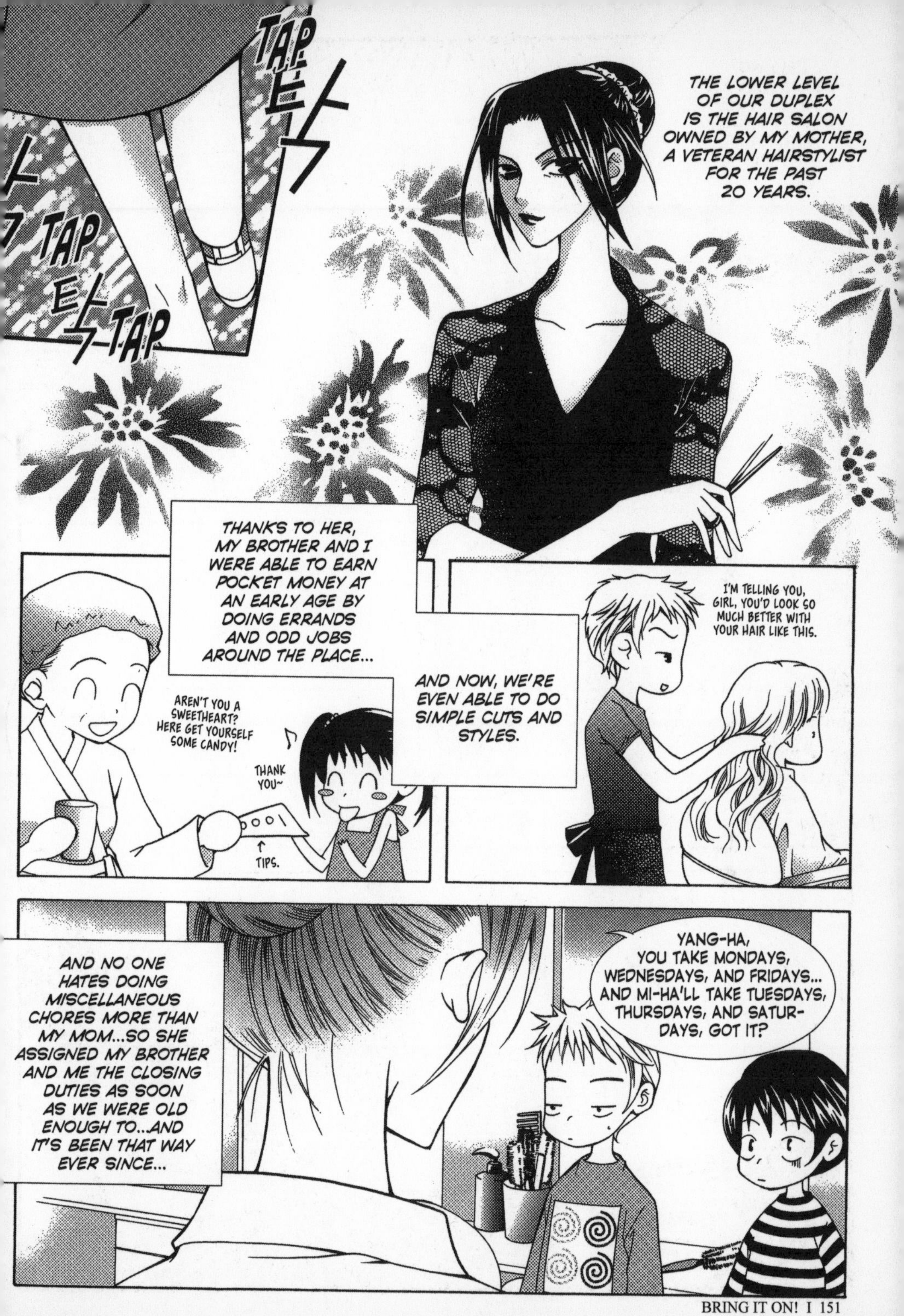
TAP
TAP
TAP
THE LOWER LEVEL OF OUR DUPLEX IS THE HAIR SALON OWNED BY MY MOTHER, A VETERAN HAIRSTYLIST FOR THE PAST 20 YEARS.
THANKS TO HER, MY BROTHER AND I WERE ABLE TO EARN POCKET MONEY AT AN EARLY AGE BY DOING ERRANDS AND ODD JOBS AROUND THE PLACE...
AREN'T YOU A SWEETHEART? HERE GET YOURSELF SOME CANDY!
THANK YOU~
TIPS.
AND NOW, WE'RE EVEN ABLE TO DO SIMPLE CUTS AND STYLES.
I'M TELLING YOU, GIRL, YOU'D LOOK SO MUCH BETTER WITH YOUR HAIR LIKE THIS.
AND NO ONE HATES DOING MISCELLANEOUS CHORES MORE THAN MY MOM...SO SHE ASSIGNED MY BROTHER AND ME THE CLOSING DUTIES AS SOON AS WE WERE OLD ENOUGH TO...AND IT'S BEEN THAT WAY EVER SINCE...
YANG-HA, YOU TAKE MONDAYS, WEDNESDAYS, AND FRIDAYS... AND MI-HA'LL TAKE TUESDAYS, THURSDAYS, AND SATUR-DAYS, GOT IT?

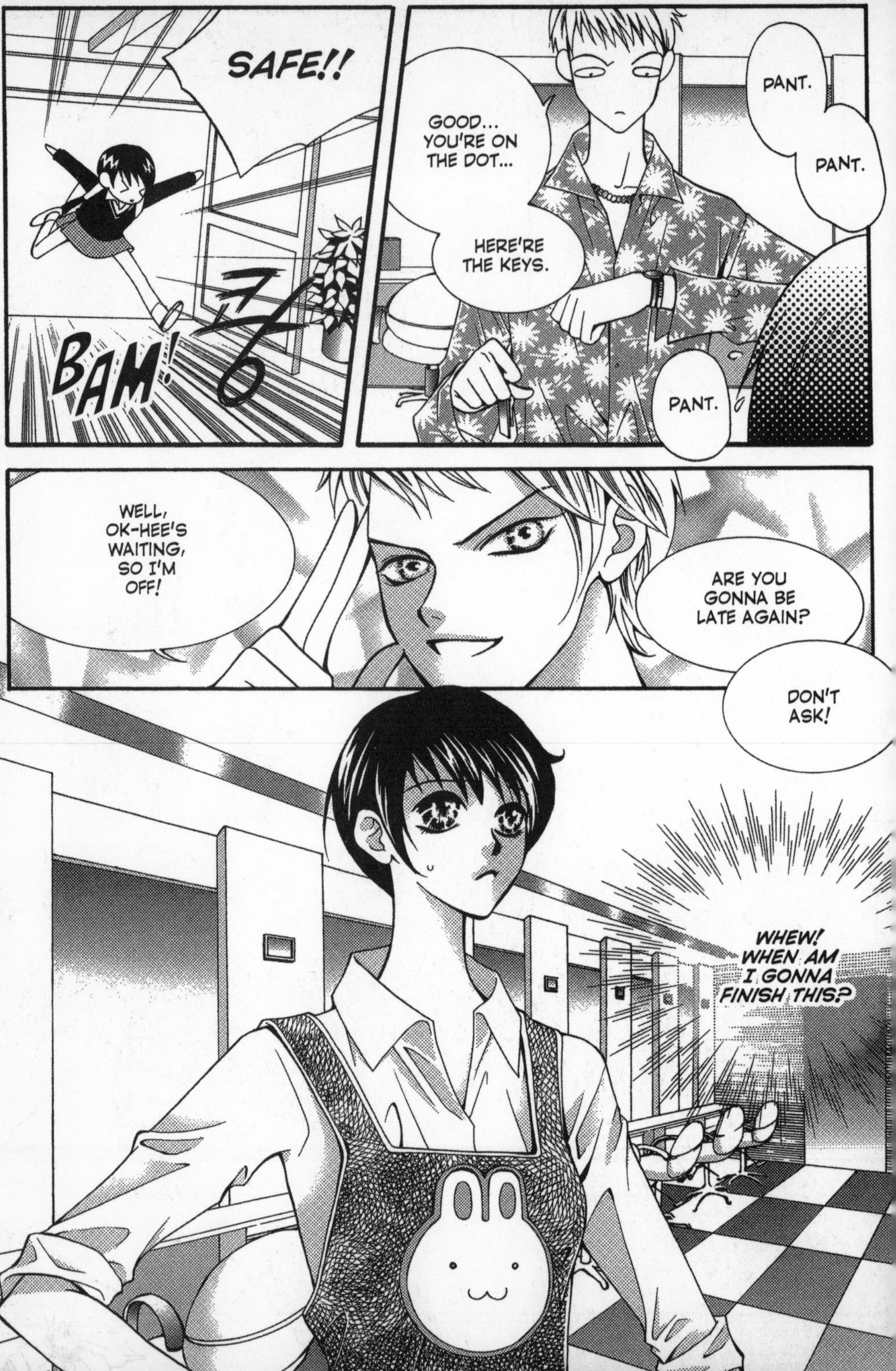
SAFE!!
BAM!
GOOD... YOU'RE ON THE DOT...
HERE'RE THE KEYS.
PANT.
PANT.
PANT.
WELL, OK-HEE'S WAITING, SO I'M OFF!
ARE YOU GONNA BE LATE AGAIN?
DON'T ASK!
WHEW! WHEN AM I GONNA FINISH THIS?

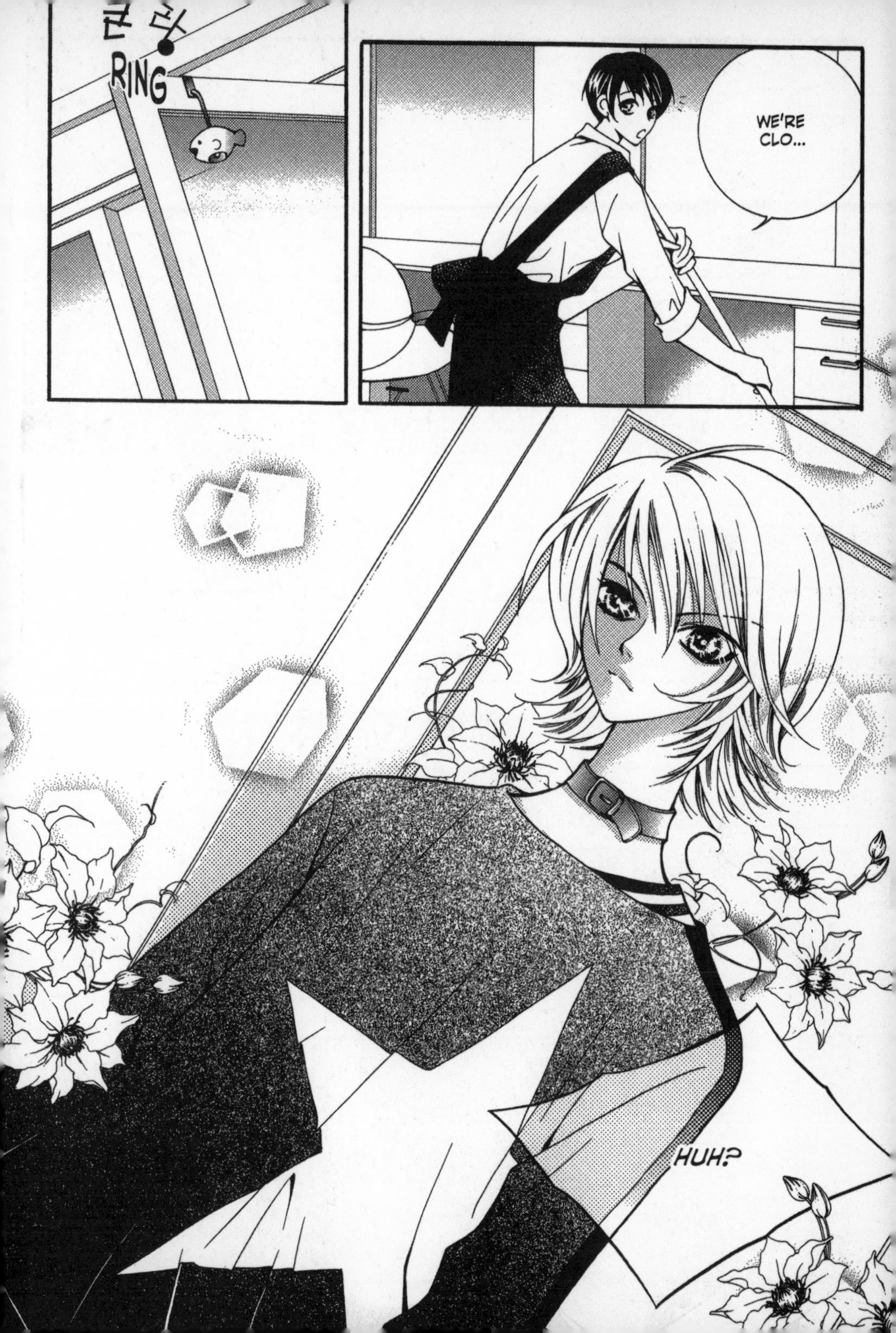
딸랑
RING
WE'RE CLO...
HUH?

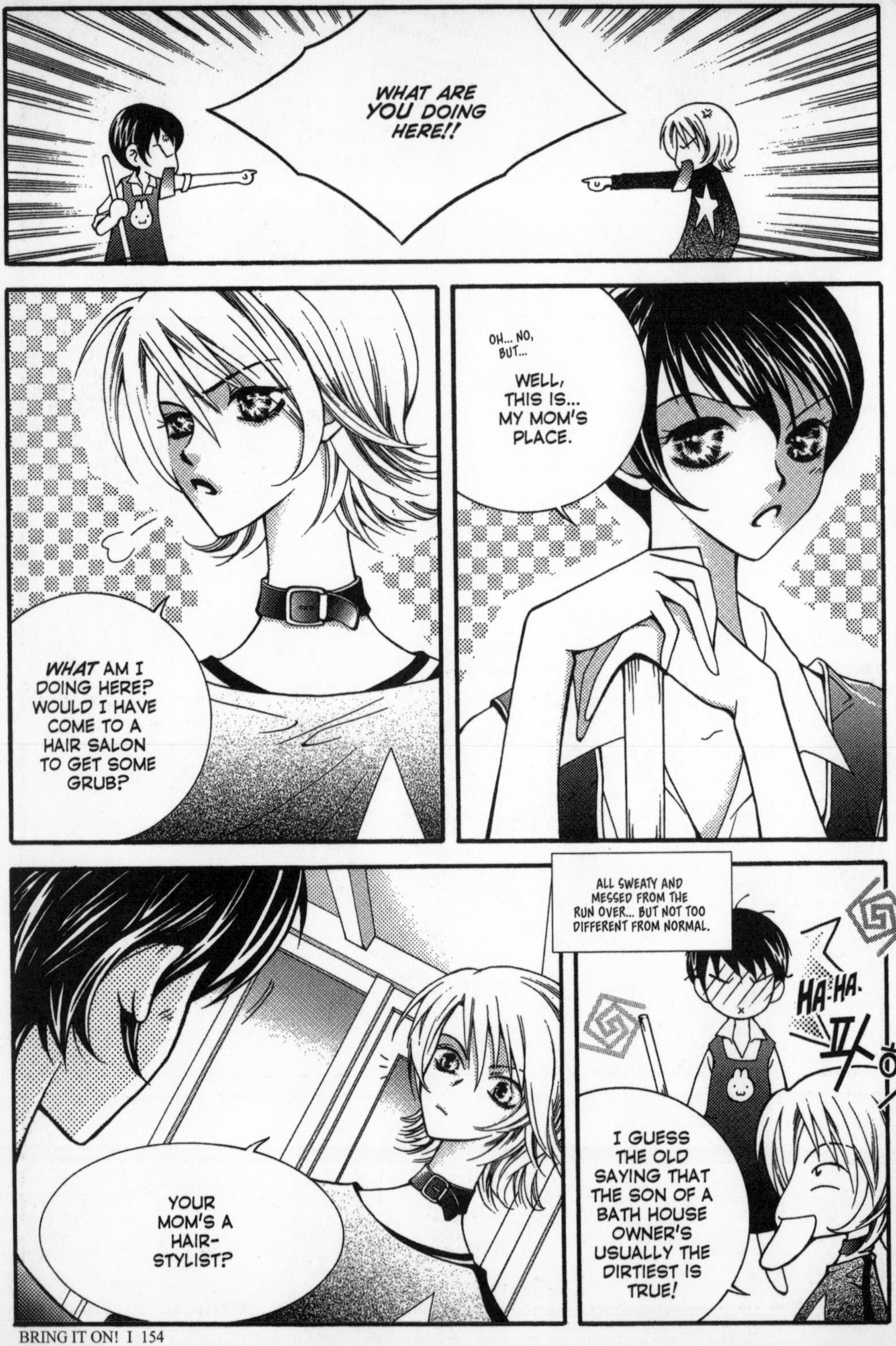
WHAT ARE YOU DOING HERE!!
WHAT AM I DOING HERE? WOULD I HAVE COME TO A HAIR SALON TO GET SOME GRUB?
OH... NO, BUT...
WELL, THIS IS... MY MOM'S PLACE.
YOUR MOM'S A HAIR-STYLIST?
ALL SWEATY AND MESSED FROM THE RUN OVER... BUT NOT TOO DIFFERENT FROM NORMAL.
HA-HA.
I GUESS THE OLD SAYING THAT THE SON OF A BATH HOUSE OWNER'S USUALLY THE DIRTIEST IS TRUE!

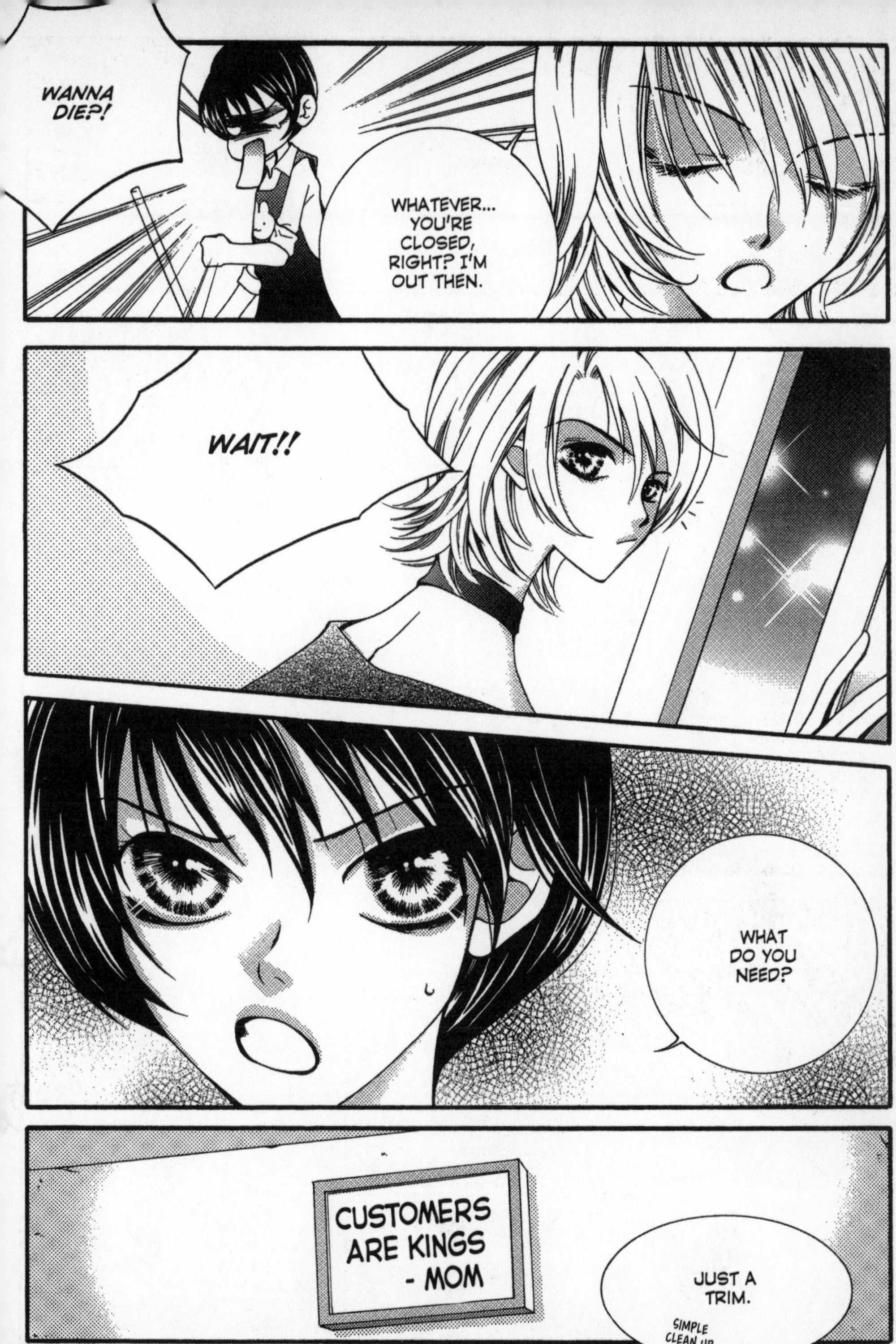
WANNA DIE?!
WHATEVER... YOU'RE CLOSED, RIGHT? I'M OUT THEN.
WAIT!!
WHAT DO YOU NEED?
CUSTOMERS ARE KINGS - MOM
JUST A TRIM.
SIMPLE CLEAN UP.

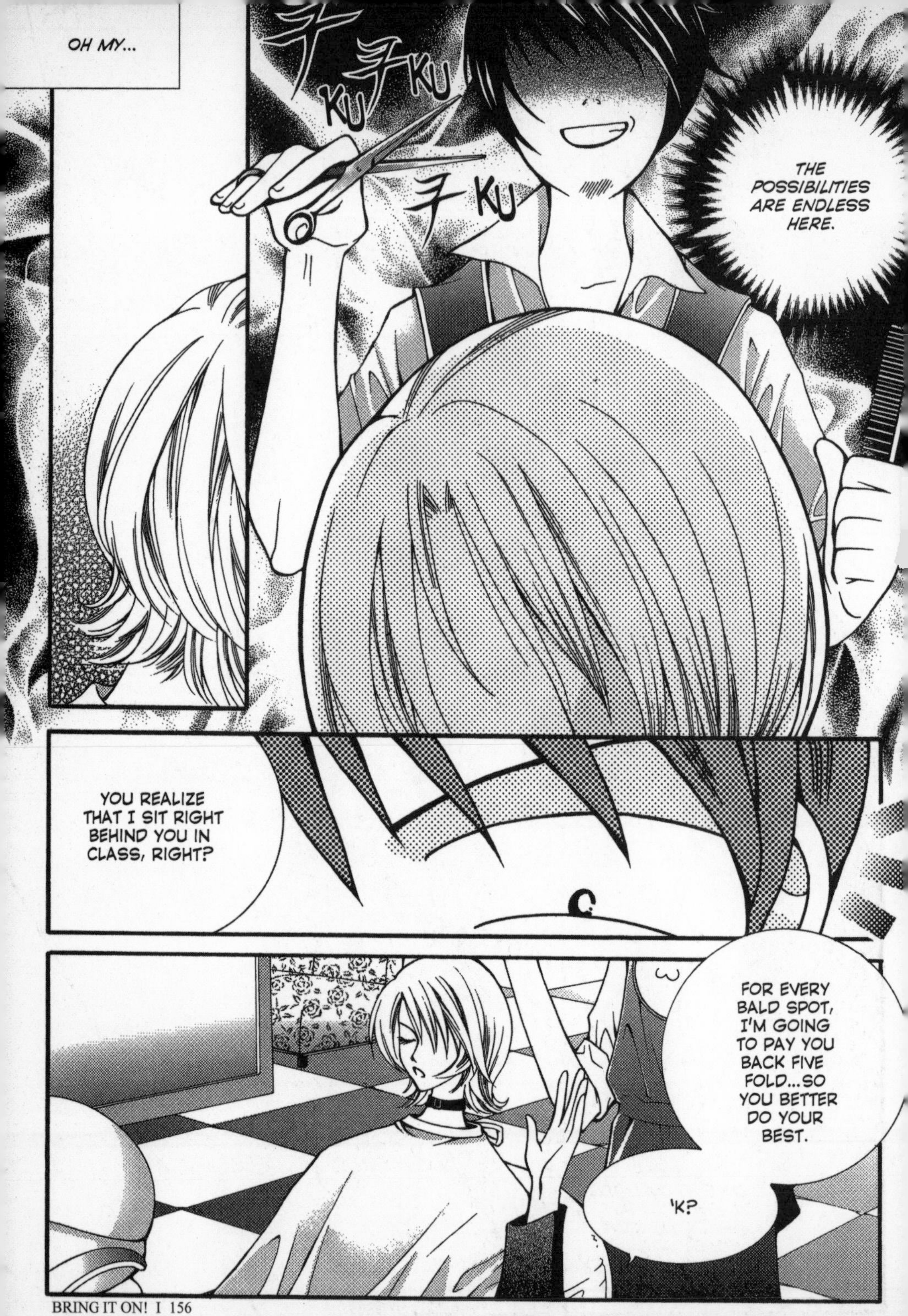
OH MY...
KU KU
KU
THE POSSIBILITIES ARE ENDLESS HERE.
YOU REALIZE THAT I SIT RIGHT BEHIND YOU IN CLASS, RIGHT?
FOR EVERY BALD SPOT, I'M GOING TO PAY YOU BACK FIVE FOLD...SO YOU BETTER DO YOUR BEST.
'K?

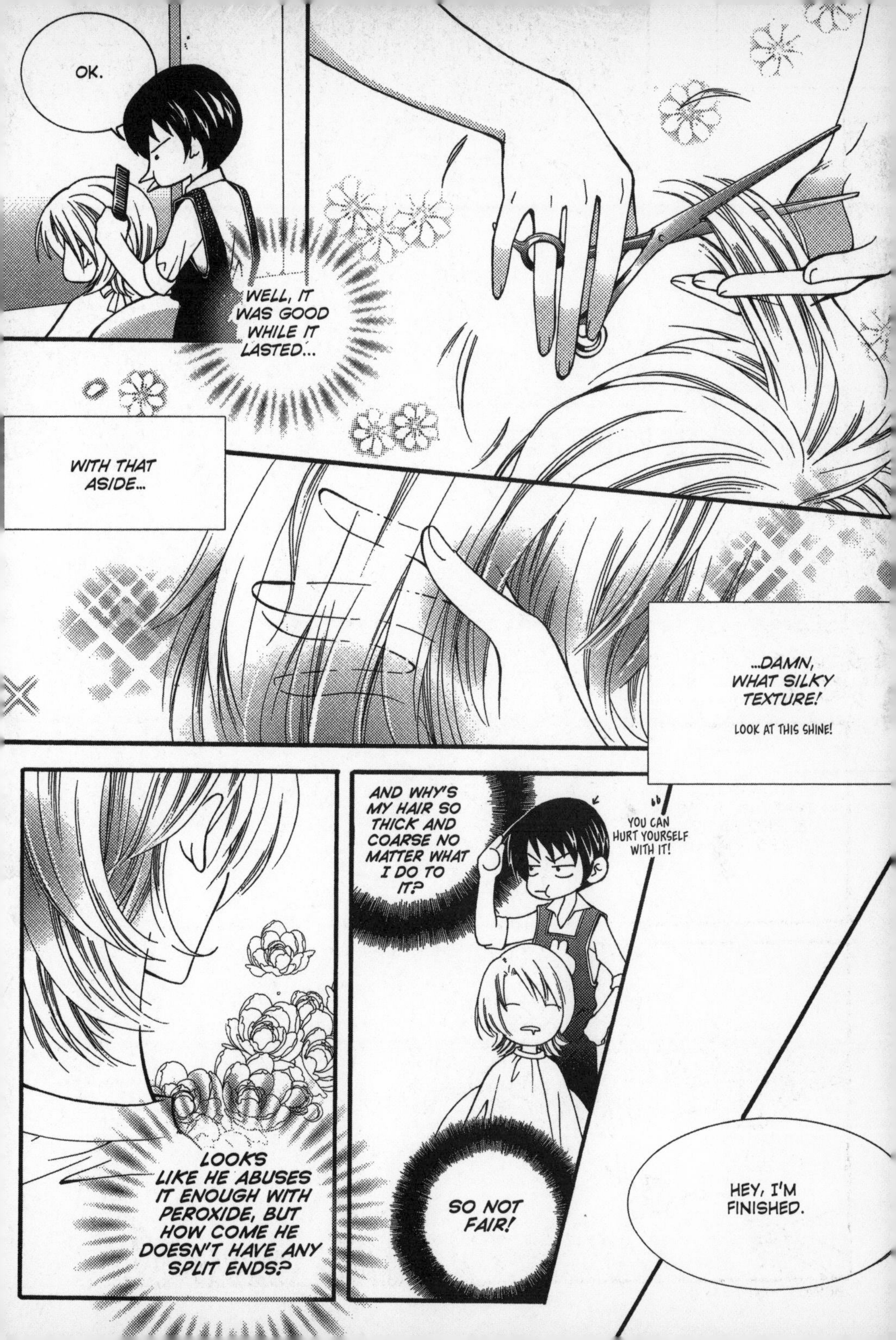
OK.
WELL, IT WAS GOOD WHILE IT LASTED...
WITH THAT ASIDE...
...DAMN, WHAT SILKY TEXTURE!
LOOK AT THIS SHINE!
LOOKS LIKE HE ABUSES IT ENOUGH WITH PEROXIDE, BUT HOW COME HE DOESN'T HAVE ANY SPLIT ENDS?
AND WHY'S MY HAIR SO THICK AND COARSE NO MATTER WHAT I DO TO IT?
YOU CAN HURT YOURSELF WITH IT!
SO NOT FAIR!
HEY, I'M FINISHED.

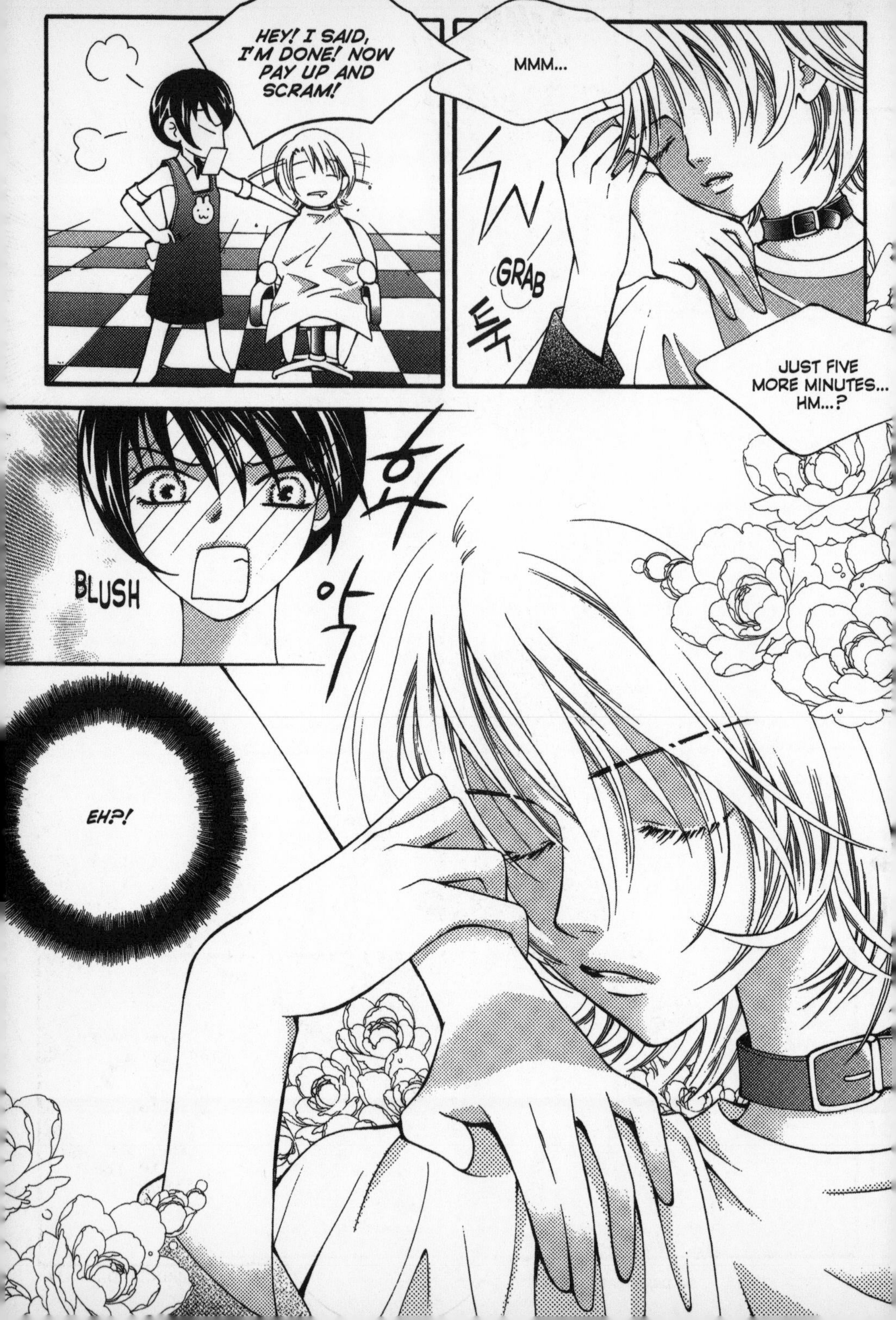
HEY! I SAID, I'M DONE! NOW PAY UP AND SCRAM!
MMM...
GRAB
툭
JUST FIVE MORE MINUTES... HM...?
BLUSH
화악
EH?!

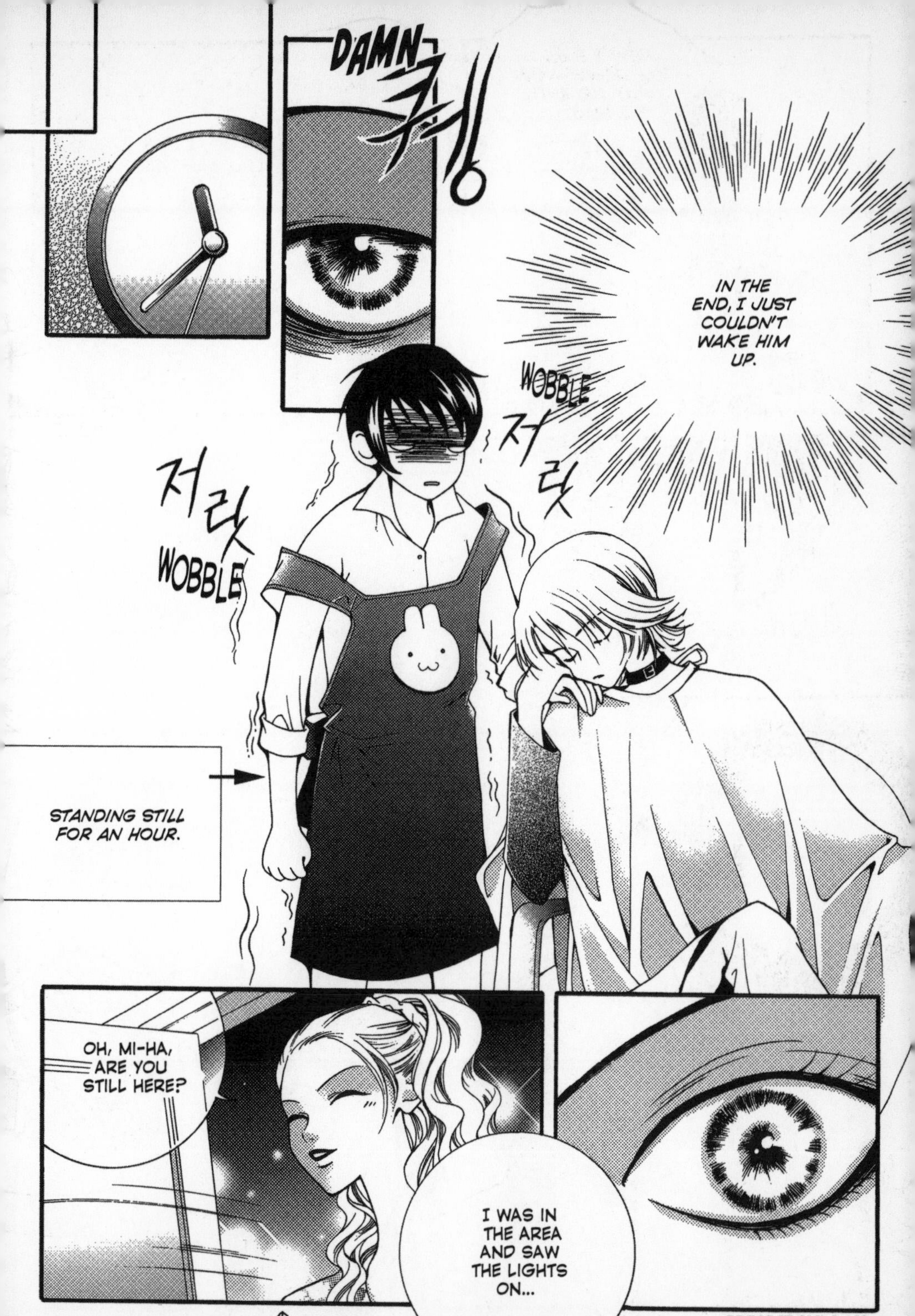

DAMN
IN THE END, I JUST COULDN'T WAKE HIM UP.
저랏
WOBBLE
WOBBLE
저랏
STANDING STILL FOR AN HOUR.
OH, MI-HA, ARE YOU STILL HERE?
I WAS IN THE AREA AND SAW THE LIGHTS ON...
MISS KIM, ONE OF THE STYLISTS

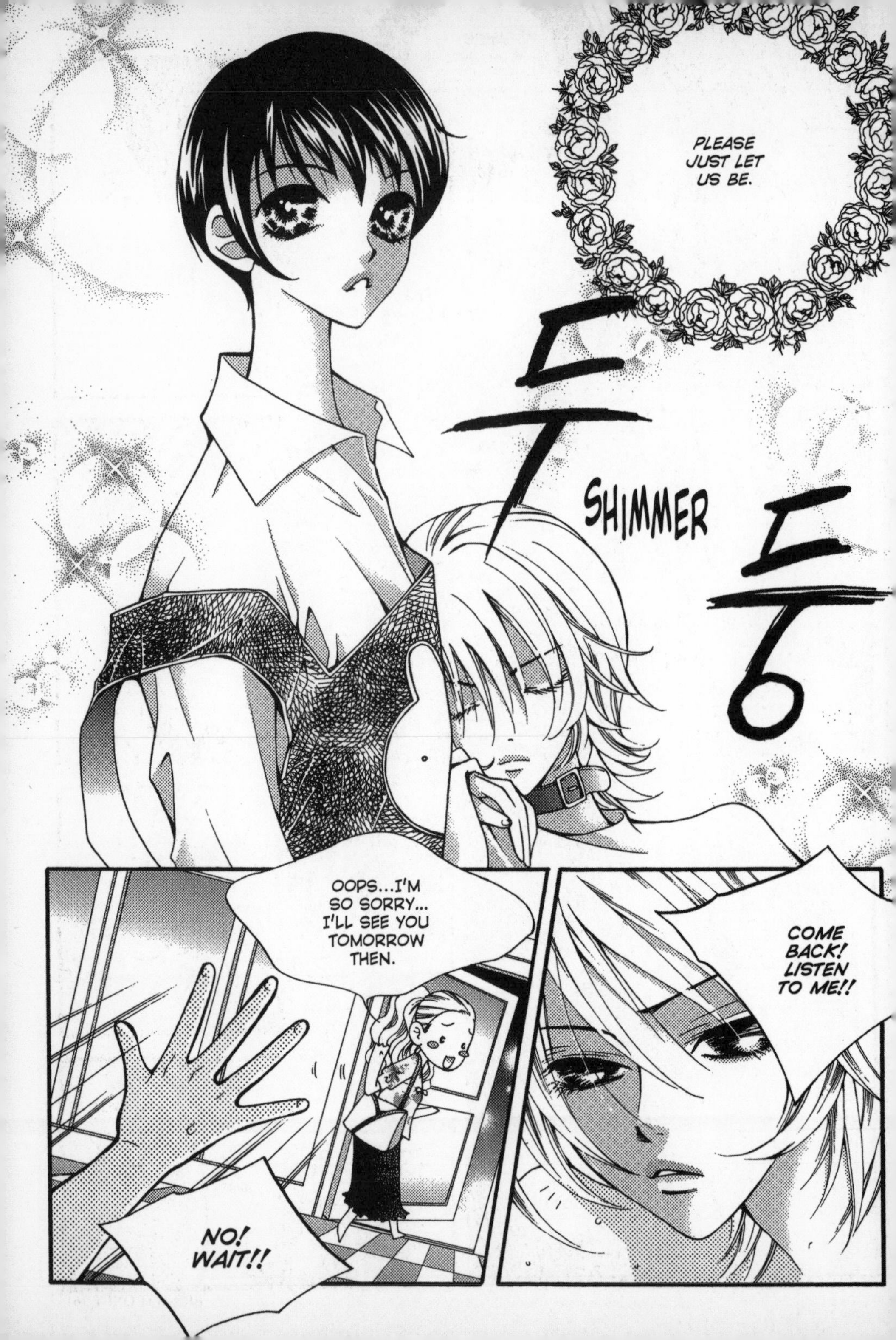
PLEASE JUST LET US BE.
SHIMMER
OOPS...I'M SO SORRY... I'LL SEE YOU TOMORROW THEN.
NO! WAIT!!
COME BACK! LISTEN TO ME!!

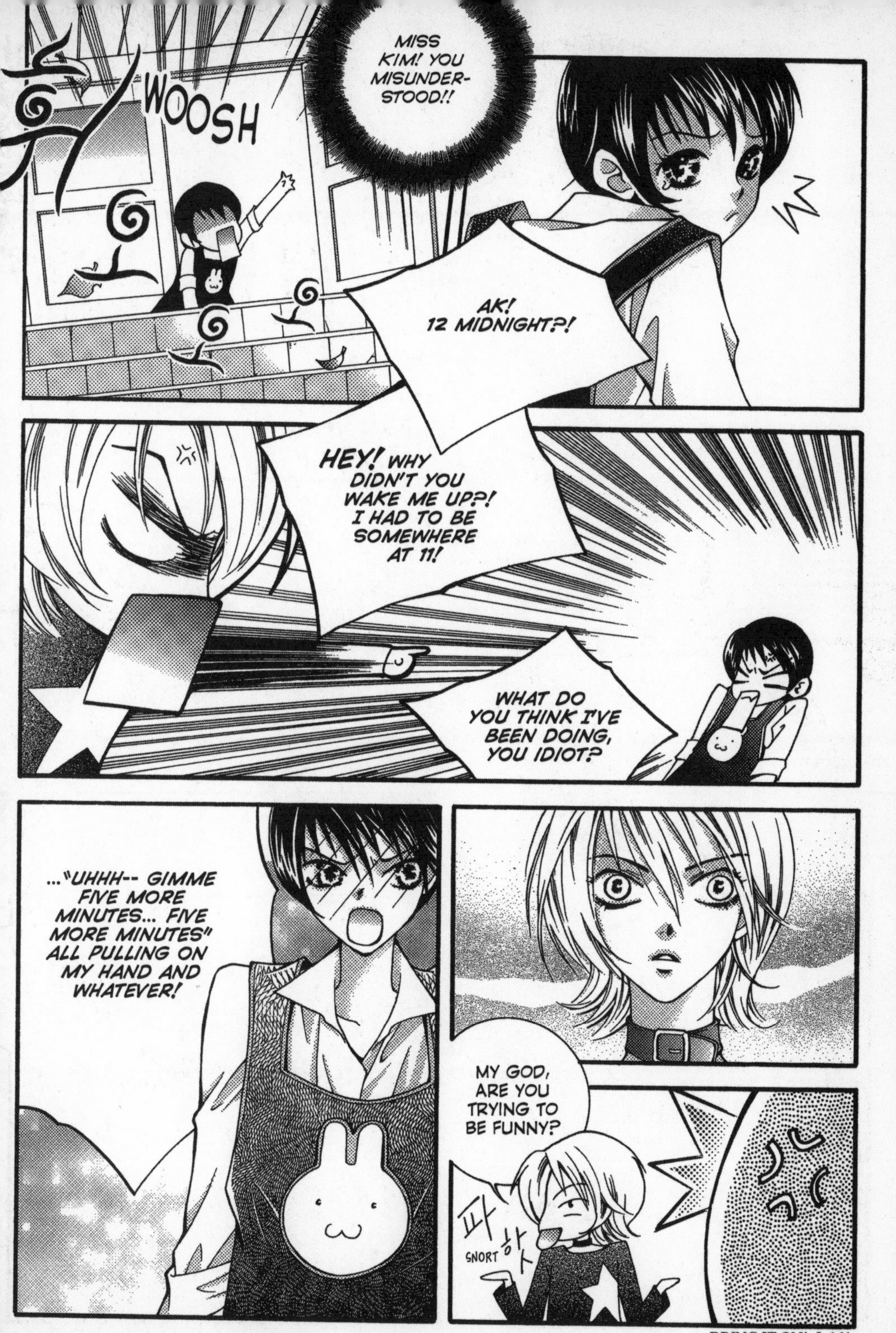
WOOSH
MISS KIM! YOU MISUNDER-STOOD!!
AK! 12 MIDNIGHT?!
HEY! WHY DIDN'T YOU WAKE ME UP?! I HAD TO BE SOMEWHERE AT 11!
WHAT DO YOU THINK I'VE BEEN DOING, YOU IDIOT?
..."UHHH-- GIMME FIVE MORE MINUTES... FIVE MORE MINUTES" ALL PULLING ON MY HAND AND WHATEVER!
MY GOD, ARE YOU TRYING TO BE FUNNY?
파핫
SNORT

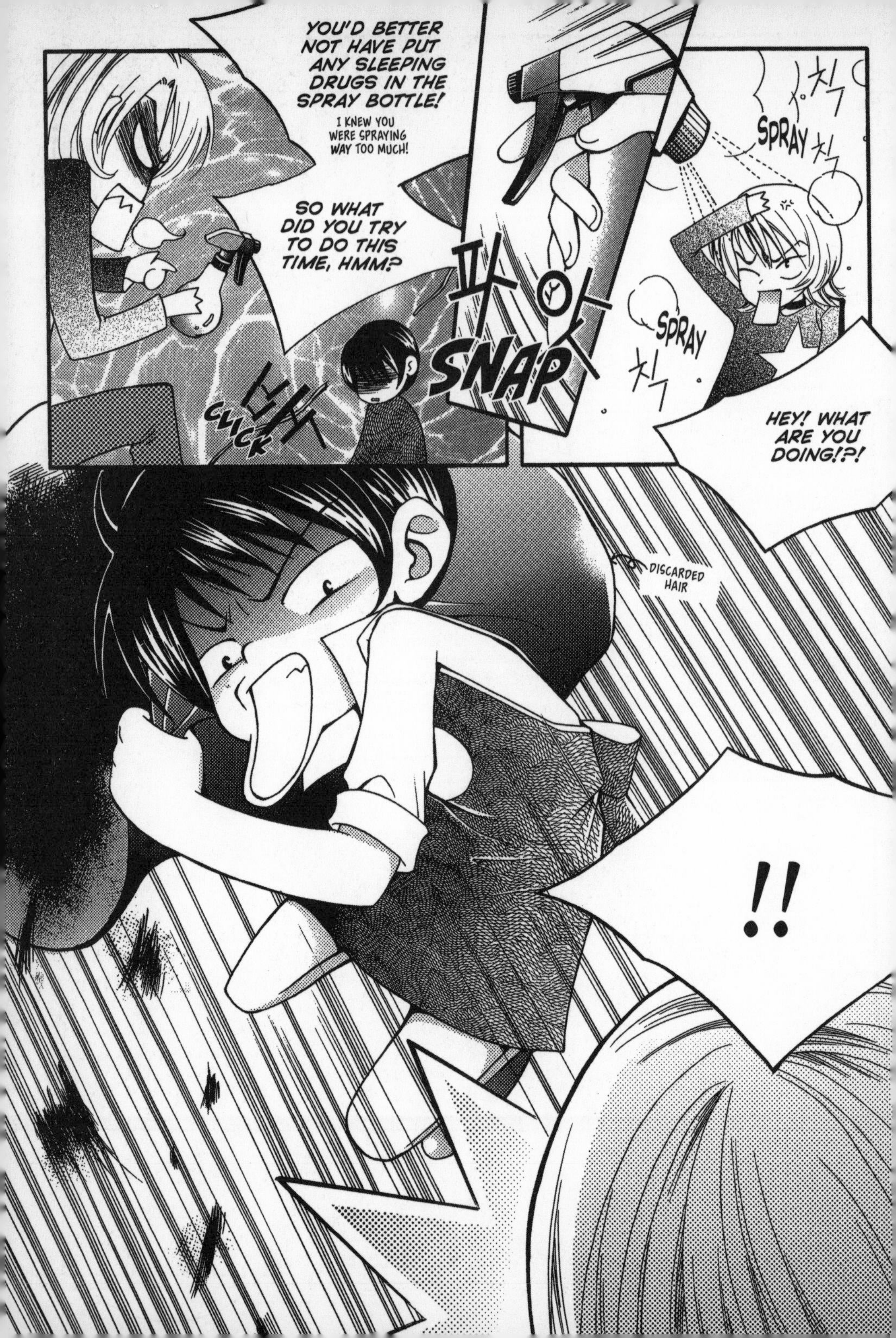
YOU'D BETTER NOT HAVE PUT ANY SLEEPING DRUGS IN THE SPRAY BOTTLE!
I KNEW YOU WERE SPRAYING WAY TOO MUCH!
SO WHAT DID YOU TRY TO DO THIS TIME, HMM?
CLICK
SNAP
SPRAY
SPRAY
HEY! WHAT ARE YOU DOING!?!
DISCARDED HAIR
!!

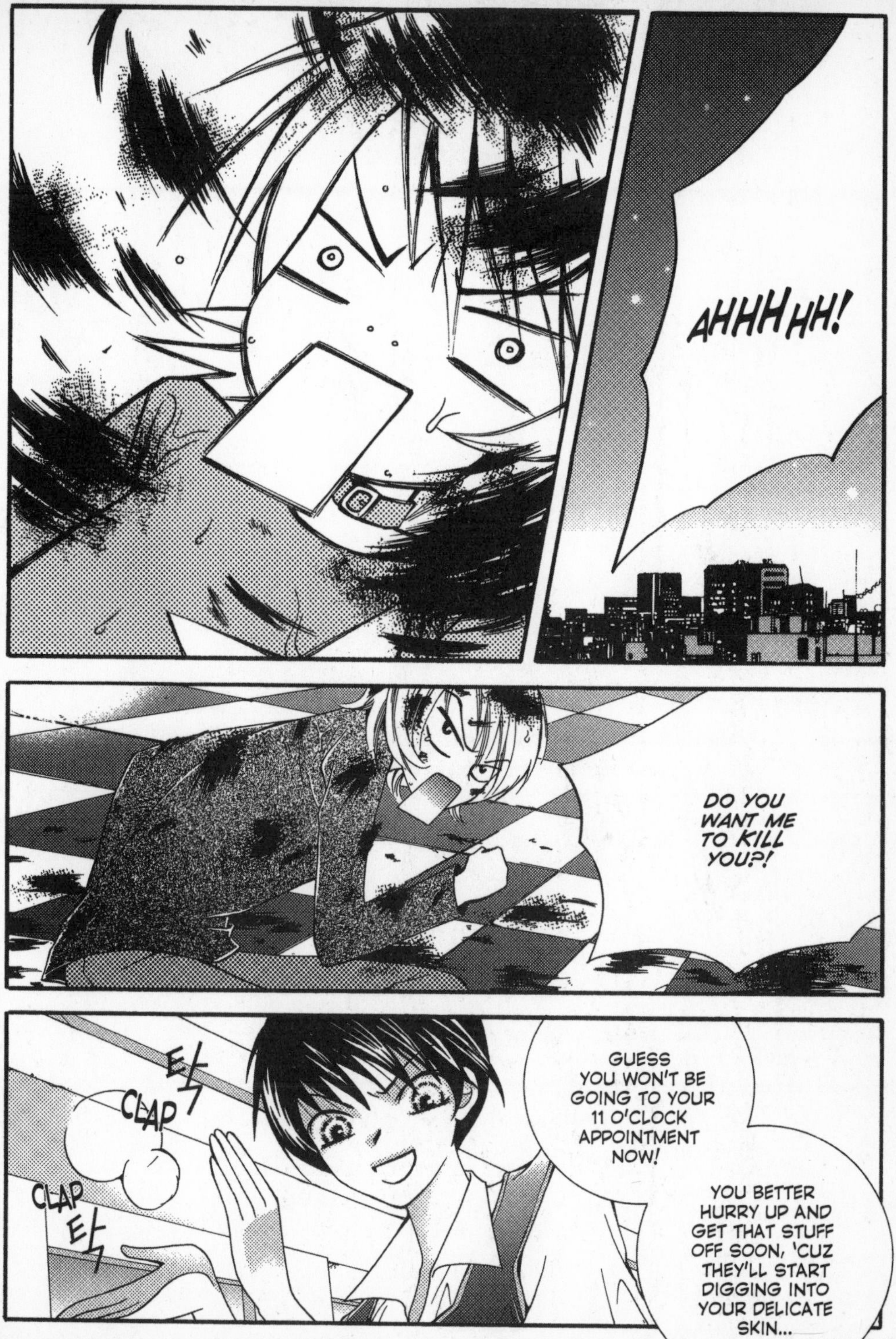
AHHHHH!
DO YOU WANT ME TO KILL YOU?!
GUESS YOU WON'T BE GOING TO YOUR 11 O'CLOCK APPOINTMENT NOW!
CLAP
CLAP
YOU BETTER HURRY UP AND GET THAT STUFF OFF SOON, 'CUZ THEY'LL START DIGGING INTO YOUR DELICATE SKIN...

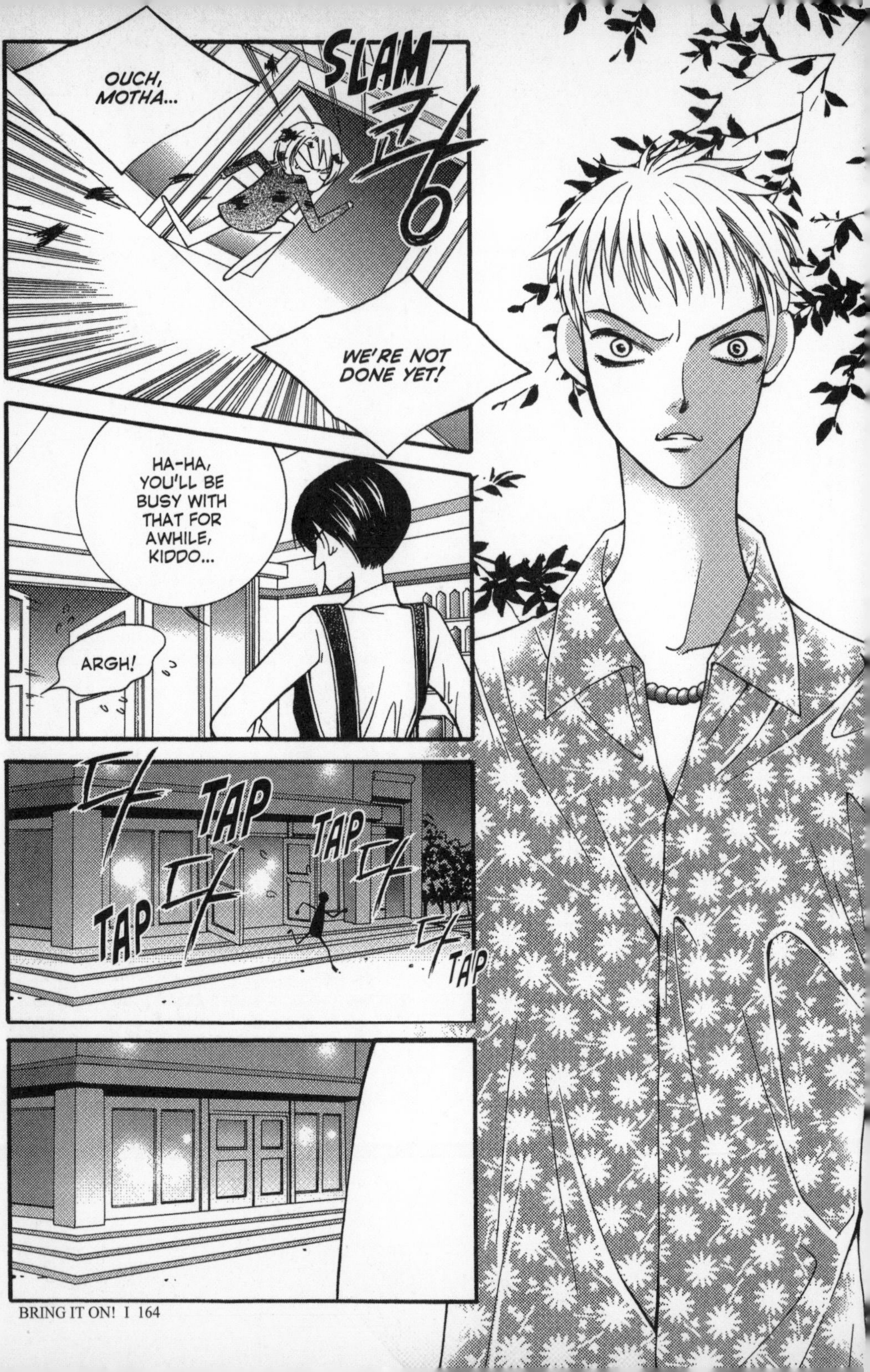
OUCH, MOTHA...
SLAM
WE'RE NOT DONE YET!
HA-HA, YOU'LL BE BUSY WITH THAT FOR AWHILE, KIDDO...
ARGH!
TAP
TAP
TAP
TAP
TAP

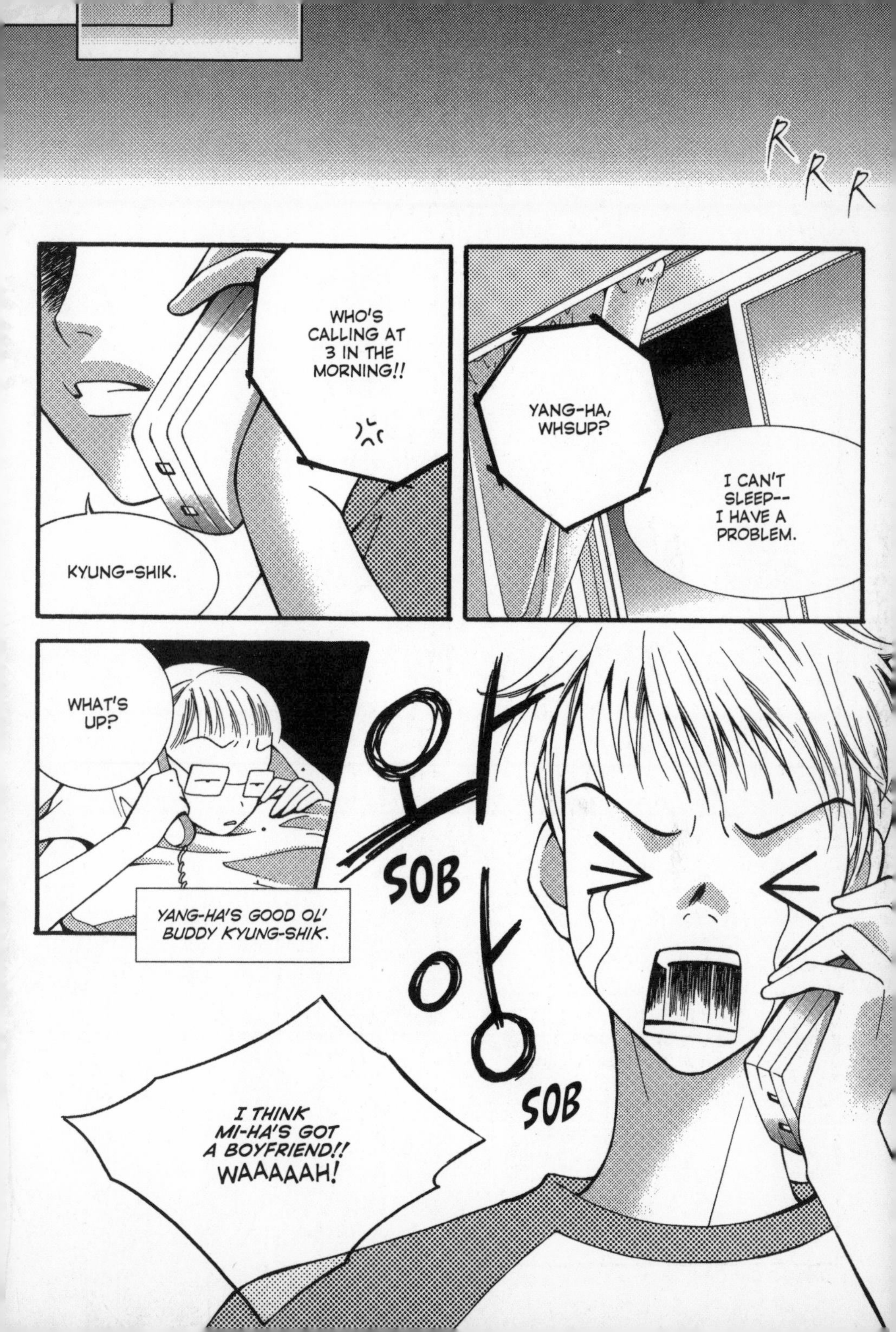
RRR
WHO'S CALLING AT 3 IN THE MORNING!!
KYUNG-SHIK.
YANG-HA, WHSUP?
I CAN'T SLEEP-- I HAVE A PROBLEM.
WHAT'S UP?
YANG-HA'S GOOD OL' BUDDY KYUNG-SHIK.
SOB
SOB
I THINK MI-HA'S GOT A BOYFRIEND!! WAAAAAH!

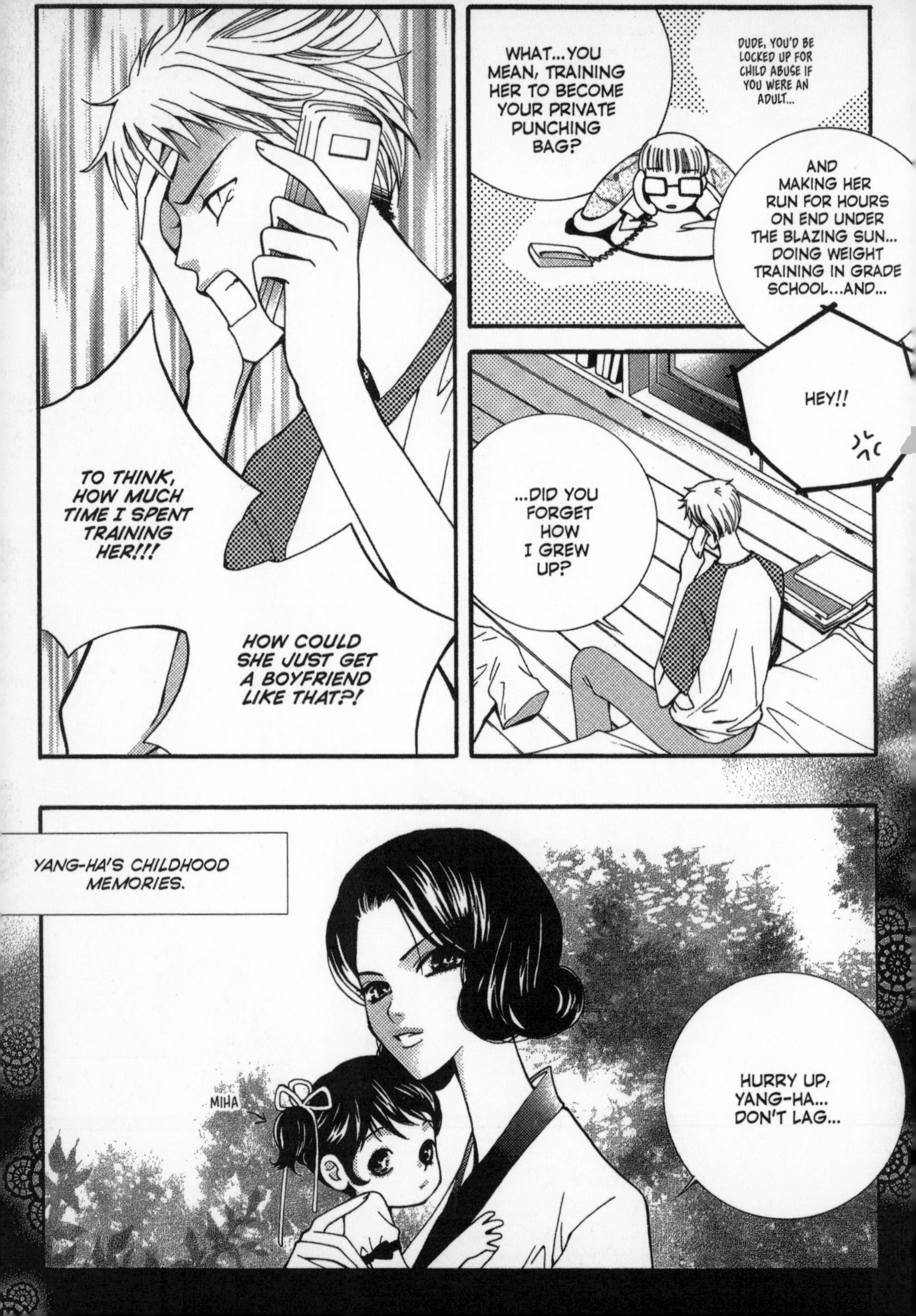
TO THINK, HOW MUCH TIME I SPENT TRAINING HER!!!
HOW COULD SHE JUST GET A BOYFRIEND LIKE THAT?!
WHAT...YOU MEAN, TRAINING HER TO BECOME YOUR PRIVATE PUNCHING BAG?
DUDE, YOU'D BE LOCKED UP FOR CHILD ABUSE IF YOU WERE AN ADULT...
AND MAKING HER RUN FOR HOURS ON END UNDER THE BLAZING SUN... DOING WEIGHT TRAINING IN GRADE SCHOOL...AND...
HEY!!
...DID YOU FORGET HOW I GREW UP?
YANG-HA'S CHILDHOOD MEMORIES.
MIHA
HURRY UP, YANG-HA... DON'T LAG...

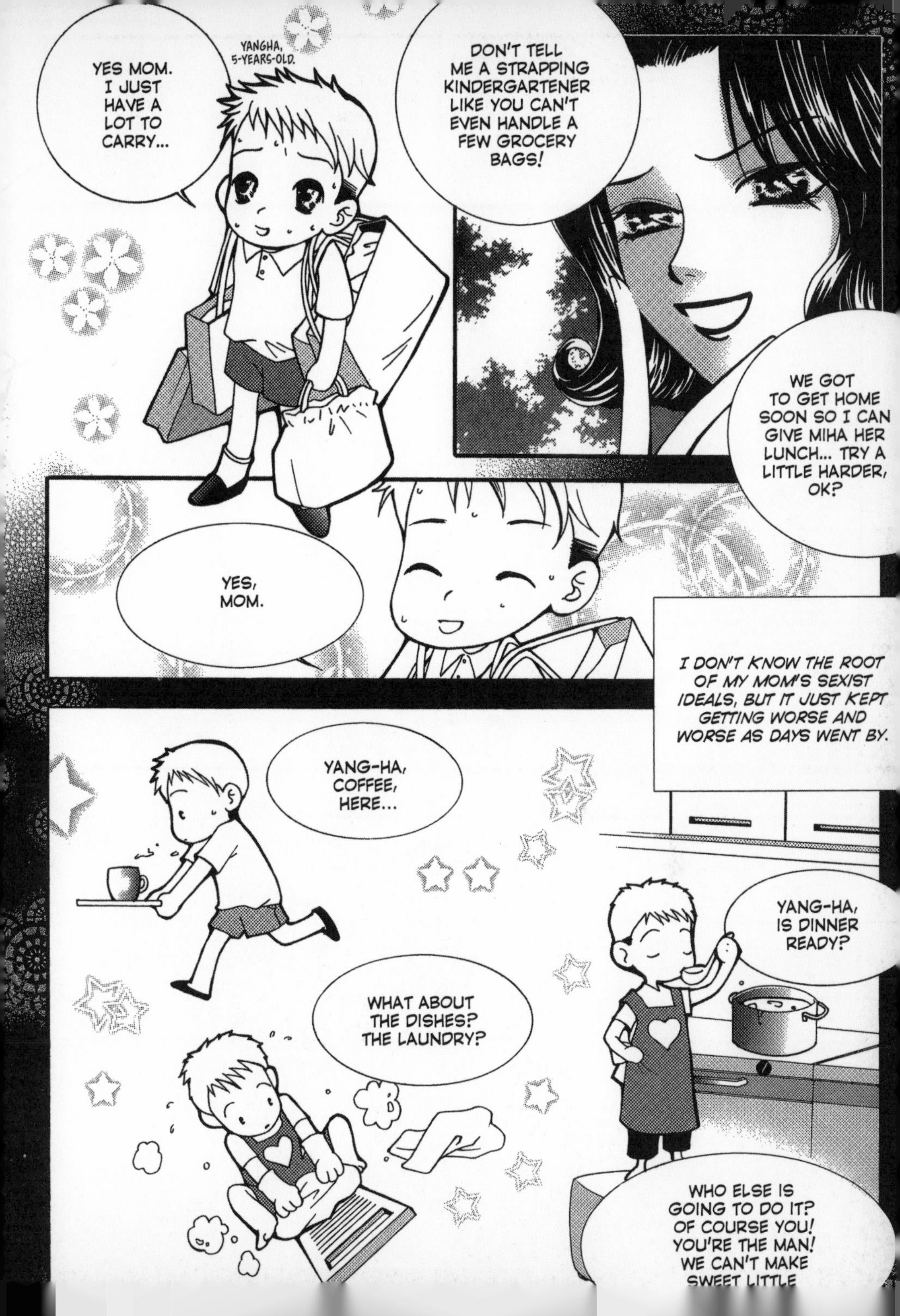
YES MOM. I JUST HAVE A LOT TO CARRY...
YANGHA, 5-YEARS-OLD.
DON'T TELL ME A STRAPPING KINDERGARTENER LIKE YOU CAN'T EVEN HANDLE A FEW GROCERY BAGS!
WE GOT TO GET HOME SOON SO I CAN GIVE MIHA HER LUNCH... TRY A LITTLE HARDER, OK?
YES, MOM.
I DON'T KNOW THE ROOT OF MY MOM'S SEXIST IDEALS, BUT IT JUST KEPT GETTING WORSE AND WORSE AS DAYS WENT BY.
YANG-HA, COFFEE, HERE...
YANG-HA, IS DINNER READY?
WHAT ABOUT THE DISHES? THE LAUNDRY?
WHO ELSE IS GOING TO DO IT? OF COURSE YOU! YOU'RE THE MAN! WE CAN'T MAKE SWEET LITTLE

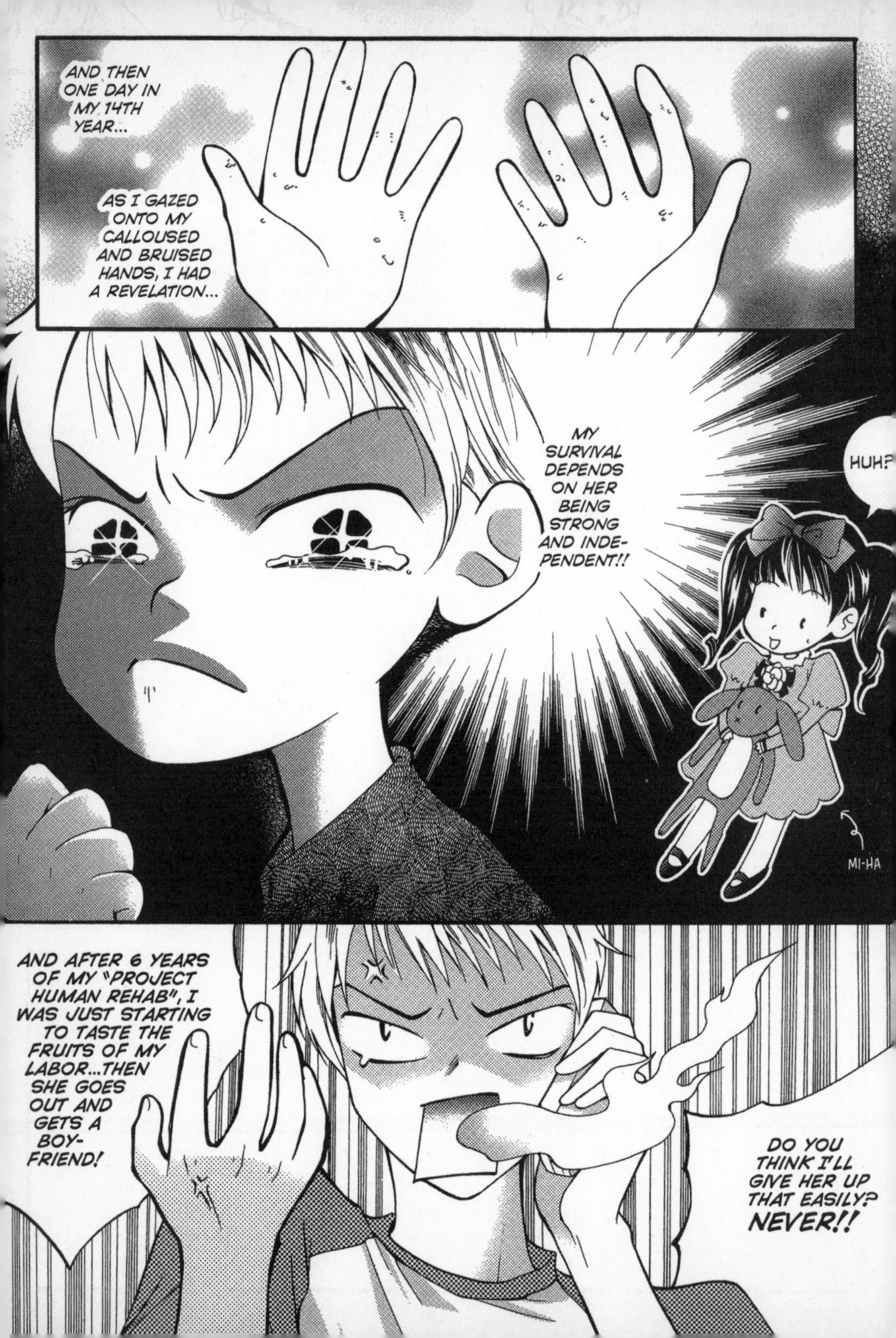
AND THEN ONE DAY IN MY 14TH YEAR...
AS I GAZED ONTO MY CALLOUSED AND BRUISED HANDS, I HAD A REVELATION...
MY SURVIVAL DEPENDS ON HER BEING STRONG AND INDE-PENDENT!!
HUH?
MI-HA
AND AFTER 6 YEARS OF MY "PROJECT HUMAN REHAB", I WAS JUST STARTING TO TASTE THE FRUITS OF MY LABOR...THEN SHE GOES OUT AND GETS A BOY-FRIEND!
DO YOU THINK I'LL GIVE HER UP THAT EASILY? NEVER!!

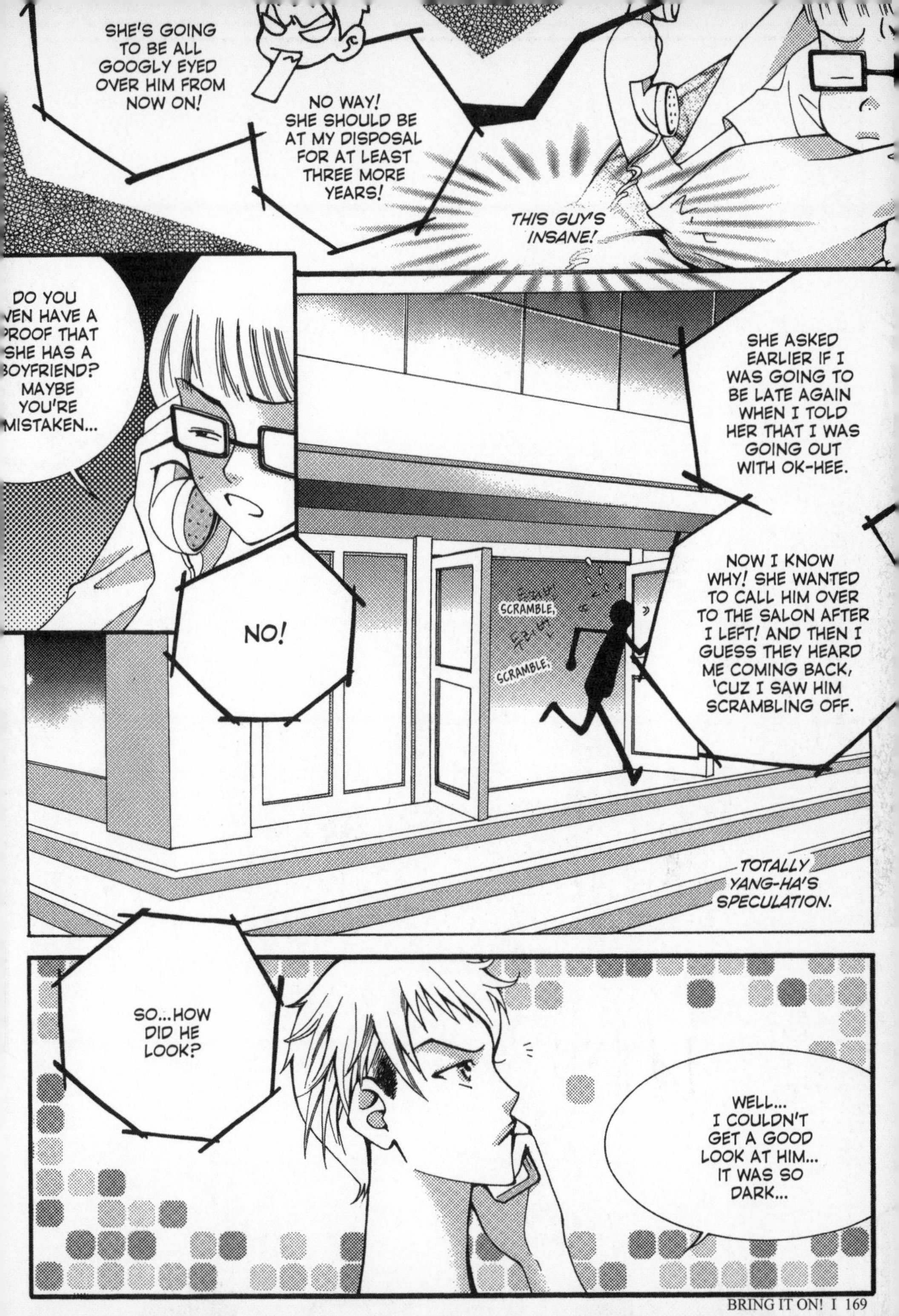
SHE'S GOING TO BE ALL GOOGLY EYED OVER HIM FROM NOW ON!
NO WAY! SHE SHOULD BE AT MY DISPOSAL FOR AT LEAST THREE MORE YEARS!
THIS GUY'S INSANE!
DO YOU VEN HAVE A ROOF THAT SHE HAS A OYFRIEND? MAYBE YOU'RE MISTAKEN...
SHE ASKED EARLIER IF I WAS GOING TO BE LATE AGAIN WHEN I TOLD HER THAT I WAS GOING OUT WITH OK-HEE.
NO!
SCRAMBLE,
SCRAMBLE,
NOW I KNOW WHY! SHE WANTED TO CALL HIM OVER TO THE SALON AFTER I LEFT! AND THEN I GUESS THEY HEARD ME COMING BACK, 'CUZ I SAW HIM SCRAMBLING OFF.
TOTALLY YANG-HA'S SPECULATION.
SO...HOW DID HE LOOK?
WELL... I COULDN'T GET A GOOD LOOK AT HIM... IT WAS SO DARK...

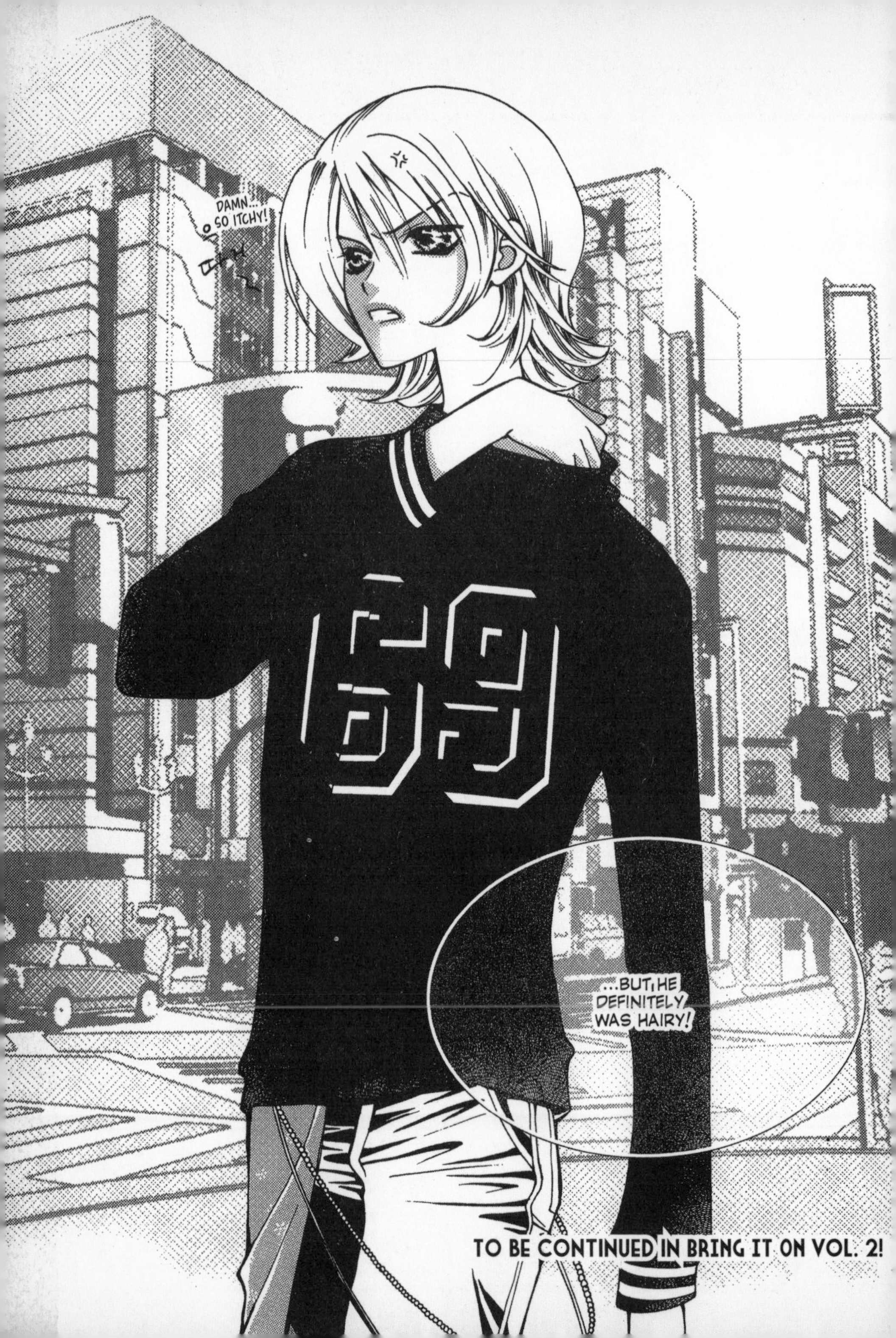
DAMN... SO ITCHY!
...BUT HE DEFINITELY WAS HAIRY!
TO BE CONTINUED IN BRING IT ON VOL. 2!

APPENDIX

Bring it on!

About the creator

● ● ● ● ● ● ● ● ● ● ● ● ●

Bring It On!
Hye-Kyung Baek
March 25th (Aries)

She debuted with <Happy
Spider>, winning the first annual
"Cake Comic Book Award".
With beautifully detailed art,
fresh characters, and a unique
sense of humor, <Bring It On!>
has become a fan favorite.

Other Major Works
<Happy Spider>, <Barbie Doll's End>,
<King of the Bandits>, <The Fan>,
<Rainy>, <ChiRo>

Quick Chat with the Creator

Innocent next door neighbor girl

Hye-Kyung Baek

Bring it on!

Hye-Kyung Baek once again brings a whirlwind of smiles and laughter with <Bring It On!> This is the story of a strong and powerful girl who uses her strength to overcome many challenging obstacles. Guys these days seem to just need good looks, so looks like it's up to us girls to stay healthy and take care of them.

What do you do to take care of your body?
Well, I tend not to like "health foods" because they taste horrible. I may look healthy and great on the outside, but I'm in pretty bad shape on the inside. -.-;; All my fat is from the herbal medicines after all.

What sort of exercise do you usually do? What works best for you?
There isn't really anything in particular that I do consistently. If I gain too much weight, I try jumping rope and hula-hooping for like four days. Hey, that's pretty good for a manhwa artist these days. I also like doing sit-ups. You might not believe it by looking at my abs, but these "wide hips" do have their benefits. Haha.

Do you have any allergies?
Men's adams apples! (There aren't any men in my family, so I'm not used to this!) When a guy is talking to me and subconsciously touches it, it makes me feel queasy.

While drawing manhwa, when do you feel most love towards it?
When a story plot first forms in my head, I feel this overwhelming sense of satisfaction that I can do anything on my own.

Then when do you have a hard time drawing manhwa?
When I can't draw the story that's in my head. I also get lonesome often since I work alone. At times like that, if a cute guy comes to cheer me on... I might drop everything and elope with him~ ^^

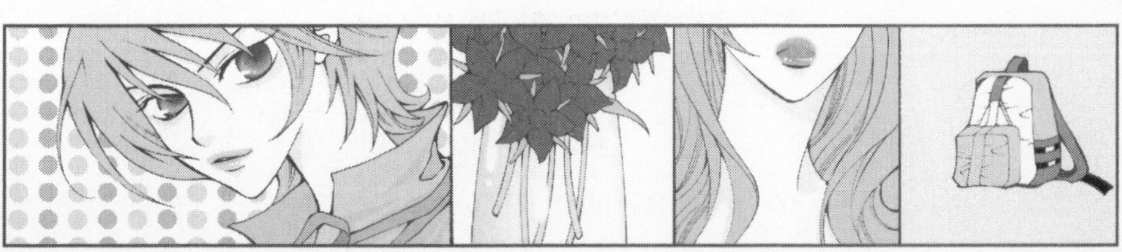

Bring It On!

by Hye-Kyung Baek

"You need to be strong if you want to get the hot guys!"

<Bring It On!> is a witty and cute school life story that will bring a smile to your face. Let's take a look at the characters that work hard to give you those smiles!

The main characters of <Bring It On!> ▶

Mi-Ha Lee

A physically(?) strong and tough girl. As a child, Mi-Ha was forced to go through vigorous workouts by her brother. Her fate changes when she thought Seung-Suh was a pervert and landed a punch on him, only to find out that he was a new student transferring into her class.

Seung-Suh Han

He is the proud transfer student who's well known for his fighting as well as his unbelievable good looks. After getting punched by Mi-Ha, he keeps on trying to get even, but he can't stand it when someone else takes his prey.

Yun-Jin Lee

Mi-Ha's cousin who uses beauty as her ultimate weapon. Unlike the radiating beauty she has on the outside, her personality is quite gloomy. She's the only one that can make Mi-Ha lose her self confidence. She earns Seung-Suh's hatred because of her actions towards Mi-Ha.

Mu-Jin Shin

Seung-Suh's friend and of course, drop-dead gorgeous! They are such close friends, people wonder about their strangely close relationship. When Seung-Suh loses control, only Mu-Jin has the power to calm him down.

ART GALLERY

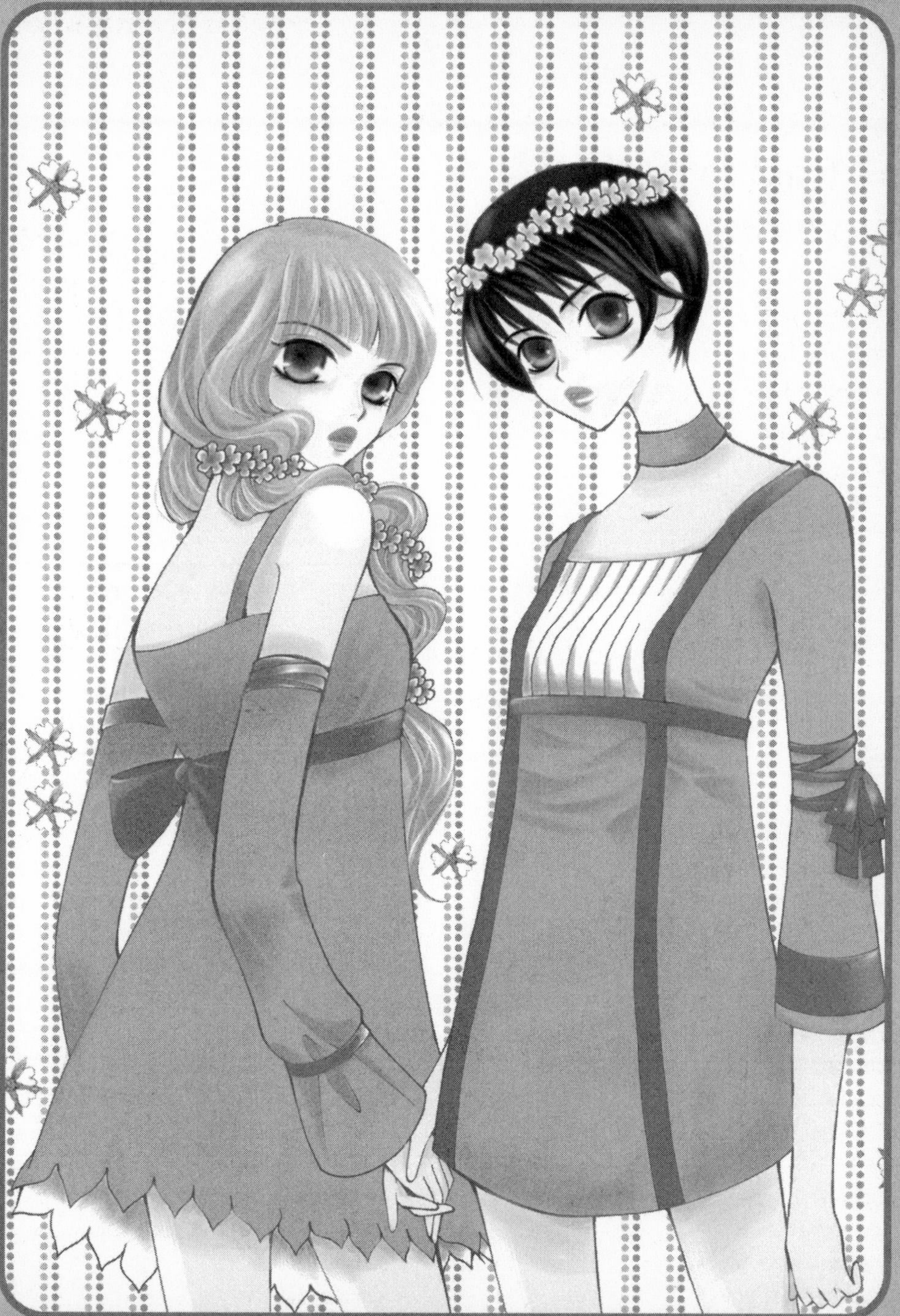

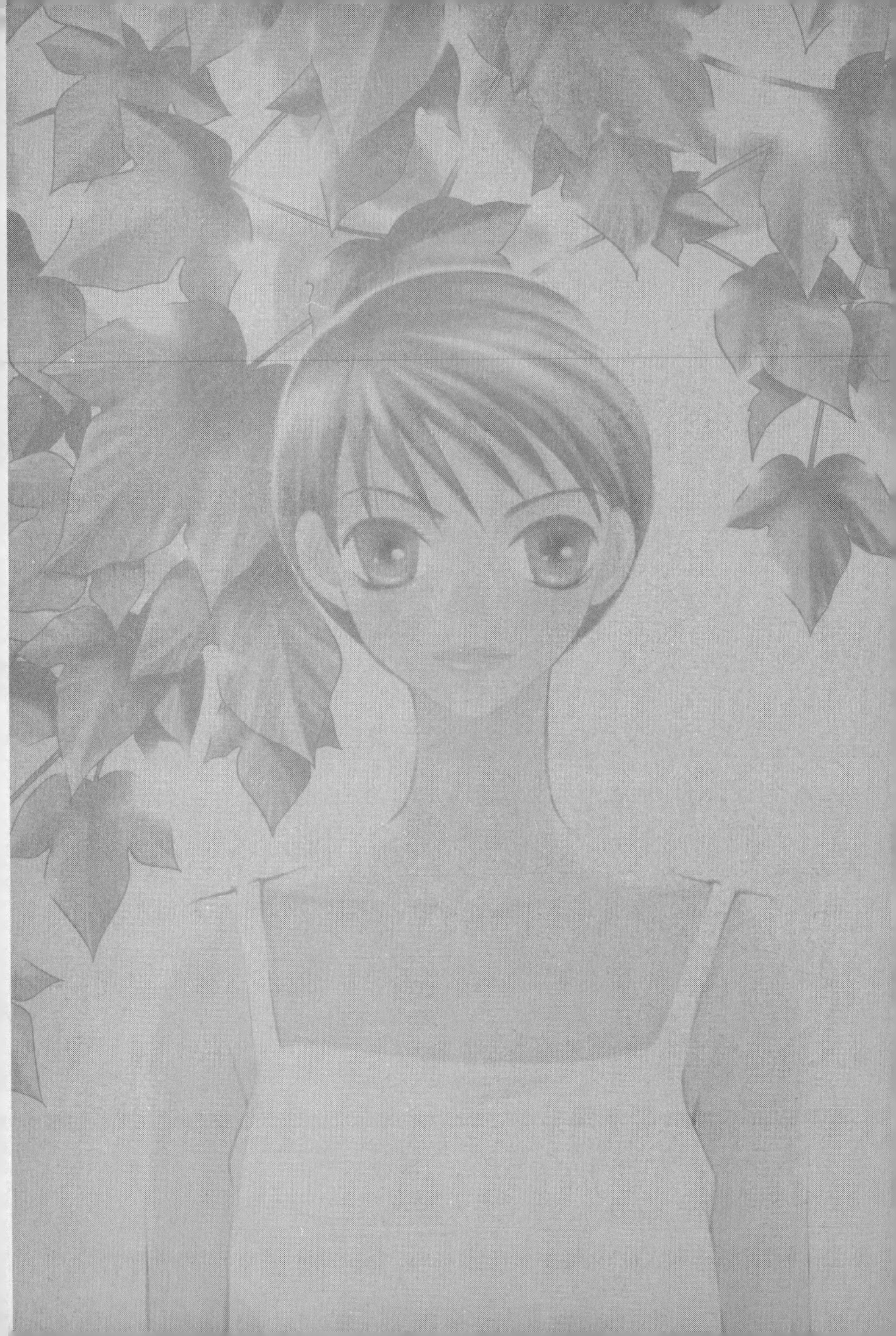

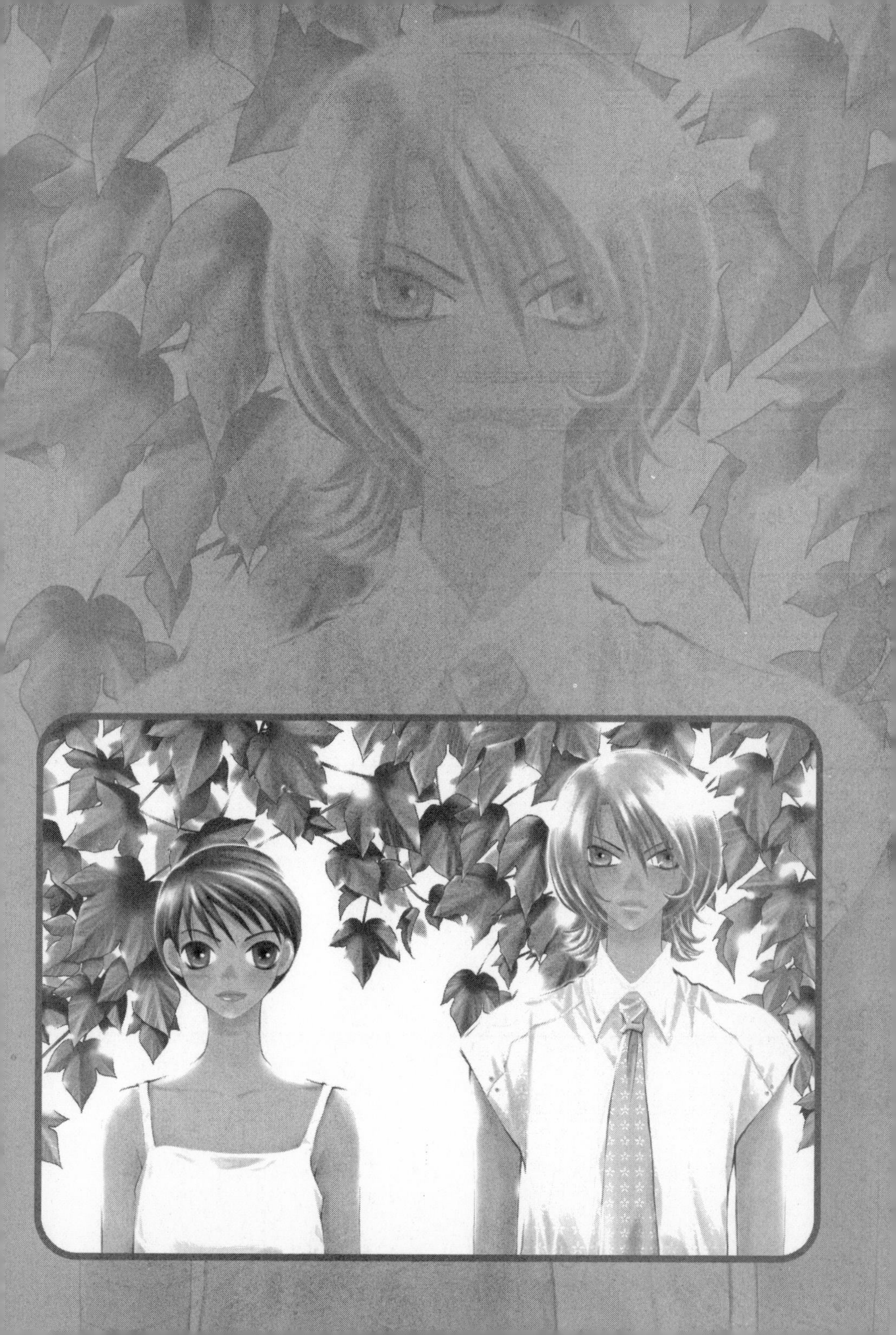

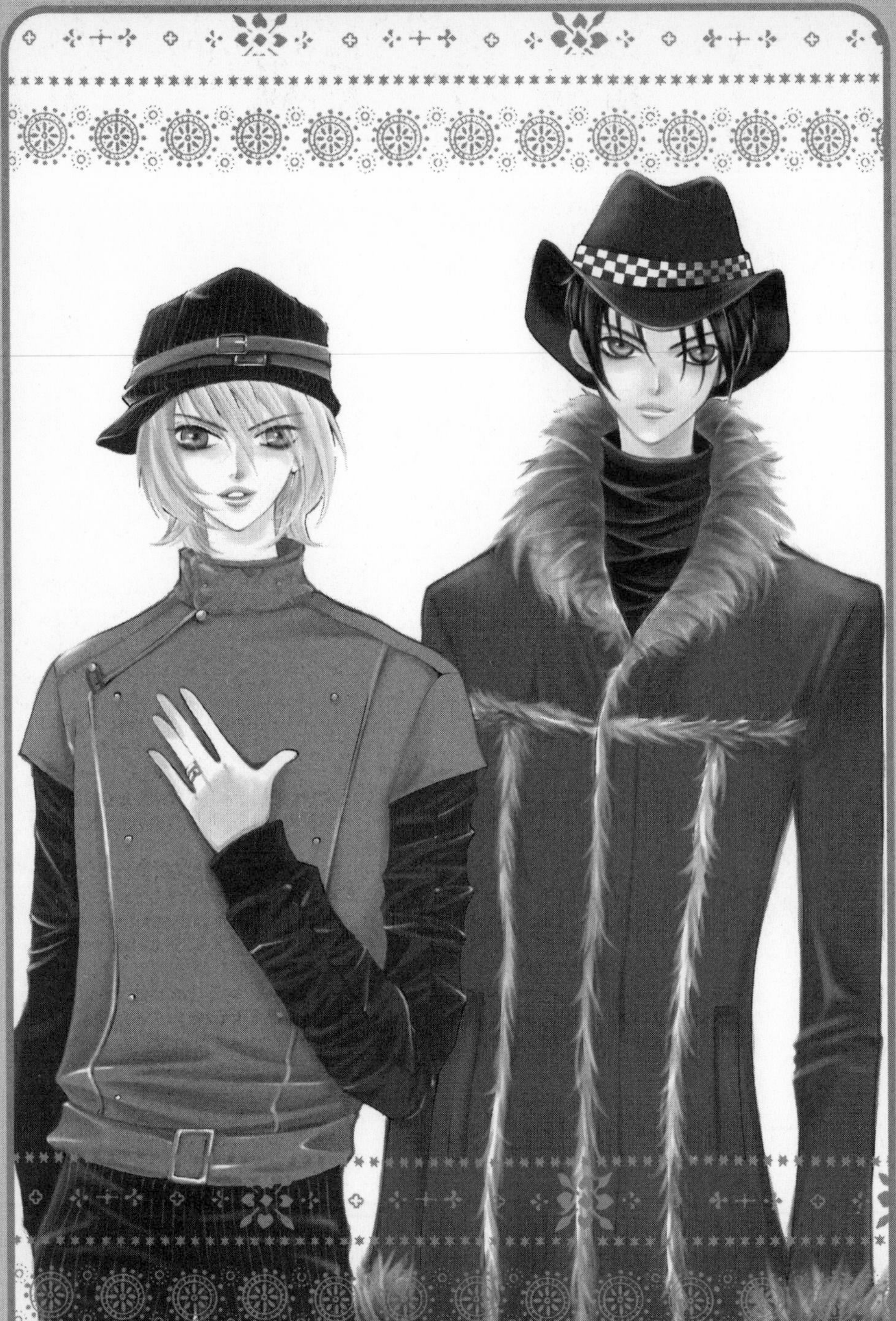

Angel Diary

vol.1

Kara · Lee YunHee

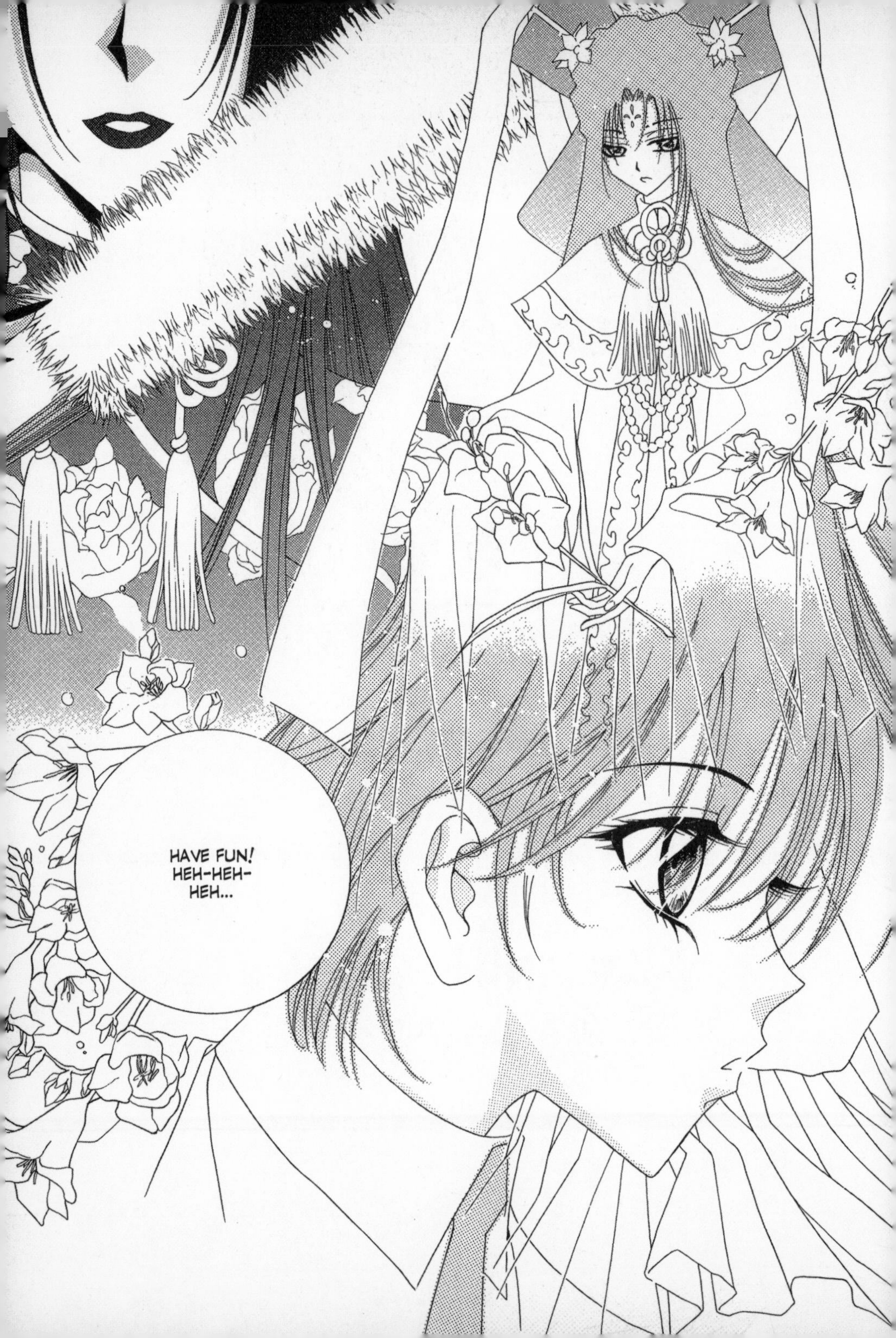
HAVE FUN! HEH-HEH-HEH...

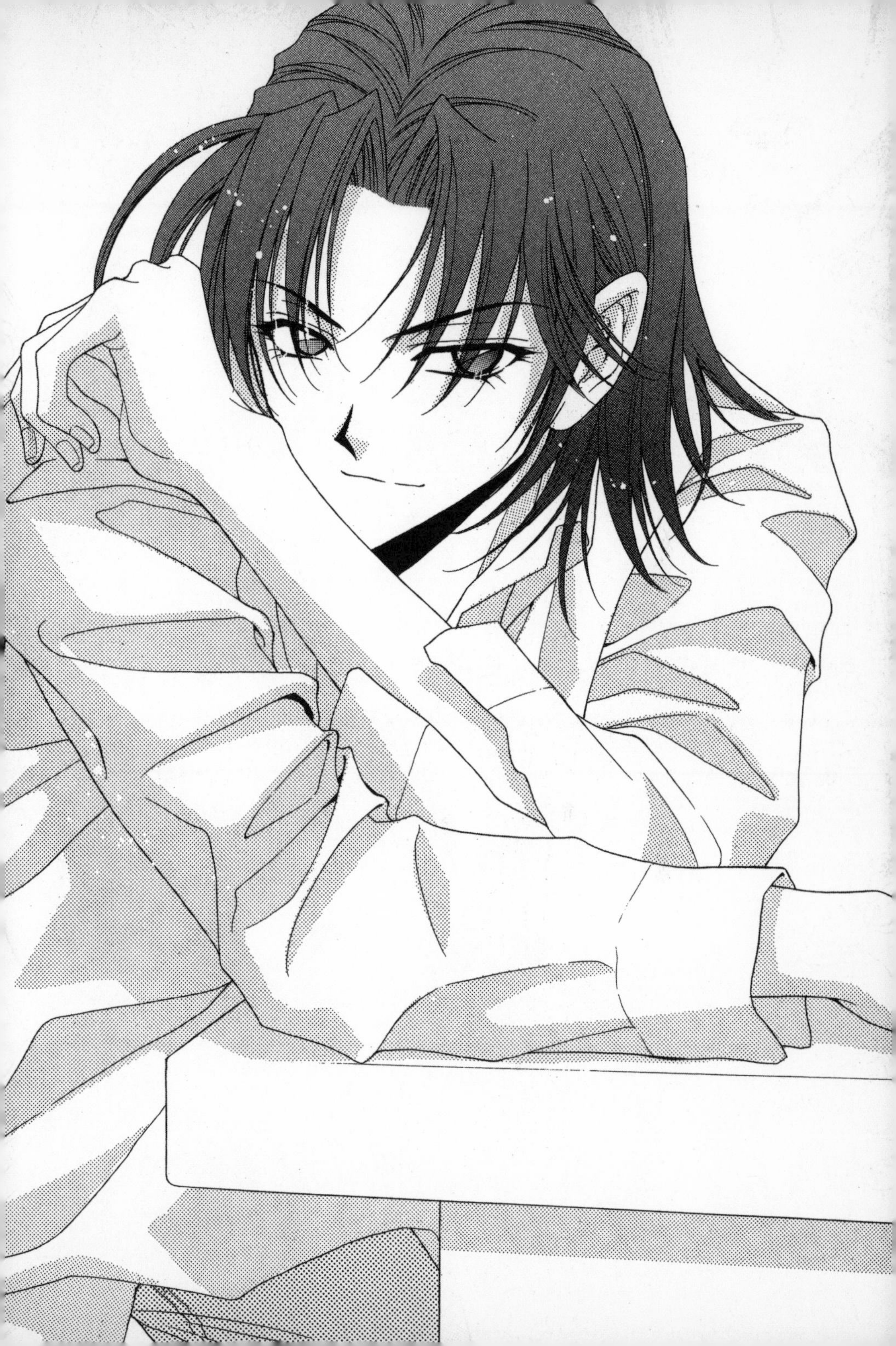

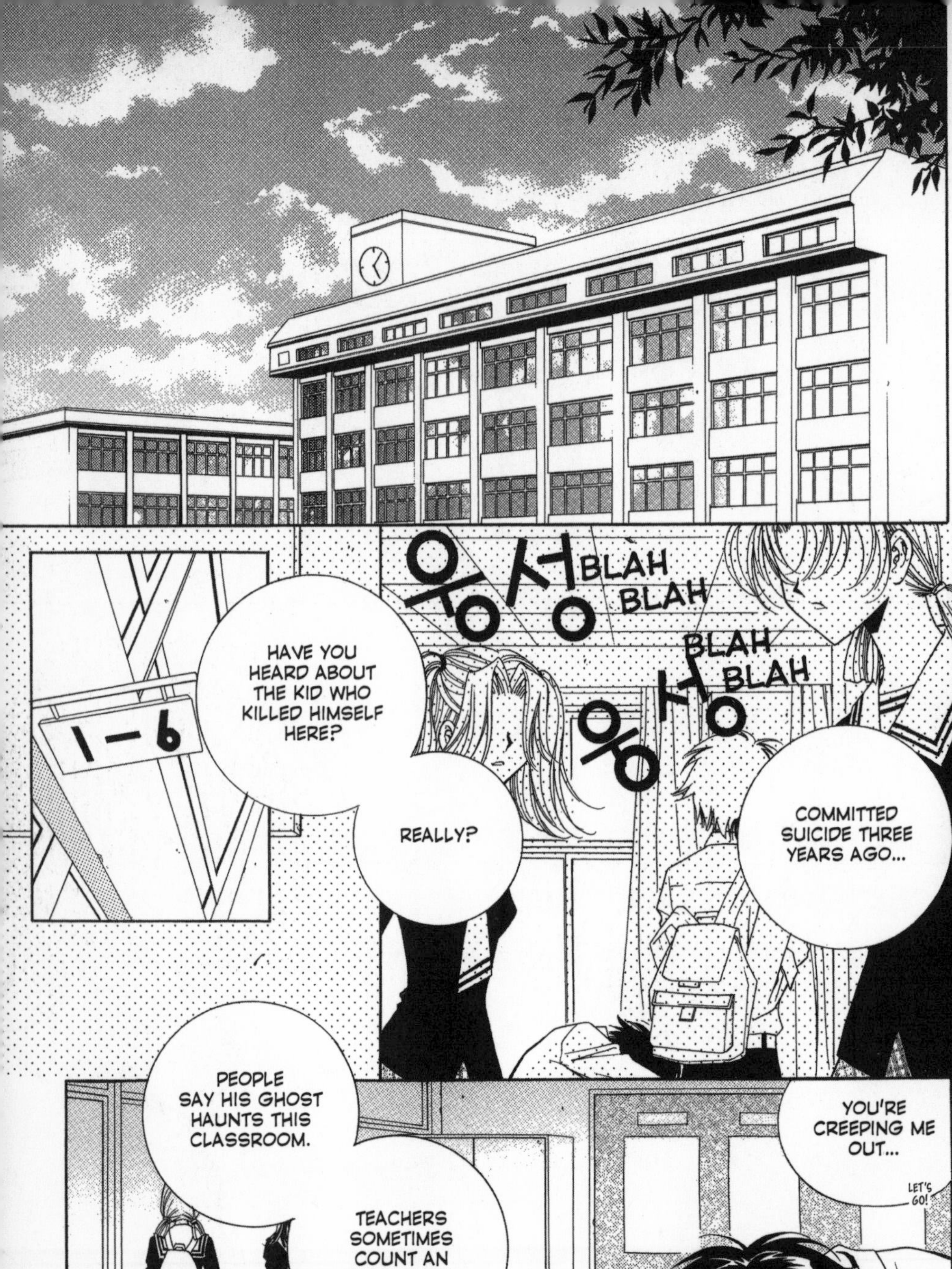
1-6
HAVE YOU HEARD ABOUT THE KID WHO KILLED HIMSELF HERE?
웅성 BLAH BLAH
REALLY?
웅성 BLAH BLAH
COMMITTED SUICIDE THREE YEARS AGO...
PEOPLE SAY HIS GHOST HAUNTS THIS CLASSROOM.
TEACHERS SOMETIMES COUNT AN EXTRA HEAD.
YOU'RE CREEPING ME OUT...
LET'S GO!

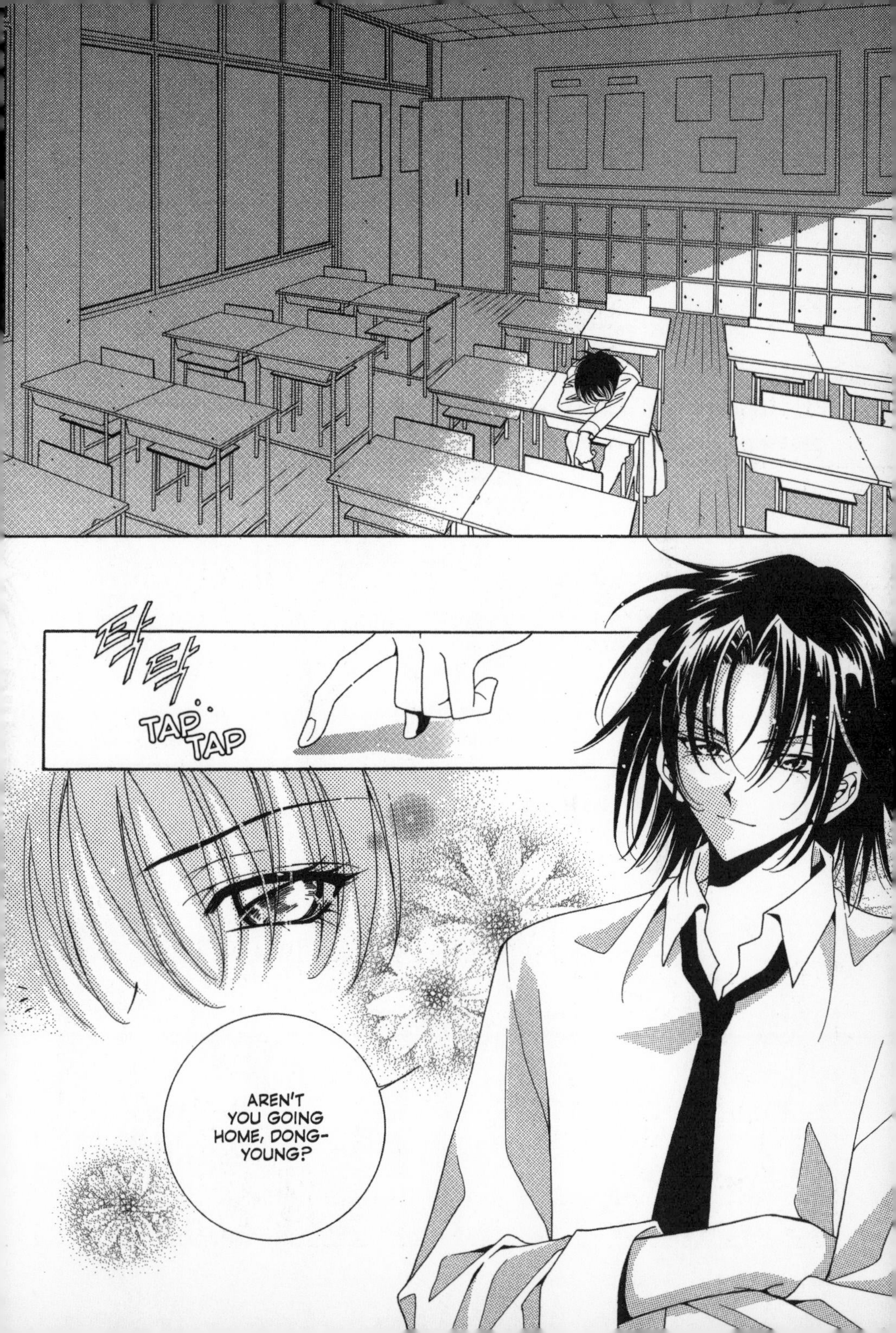

탁 탁
TAP TAP
AREN'T YOU GOING HOME, DONG-YOUNG?

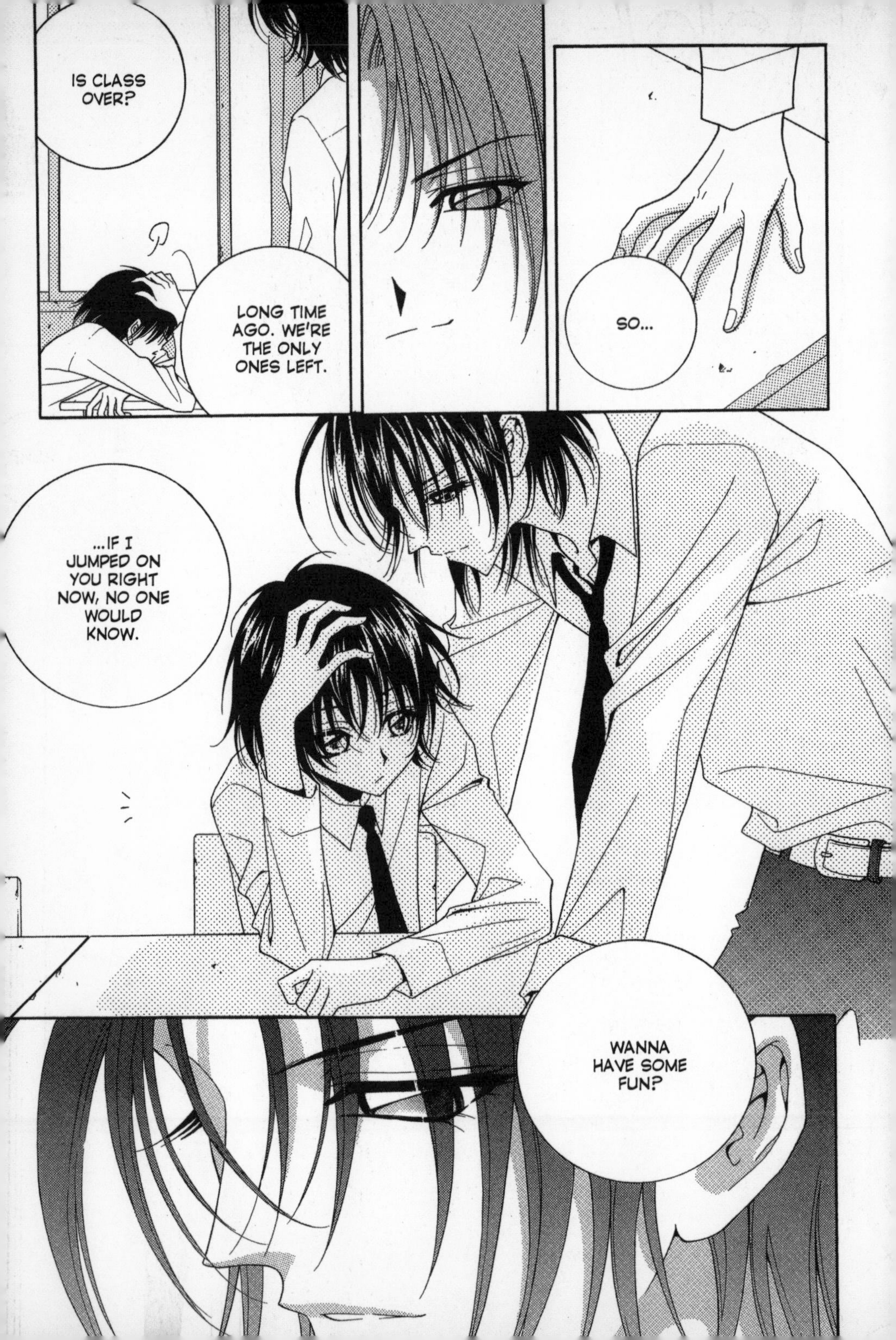
IS CLASS OVER?
LONG TIME AGO. WE'RE THE ONLY ONES LEFT.
SO...
...IF I JUMPED ON YOU RIGHT NOW, NO ONE WOULD KNOW.
WANNA HAVE SOME FUN?

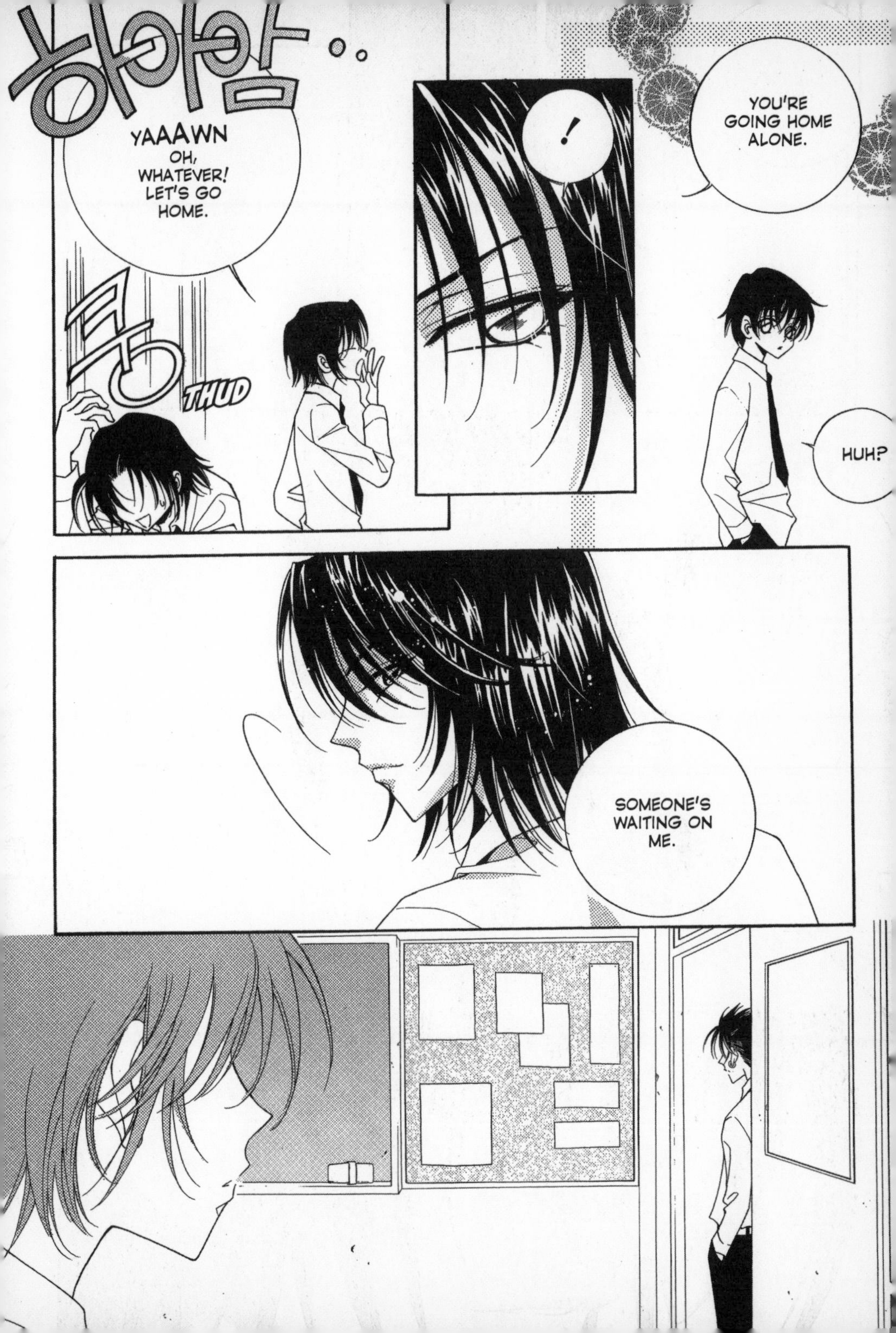
하아암..
YAAAWN
OH, WHATEVER! LET'S GO HOME.
툭
THUD
!
YOU'RE GOING HOME ALONE.
HUH?
SOMEONE'S WAITING ON ME.

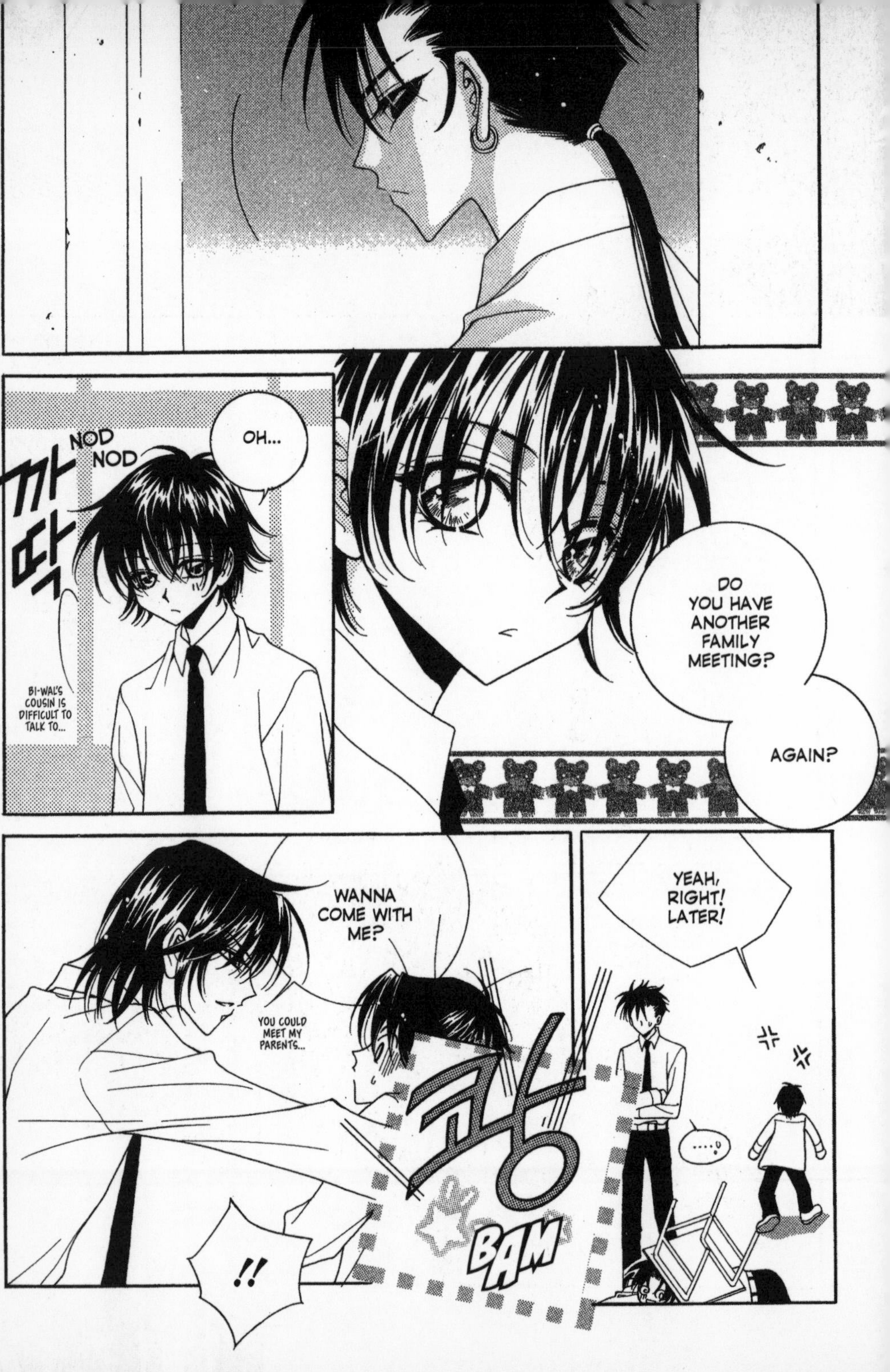
NOD NOD
까딱
OH...
BI-WAL'S COUSIN IS DIFFICULT TO TALK TO...
DO YOU HAVE ANOTHER FAMILY MEETING?
AGAIN?
WANNA COME WITH ME?
YOU COULD MEET MY PARENTS...
!!
쾅
BAM
YEAH, RIGHT! LATER!
....?

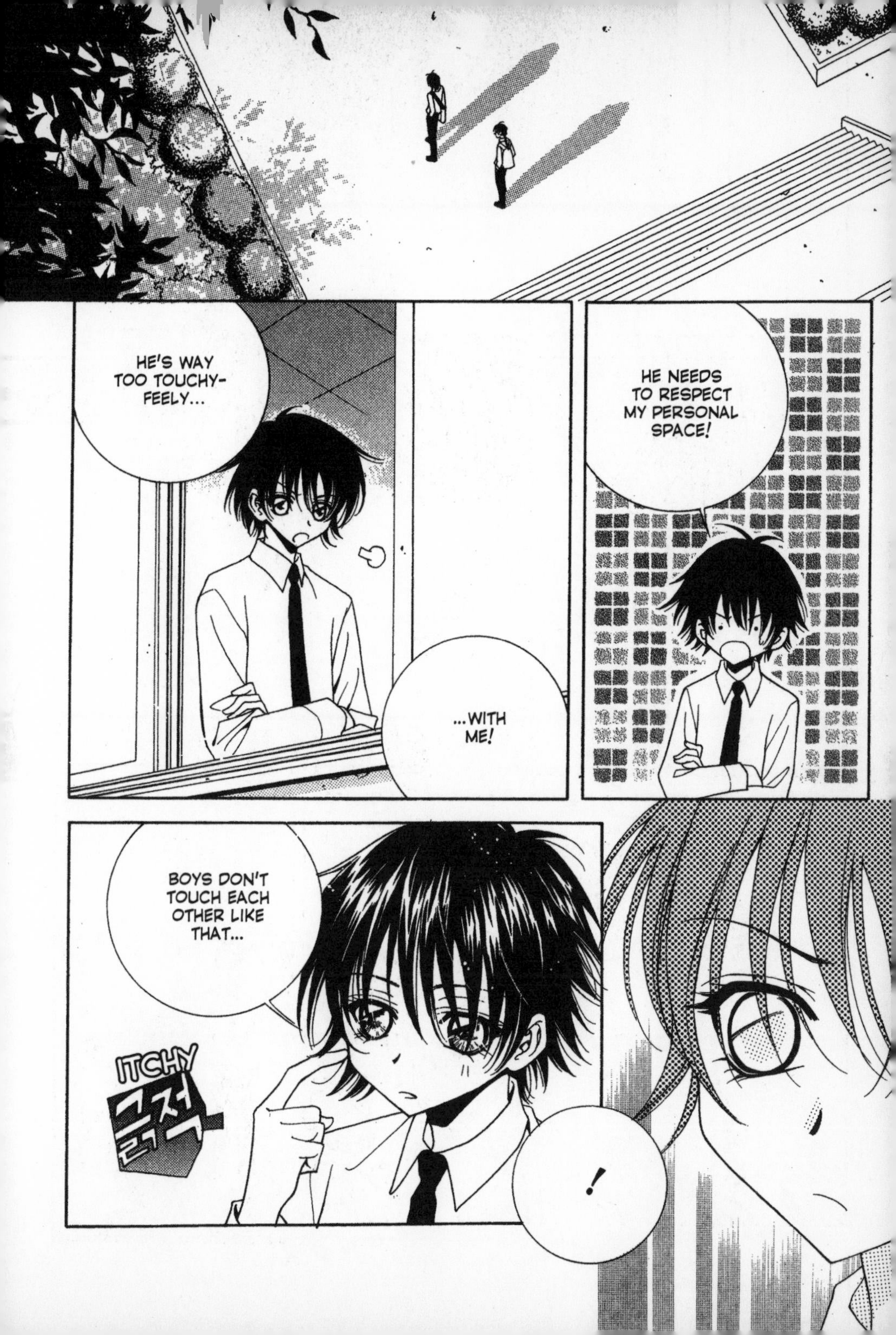
HE'S WAY TOO TOUCHY-FEELY...
...WITH ME!
HE NEEDS TO RESPECT MY PERSONAL SPACE!
BOYS DON'T TOUCH EACH OTHER LIKE THAT...
ITCHY
긁적
!

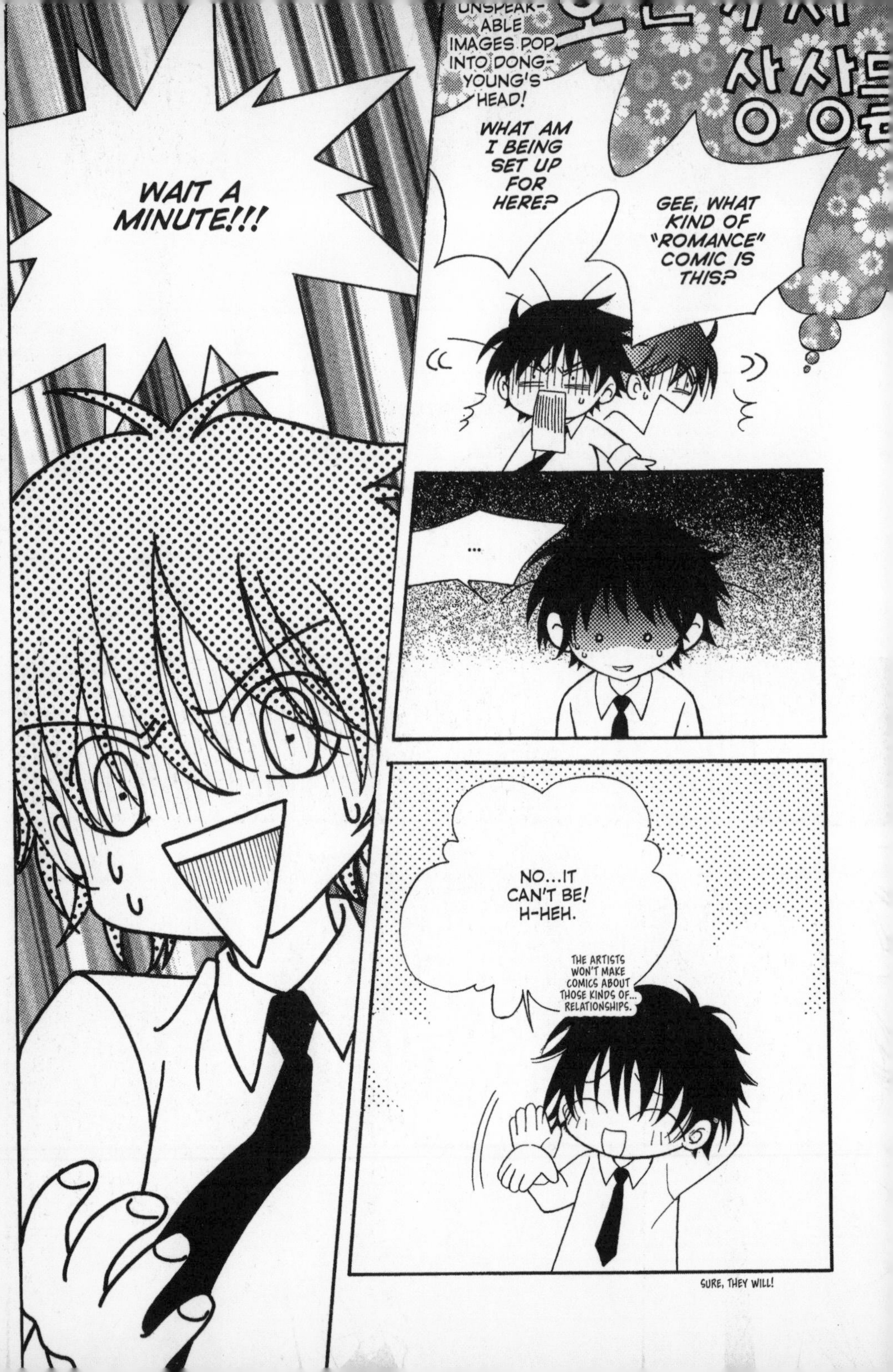
WAIT A MINUTE!!!
UNSPEAKABLE IMAGES POP INTO DONG-YOUNG'S HEAD!
WHAT AM I BEING SET UP FOR HERE?
GEE, WHAT KIND OF "ROMANCE" COMIC IS THIS?
...
NO...IT CAN'T BE! H-HEH.
THE ARTISTS WON'T MAKE COMICS ABOUT THOSE KINDS OF... RELATIONSHIPS.
SURE, THEY WILL!

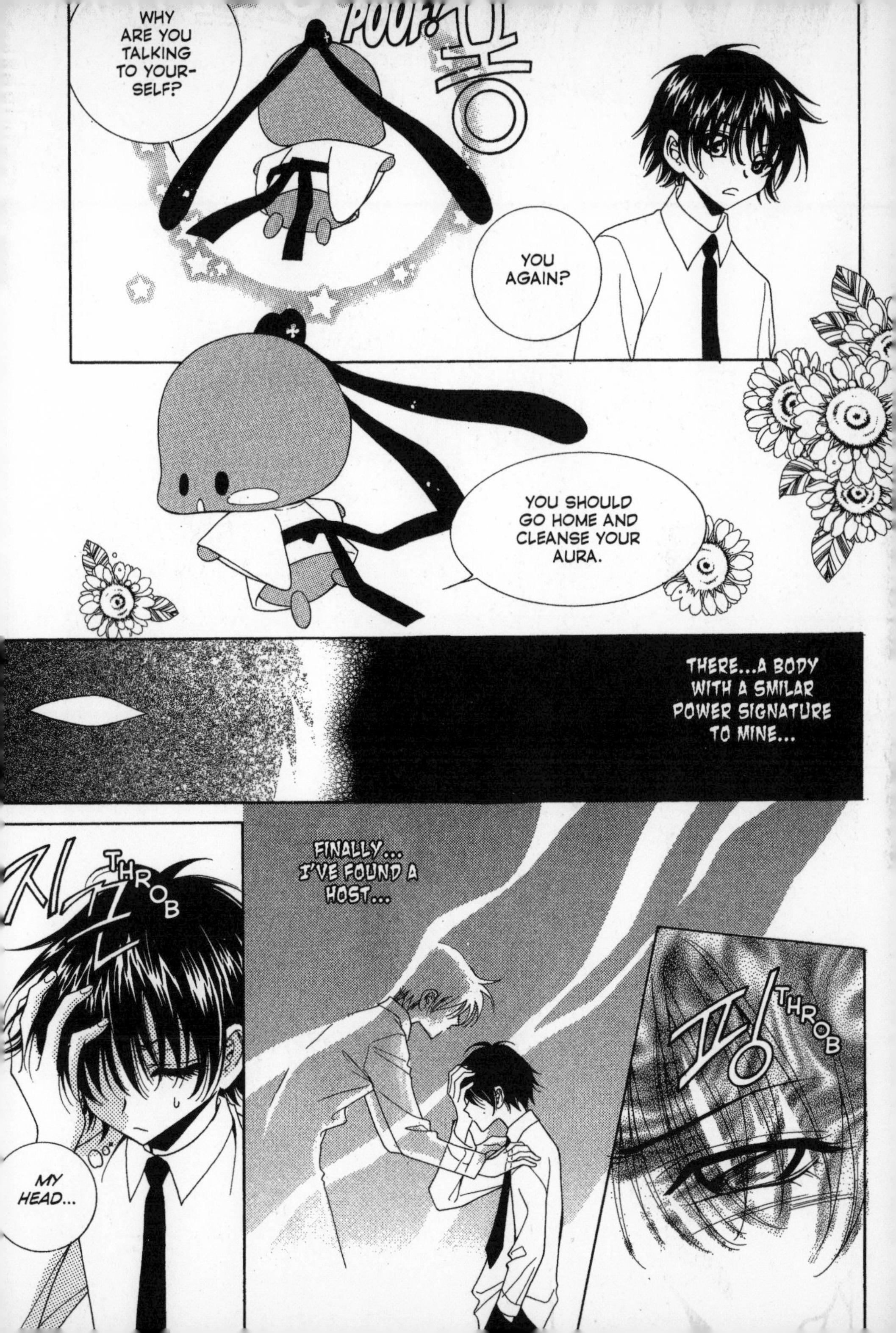
WHY ARE YOU TALKING TO YOUR-SELF?
POOF!
YOU AGAIN?
YOU SHOULD GO HOME AND CLEANSE YOUR AURA.
THERE...A BODY WITH A SMILAR POWER SIGNATURE TO MINE...
THROB
MY HEAD...
FINALLY... I'VE FOUND A HOST...
THROB

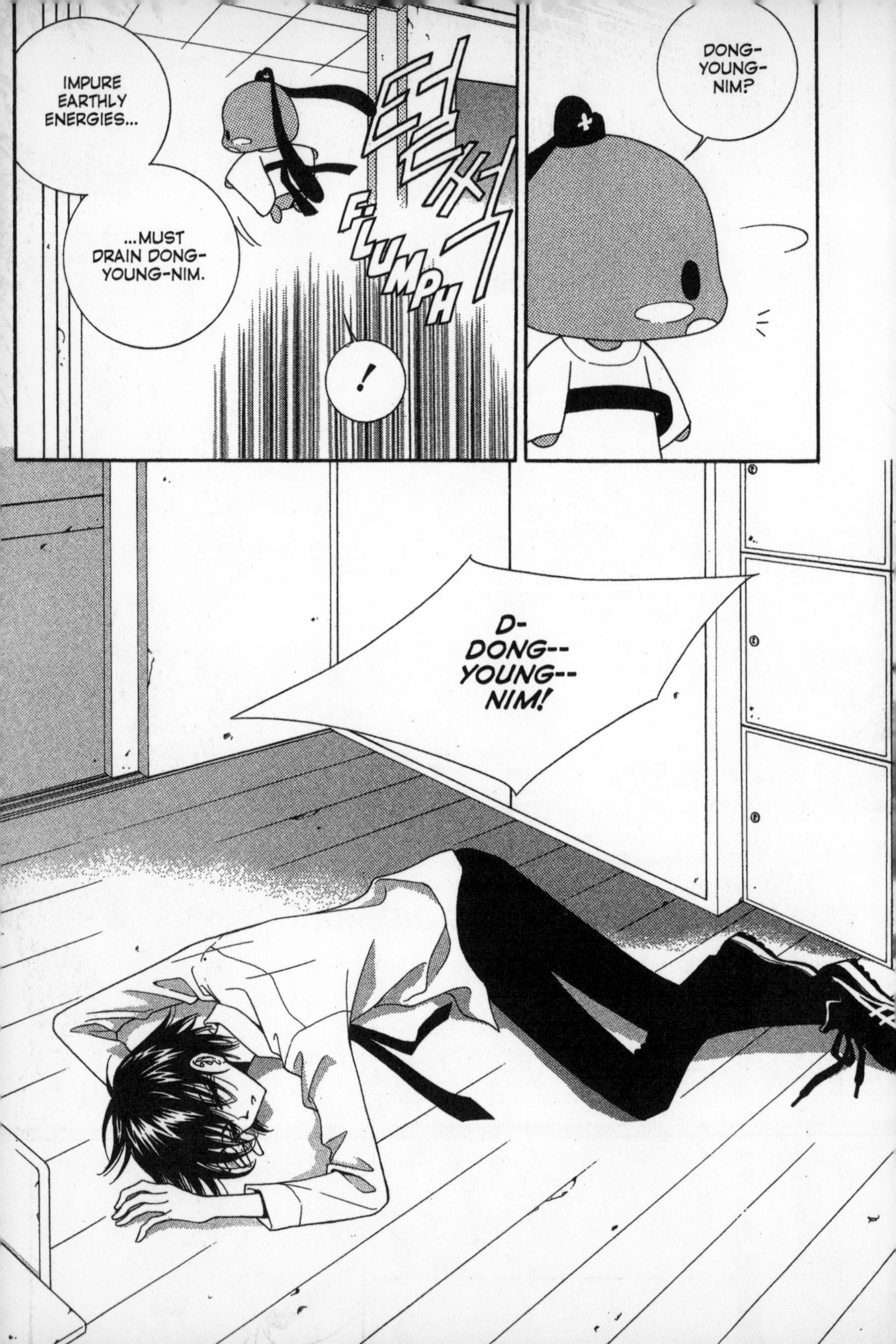
IMPURE EARTHLY ENERGIES...
...MUST DRAIN DONG-YOUNG-NIM.
털썩
FLUMPH
!
DONG-YOUNG-NIM?
D-DONG--YOUNG--NIM!

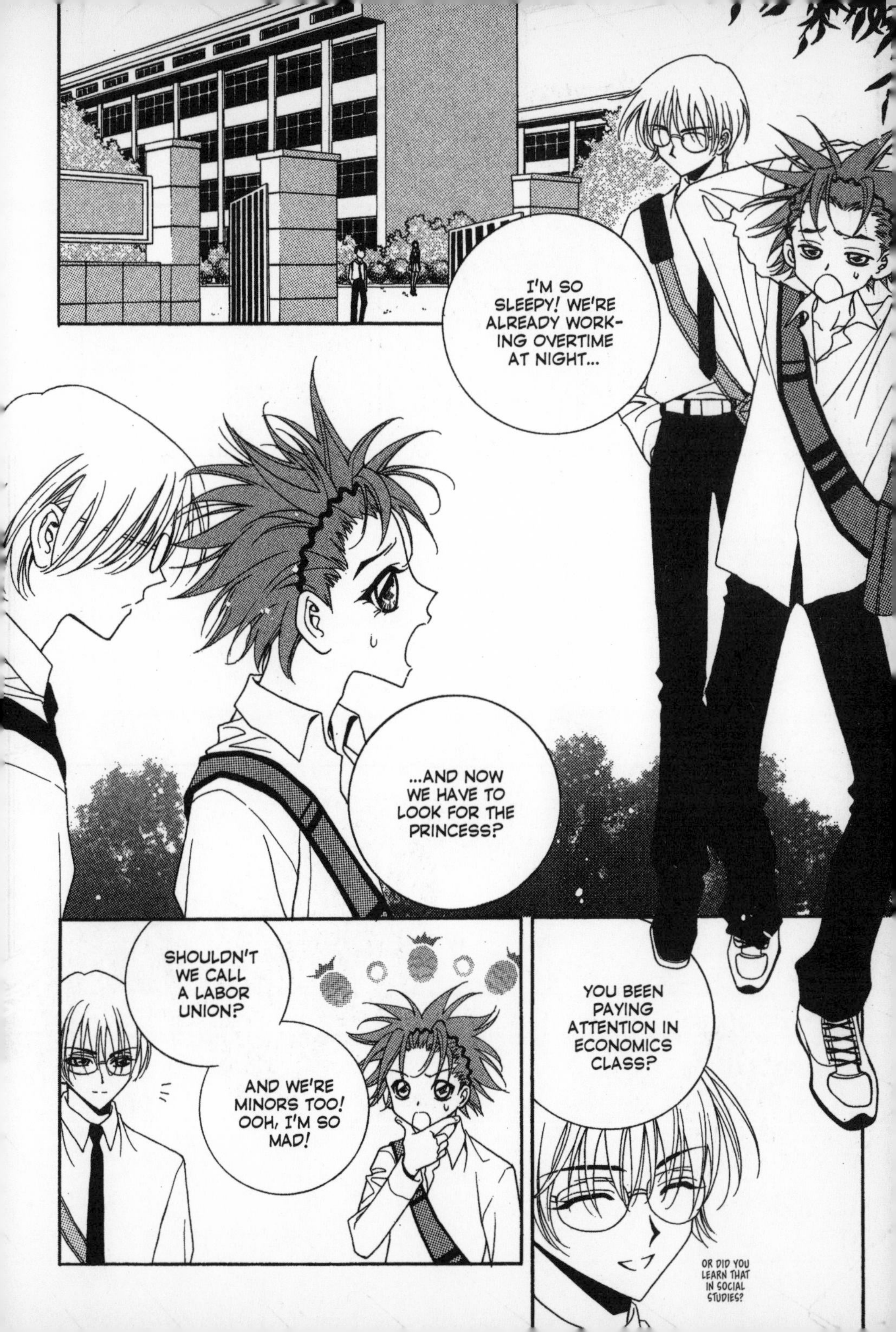

I'M SO SLEEPY! WE'RE ALREADY WORKING OVERTIME AT NIGHT...
...AND NOW WE HAVE TO LOOK FOR THE PRINCESS?
SHOULDN'T WE CALL A LABOR UNION?
AND WE'RE MINORS TOO! OOH, I'M SO MAD!
YOU BEEN PAYING ATTENTION IN ECONOMICS CLASS?
OR DID YOU LEARN THAT IN SOCIAL STUDIES?

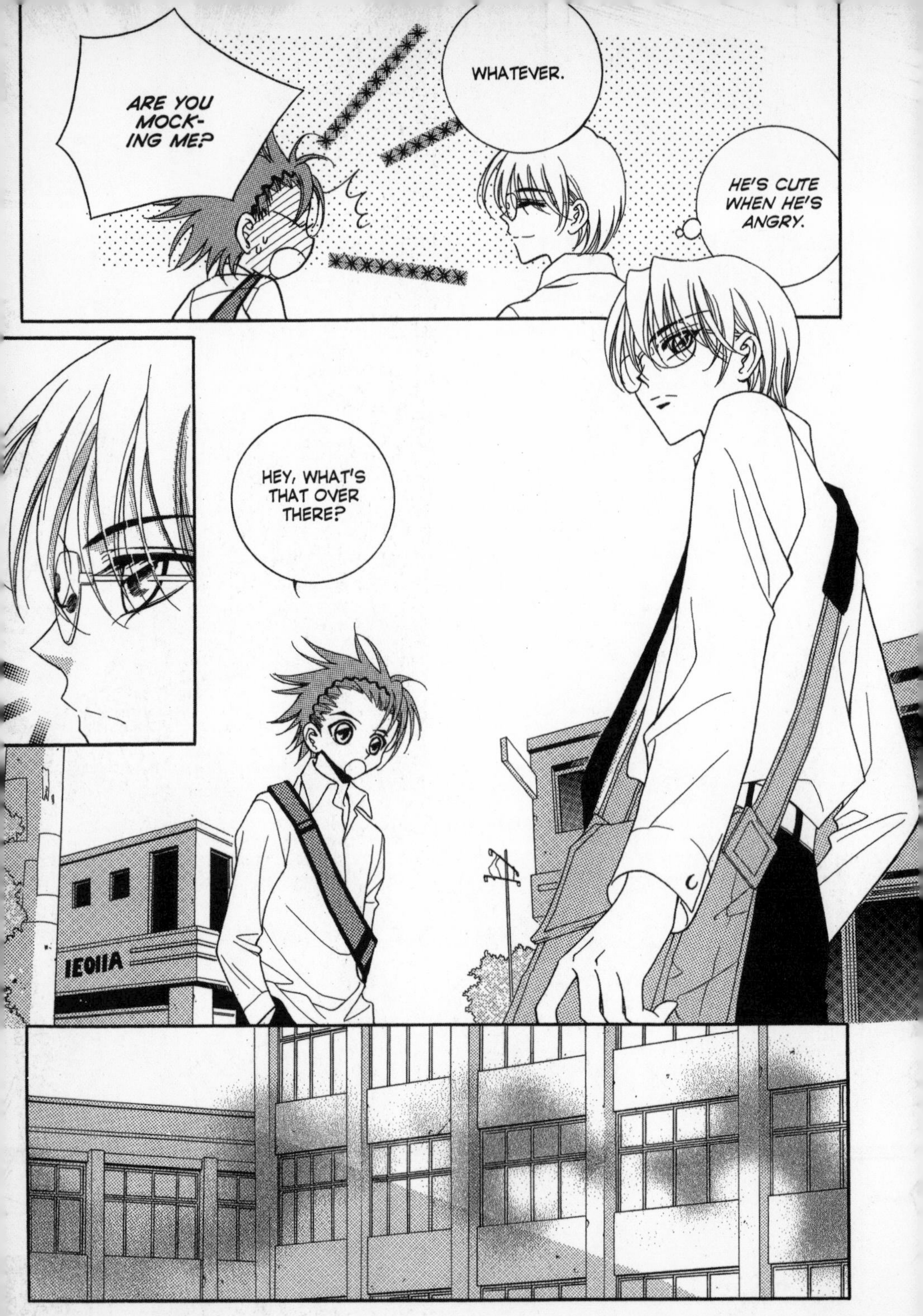
ARE YOU MOCK-ING ME?
WHATEVER.
HE'S CUTE WHEN HE'S ANGRY.
HEY, WHAT'S THAT OVER THERE?
IEOIIA

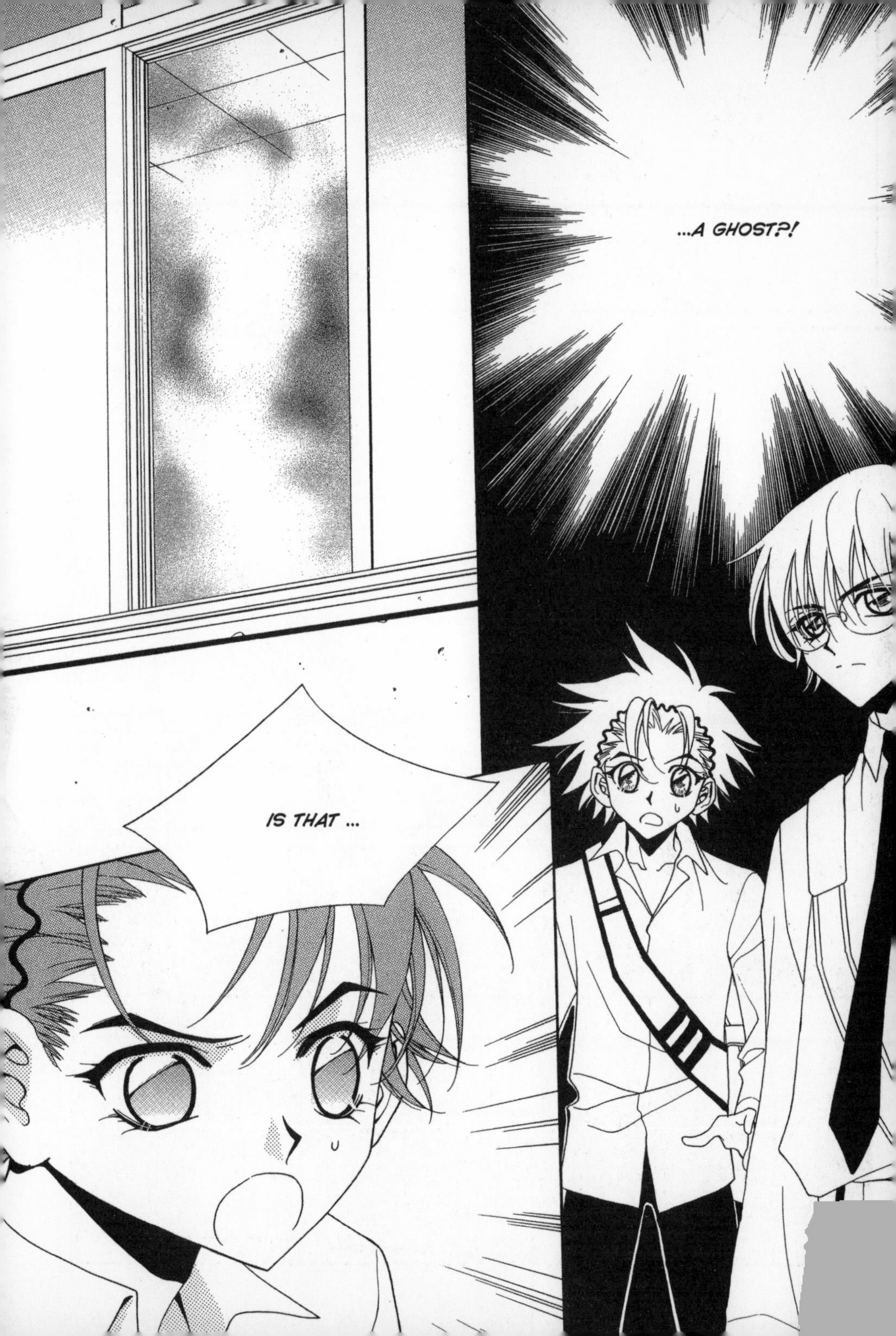
IS THAT ...
...A GHOST?!

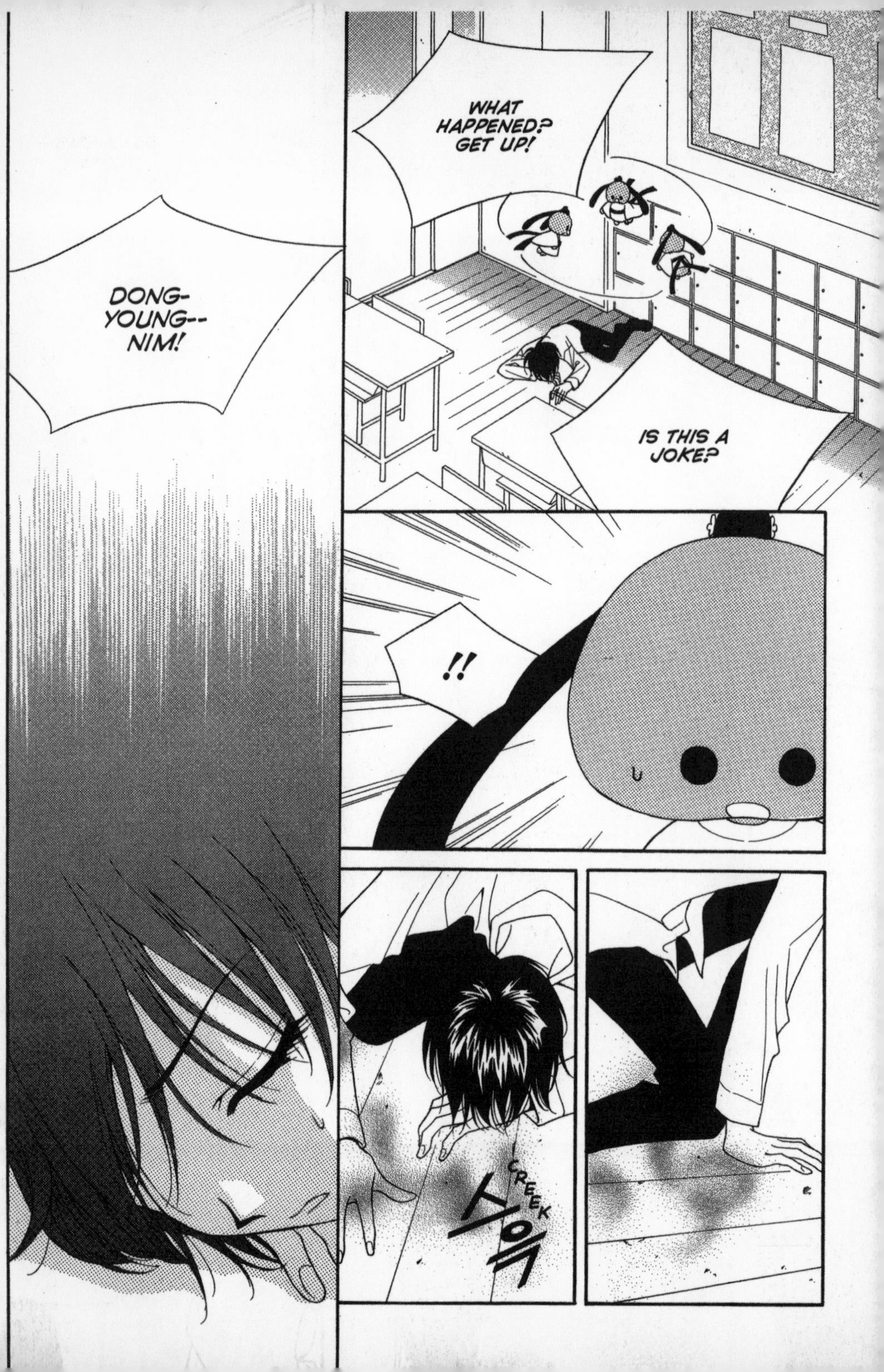
DONG-YOUNG--NIM!
WHAT HAPPENED? GET UP!
IS THIS A JOKE?
!!
CREEK

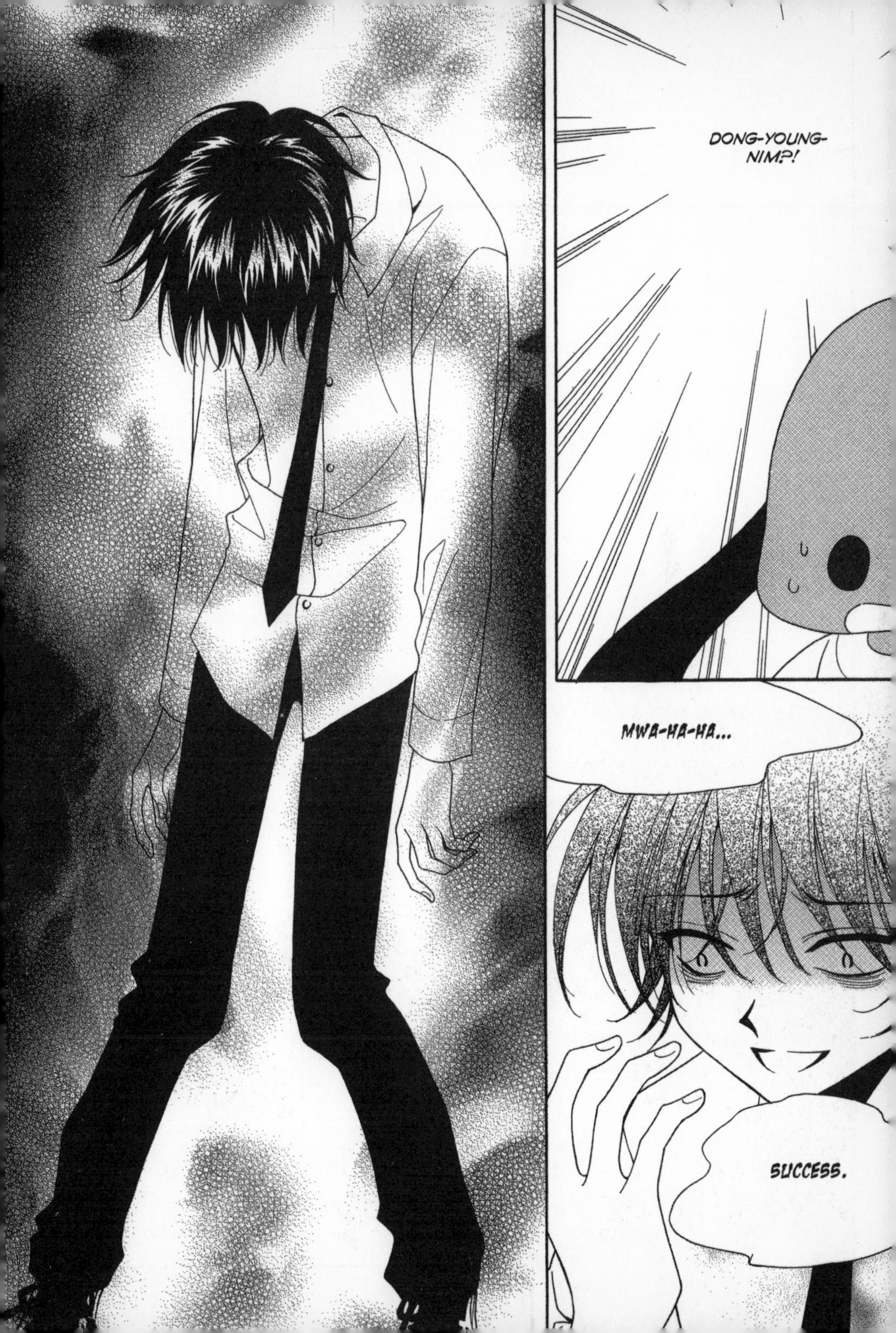
DONG-YOUNG-NIM?!
MWA-HA-HA...
SUCCESS.

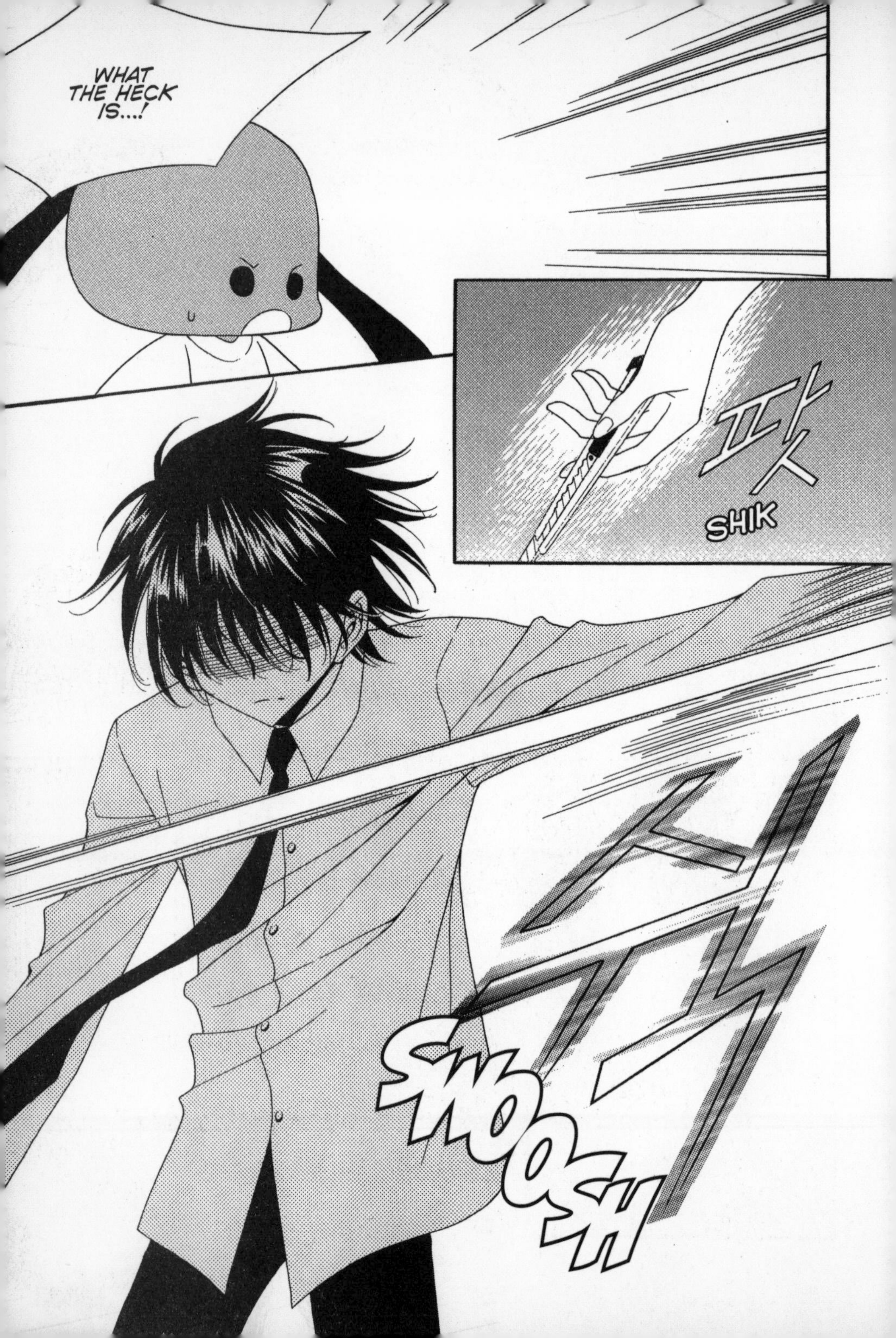
WHAT THE HECK IS...!
팟
SHIK
SWOOSH

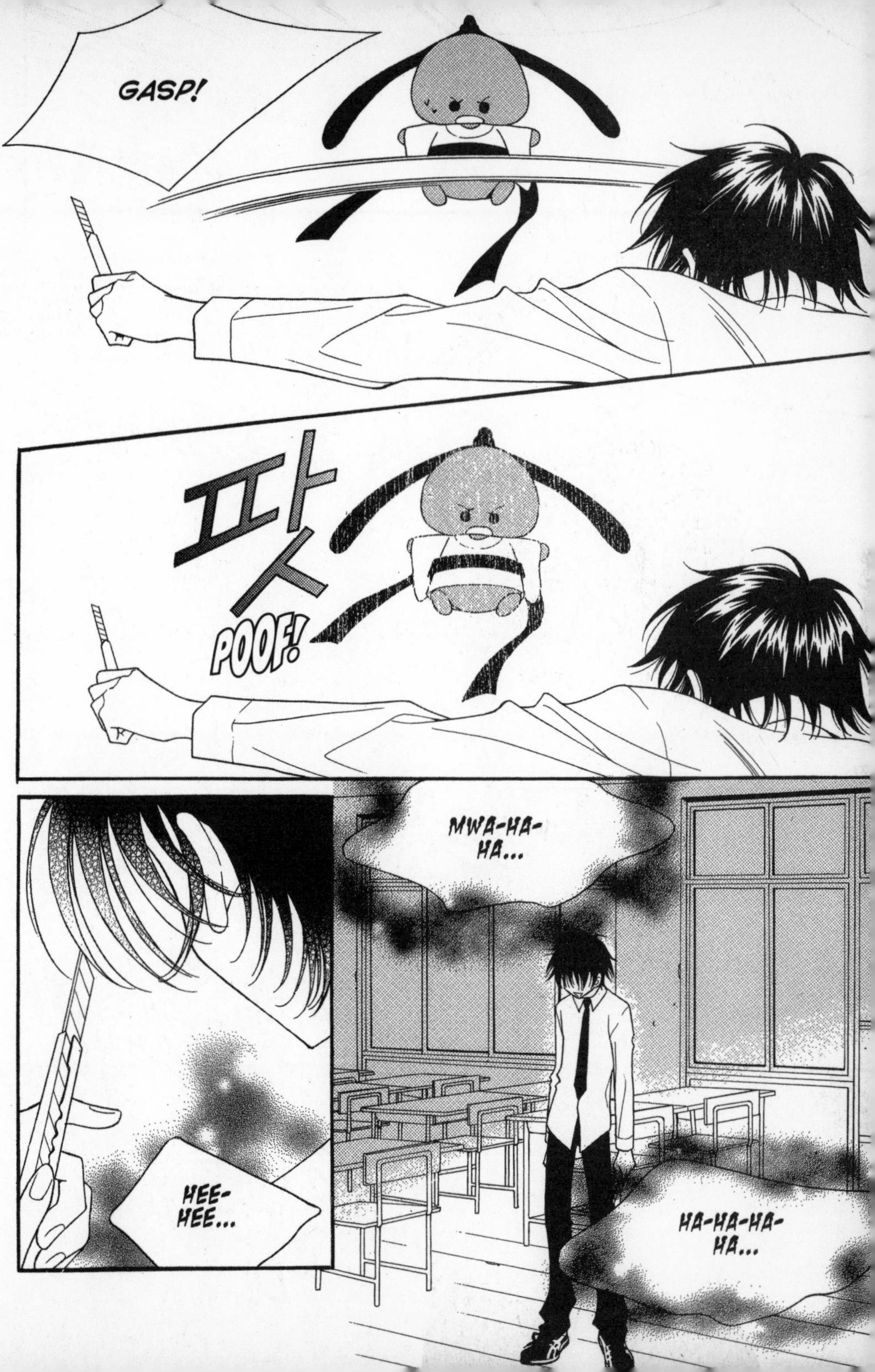
GASP!
팟
POOF!
HEE-HEE...
MWA-HA-HA...
HA-HA-HA-HA...

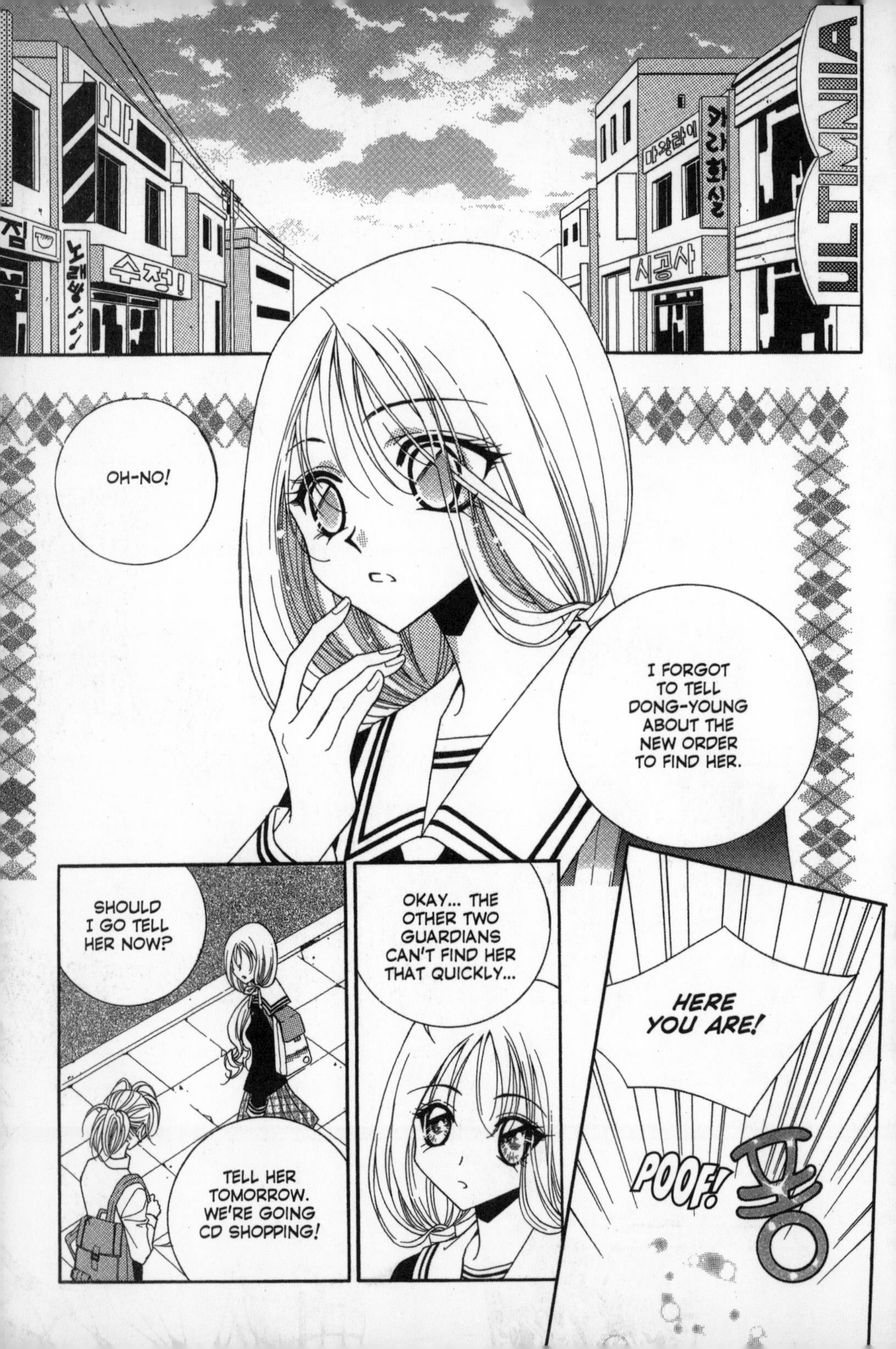
OH-NO!
I FORGOT TO TELL DONG-YOUNG ABOUT THE NEW ORDER TO FIND HER.
SHOULD I GO TELL HER NOW?
TELL HER TOMORROW. WE'RE GOING CD SHOPPING!
OKAY... THE OTHER TWO GUARDIANS CAN'T FIND HER THAT QUICKLY...
HERE YOU ARE!
POOF!
퐁

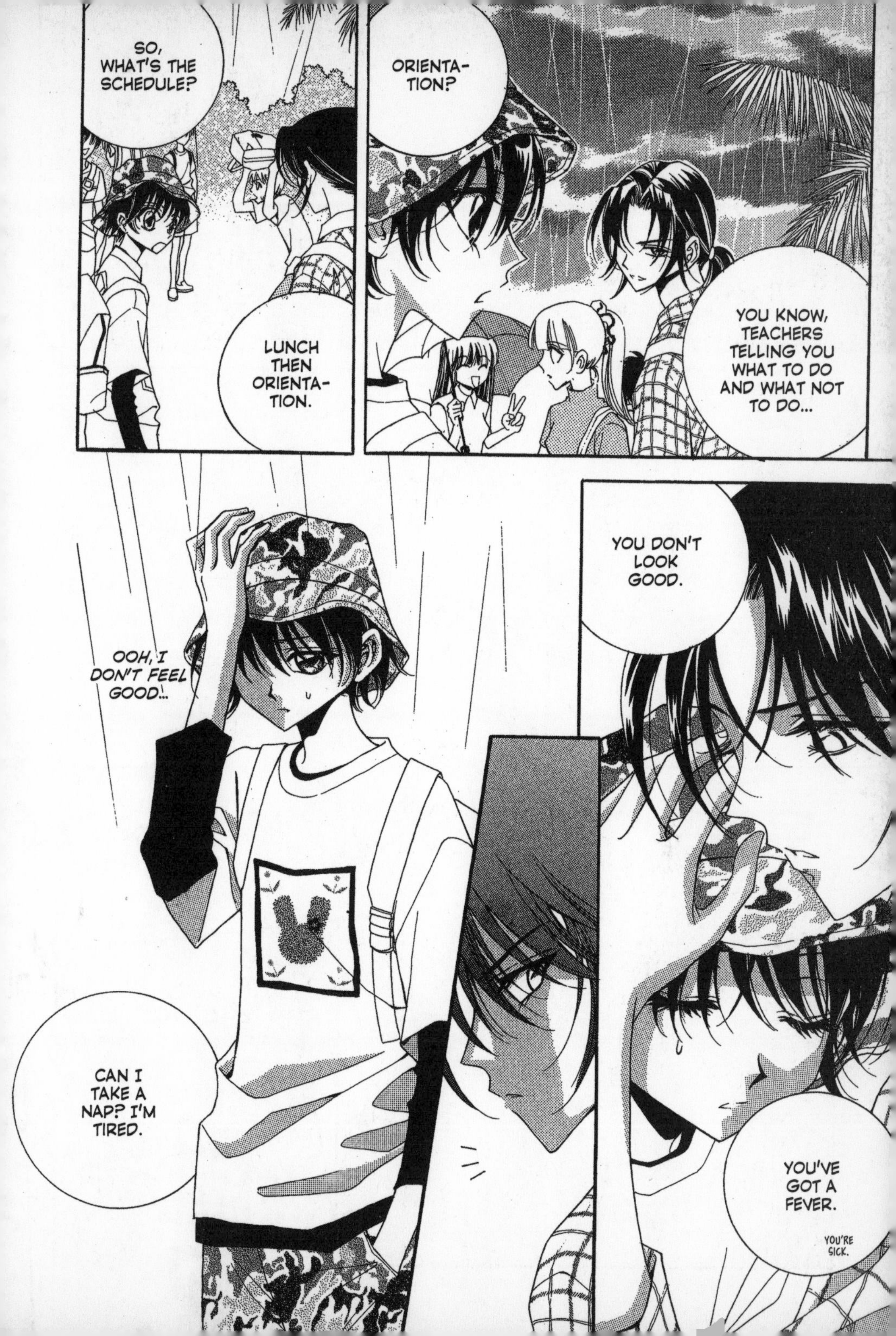
SO, WHAT'S THE SCHEDULE?
LUNCH THEN ORIENTA-TION.
ORIENTA-TION?
YOU KNOW, TEACHERS TELLING YOU WHAT TO DO AND WHAT NOT TO DO...
OOH, I DON'T FEEL GOOD...
CAN I TAKE A NAP? I'M TIRED.
YOU DON'T LOOK GOOD.
YOU'VE GOT A FEVER.
YOU'RE SICK.

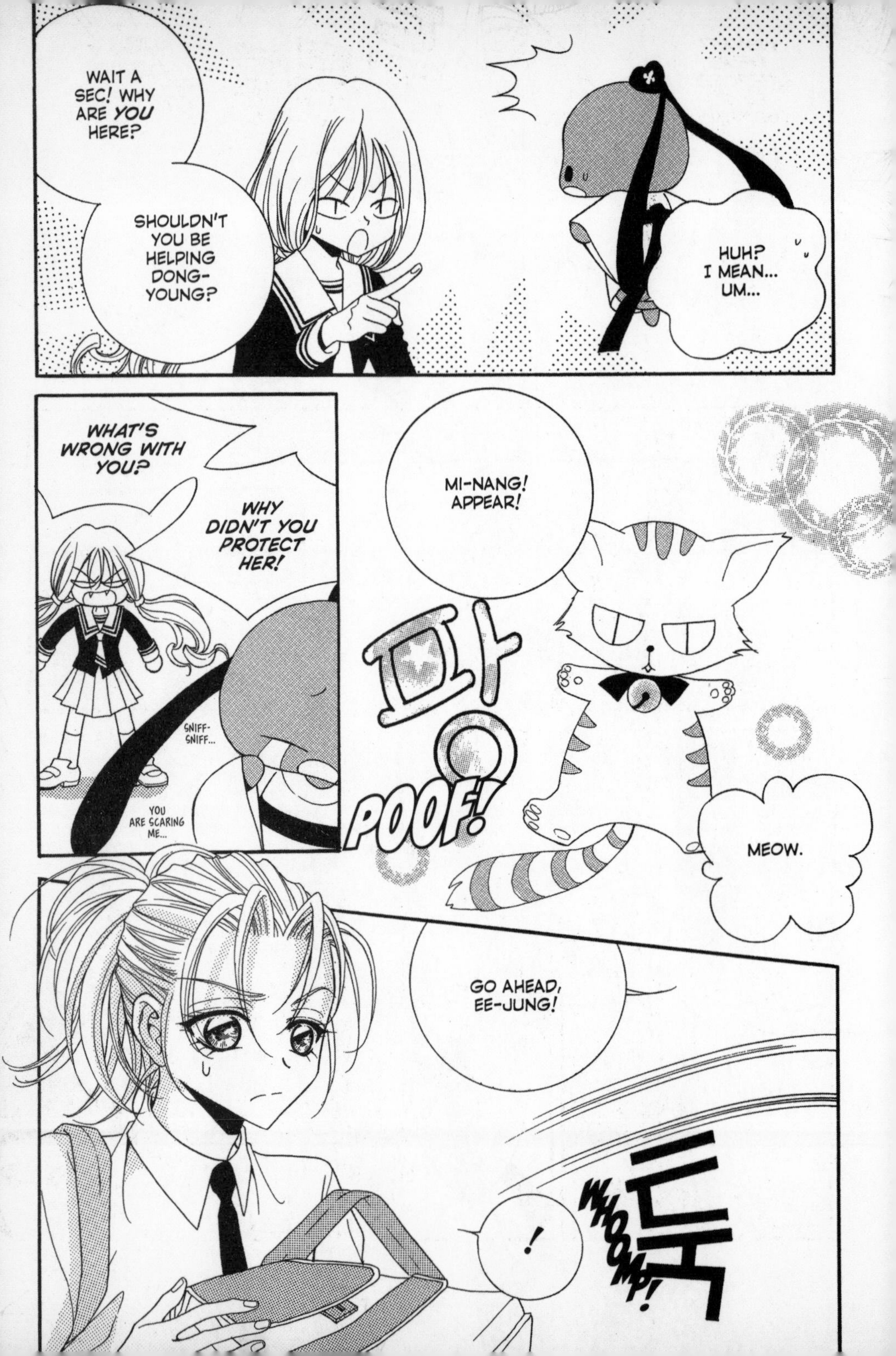
WAIT A SEC! WHY ARE *YOU* HERE?
SHOULDN'T YOU BE HELPING DONG-YOUNG?
HUH? I MEAN... UM...
WHAT'S WRONG WITH YOU?
WHY DIDN'T YOU PROTECT HER!
SNIFF-SNIFF...
YOU ARE SCARING ME...
MI-NANG! APPEAR!
파앙
POOF!
MEOW.
GO AHEAD, EE-JUNG!
!
드다
WHOOMP!

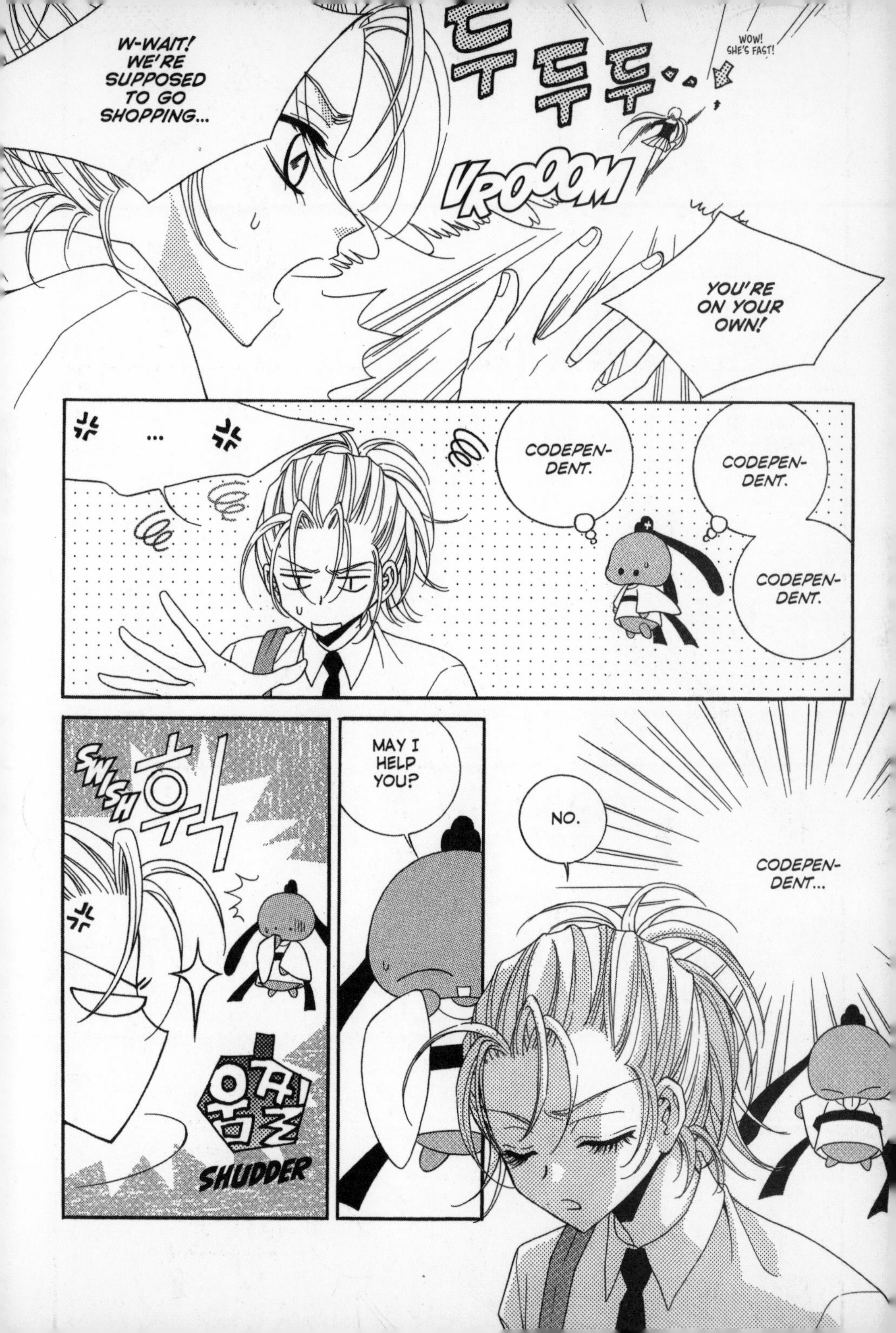
W-WAIT! WE'RE SUPPOSED TO GO SHOPPING...
두두두..
WOW! SHE'S FAST!
VROOOM
YOU'RE ON YOUR OWN!
...
CODEPEN-DENT.
CODEPEN-DENT.
CODEPEN-DENT.
SWISH
휙
SHUDDER
MAY I HELP YOU?
NO.
CODEPEN-DENT...

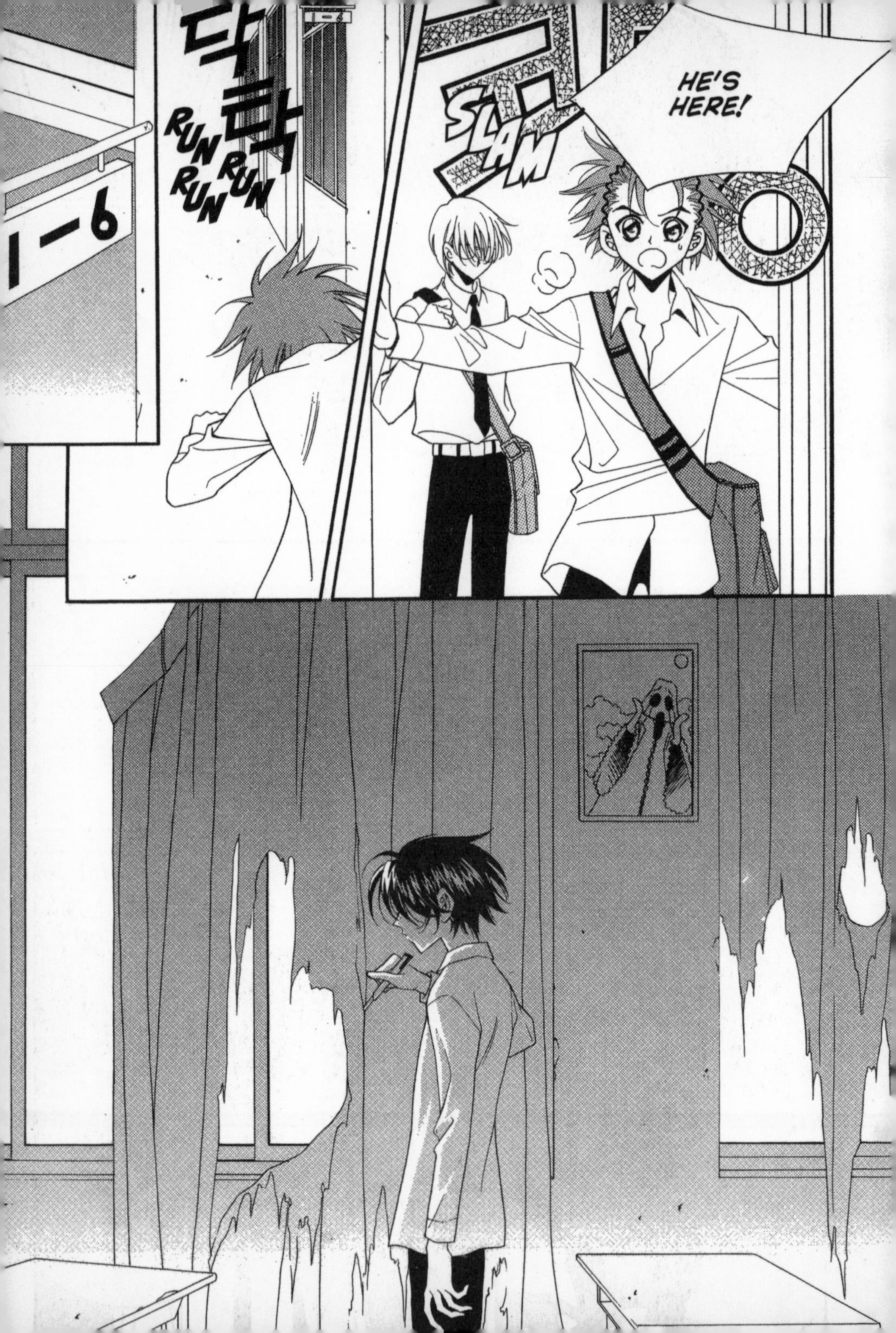
1-6
다닥
RUN RUN RUN RUN
SLAM
HE'S HERE!

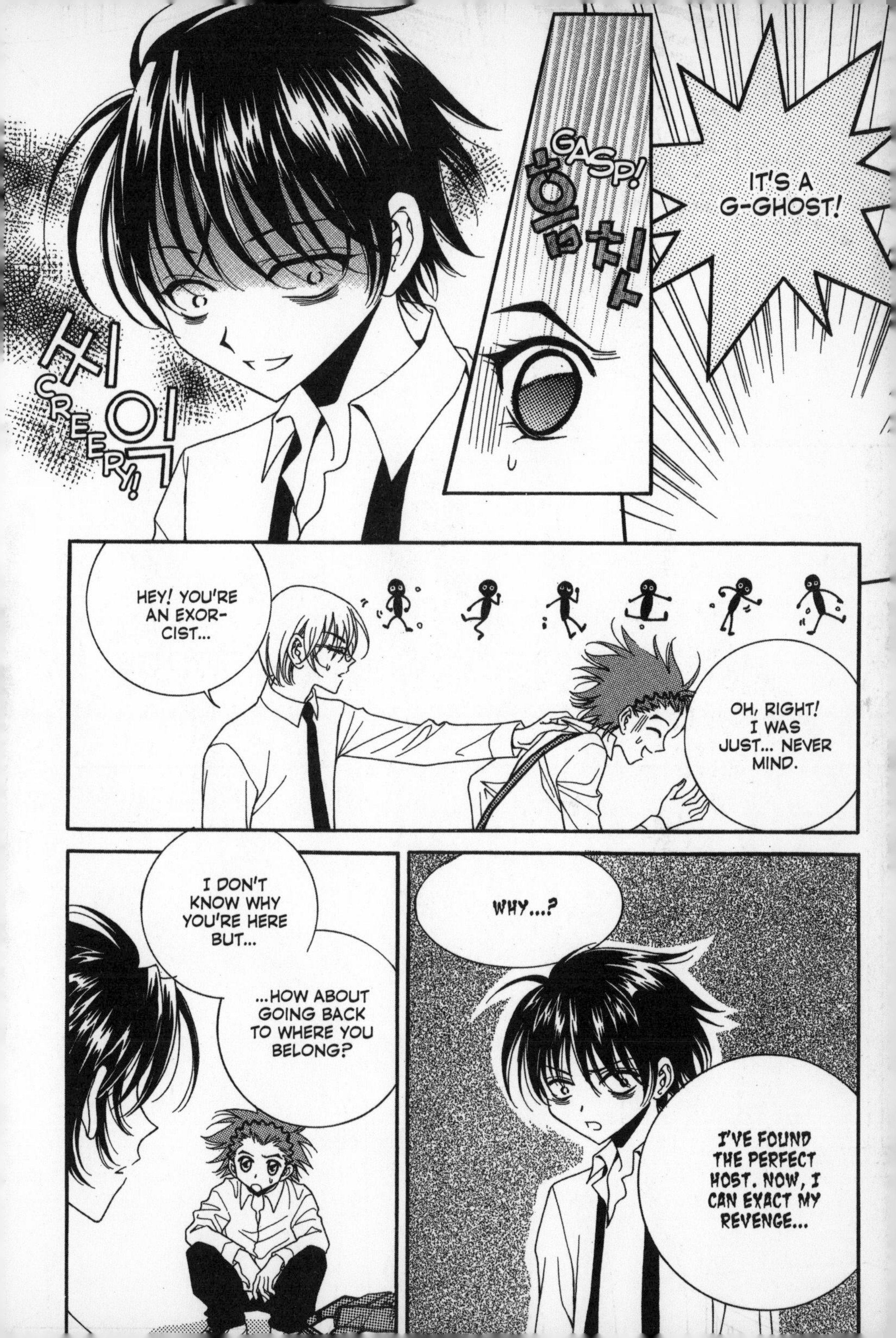
CREERY!
GASP!
IT'S A G-GHOST!
HEY! YOU'RE AN EXOR-CIST...
OH, RIGHT! I WAS JUST... NEVER MIND.
I DON'T KNOW WHY YOU'RE HERE BUT...
...HOW ABOUT GOING BACK TO WHERE YOU BELONG?
WHY...?
I'VE FOUND THE PERFECT HOST. NOW, I CAN EXACT MY REVENGE...

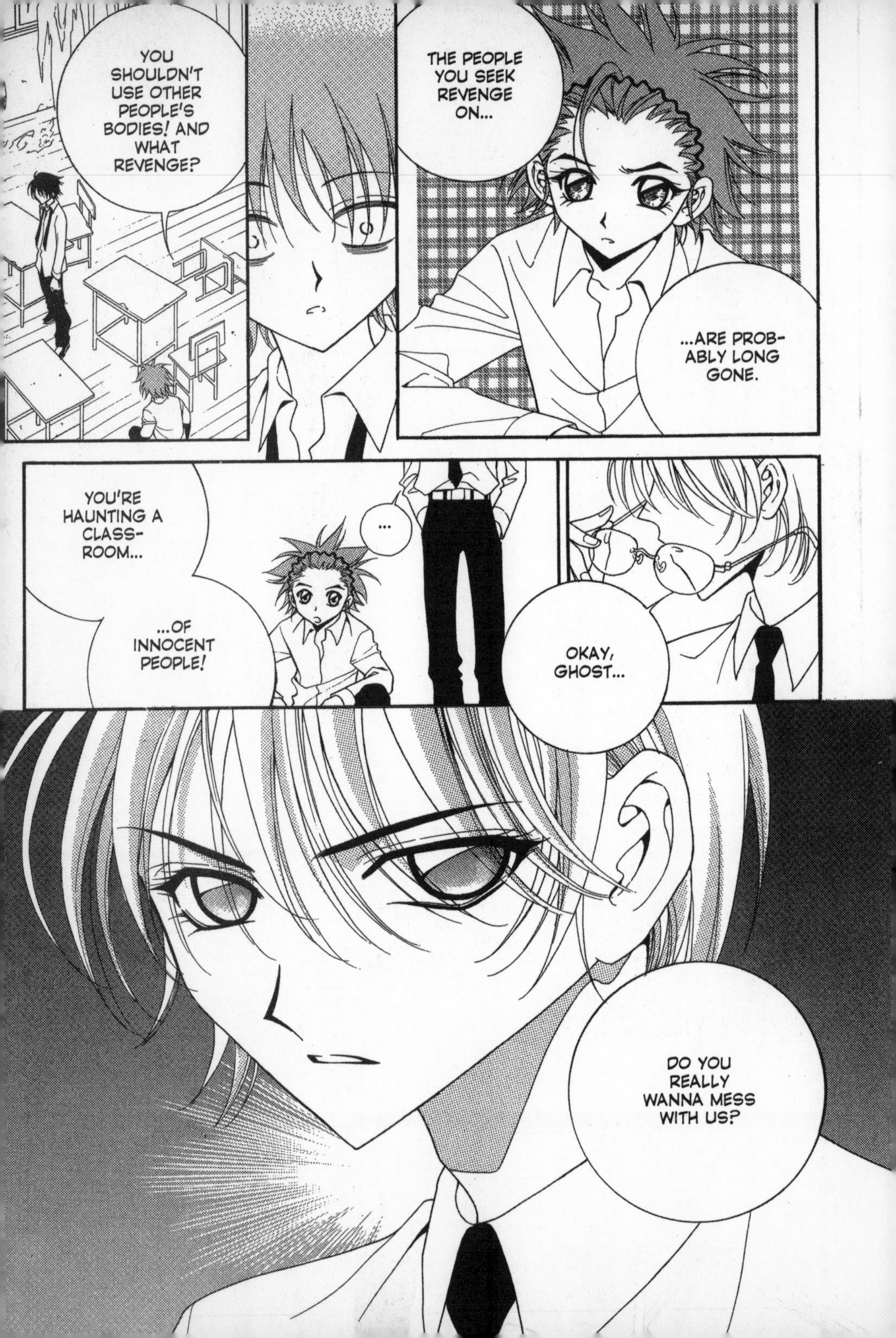
YOU SHOULDN'T USE OTHER PEOPLE'S BODIES! AND WHAT REVENGE?
THE PEOPLE YOU SEEK REVENGE ON...
...ARE PROBABLY LONG GONE.
YOU'RE HAUNTING A CLASS-ROOM...
...OF INNOCENT PEOPLE!
...
OKAY, GHOST...
DO YOU REALLY WANNA MESS WITH US?

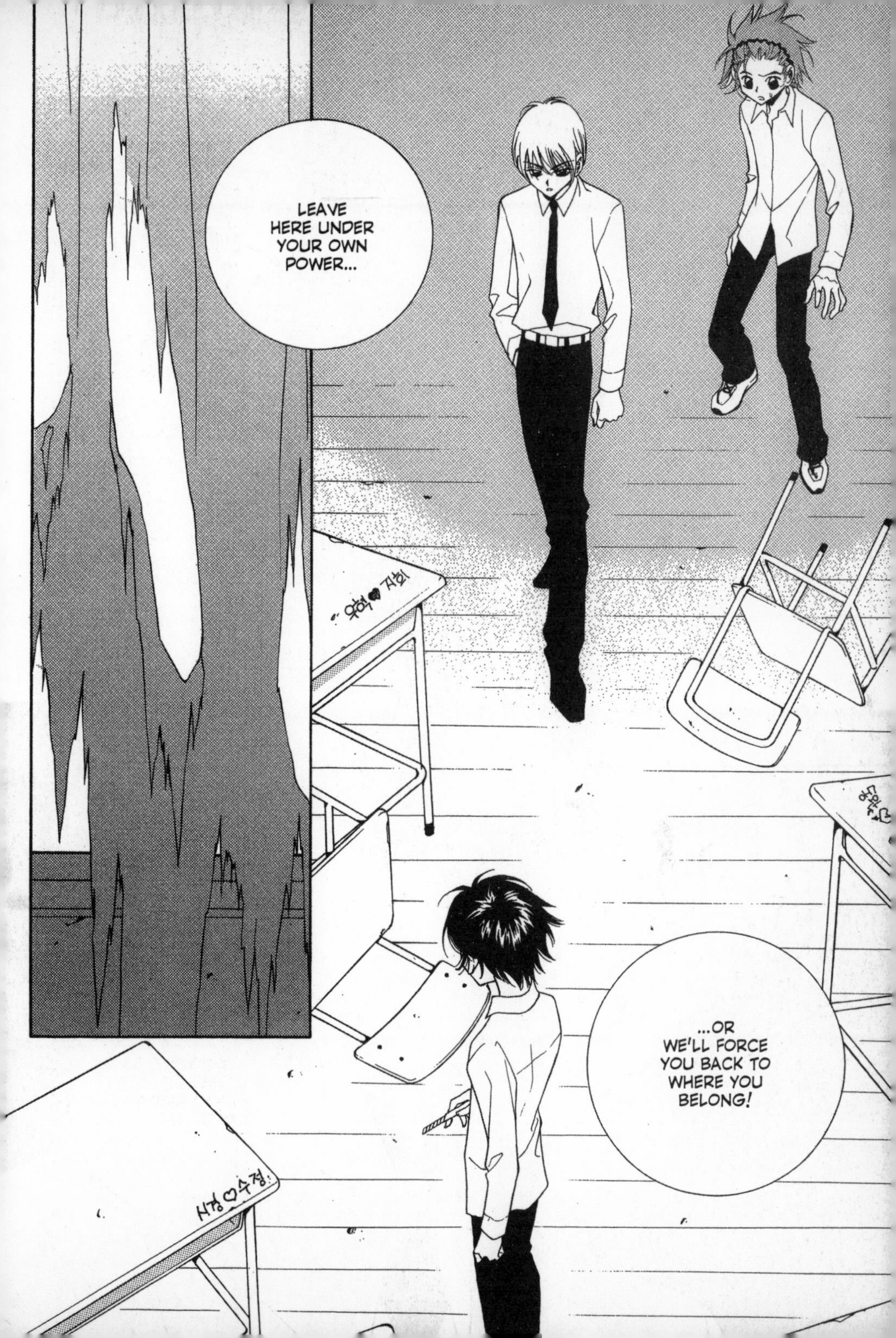
LEAVE HERE UNDER YOUR OWN POWER...
...OR WE'LL FORCE YOU BACK TO WHERE YOU BELONG!

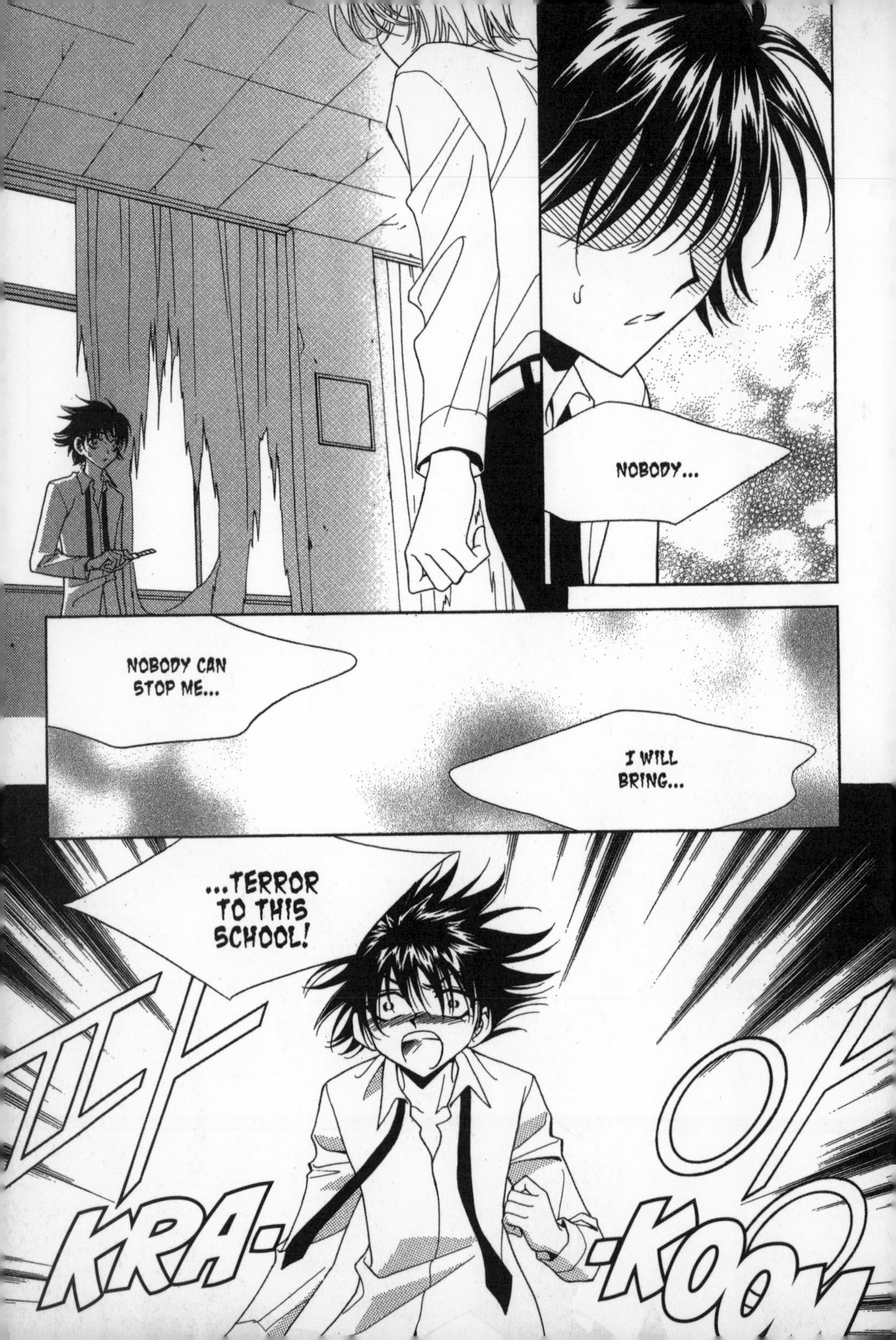
NOBODY...
NOBODY CAN STOP ME...
I WILL BRING...
...TERROR TO THIS SCHOOL!
KRA- -KOOM

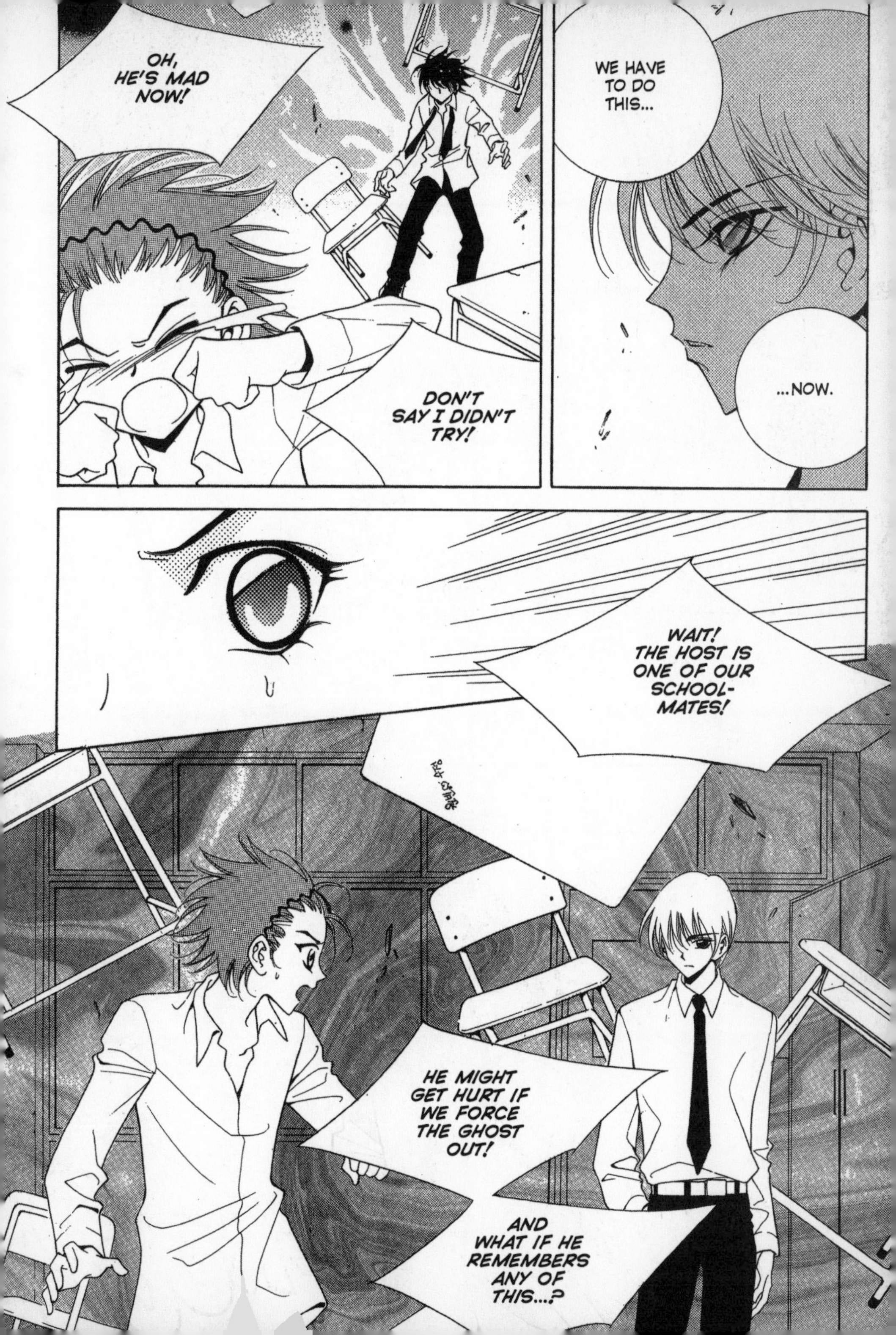
OH, HE'S MAD NOW!
DON'T SAY I DIDN'T TRY!
WE HAVE TO DO THIS...
...NOW.
WAIT! THE HOST IS ONE OF OUR SCHOOL-MATES!
HE MIGHT GET HURT IF WE FORCE THE GHOST OUT!
AND WHAT IF HE REMEMBERS ANY OF THIS...?

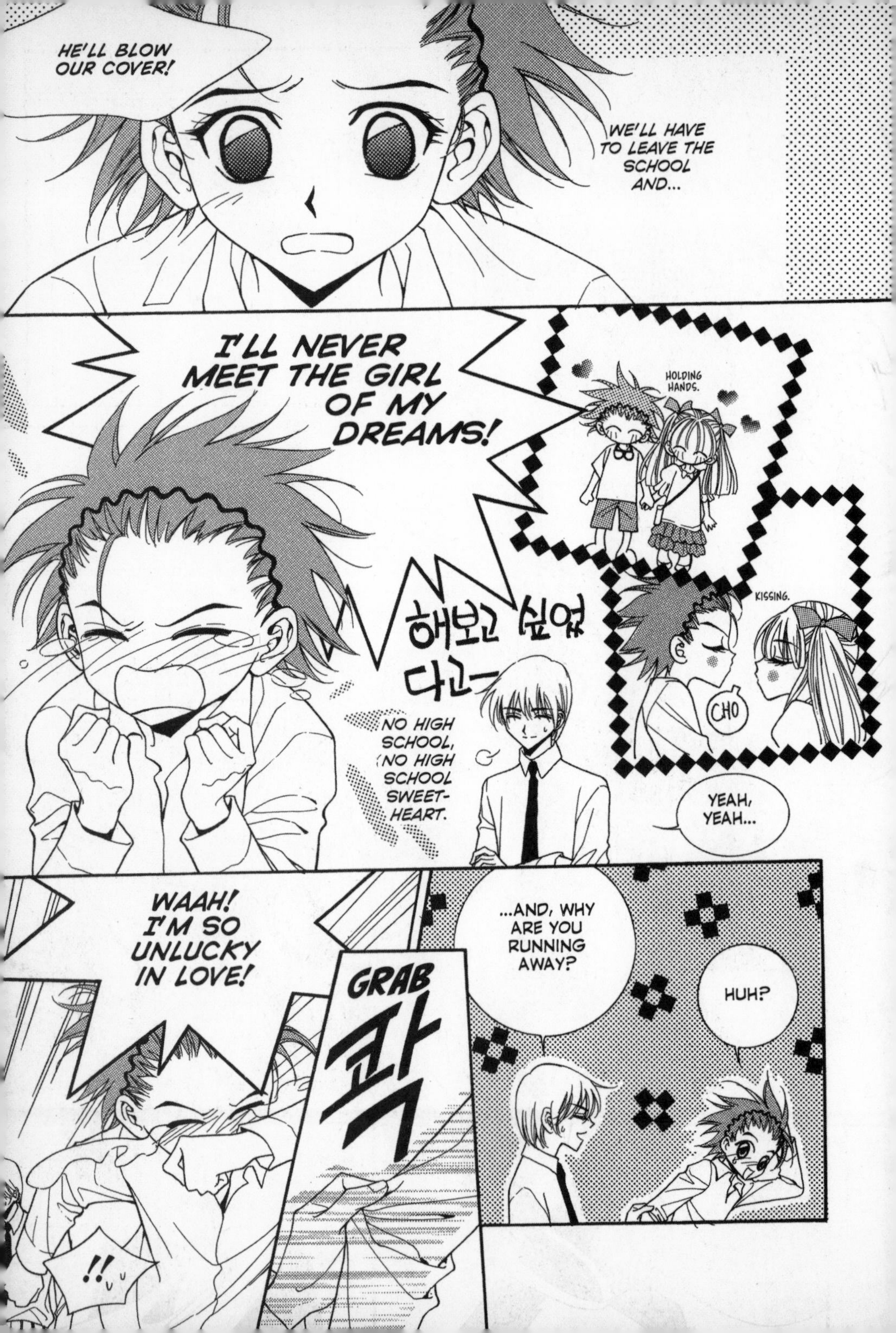
HE'LL BLOW OUR COVER!
WE'LL HAVE TO LEAVE THE SCHOOL AND...
I'LL NEVER MEET THE GIRL OF MY DREAMS!
HOLDING HANDS.
KISSING.
CHO
해보고 싶었다고—
NO HIGH SCHOOL, NO HIGH SCHOOL SWEET-HEART.
YEAH, YEAH...
WAAH! I'M SO UNLUCKY IN LOVE!
!!
GRAB
콱
...AND, WHY ARE YOU RUNNING AWAY?
HUH?

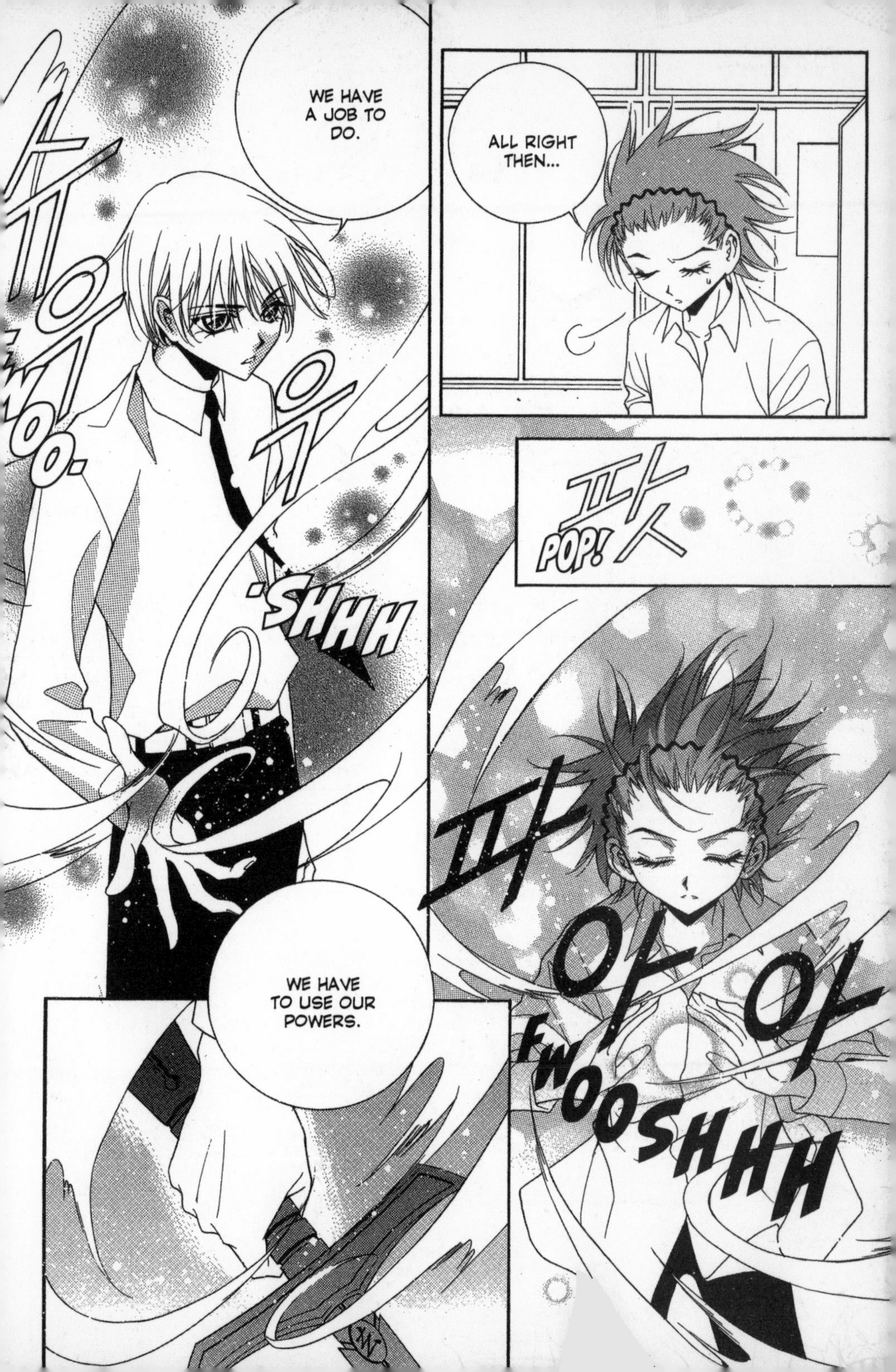
WE HAVE A JOB TO DO.
FWOO..
SHHH
WE HAVE TO USE OUR POWERS.
ALL RIGHT THEN...
팟
POP!
파아아
FWOOSHHH

Danbi Original

Bring it on! vol.1

Story and art by HyeKyung Baek

Translation Eugene Chung · Sunny Kim
English Adaptation Sunny Kim
Touch-up and Lettering Marshall Dillon
Graphic Design EunKyung Kim · YoungAh Cho
Assistant Editor Jackie Oh
Editor JuYoun Lee

ICE Kunion

Project Manager Chan Park
Marketing Manager Erik Ko
Editor in Chief Eddie Yu
Publishing Director JeongHyun Chin
Publisher and C.E.O. JaeKook Chun

Bring it on! © 2005 HyeKyung Baek
First published in Korea in 2002 by SIGONGSA Co., Ltd.
English text translation rights arranged by SIGONGSA Co., Ltd.
English text © 2005 ICE KUNION

Published by ICE Kunion
SIGONGSA 2F Yeil Bldg. 1619-4, Seocho-dong, Seocho-gu, Seoul, 137-878, Korea

ISBN : 89-527-4451-9

First printing, October 2005
10 9 8 7 6 5 4 3 2 1
Printed in Canada

www.ICEkunion.com/www.koreanmanhwa.com